D1423460

TEST
PILOTS

TEST PILOTS

The Story of
British Test Flying
1903 – 1984

DON MIDDLETON

WILLOW BOOKS
Collins
8 Grafton Street, London W1
1985

A superior pilot is a man who uses his
superior judgement to avoid the use of
his superior skill

from a Royal Air Force flight safety poster by courtesy of
Air Vice Marshal Kenneth W. Hayr CB, CBE, AFC
RAF Inspector of Flight Safety, 1976–79

Willow Books
William Collins Sons & Co. Ltd
London · Glasgow · Sydney · Auckland
Toronto · Johannesburg

All rights reserved

First published 1985

© Don Middleton 1985

BRITISH LIBRARY CATALOGUING IN PUBLICATION DATA
Middleton, D. H.
Test pilots: the story of British test
flying 1903–1984.
1. Airplanes – Great Britain – Flight testing
I. Title
629.134'53'0941   TL671.7
ISBN 0-00-218098-7

Designer: Lee Griffiths

Set in Linotron Sabon by
Rowland Phototypesetting Ltd
Bury St Edmunds, Suffolk
Made and printed in Great Britain by
William Collins Sons & Co. Ltd, Glasgow

CONTENTS

FOREWORD

by Sir Arnold Hall, FRS, MA, FRAeS

Test flying covers both the flying of aircraft to establish and improve their own performance and safety, and the use of aircraft as an essential tool of research into many other areas of knowledge, typified by aerodynamics, meteorology, and instrumentation. The men and women who handle the aircraft, and who additionally often take major parts in the observation of results, are 'the test pilots'.

Public knowledge of the work they do varies from 'high profile' to 'unknown'. That the work of a particular test pilot is a matter of high public interest neither detracts from, nor adds to, the technical significance of the work he does, and at the other extreme, lack of public knowledge or interest detracts nothing from the very significant contribution made to the advance of knowledge. All are characterized by a high degree of professionalism, by an ability to work closely and in harmony with the scientists and engineers involved in the project – who themselves often fly as observers in the experimental flight programme – and by a 'feel for the air' which brings quality to their work as well as enjoyment of the environment of flight.

In the earlier days of flying when the art was less advanced, and much less supported by the development of understanding, particularly of the aerodynamic and structural factors involved, the test pilot faced a whole spectrum of unknowns. Sadly, this has resulted in the loss of many outstanding people. As a result of the work done, as well as the development of theoretical understanding and of laboratory backing, some areas of risk were diminished, but with aircraft advancing in so relatively short a period of time from vehicles that could, at the most, carry two people a short distance at low speed, to the very high speed, long range, high load carrying capacity machines of today, the unknown was, and still is, constantly encountered and faced by those engaged in test flying and observing.

They have made a major contribution to what is in many ways an astounding rate of advance. In doing so, they, and all others engaged in aeronautical development, have helped to bring about a major change in the world. Anyone who doubts this should stand for a few moments in any major airport, and note how people of all races, colour, origin and outlook, have been intermingled by the aeroplane as – in such large numbers – they criss-cross, in their travels, a world that has become so much smaller. The social and political consequences of this, already manifest in many ways, have yet further to go in their decisive influence on the fate of mankind.

This book tells the story of some of the eminent people who have taken part in this process and enables the reader to share, at a distance, the thrills, upsets, stresses, and achievement of their remarkable activities. Having myself known, worked and flown with some of them, I see them not quite as 'a race apart' – though in some ways they are, particularly when facing alone the latest frontiers of our knowledge – but as enthusiastic, gallant, warm and highly professional people, doing the job they like and enjoy.

A. A. Hall

ACKNOWLEDGEMENTS

It was my original intention to write a definitive history of test flying in Britain; to that end a chronological chart was prepared naming pilots from 1903 to the present day. It soon became clear that within the compass of a normal sized book such a comprehensive survey was not practicable. Additionally, as some of the British aerospace companies no longer possess archive material regarding the flying activities of their predecessors, details of the work of many test pilots did not exist. This book is, therefore, directed towards the more important aircraft and events which link the machines and their pilots to contemporary technology.

It will be appreciated that the demands of war-time production called for a major increase in the number of test pilots required to fly production aeroplanes. An invaluable contribution was made by pilots who flew in bad weather, without radio, and regardless of serious navigational problems. Space limitations preclude mention of their work and that of their peace-time colleagues, other than in the course of experimental flying.

It is hoped that this book will be accepted as a tribute to all test pilots and that those who are not named will accept the author's apology and his dedication of the book to all of this talented breed who have served the British aircraft industry — and their country — with such dedication in peace and war. The contribution of their wives must also be recognized.

A list of test pilots, and others, who have assisted with interviews, reminiscences and the loan of photographs, will be found on a later page. I express my thanks for their kind cooperation.

I am particularly indebted to Sir Arnold Hall who has contributed the foreword to this book. He was one of the most distinguished of a long line of distinguished directors of the Royal Aircraft Establishment at Farnborough and his name will always be linked with the remarkable success, under his direction, of the investigations into the Comet I disasters.

I thank Richard T. Riding, editor of *Aeroplane Monthly*, for permission to quote from my articles on British test pilots already published in that journal, and for his cooperation in permitting access to his photographic library.

I must make particular reference to a series of books, covering the history of British Aviation, written by Harald J. Penrose, himself a very experienced test pilot, an outstanding aviation author and a marine architect. These volumes formed an invaluable source of reference and I am grateful to Mr Penrose for his advice and encouragement.

I am indebted to the commanding officers and the staffs of the Aeroplane and Armament Experimental Establishment, the Empire Test Pilots School and the Royal Aircraft Establishment for permission to visit their organizations and for the assistance and hospitality I enjoyed there. Brian Kervell and William Chinn, at RAE, and Terry Heffernan, at Boscombe Down, were especially helpful in resolving historical problems, as was the MoD RAF Personnel Management Centre at Gloucester.

Several of the British Aerospace divisions were most cooperative in providing data and photographs, and in arranging interviews with pilots.

With the demise of the early aero-engine companies little data was available for use in preparing a satisfactory account of the work of their test pilots, so it was decided to use Rolls-Royce Limited as an exemplar in this vitally important area. I am extremely grateful to Michael Evans, Captain Cliff Rogers, Jim Heyworth and Jack Titley for their assistance.

My thanks are also due to the Royal Aeronautical Society, and to J. L. Nayler, the Librarian, for access to their records.

Mr B. Limbrey, of Martin Baker Aircraft Company Ltd provided valuable data on their aircraft and ejector seats.

Finally my thanks must go to my wife, and to Hilda Benham, who have read all the drafts and made most valuable suggestions.

Don Middleton
November 1984.

INTRODUCTION

The desire to fly was one of man's earliest aspirations. Ruins of the ancient Inca civilization are evidence of this, the angels of religious tradition and the Greek legend of Icarus confirm the preoccupation with the principle of flying. Icarus was the son of Daedalus, a Greek architect who planned the Labyrinth at Crete for the Minotaur. Having completed the design he was imprisoned there. Unable to escape by sea his thoughts turned to the air and the legend describes how he constructed wings for Icarus and himself. The feathered assemblies were fixed with wax to their backs. Despite the warnings of his father the impetuous youngster flew too near the sun, the wax melted, and the unfortunate boy fell into the sea whilst his prudent parent flew serenely to safety. A modern accident investigation inspector would probably report that the pilot exceeded the thermal limits of the craft thus inducing structural failure and loss of control.

History records many tower-jumpers whose experiments usually resulted in injury or death. In 1110 Eilmer, a Benedictine monk in Malmesbury Abbey, made a set of wings and leaped from the top of the Abbey, breaking his limbs as he landed after a 'flight' of more than a furlong. Eilmer wrote a reasoned test report attributing his accident to the absence of a tail. His approach was in the best tradition of the Aeroplane and Armament Experimental Establishment, located eight centuries later nearby on Salisbury Plain. The Abbot was not impressed, and expressly forbade his wayward monk to carry out further experiments.

Eilmer's flight is commemorated by a stained glass window in the Abbey; a local public house is called *The Flying Monk* and the RAF occasionally re-enact the event at local carnivals, prudently using a wire cable to establish the glide path!

In November 1783 after a few tethered 'flights' to check performance and prove operating procedures, the Frenchmen, Pilâtre de Rozier and the Marquis d'Arlandes made the first manned flight in a Montgolfière hot air balloon from the Bois de Boulogne in Paris. M. Charles was, at the same time, developing a hydrogen balloon. Both groups proceeded logically until de Rozier conceived the disastrous idea of combining hot air and hydrogen. In the inevitable conflagration de Rozier and his passenger, Pierre Romain, died.

The heavier than air flying machine is the subject of this book and the narrative follows broadly the main stages of aircraft development, the years of adventure, and the acquisition of a more scientific approach through the research establishments, the manufacturing industry, the RAF and the civilian operators of aeroplanes. This phase leads directly, in the early 1930s, to the widespread consideration of the all-metal monoplane formula whch led to the great bombers and fighters of the Second World War. By 1945 the gas turbine had emerged as the powerplant of the future, and problems of control were arising as fighters were approaching the speed of sound.

The next ten years, the transonic era, was unquestionably the most dangerous period in the development of aeroplanes. Structural vibration could arise at a very high amplitude with no warning and catastrophic failure of the airframe could follow instantly. Ben Gunn's experience in the Boulton Paul P.120 research delta aircraft was a classic example, Gunn was lucky – he had an ejector seat – and survived when the machine disintegrated in 1952.

When, on 1 May 1951, the Handley Page H.P. 188 research aircraft broke up over Stansted airfield, due to control problems at 200 ft, Douglas Broomfield, Handley Page's test pilot became the thirty-second British test pilot to be killed since the war. Later, on 14 July 1954, Ronald Ecclestone of Handley Page, with his crew of three, were killed at Cranfield when the prototype Victor bomber, for which the HP. 188 had been built as a research aircraft, lost its tailplane due to fixing bolt fatigue during a low level high speed run over the airfield. This was the price in lives of test crews to be paid for developing one of the world's finest bombers.

It is important not to over-dramatize the role of the test pilot, and none would accept for a moment that their role has been dramatic. Nevertheless that period of solving the problems of passing safely and easily through the speed of sound, or Mach 1.0 as it is known, produced some very dramatic moments, which will be narrated in later chapters.

From 1960 onwards the principles of supersonic flight became much clearer, and the accent was upon the development of new materials to withstand the greater mechanical stresses arising in high speed flight, and the new problems of thermal stresses inseparable from the passage of an aeroplane through the air at ever increasing speeds. The design of gas turbines and the complexities of their air intakes was, and still is, a major consideration of the aircraft designer. The story of the development of the brilliant Concorde reveals the massive talent which our industry can bring to bear on such abstruse problems, and the standard of test flying which can be deployed to support the designers and scientists.

Since the 1960s the test pilot has been more secure in the air by his ability to use the very sophisticated techniques of simulation and computer analysis to predict what is likely to happen under various conditions of flight. Occasionally an unexpected failure occurs in spite of advanced technology. In 1959 a Victor bomber on test from the A&AEE at Boscombe Down disappeared without trace. It was found to have dived vertically from 54,000 ft into the Irish Sea for no apparent reason. This was most serious and a major two year salvage operation took place. Almost 600,000 fragments were recovered, only to prove that a pitot head had broken away from the wing causing the autostabiliser to put the machine into the fatal dive.

Civilian flying today is as unremarkable as travelling by bus. Sadly, however, it is not always as comfortable. Business men use their executive aeroplanes with no more sense of adventure than when using their cars. Helicopters fly in appalling weather to succour shipwrecked mariners or service oil rigs in the North Sea and holiday makers fly in thousands to all parts of the world on package deals.

A common thread links all these activities – the dedicated work of the test pilots and test crews who have perfected the end product of clever designers and engineers and proved beyond doubt that it is fit to be flown by normally competent pilots and carry passengers in safety with reliability. The influence of the test pilot upon the 'personality' of the aeroplane is considerable. The late Geoffrey de Havilland Junior, sadly killed in the D. H. 108

tail-less research aeroplane at the height of his career, had an enviable reputation for his work on the control responses of the aeroplanes he tested. Pilots recognized the hand of the master in the de Havilland aircraft flown from the 1937 Albatross airliner onwards – they were 'pilots' aeroplanes.

What then makes a good test pilot? Certainly not the characteristics manifest in such Hollywood screen epics as the pre-war 'Test Pilot'. Requirements have changed over the years but at no time was he a reckless fool who threw the new aeroplane into a vertical terminal velocity dive, judging it a good machine if it could be pulled out without the wings coming off! In the 1930s, a major development period in aircraft design, the test pilot was a good airman who, from his years of experience, could assess the worth of his aeroplanes, and, from his engineering knowledge, could usually recommend corrective action to overcome a problem. Aircraft companies varied in the degree of acceptance of their test pilots and it is probably true to say that the excellence of the product was in direct ratio to the depth of involvement of the pilot in all the stages of design and development.

The really intuitive and analytical test pilot as exemplified by such men as P. W. S. 'George' Bulman of Hawker, Jeffrey Quill of Supermarine and Harald Penrose of Westland began to set the pattern for the future and, as aeroplanes became more complicated, heavier and faster, the problems and dangers multiplied to a level which necessitated a more scientific approach. The rapid technological advances essential in war demanded standardization of test techniques, so the United Kingdom led the way in forming the Empire Test Pilots School. Since then most leading test pilots have been drawn from the ranks of its Graduates. They form a proud élite of some of the world's finest pilots. From the E.T.P.S. British pilots must serve three years with one of the Test Establishments, A&AEE* at Boscombe Down, or the Royal Aircraft Establishment at Farnborough or Bedford. These Establishments have made, through their scientists, engineers and test pilots, a massive contribution to the deservedly high prestige which the British aircraft industry enjoys throughout the world.

---

* Aeroplane and Armament Experimental Establishment.

1

THE EARLY PIONEERS AND THE PRESSURES OF WAR

The test pilot's profession is, by definition, as old as flying itself. In 1783 the Montgolfière brothers rose from the ground in their hot air balloon, so, at that time test flying may be said to have commenced. Testing is primarily associated with powered heavier-than-air machines, but important work was carried out in the development of gliders during the nineteenth century. Adequate lightweight power plants were non-existent so pioneers either built gliders or struggled with steam engines.

The first test pilot to be employed was probably a coachman on the staff of Sir George Cayley, the Yorkshire baronet who formulated the aerodynamic theory of flight and inscribed it on a silver disc; on the obverse was an engraving of a glider embodying his principles. In 1849 he built a glider which he did not fly himself. After ballasted flight he launched a boy who lived on his estate, he survived and, in 1853, his coachman was called upon to fly an improved glider across a valley on the estate. Happily, he too landed safely, resigning his post immediately!

Engines were the Achilles heel of aeroplane builders. In 1906 the 50 hp Levavasseur Antoinette became available, it was light and reliable and was used by Hubert Latham in his attractive Antoinette monoplane in an attempt to cross the Channel two days after Blériot's triumph. It was the Antoinette's first flight and it finished in the sea.

By the end of 1909 Europe was the centre of world aviation. A major flying event was La Grande Semaine d'Aviation de la Champagne held near Rheims from 22 to 29 August under the patronage of the President of the French Republic. Many handsome prizes were offered by the champagne industry, and it set the pattern for many other competitions through which aviation developed rapidly. By 1913 pylon racing, spot landing competitions and dummy bombing attacks with flour bags were commonplace, and many of the pilots named in the competitions were to achieve eminence in the aeronautical world; names such as J. T. C. Moore Brabazon, Geoffrey de Havilland, Tom Sopwith, Harry Hawker, Hon C. S. Rolls and Louis Paulhan. All of these pioneers who left the ground in their remarkable flying machines were test pilots in the rudimentary fashion of the day, the risks they ran on every flight were considerable; aerodynamic factors were little understood, the effect of them upon structural strength was highly problematical, and stability was marginal. Their flying was often of the 'seat of the pants' variety, and in so many cases an ability to achieve a logical analysis of the problems faced in the air eluded them. An exception was John William Dunne, probably better known for his book *An Experiment with Time*, and his theories of the universe.

Dunne was a brilliant man who conceived the idea of a swept-back wing as a means of achieving inherent stability. He studied the science of aerodynamics, so far as it existed, and made models to achieve his aim of building an aeroplane which would almost fly itself regardless of wind or weather. He believed that inherent stability and inherent safety were synonymous, an entirely different approach from that of his contemporaries, including the Wright brothers, who purposely built instability into their machines so that the pilot should have over-riding control. Dunne studied falling leaves and gulls and decided that the swept wing was correct; not based upon a bird or a leaf but developed from his own empirical calculations.

In June 1906 Dunne joined the staff of the Army Balloon Factory at South Farnborough and built a succession of model gliders. In 1907 his full size glider came to grief at Blair Atholl in Scotland but not before he was satisfied that his theories were sound. In October 1908 he flew a glider in a wind of over 30 mph. He installed a 30 hp engine but the results were poor. An appeal to the Army for a 50 hp engine to enable the machine to fly at 40 mph, the minimum he considered feasible for controlled flight, drew from the generals the discouraging retort that such a venture was utter nonsense, it would be impossible to see anything from an aeroplane moving at such a speed! Furthermore, if aeroplanes required such expensive engines there was no future for them.

So Dunne returned to the private enterprise fold and was backed by Lord Tullibardine, heir to the Duke of Atholl, and a group including the great Oswald Short, who, with his brothers Horace and Eustace, was to achieve such eminence in aviation. In 1910 a new machine, the Dunne D5, was ready for trials at Eastchurch on the Isle of Sheppey. Initially its performance was very disappointing, the flight ending as the engine stopped after three minutes. Nevertheless for a machine of such radical design it was a fairly encouraging start. The significance of Dunne's flights to this narrative lies in the reports which he wrote afterwards based upon his notes made in the air, describing in great detail the progress of the flight. He diagnosed quickly and precisely the phenomena which he experienced and had sufficient skill and knowledge to analyse the facts and make the necessary alterations to the machine to overcome difficulties.

In April 1913 J. W. Dunne addressed the Aeronautical Society of Great Britain on the subject of 'The Theory of the Dunne Aeroplane'. This learned body commented upon his paper and he ended his reply: 'My work has been done by practical experiments, it is not the experimental facts which are in question but the theory which I have evolved to cover those facts, which theory I submit to this learned Society for criticisms. But the facts are unquestioned. The aeroplane does do these things, and if the theory does not give warranty for the practice then it is the theory which is wrong.' Few test pilots today would dispute that philosophy of their calling.

Dunne had a weak heart and worked far too hard. In May 1914 he withdrew from flying on medical advice, a man dedicated to aircraft design, years ahead of his time, and swimming against the mainstream of contemporary aeronautical wisdom. Men before him had built and flown various types of flying machine, so to a degree could be called test pilots. Not one had documented his

J. W. Dunne's swept-wing biplane.

findings as had Dunne, so he can, with conviction, be described as Britain's, if not the world's, first true test pilot as we understand the function today. It was proper that, before he died during the Second World War, he saw the reality of the tail-less concept in the Westland-Hill Pterodactyl and in the published data of Alexander Lippisch and the Horten brothers, the German aerodynamicists who were probably influenced by his work.

In the second decade of the twentieth century a passion for aviation was sweeping through Europe. By 1908 one whose imagination had been stimulated was a young motor engineer named Geoffrey de Havilland, whose name will long be remembered as probably the greatest of all the British pioneers and whose everlasting memorial must be the D.H.98 Mosquito, which, with the Supermarine Spitfire, had a greater degree of versatility and development potential than any other aeroplane.

With his friend, Frank Hearle – later to become managing director of de Havilland – and £1,000 given by his grandfather, D.H. began, in 1908, to build a biplane powered by a petrol engine which he designed himself. In his autobiography *Sky Fever* Sir Geoffrey quoted a price of £220 for the engine and the tools to build the aeroplane cost less than £20. Frank Hearle was paid 35 shillings (£1.75) per week. Neither of them had ever seen an aeroplane in flight when they were visited in their wooden shed in Fulham by A. V. Roe, who thereupon invited them to his shed at Lea Marshes. His machine was developing satisfactorily but, on the occasion of their visit, was unable to fly.

In May 1909 Geoffrey found time to get married and his new wife was immediately recruited to sew the wing fabric in place and provide tea. In December the aeroplane was ready for its trials at Seven Barrows near Beacon Hill in Berkshire. Measuring thrust with a butcher's spring balance, the first engine runs were discouraging as they revealed inadequate power, one of the bevel gear boxes in the propeller drive failed and frustrations were legion. A sloping take-off path was found and the machine accelerated until Geoffrey pulled back the elevator control to rise from the ground. The control was too powerful and the wings collapsed at a height of 20 ft. The pilot struggled out of the wreck almost uninjured but he realized that the structure was much too weak and his choice of timber distinctly suspect. All that could be salvaged was the engine, which they now knew would be installed in an aeroplane which would fly.

D.H.1 at Seven Barrows. Geoffrey de Havilland in the pilot's seat; and during flight.

By the summer of 1910 D.H. and Hearle were back at Seven Barrows with a new improved machine which proved to be highly satisfactory. Visitors to the Carnarvon Arms public house on the Winchester road outside Newbury will see an interesting series of photographs of the trials of this aeroplane. Geoffrey and Frank Hearle stayed at the inn during this period. Significantly, a few months later his son Geoffrey Raoul de Havilland was born as his father was beginning to fly higher and further. With his brother John he became a test pilot in his father's company and, like John, met his death in a de Havilland aircraft on a test flight.

The satisfactory results achieved with Number Two left D.H. in a dilemma: he had spent all his money building it but saw no commercial future for it. By coincidence, at the 1910 Olympia Motor Show, he met a friend, Fred Green, who was on the staff of the Government Balloon Factory at Farnborough. Geoffrey explained his problem and Green suggested that as there had been talk of buying an aeroplane he should write to the new Superintendent, Mervyn O'Gorman, offer him the aeroplane and ask for a job!

The negotiations were highly successful; provided that the machine was seen to do a test flight of one hour duration he would be paid £400 for it and both men would be employed at the Factory to develop heavier than air machines. In 1912 the establishment was re-named the Royal Aircraft Factory, and de Havilland soon became chief aircraft designer and test pilot. He was an empirical designer, knowing little of stressing and not much more about the finer points of aerodynamics. He said, in later years: 'An aeroplane designed purely by mathematics may be a terrible looking thing and hopeless to fly . . . an aeroplane that looks right, really right, will be right in other ways.'

On 7 February 1911 D.H. was awarded Royal Aero Club Aviator's Certificate No 53 and on 9 January 1912 he qualified for the RAC Special Certificate which required a non-stop out-and-home flight of 100 miles and a landing from 500 feet within 100 yards of the starting point without using the engine. His certificate was the fourth one to be issued.

So began the career which, in the First World War, gave the Royal Flying Corps a large number of de Havilland designed aeroplanes, test flown by the designer. In later years Frank Hearle said: 'I am always amazed at the way de Havilland managed with that £1,000 provided by his grandfather – designing the engine, getting it made and tested by the Iris Company, renting the workshop, buying tools and materials, transporting the machine for testing, buying the hangar, living expenses for both of us for about eighteen months including purchasing and running the Panhard car – and then to start all over again. I have always had the greatest admiration for him. He never gave orders, just talked matters and problems over and you knew what he wanted and did it. From the beginning he seemed like an elder brother to me.'

After the Second World War Captain de Havilland attributed his success to his ability to test and fly machines of his own design. There is little doubt that the remarkable achievements of his company's products, first built at Stag Lane from 1920 to 1934, and at Hatfield thereafter, were in large measure due to the philosophy with which this modest man directed his organization, taking an active part from design onwards.

Contemporary with de Havilland were other talented pioneers whose names were known throughout the world until their famous companies were absorbed into the monolithic aircraft corporations of the 1960s and '70s or paid the supreme

A. V. Roe (above) *with his triplane at Blackpool, 1910; and Frederick Handley Page in HP.1 (1909).*

penalty of closure, as did Handley Page who wished to remain independent.

Alliott Verdon Roe – AVRO – Frederick Handley Page, the Short brothers, Robert Blackburn, Tom Sopwith and Charles Fairey were the leaders. Fairey took up a full time post in aviation through J. W. Dunne. He worked at Finchley Power Station where he was due to be promoted to manager. In 1910 he built flying model aeroplanes, one of which won gold medals and a silver cup in a competition at the Crystal Palace in South London. He thought he might be able to build a business around his hobby and decided to discuss the idea with A. W. Gamage, the London store which already had a kite and model aeroplane department. They were interested and made an arrangement with him.

J. W. Dunne saw one of his models in the store and wrote to say that one of his twisted and swept wing patents had been infringed. Fairey decided that a meeting with Dunne was the best way to

deal with the situation. He liked Dunne, who was, in turn, impressed by the young man who offered him a job in his own aircraft manufacturing facility at Eastchurch. Next day, to the dismay of his mother and stepfather, young Charles resigned his job at the power station to join Dunne.

Another great pioneer was Thomas Sopwith, better known as 'Tommy', who built and flew aircraft at Brooklands. His Sopwith Camels and Triplanes were prominent over the Western Front in the First World War. Afterwards the company name was changed to the Hawker Aircraft Company Limited. In 1910 Sopwith won the Michelin Prize of £4,000 for the longest non-stop flight from any point in England to anywhere on the Continent. On 18 December he flew from Eastchurch to a field near Beaumont in France, a distance of 169 miles in 3½ hours.

This event was marred by the death of the first test pilot to be employed by a British constructor. The victim was Cecil Grace who flew Oswald Short's aeroplane. Adverse winds caused him to abandon his flight after crossing the Channel. On

T.O.M. Sopwith with Sopwith Tabloid (1913).

his return, having scrapped his flotation gear to save weight and his compass, believing it to be inaccurate, he flew on a wrong heading, missed the North Foreland and was never seen again.

The Military Aeroplane Competition in 1912 stimulated much interest among constructors and the Farnborough Royal Aircraft Factory was a hive of industry with a number of submissions against the requirement for a reconnaissance aeroplane which had been issued in the previous year. Geoffrey de Havilland was inundated with work and Mervyn O'Gorman began to recruit pilots to help him. Lieutenant S. C. Wimperis Smith, an Army officer enthusiastic about flying, and one Ronald Kemp were among the first. O'Gorman also formed the nucleus of the remarkable scientific teams at Farnborough, Thurleigh and Boscombe Down which have ensured, in spite of the machinations and destructive edicts of governments of all political shades, that British aviation technology is in the forefront.

One of the first recruits was one of O'Gorman's own relations, Edward Busk. Holding a Mechanical Sciences tripos he was inventive and had that talent for technological investigation which is a characteristic of all good test pilots. A contemporary of Rupert Brooke, the poet, at King's College Cambridge, he was influenced by Dr F. W. Lanchester, that great experimental engineer who, at the end of the nineteenth century, explained precisely how lift was generated and could be calculated fairly accurately. In 1894 he built rubber powered model aeroplanes which he launched from the bedroom window of his house in Warwick. From them he developed the theory of aircraft stability and control which stood the test of time. In a sense Lanchester was a competitor of J. W. Dunne, but followed the theory that the stable aeroplane configuration would have the cruciform fuselage, wing, tail plane, rudder arrangement, and not swept-back wings.

Busk hoped to build his own aeroplanes based upon Lanchester's theories. He built many models, learned to fly in 1912 at Hendon aerodrome, which had just opened, and was becoming the mecca for all would-be aviators. He soon realized that his private resources were inadequate to finance his ambition and was delighted to be offered a post at Farnborough, where he could be paid to carry out the work he enjoyed so much. So RAE recruited one of its brightest stars. He studied the rudimentary 'wind channel' experiments taking place at the National Physical Laboratory at Teddington and quickly realized the gulf that existed between

theory and practice when he tried to brief the Farnborough pilots in the experiments which were very clear in his own analytical mind, but not easy to put across to those without this talent. After nearly a year he had to admit to his chief that he could not obtain the results he sought unless he flew the machines himself. O'Gorman saw the strength of his argument and instructed Geoffrey de Havilland to train him in the art of test flying using the BE.2C biplane which de Havilland had designed.

The two men set the pattern for test flying procedure which developed over the years and was not changed radically until the jet age dawned and telemetry relieved the pilot of much of the data gathering function of the job, by transmitting it automatically to recording stations on the ground. Busk knew well what every good test pilot knows, that the pilot must know exactly what he is doing and why he is doing it, an obvious truth but not widely understood in those early days. His own mental agility outstripped the capability of the rudimentary test equipment available to record data in flight so he developed acute powers of observation, powers certainly shared by other pilots but not so widely accepted as a vital requirement in a test pilot. Busk's advocacy soon changed this. Acceptance of this conviction was a milestone in the history of the craft of test flying and Busk made a major contribution during his all too short period at Farnborough.

On 5 November 1914, he was airborne in a BE.2C; Geoffrey de Havilland, flying at the same time, saw in the twilight an aircraft trailing flames going down into the dusk to crash on Laffans Plain. Ted Busk had made his last flight. His passing, at the age of 28, was an immense loss to aviation.

In 1910 A. V. Roe had a pupil, a sad faced young man with a drooping walrus moustache. To pay for his tuition, Howard Pixton worked for nothing as a mechanic in Roe's Manchester factory. By April of the following year he had made such good progress in his flying training that he was appointed a test pilot at £2 per week and a share of any prize money the Roe aeroplane might win.

In the same year Frederick Handley Page appointed Robert Fenwick as his test pilot but he was instantly dismissed soon afterwards for wrecking Page's D Monoplane on the Saturday before the important Circuit of Britain Race. He was replaced by Edward Petre, a Norwegian with only limited command of the English language.

B. C. Hucks, the inventor of the Hucks Starter for aircraft, was a mechanic with Claude

Grahame-White and was learning to fly. Robert Blackburn was preparing his new aeroplane, the Mercury, for display at the 1911 Aero Show at Olympia. He had met Hucks at a Blackpool flying event, was impressed with him and offered him a job assisting him in the flying trials. Blackburn soon realized his ability and left him to do all the flying; he was testing even before he was awarded his pilots certificate.

The British and Colonial Aeroplane Co Ltd, later to be the British Aeroplane Co Ltd, had been formed by Sir George White Bt., the formidable Bristol financial magnate. Among his appointments to the flying staff was Eric Gordon England who flew Boxkites to flying meetings all over the kingdom. He became a designer, having shown much ability as a practical man. He said that his design qualifications were nil but he was a born mechanic with a flair for design: 'We did not worry about stresses in those days!' Howard Pixton moved from A. V. Roe to Bristol and by the end of 1911 both Fred Handley Page and Blackburn were in serious trouble. Edward Petre crashed his new HP. 'E' type after an engine failure, the machine was a write off, but the pilot, escaped. Hubert Oxley, Blackburn's new test pilot, was killed when the Mercury broke up during a shoot-up over the seaside resort of Filey.

Crashes were commonplace in those early days. Often the light structure absorbed the shock and the pilot escaped serious injury but the monoplane formula became very suspect after some serious accidents. Graham Gilmour, flying a Handasyde, was killed near Richmond on Thames when the port wing broke in turbulence at 400 ft. E. V. B. Fisher, one of A. V. Roe's early assistants was killed when his Flanders F3 monoplane stalled and dived into the ground. It could equally easily have occurred with a biplane but it proved to be a useful stick with which to beat the opposition. Captain E. B. Lorraine, one of the most competent pilots in the Royal Flying Corps, followed by stalling, with a passenger, at 400 ft; both were killed. The Bristol School at Brooklands was the next to experience disaster with a monoplane. Lindsay Campbell, who was taking a flying course prior to organizing an Australian Flying Corps, had an engine failure and did not lower the nose to a gliding attitude. He stalled and was killed. At the Larkhill military trials later in the year yet another monoplane, a Deperdussin Gnome, broke up in the air, the two occupants losing their lives.

Most of the companies were working on monoplane designs and they were shocked when Colonel Seely, the Under Secretary for War, issued an order prohibiting all RFC pilots from flying monoplanes. It was, of course, a red herring: there was nothing intrinsically wrong with the monoplane formula but it was certainly more difficult to combine structural strength with lightness and stress calculation was a little understood art at that time. The effect on military aircraft design was serious and the monoplane was suspect in official circles for two decades.

The 1912 Military Aircraft Trials were conducted on the basis of very rudimentary scientific parameters; pocket barographs, aneroids and stop watches were used by pilots, loading was checked accurately and flights were timed most carefully on upwind and downwind legs of a set course. Geoffrey de Havilland's B.E. biplane was awarded most marks. Farnborough was beginning to relate practical considerations to theory and this aeroplane was the catalyst. One of its pilots was Edward Busk who, as previously recorded, died in one of them when, it is believed, a hush-hush experimental incendiary bomb ignited in the cockpit.

The First World War found Farnborough with a galaxy of talent on the scientific and technical side. Melvill Jones, later Professor Jones, had come from Vickers airship works at Barrow, William Farren, later Sir W. S. Farren, Hermann Glauert, the Nobel prizewinner, F. W. Aston and Major R. H. Mayo who was responsible for the remarkable Short composite aircraft in 1938, also joined them.

Mervyn O'Gorman's dynamic leadership of the team was of immense value to wartime aviation. A major terror of pilots was the spin. Research was carried out to find out why pilots stalled and spun in when turning downwind near the ground – a phenomenon which was all too frequent wherever men flew. One of the scientists at the Factory was Frederick Lindemann, highly qualified, very energetic and a close friend of Winston Churchill. He built for himself the reputation of having carried out most of the significant test flying associated with the spinning research programme. There is, however, some controversy about this as there is little doubt that Major Frank Goodden, the chief test pilot of the Royal Aircraft Factory, deserved most of the credit for this very hazardous work. Much had also been done by Harry G. Hawker, Sopwith's chief test pilot, who received little credit in official circles at the time. Lindemann achieved a meteoric rise to fame during the Second World War as Churchill's scientific adviser, being awarded a peerage as Lord Cherwell for his services.

Among the problems to which the scientist pilots turned their attention during the war of 1914–18 was controllability of aircraft and flight instrumentation, vital considerations for the successful accomplishment of bad weather and night flying, which could at that time so easily lead to pilot dis-orientation and the dreaded spin.

During the war the aircraft manufacturing industry grew rapidly and tension arose between the Farnborough factory and other constructors. Mervyn O'Gorman had made an enemy of the vitriolic founder editor of *The Aeroplane*, Charles G. Grey, by refusing him entry into the factory. Grey took every opportunity to lambast O'Gorman and his organization both in print and through his parliamentary contacts. Unquestionably the BE.2C which was the mainstay of the RFC two seater force was hopelessly outclassed by the German Fokkers in 1915–16 and casualties were appalling. It must not be forgotten that crews were not provided with parachutes. The War Office considered that such life saving equipment would encourage crews to abandon the aircraft rather than try to fly it back to base. Some of Grey's supporters even suggested that it was O'Gorman's policy to damage the private constructor as much as possible to allow Farnborough to dominate the scene. Geoffrey de Havilland was deeply upset by these attacks and never forgave Grey, who was never welcome at Hatfield in later years. Indeed Sir Geoffrey tried to keep the press as far away from his works as possible.

C. G. Grey won his battle, a committee of enquiry was set up and, in 1916, it was decided that Farnborough would cease to design and build aeroplanes but would concentrate entirely on research projects, with the results of their researches being made available to the industry as a whole. O'Gorman's contract was not renewed. His successor was H. W. Fowler.

Farnborough built one more aeroplane known as the Tarrant Tabor. A giant triplane, 131 ft in span, with four engines, two of them mounted high up between the centre and upper wings, it was designed by W. H. Barling of the Aerodynamics Department. Much of the structure was built by a Byfleet firm called Tarrant whose name it bore to avoid the ultimate fate of termination as a result of the 1916 Government edict. In the event it is unfortunate that it was not abandoned as it cost the lives of the two test pilots who were to make its maiden flight in 1919. Captain F. G. Dunn and his co-pilot Captain P. T. Rawlings with a crew of two observers taxied out for take-off, the engines were at full throttle, the great aircraft began to move. Suddenly its nose went down and bored into the ground, killing the pilots who had opened up the upper engines too early in the take-off run with the result that, at low speed, elevator control was inadequate to counteract the thrust of the high mounted pair of engines.

Farnborough's loss of design and constructional work was the industry's gain. Many of the highly qualified and experienced staff were directed to take up posts in the private sector of the industry where their talents were given free rein.

2

POST-WAR EUPHORIA I

When the First World War ended in 1918 the effect on the British aircraft industry was devastating. An average of 2,668 airframes and 1,841 engines were produced in each month of 1918 and the cancellation of all military contracts left most of the companies in dire straits. Farnborough was reduced to almost a quarter of its wartime strength of 5,000 people, but the test pilots were as busy as ever on the basic problems which emerged in almost every new aeroplane they flew. Control and stability, engine reliability and vibration were the major ones. Vibration could be a serious phenomenon as it was largely unpredictable; most dangerous of all was flutter, a high frequency vibration which could occur so suddenly and violently that a wing or control surface could begin to disintegrate in seconds.

The test pilots were no more fortunate than their Service contemporaries in the provision of parachutes. A. Hessell Tiltman, co-founder with Nevil Shute Norway of Airspeed Limited, recalled his early days as a designer at de Havillands when he was persuaded to fly with the test pilot W. L. Hope. Hope was privileged; he had a 'chute, his observer appeared to be expendable, so Tiltman visited his chief, Frank Hearle, to suggest that such a situation was unfair to both pilot and observer. Hearle said that the firm could not afford another parachute, so he would have to make the best of the situation. Tiltman thought that this was cold comfort if the wing was about to come off and remembered slamming the door in pique as he left the office!

Various official establishments for the testing of aircraft were formed during the war. Two were in the Ipswich area, Martlesham Heath and the Royal Naval Air Station at Felixstowe. At the beginning of the war an Experimental Flying Section was formed at the Central Flying School, Upavon, Wiltshire. By 1915 it had been decided that it absorbed too much of the flying training time at CFS. First the Armament Flight moved to Orford-ness in Suffolk, but it was soon realized that the distance between the two parts of the Section, by then a Squadron, was a handicap, so a new site was sought by two officers, one being Lt Henry Tizard, later Sir Henry Tizard, a most distinguished aviation scientist. Martlesham Heath was selected and the Station opened on 16 January 1917, the Armament Flight soon moving in.

Martlesham had achieved some prominence in May 1916 when a large Porte flying boat flown by Sqn Cdr John Porte, its designer, took off from RNAS Felixstowe with a Bristol Scout fighter piloted by Lt M. J. Day, mounted on its upper wing centre section. At 1,000 ft the engine of the fighter was started, the locks released and the Scout climbed away from the flying boat to land at Martlesham; the first pick-a-back aircraft but by no means the last.

The major aircraft constructors at the end of the war were Airco at Hendon, Blackburn at Leeds, Bristol at Filton, Fairey at Hayes, Gloster at Gloucester, Hawker at Kingston, Handley Page at Cricklewood, A. V. Roe at Manchester, Shorts at Rochester, Vickers at Joyce Green and Westlands at Yeovil, with a few smaller ones such as Martinsyde. Their main pre-occupation was to try to keep a workforce of sorts together during the locust years in the hope that military orders would be forthcoming and that the burgeoning civil aviation market would develop quickly.

A syndicate headed by Handley Page had bought 10,000 surplus wartime aircraft and large stocks of engines and spares to a total value of £5.7 million for the sum of one million pounds. The purpose this deal was said by HP to be 'To ensure the future of the British aircraft industry.' Nothing could have been further from the truth. The whole operation was a great embarrassment to the industry who, to add insult to injury, were invited to buy back their own aeroplanes from the consortium.

Geoffrey de Havilland, after a period as a pilot in the Royal Flying Corps, had joined the Aircraft

Manufacturing Co – Airco, where he designed and test flew many famous aeroplanes from the D.H.1 in 1915 to the D.H.18 in 1919. By October 1918 the newly formed Royal Air Force had 3,877 de Havilland designed machines in service. In the period 1918/19 Airco made £129,000 profit after tax on a capital of £402,500. In spite of this excellent performance it went into liquidation in the middle of 1920 when Britain had 700,000 unemployed. The company was taken over by Birmingham Small Arms who closed down the aviation side of it.

Since the crash of the Tarrant Tabor at Farnborough, the authorities had considered the airworthiness requirements for the new breed of aeroplane entering service. Regulations were promulgated covering the licencing of air and ground crews and technical standards applicable to the machine itself. A crucial element in the stability and controllability of an aeroplane is the location of the centre of pressure in relation to the chord or width of the wing. Hitherto it had sometimes been a hit and miss affair. If it was right in the first test flight, splendid! If not, someone was likely to be hurt.

Requirements were published for certain strength factors to be built into every design and also for centre of pressure locations to be established in wind tunnel tests of scale model wings.

Little had been achieved in building wind tunnels since the N.P.L. 'wind channel' experiments which interested Edward Busk in 1916. Airco and Handley Page built one during the war. Bristol and Westland followed suit in 1919 whilst Vickers were considering the construction of one.

Shorts were building bus bodies and trying to diversify into marine craft from electric canoes to 500 ton sea going barges, their location on the River Medway making this a fairly natural choice. Martinsyde built sporting motor cycles as did Sopwith. Blackburn had submitted to the Air Ministry a design for a torpedo carrying aircraft as a private venture whilst he followed the motor vehicle body path and sold aircraft general stores such as turnbuckles, nuts, bolts and small fittings.

Vickers, already well diversified, were not in such a parlous plight as the other firms, since they were developing the Vimy bomber as a passenger aircraft. The Instone shipping firm bought one for a cross-Channel service which had been operating for several months, albeit for the most courageous of passengers, who had to be prepared for a forced landing in a field if the pilot became lost flying from Hounslow to Le Bourget! Worse, an engine might fail – with luck, over land. Turbulence at the low altitudes of the flights made the cross-Channel ferry seem the epitome of gracious travel.

There was a report of a flight in gale force winds with twenty unfortunate passengers fortified with brandy. One passenger's bowler hat brim was round his neck; fortunately the crown acted as an effective crash helmet as he hit the cabin roof which also suffered from the impact! The machine had to be re-rigged when it landed at Hounslow. From these inauspicious beginnings grew the great air travel industry as we know it today.

Twenty-five Vickers Vimys were built by Westlands at Yeovil in 1918–19 adding to their wartime tally of over 790 other aeroplanes, most of them designed by other companies. Of the few which came from the Yeovil drawing office none was sufficiently successful to build in quantity so the main activity was the repair and overhaul of RAF D.H.9s and 9As of which they had built 390. Test flying at Yeovil was occasionally carried out during the war by the famous Harry Hawker, chief test pilot of the Sopwith company, who would sometimes arrive by train in the middle of the afternoon, put three or four new aeroplanes through their paces and return to London in the evening – a measure of the rather perfunctory nature of test flying in those simple times.

The Vimys were flown by Sqn Ldr Rollo de Haga Haig, a dashing young officer from the Martlesham Test Establishment. At the end of 1918 Capt A. S. Keep was demobilized from the RAF after distinguished service with Trenchard's Independent Air Force in France. He applied for a job as test pilot at Westlands and was invited to Yeovil for interview. He decided to arrive in a manner befitting his hoped-for position so borrowed a Bristol Fighter to fly from Filton. It was late before he took off on his return flight and he soon realized that, in his preoccupation with the possibilities of his new job, he was lost; as dusk was falling he decided to land in a field where he spent an uncomfortable night. In the morning he taxied into a stone wall as he prepared for take-off. It took a further two days to find and fit a new propeller. Keep hoped that his new employers would not hear about this most inauspicious start to his new career.

An ugly abomination built to meet a naval requirement was the Walrus, based on a D.H.9A airframe. On the first flight Stuart Keep took the foreman of the erecting shop, one Harry Dalwood as ballast. The flight was uneventful until Keep closed the throttle, the nose went down ominously

Westland Walrus.

so the test pilot opened up again. Clearly a landing could not be made at full throttle, so Dalwood courageously climbed out of the cockpit and worked his way along the top of the fuselage until the centre of gravity was in the right position for a safe landing. Mr Dalwood was known as a very sober man with a lined face – hardly surprising after such a flight! The works superintendent, W. G. Gibson, was hit on the head by the propeller of this machine as he tried to start the engine. A crowd gathered around his recumbent body, Keep took one look and said 'He's dead!' throwing his heavy flying coat over Gibson who immediately sat up. 'Damn me!' said Keep, 'I thought you were dead!' 'I think I am,' replied the victim.

Handley Page dominated the British airliner scene in the 1920s, although, after the war, the factory capacity which had been fully occupied in building large 0/400 bombers and the even larger V1500 four-engine type, was under-employed, and a part of it was let to a gentleman named Smith who marketed fried sliced potatoes which he called potato crisps. A converted 0/400 bomber, operated by No 86 Communications Wing RAF and named 'Silver Star', had the distinction of being the first aeroplane to be used on a cross-Channel service and the first to undertake a night passenger service to France. It carried six passengers and was used to ferry delegates to the Peace Conference in Paris.

In 1919 Handley Page Transport Ltd was formed and immediately began operations from Cricklewood, where their factory provided full repair and service facilities. A route to Paris was established, later extended to Brussels and Amsterdam. One of the pilots became Marshal of the RAF Lord Douglas of Kirtleside. After the Second World War he was appointed Chairman of British European Airways. Handley Page's talent for building heavy bombers had given the company a head start in the civil market but they had their problems. The 0/400s operating out of Croydon were extremely marginal in performance. One of them failed to climb the hill when taking off towards Purley and, in full flight, dropped into a field. Another, taking off downhill, had to land again as soon as it had crossed the Brighton road. The passenger capacity had to be reduced to an uneconomical five in the interests of safety.

Nevertheless, the operation of these converted bombers gave a much needed boost to the industry which began to see, at last, a glimmer of hope for its future in the civil market.

Handley Page's success was due partly to the remarkable drive created by HP himself, for he was certainly one of the great characters of his time. His test pilots, too, made a valuable contribution, Frank Courtney operating on a free-lance basis, and Captain G. T. R. Hill concentrating primarily upon research flying.

Joy riding began to show the British public the pleasures of aviation. 26-year-old Alan Cobham was flying for the Berkshire Aviation Co, owned by Fred Holmes and John Leeming, one of the original sponsors of Barton aerodrome, which became Manchester's first municipal aerodrome. E. W. 'Jock' Bonar, later to become a test pilot with Rolls-Royce and Napier, recalled the memorable charter flight from Barton when the Lord Mayor

D.H.9 with covered passenger seats.

of Manchester and the Chairman of the Airport Committee were flown to Croydon to receive from the Air Minister the operating licence for the new airport. The two gentlemen travelled in a converted D.H.9 with a coach roof over the two open cockpits. The machine was to be escorted by two Avro 504s, one of which was flown by Jock who, to maintain the dignity of the occasion, visited a pawn shop to buy a bowler hat! The flying gear of the two dignitaries was morning suit, top hat and the chain of office. Thus arrayed, the formation took off for Croydon. After a bumpy flight they performed a figure of eight over the airport, 'just to show them that we really can fly'! As they arrived at the dais where the official welcoming party was waiting, the lid was removed from the D.H.9 to reveal two extremely unhappy and undignified passengers using their toppers for a most irregular purpose. They decided, understandably, to return to Manchester by train.

The Air Ministry had sponsored a competition in 1920 for a large airliner. Vickers entered the Vimy conversion which benefitted from the prestige of Alcock and Brown's flight across the Atlantic. Bristol had converted the Braemar triplane bomber and Handley Page entered his 15 seat W.8, the world's first large commercial aeroplane designed as such. At that time, three airlines were operating in UK; Instone, Daimler and Air Transport and Travel in competition with HP. A.T.T., a subsidiary of the ill-fated Airco, was forced out of business

by subsidized foreign competition in 1920 whilst the other three merged in 1924 to form Imperial Airways.

Sopwith was of the opinion in 1920 that the day of the large aeroplane had not arrived so he concentrated upon small high speed single engine machines.

Two very competent engineers, Major Green and John D. North, later chief designer of Boulton Paul Aircraft, joined a firm called Siddeley Deasy which was taken over by Armstrong Whitworth to become Sir W. G. Armstrong Whitworth Aircraft Ltd. North designed the famous A. W. Siskin fighter which was test flown by Frank Courtney, an elegant man with pince-nez spectacles. The Siskin revealed handling and performance characteristics which he thought were superior to any machines in service at that time. The Siskin had the unique distinction of marking indelibly pilots who were unfortunate enough to turn it over when landing. They were often thrown forward against the gun sight which left the proboscis recognizable as the 'Siskin nose'.

Avro were building bodies for Crossley motor vehicles and a small aeroplane called the Baby which Bert Hinkler flew. He joined the firm as test pilot when he left the RNAS and flew the Baby to Turin, a distance of 650 miles in 9½ hours, using 20 gallons of fuel. This aeroplane was a highlight at the great Aircraft Exhibition at Olympia in 1920. The new Bristol Pullman four engine 14 seat triplane caused a major sensation, but unfortunately the test pilots at Martlesham Heath objected so strongly to the enclosed cockpit that the project was abandoned.

Oswald Short's all-metal pace setter, the single seat Swallow mailplane, was a most contentious exhibit. The rest of the industry, who were not as enterprising, averred that Short was too far ahead of his time. Supermarine showed the Sea King single engine flying boat with a planked, highly polished mahogany hull, a superb example of the boat builders art. Charles Fairey exhibited his Pintail amphibious seaplane with its wheels inboard of each float, whilst the Blackburn T.1 Swift single seat biplane reflected the state of the art at Leeds. Handley Page displayed a W.8 airliner and Vickers the Vimy Commercial. There were many minor exhibitors and a fine show of aero engines including Roy Fedden's Cosmos Jupiter. Cosmos patents and designs were taken over by Bristol Aeroplane Company and Fedden was instructed to form the Bristol Aero Engine Division as Chief Engineer. So began his distinguished career with the Company, and the famous range of Bristol radial engines, which culminated in the 2,850 hp sleeve valve twin row Centaurus, unquestionably one of the finest engines built anywhere in the world, powering such aeroplanes as the Bristol Britannia, Airspeed Ambassador, Blackburn Beverley, Hawker Tempest and Sea Fury. Rolls-Royce and Napier were the other important exhibitors.

Handley Page W.8 airliner.

In July 1920 the Aerial Derby at Hendon stimulated even more interest in aviation. One of the competitors was Cyril F. Uwins who had been seconded from the RAF shortly after its inception in 1918 to test fly Bristol aeroplanes. After demobilization he joined the staff on 1 April 1919. He made the second flight of the Bristol Scout fighter with the nine-cylinder Bristol Mercury engine. The first type he handled entirely on his own responsibility was the Badger two seat fighter. He carried out the first flights of all Bristol aeroplanes up to the Type 170 Freighter in 1945, retiring in 1946, having made 53 first flights.

The Air Ministry Competition at Martlesham Heath was the next major event which the industry saw as an opportunity to rebuild its fortunes. Avro entered a triplane flown by H. A. Hammersley; its take-off and landing performance was poor and a bad landing weakened the rear undercarriage struts. Harry Hawker was flying Sopwith's Atlantic with a curious four wheel undercarriage; to enable him to land, the damaged Avro had to be rather unceremoniously dragged aside. Hawker forgot to release his wheel brakes before touching down, so, as he did so, three loud reports heralded burst tyres as the machine pulled up most abruptly near to the Avro, which promptly subsided upon its belly as its weakened landing gear gave up the struggle. As is so often the case, flying incidents or accidents happen in threes. An RAF pilot landed his single seater fighter very heavily and wrote it off. Within

Vickers Viking amphibians.

the space of three minutes three bent aeroplanes littered the aerodrome to the great amusement of the spectators. Fortunately there were no injuries other than to the ego of the pilots concerned.

The HP W.8 was in trouble with a damaged propeller. During an air test of the replacement, Major Brackley, at the controls, noticed that fabric was tearing away from the port upper wing. After the necessary repairs had been carried out and the replacement fabric doped to tighten it, one of the workmen on a trestle fell through the fabric of the lower wing, and fearful of summary retribution at the hands of Handley Page, he fled precipitately. In spite of these problems 'Brackles', a famous name in the history of civil aviation, put up a first class performance. Westland's Limousine flown by their test pilot, Captain Stuart Keep was impressive.

The amphibious section of the Competition was judged at Martlesham, the waterborne trials taking place at Felixstowe. Supermarine entered the Commercial amphibian, flown by Captain Hoare, and a touch of light relief was given to the proceedings by Captains Broome and Cockerell of Vickers with 'Viking III' on their jaunty sailors cap ribbons as they demonstrated their Company's Viking. Lt Col Vincent Nicoll of Faireys, almost as tall as his chief, arrived in the Pintail after a very choppy landing on the Orwell off Felixstowe.

It was generally agreed that the amphibians showed a degree of technological advance superior to the land planes, in which class no first prize was awarded. Handley Page was second and Vickers third. In the class for small aeroplanes the Westland Limousine was first, followed by Sopwith. Of the amphibians, Vickers took first prize, Supermarine was second with Fairey third, take-off problems having handicapped the Pintail.

Sam Saunders, the Isle of Wight boat-builder, had joined forces with A. V. Roe to form Saunders-Roe at Cowes. They produced a rather unconventional biplane flying boat, the Kittiwake. Captain Norman Macmillan, Avro's test pilot, came to Cowes to test it. The first flight nearly ended in disaster when, at 500 ft, a large section of the leading edge broke away from the upper wing. By very skilful flying, Macmillan managed to bring the almost uncontrollable aircraft safely back to the water, where he ran over a rock doing slight damage to the hull. The Kittiwake had serious control problems which resulted in a serious crash when being flown by an Air Ministry pilot.

Flying was considered a dangerous activity and, in 1920, as now, an air crash was a major headline in the press. With the prospects for civil aviation improving steadily safety became a major objective. Juan de la Cierva, the Spanish engineer, took out a patent for a design which became the autogiro, whilst Frederick Handley Page worked on the principle of the slot, in which a small auxiliary aerofoil, curved to follow the profile of the leading edge of the wing, was mounted just above the leading edge of the wing to guide the airflow and delay its breakaway in a steep climb. Both inventions were a major contribution to safety in the air although the application potential of the slot was much greater than that of the autogiro.

The aircraft industry in Britain staggered from one financial crisis to another. In September 1920 the great Sopwith company went into voluntary liquidation with, however, a useful surplus of assets

positions in the company in later years, the D.H. company was formed on 5 October 1920, and housed in four huts on Stag Lane aerodrome in North London. One of the previous tenants had been a chocolate manufacturer who had left in a hurry. The mess was indescribable. Before the Drawing Office could be established in it the stock of chocolate had to be sold at bargain prices for 14 lb slabs.

The two staff huts were very cold in the winter so Capt de Havilland would summon the staff for a ten minute football session to warm up. Lunch was a packet of sandwiches eaten in hangar or office. In the summer the venue changed to the trees outside, one of which came to be regarded as the director's lunch shelter.

Various Air Ministry contracts were secured, D.H.9s were repaired, and the D.H.18, specially designed as a civil aeroplane in the Airco days, was put into production. D.H., Walker and Hearle shared one of the huts which, to this day, is preserved at the British Aerospace works at Hatfield as the de Havilland Museum. It is sad that so little of that famous marque has been preserved.

The airline business was also in dire trouble, prolonged bad weather having caused many cancelled flights on the London–Paris route. Air Transport and Travel with Handley Page Transport were near to bankruptcy. Each of HP's eight converted 0/400 bombers averaged 30 minutes flying a day and over one hundred forced landings were made. One crashed into a tree near Cricklewood killing the crew and two passengers. Nevertheless the line

over liabilities. It was immediately re-organized under the name of H. G. Hawker Engineering Co Ltd, the Hawker being Harry, their famous test pilot – surely the first and only time in the history of aviation that a test pilot was so honoured.

Geoffrey de Havilland decided to invest £3,000 to start his own company with his colleague Charles C. Walker, who invested £250 and rose to become the highly respected technical director of the de Havilland Aircraft Company. Holt Thomas, the owner of Airco, generously promised to invest £10,000 over a period, so with Frank Hearle and other Airco people, many of whom held senior

Fairey Pintail.

D.H.29.

had a good record: 320,000 miles with 4,000 passengers without a fatal accident was extremely creditable, but these unhappy events gave more ammunition to the protagonists of the airship which was considered to be the airliner of the future.

In 1921 Richard Fairey was still trying to overcome the control problems of his Pintail amphibian. Norman Macmillan left Avro to join him as chief test pilot when Colonel Nicholl contracted a serious illness.

The second RAF Pageant at Hendon in July stimulated public interest in flying and an Aerial Derby was to be held on 16 July. Two days before the race, Harry Hawker, while testing his Nieuport Goshawk, was killed when the machine went out of control. This was not the sort of publicity needed although it was later reported that he suffered from a tubercular spine and would, in any case, have lived for only a short time. It was suspected that the condition caused him to lose control and crash. Recent research, however, suggests that his machine may have caught fire in the air.

Aircraft companies saw these racing events as excellent opportunities to show off the capabilities of their aeroplanes, and they would usually be flown by the test pilots. 'Cy' Uwins flew the Bristol Bullet with clipped wings in the Derby, and Hubert Broad's mount was a Sopwith Camel. Still the industry remained in the doldrums. The new de Havilland company had an order for a military machine, the D.H.29, which proved to be extremely troublesome with control characteristics at variance with the data established in the wind tunnel. Geoffrey de Havilland was very worried as the whole future of the company was at stake. The outcome of one of his alarming test flights was the invention by Arthur Hagg, his chief designer, of

differentially controlled ailerons which, in a turn, caused the aileron rising to lower its wing to move through a greater angle than the other one, thus reducing drag on that side. This was a device of fundamental importance and has been used almost universally by aircraft manufacturers ever since. The monoplane D.H.29 was quickly replaced by the biplane D.H.32.

The revolutionary Short Silver Streak all metal biplane, shown at the 1920 Olympia Show as the Swallow, was first flown at the Isle of Grain airfield on 20 August of that year by John Lankester Parker, who spent the whole of his distinguished test flying career as chief test pilot to Short Brothers. The son of a flour miller at Barton Mills, Suffolk, he suffered from polio but became utterly bored with the prospect of a life milling flour. He persuaded an uncle to finance flying training at the Vickers School, Brooklands in 1913 and soon developed the critical faculty which built his reputation as one of the finest marine test pilots in the world. He concluded that the Bristol Boxkite on which he trained with hardly any instruments had a top speed of 33 mph, a landing speed of 27 mph and a zero rate of climb! The 50 hp Gnome engine had no throttle, just a 'blip' switch, on or off. The pilot had to remember to put the nose hard down before switching off in the air, otherwise the machine would stall. No dual control was fitted and as the occupants were fully exposed to the weather without even a windscreen, they tucked the bottoms of their trousers into the tops of their thick socks to stop the draught going right through. Navigation was a primitive art, and Lankester Parker recalled being instructed to steer for a particular advertising hoarding.

In June 1914 he was awarded his Royal Aero Club Aviators Certificate No 813 but had to cease flying as his money ran out. His disability prevented him from joining the Royal Flying Corps so he became an unpaid instructor at a Hendon flying school. Raising a further £25, he decided to learn to fly seaplanes at Windermere, where Roland Ding was operating a small machine called the Waterhen, in which the pupil sat in the rear cockpit and leaned over the instructor to take the controls. Not surprising, Parker's first take-off was traumatic for both Ding and himself. His mentor grounded him for ham-fistedness and went away for the weekend to recover from the experience, leaving behind a group of disgruntled pupils who expected to continue their training. Parker immediately took the machine out of its shed and gave the pupils their instruction, making an unprecedented fifty flights in the weekend. He even sent one of them solo and awaited the return of Roland Ding with some apprehension.

To John's surprise his enterprise was well received and rewarded with promotion to instructor – without pay. At least he was able to build up his total flying hours. The aircraft were poor things, underpowered, unreliable and almost incapable of leaving the water on the primitive floats fitted to them. So, with two helpers, Parker set out to improve float performance, making models of different designs and towing them alongside a motor boat by means of a fishing rod and line, to study the characteristics of them as speed rose. Useful improvements were made and his interest in hydrodynamic theory stimulated.

He could not afford digs so lived in a packing case in the corner of a hangar, even selling his bicycle to enable him to subsist. Three months later

Short Silver Streak.

Ding paid him 30/- (£1.50) per week, and soon afterwards, to his delight and amazement his salary was raised to six pounds. He taught seventy-five pupils to fly, none was killed – a record for that era of flying. In 1916 the school was taken over by the Admiralty for war purposes. Parker met Rear Admiral Murray Sueter who asked him if he would like to be test pilot to a friend of his – Horace Short. John rode his motorcycle to Eastchurch to see Horace who was of alarming appearance, his head being about twice normal size, and usually of most angry mien. He had a sense of humour but it rarely showed. Relentless in his pursuit of quality his technical ability was remarkable. He had two younger brothers; Oswald, 'the Kid', as Horace called him, who worked with him whilst Eustace, the middle one, was building balloons.

Short's chief pilot was Ronald Kemp, an ex-Farnborough pilot officer, overloaded with work, who welcomed Parker's assistance. Horace appointed the young man on three months unpaid trial but he was not allowed to fly any of the machines; he protested to Horace, saying that he would leave if he was not given the opportunity to prove his worth. His chief relented and told him to fly four large bombers awaiting test. He flew them all on the same day, apprehensive of their size after the small aeroplanes to which he was accustomed. Horace and 'the Kid', watching from the sheds, were very impressed by his flying, particularly when the engine of one of the bombers failed and he force-landed in a small field – he had in fact aimed for a larger one next to it!

In his early days with Short there was not sufficient work to keep him fully occupied so he

Bert Hinkler (centre) *with Avro Avian (1927).*

became involved with one of the very few freelance test flying organizations, run by an American called Prodger. Routine test flights commanded a fee of £10, prototypes were negotiable at a higher fee. So Lankester Parker amassed valuable experience in a wide range of aeroplanes. He could almost tell by looking at it whether a machine would fly well or not. His first Short prototype was the Scout, a twin float seaplane; initially a troublesome design, at which he worked until he turned it into a reasonably good machine. In January 1918 he nearly died on one of his freelance flights. Flying a Norman Thompson flying boat over water, out of sight of land en route to Southampton, the pusher propeller came off and wrecked the tail. The boat dived into the water, and Parker was picked up by a minesweeper eight hours later, fortunately uninjured.

In the same month he replaced Ronnie Kemp as chief test pilot, a post he held until his retirement in 1946. His first prototype test flight was the Short Shirl, a torpedo carrying landplane of inferior performance. He flew the Silver Streak which proved to have excellent handling characteristics and was fast. Its arrival at Martlesham for Service trials in June 1921 aroused great prejudice. The first test flight had revealed ripples and buckles in the thin aluminium skin and five months were spent in rebuilding it with a tougher duralumin alloy skin. After tentative flight trials which resulted in agreement that 'the aeroplane was astonishingly good, easy to control and had excellent manoeuvr-

ability', strength tests were carried out. These were remarkably successful, entirely vindicating the unique method of construction which was, of course, years ahead of the rest of the industry and, in the true British tradition, left to the Americans to develop and exploit in their pioneering metal aeroplanes of the 1930s.

By 1922, Bert Hinkler, the Australian whose name is linked with a number of record breaking flights in small aeroplanes with a single engine, was chief test pilot to A. V. Roe. He flew their first post-war service type, a brutish and ugly Fleet Spotter. This too showed serious symptoms of incurable instability and was abandoned.

1922 also saw the appointment of a director of research under the Air Ministry. Air Commodore Brooke-Popham was posted to be Air Member for supply and research. He soon emphasized the crucial importance of research into instrument design and reliability essential to the development of blind flying, without which military and civil aviation in Europe was so seriously handicapped as to be ineffectual.

All research into navigation, meteorology, instruments, wireless and signals was to be concentrated first at RAF Biggin Hill and later at RAE Farnborough, where it became a major element in the work of the Establishment.

On 24 November 1922 Vickers chief test pilot, Stan Cockerell flew the prototype Virginia bomber from Brooklands. A mere 39 years later G. R. 'Jock' Bryce flew Vickers last bomber, the superb Valiant, from the same aerodrome. The contrast could hardly be more dramatic and illustrates clearly the remarkable strides made in aircraft design in such a short time. The lumbering twin engined biplane cruised with 3,000 lb of bombs at around 100 mph and had a range of 958 miles. The sleek four jet monoplane 'V' bomber carried 21,000 lb of bombs 4,000 miles at over 560 mph 54,000 ft above the earth. Nevertheless the 'Ginnie' served the RAF well, and as late as 1940 was to be seen on parachute training sorties at Henlow, with the parachutist gripping the inter-plane strut as he stood on the wing ready to pull his rip-cord and be dragged off his windy perch. One clutched it so tightly that he took the strut with him!

Short made yet another attempt to interest the Ministry in all metal construction by building a two seater fighter, the Springbok. John Lankester Parker flew the prototype at Martlesham Heath in April 1923 and, once again, problems arose with the thin wing cladding which failed at the trailing edge through vibration. The wings were re-covered in fabric, whilst a second prototype was built with a thicker duralumin skin. There were stability problems with the Springbok, the second prototype killing its RAF pilot in a crash following a spin from which he was unable to recover. The frequency of instability reported in new aeroplanes illustrates clearly the gulf between wind tunnel tests and practical results in the air, which so often led to fatal accidents.

The Service did not like the Springbok although three more were built, suitably modified to overcome the spinning problem. Structurally it was another machine too advanced for its time. In spite of the low maintenance demands of the metal aircraft, there were simply no skilled men available who were familiar with the problems of thin sheet metal structures. Not until the development of the Spitfire in 1936 was the RAF conditioned to accept a stressed skin metal airframe, and even that was almost cancelled in favour of the Hurricane and orthodox fabric covered metal construction.

As a diversion from such serious matters as military aircraft development, Lankester Parker became involved in the rush to build ultra light aircraft, stimulated by the offer of a £500 prize by the Duke of Sutherland, the Under Secretary of State for Air. The Duke envisaged the development of, in effect, an airborne motorcycle.

A lecture to the Institution of Aeronautical Engineers by Sqn Ldr Maurice Wright, the Air Ministry's chief test pilot, on the subject of low powered flying gave added stimulus to even the larger firms still suffering severely from a dearth of orders. English Electric built the Wren, a tiny machine with a single 400 cc motorcycle engine. Maurice Wright test flew it and was most alarmed when the wing twisted as soon as aileron was applied. It was so low slung that only on very smooth grass could it accelerate for take-off, otherwise a push start was necessary. Contemporary motor cyclists, however, would be accustomed to such a technique. Together with de Havillands D.H.53, the Humming Bird, the Wren is preserved in the Shuttleworth Collection at Old Warden, Bedfordshire.

Roy Chadwick of Avro, later to design the famous Lancaster bomber and to lose his life on a test flight in a Tudor airliner, designed an entrant for what became the *Daily Mail* Motor Glider Competition. Glosters, or Gloucestershires, as they were known at that time, built a small machine as did Handley Page and Vickers whilst a pretty little entrant, the Gnosspelius Gull, in which Shorts had an interest, was test flown by Lankester Parker. On the first flight he mis-judged his landing, stalled the Gull and broke his seat when it hit the ground fairly hard. Both the Avro machine and the E. E. Wren won prizes but the ultralight formula languished as a rather unpractical diversion until it was superseded by de Havilland's Moth in 1926, and resurrected in the late 1970s by the home-built microlight movement.

Boulton and Paul of Norwich, who built military aircraft during the war, produced a remarkable aeroplane called the Bodmin. John North, the chief designer, was determined to follow the path of metal construction, which he saw as the only way to build aeroplanes as an industrial product rather than a craft product. Spars, struts and longerons were all in rolled and flanged high tensile steel. The twin Napier Lion engines were mounted in tandem in an 'engine room' in the fuselage, the radiators being located between the fuselage and the propellers which were driven by bevel gears and shafts. Two tractor propellers were connected to the forward engine and two pushers to the aft engine.

The Bodmin was the first serious attempt to increase long range reliability by designing the engine installation for accessibility in flight. The press representatives were intrigued by this very advanced aircraft which Frank Courtney flew, and were anxious to know what would happen to the engineer, located between the engines, in the event of a crash, which they considered very probable as a result of the vulnerable mass of shafts and gears. Possibly to their disappointment the first flight was very successful and Courtney was taken by the news hounds to a Norwich hotel for lunch. As he was leaving the hotel, a careless messenger on a

Armstrong Whitworth Sinaia (above); and Frank Courtney with Boulton Paul Bourges (1922).

cycle crashed into Courtney, knocking him into the gutter. So the Press had their 'scoop' after all: 'Famous test pilot injured in collision with bike!'

One of Courtney's narrowest escapes from total disaster was whilst testing the Armstrong Whitworth Sinaia, a twin engined bomber of 90 ft span powered by two 500 hp Armstrong Siddeley Tiger engines which had been inadequately developed, with only rudimentary bench tests. He flew it at Farnborough and had difficulty in persuading both engines to run at the same time. During a landing approach he noticed slackness in the elevator control so the machine was taken into the hangar for inspection. On the way the fuselage suddenly sagged in the middle and collapsed, some bracing wires having parted. The Sinaia was abandoned.

3

MILITARY STIMULI

Fortunately for the industry, 1923 saw a Government commitment to establish an effective Home Defence Air Force by increasing the number of Squadrons from 34 to 52. Air racing continued to improve the breed and the Schneider Trophy race for seaplanes was being recognized as a major technological challenge. Blackburn and Supermarine competed against French and American entrants, the American Curtiss Navy racer winning at 177.3 mph. Blackburn's chief test pilot, Kenworthy, had a narrow escape in the Pellet flying boat. Longitudinally unstable it porpoised badly, so that on take-off tests it bounced across the water, a wing touched the surface, slewed it round and caused it to dive straight to the bottom with the pilot still in the cockpit. Fortunately he managed to escape and rose to the surface hauled out by rescuers in boats which had rushed to the scene.

In September 1923 Fred Raynham, Handley Page's freelance pilot, flew to Martlesham for evaluation the HP.21, a new cantilever monoplane fighter for shipboard use. A lineal descendent of the Short Silver Streak it was well ahead of its time, and a very impressive design. Yet again, stability problems bedevilled it and vibration was another cross the pilots had to bear. Before the service test pilots could fly it, the control column broke at the root, and the unfortunate Raynham had to bend down in the cockpit trying to fly and land the machine by grasping the short column mounting. He 'landed' blind and survived the ensuing crash uninjured. No further work was done on this very interesting aeroplane which was built as a wooden monocoque.

Controversy raged over the merits of all metal construction which, if it were to be widely used, would increase building costs substantially. Hitherto the simple wooden aeroplanes were relatively cheap and easy to build, so modification, indeed complete replacement, was within the financial resources of the larger manufacturers who were the trend setters.

Junkers, in Germany, was pioneering duralumin structures with corrugated metal skinning; his only British disciples were Shorts. Harald Penrose tells the story of Handley Page who, at a conference, told the audience that the first Junkers he saw had crashed on landing, breaking the fuselage just behind the K of the name Junkers painted on its side. He read it as J-U-N-K! In spite of this little bit of malicious humour HP knew as well as any constructor that the writing was on the wall for the current wooden techology. There was, however, more interest in steel tube frames with fabric covering which began to be more widely used, and the purchase by the Air Ministry of a Junkers J 10 for evaluation created a minor sensation.

The RAF Expansion Scheme stimulated a number of new designs which emerged in 1924. Hawkers produced the Woodcock, which, in its original form was a clumsy looking single-seat night fighter. Fred Raynham reported, after his first flight, that the rudder was completely ineffectual and he would not risk a spin in the machine. A major re-design was necessary and the designer was dismissed. He was replaced by George Carter who had been chief draughtsman at the Sopwith Company. Fred Raynham introduced to him a tall hook nosed draughtsman who swore like a trooper but appeared to be very able. His name was Sydney J. Camm, later Sir Sydney, the designer of the beautiful and superbly efficient Hawker biplanes, the Hurricane, Typhoon, Tempest, the elegant Hunter and the unique Harrier. The name of this brilliant man is immortalized in the display of his aeroplanes at the RAF Museum, Hendon.

The new Woodcock was rather more satisfactory, but Raynham found that, at altitude, the exposed valve gear of Fedden's Bristol Jupiter radial engine iced up. Fairings were fitted over the cylinder heads to overcome the problem.

Gloucester had produced the Grebe single seater fighter, a two seat prototype which had been flown in the 1923 King's Cup Air Race by Flt Lt R. L. R.

Fairey Fox.

Atcherley, the famous 'Batchie'. The Grebe was shown in RAF livery at the Hendon Pageant in June. It was a remarkably manoeuvrable aeroplane with well balanced controls, ideal for the relatively inexperienced young pilots joining the new squadrons. 132 Grebes were built.

Armstrong Whitworth decided to join the metal construction brigade and produced the Siskin which was the first metal airframe to go into production. The covering was, of course, fabric. Martlesham test pilots liked it, pronouncing that it was 'uncouth but had a heart of gold.' Praise indeed from these hard headed professionals. It was certainly the best single seater in terms of viceless handling characteristics, provided that one did not turn it over and acquire the 'Siskin nose'.

Richard Fairey was becoming increasingly disenchanted with the Government specification for a general purpose aeroplane, which he was convinced was intended to do so many jobs that it could do none of them properly. He saw the progress the American Curtiss Company had made in the design of high speed single seat fighters, in which their own in-line engine drove a very efficient propeller, made from a slab of twisted duralumin, machined to thin sections impossible to make with wood. The performance of the Curtiss Racers in the 1923 Schneider Trophy Race galvanized him to action. In the absence of Government support, he raised a large sum of money mostly by mortgaging his own company and sailed to America, where he carried out some shrewd negotiations and returned with the rights for the Curtiss D.12 engine, the Reed metal propeller, wing surface radiators and other design features. He gathered together an expert staff, including Captain Norman Macmillan as test pilot and, in considerable secrecy, started the design of the revolutionary Fairey Fox.

By May 1924 a new and radical Westland design was ready for its maiden flight. The Dreadnought was built under an Air Ministry Contract to the design of a Russian, M. Woyevodsky. The fuselage blended into the wing as a continuous aerofoil and it was powered by a single Napier Lion engine. After several hops Stuart Keep took off in this remarkable prototype. It was soon apparent that it was tail heavy; for even with the elevator full down Keep was in dire trouble. It stalled and crashed from 100 ft. The nose section, with the cockpit, broke away, the pilot being severely injured, losing both his legs. His approach to this tragic end to his flying career was characteristic of his counterpart of more recent years, the late Sir Douglas Bader. Keep, also, courageously mastered the art of walking on a pair of 'tin' legs and became Westland's general manager, retiring in 1935.

Stuart Keep was succeeded as chief test pilot by Major L. P. Openshaw who had served during the war at the Isle of Grain experimental establishment operated by the Navy. Both Keep and his successor were university graduates; unusual qualifications for test pilots in those days of empirical flying.

The 1920s saw the introduction of a more advanced range of flight test instrumentation and the next decade developed techniques much further. Harald Penrose, in his study of test flying in the centenary issue of the Royal Aeronautical Society Journal refers to the existence of special instruments such as flow meters, an air-log to check position error in the location of the air speed indicator pitot tube, and a form of desynn, an instrument to record the exact position of a control surface on light sensitive film, so that synchronous recordings could be made. Acceleration and rate of turn recorders were used and control column

Westland Dreadnought.

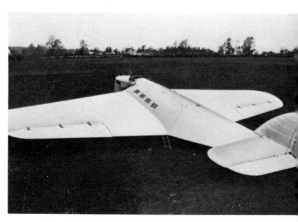

forces could be measured accurately. A hot wire anemometer formed the basis of a rate of descent meter and a cine camera focused on the instrument panel pioneered the automatic observer.

Wind tunnel techniques were developing to a point where the correlation between theory, wind tunnel data and full scale flight test data could be established with a fair degree of accuracy and certainty. Company test pilots were primarily concerned with the final stage of aircraft development. For all the knowledge which had been so painstakingly acquired at Farnborough, Martlesham, and later, at the Marine Aircraft Experimental Establishment at Felixstowe, prototypes were often erratic in one aspect of handling or performance, sometimes in both. Some were utterly dangerous and broke up in the air.

The most important experiment in the testing of aeroplanes was, and indeed still is, the establishment of lift and drag data. In the early days this was done by means of the 'prop stopped glide', the propeller being stopped to eliminate the inconsistencies in results due to the propeller. Weather conditions had to be almost perfect and as the ceiling of these machines was a mere 9,000 ft or so, and time had to be allocated for a dive of probably 3,000 ft to re-start the engine, there was little time on each sortie for the data to be gathered. A method used to compare model results with full scale practice, was the fitting of a water manometer connected to twenty or so sampling points, to measure pressure distribution over the wing surfaces. Scientists at Farnborough developed in the early 1920s an ingenious instrument for measuring the pressure distribution over a rotating propeller blade. From this date interest in variable pitch propellers began.

The stall, leading to a spin, was still the most dangerous flight aberration and pilots were continuing to meet their deaths as a result. Much experimental work was done at the National Physical Laboratory and the Royal Aircraft Establishment where the mechanics of the elusive and more lethal flat spin was postulated by the scientists. Complex instrumentation was devised to record the spinning motion and much work was carried out on a Bristol Fighter and later the Gloster Gamecock.

The Bristol had a predictable flat spin and would recover easily, but the Gamecock had all the hallmarks of a bad and dangerous spin-prone aeroplane, which rotated fast and flat. A hazardous series of flights was carried out by Flt Lt C. E. Maitland at Farnborough. He loaded the aircraft to what was supposed to be a fairly safe trim and climbed to 15,000 ft initiating a spin at that height. It was his intention to pull out after a few turns, and onlookers were horrified to see the Gamecock spinning down through no less than 40 turns, at a rate computed later of 50 turns per minute. He taxied back to report a very harrowing experience in dis-orientation which proved beyond doubt that the Gamecock was a rather nasty spinner. Maitland volunteered to repeat the flight with more instrumentation on board. This time he pulled out after thirty-four turns, twenty-five of them unintentional! He was awarded a well earned AFC for these flights.

The scientists had decided that location of the tailplane on top of the fin, as in so many modern jet aircraft, would solve the spin problem, so the Gamecock was suitably modified. It worked perfectly; the spin was slower and recovery rapid. Unfortunately the location of the tailplane in this position introduced strength and weight penalties at the tail so few designers availed themselves of this expedient, whilst people continued to be killed in spinning accidents.

It is time to introduce into the narrative one of the greatest test pilots of all time, one whose name is spoken of in great affection and admiration by the old-timers who were his contemporaries – 'George' Bulman. Group Captain Paul W. S. Bulman was cursed with a poor memory for names and, during the First World War, in which he served with distinction, he called everyone Colonel or General. This was hardly appropriate in peacetime so his friends and acquaintances became Georges – they in turn responded with George.

The son of a Bedfordshire clergyman, he was destined for a career in the Bank of England. Joining the RFC a year before it became the RAF in 1918, he flew Sopwith Pups in No 46 Sqn and Camels with No 3 Sqn. No 3 pioneered the techniques used by the Camel's descendant, the Hawker Typhoon or 'Bomphoon' as it was sometimes called in its bombing role. The Camel carried four 20 lb bombs and operated in conjunction with tanks, as did the heavily armed Typhoons which created such havoc among the *Wehrmacht* in the Falaise Gap battles after the invasion of Europe.

George talked little of his wartime experiences and would not reveal the number of his victories, saying, simply 'We flew as a Flight, the victories were the Flight's.' Nevertheless, he received the MC for his services. In 1918 he was granted a permanent commission, and immediately took up his first test flying position at the Daimler airfield at Radford, where SE.5As and Sopwith Snipes were produced. He moved to a ferry pool at Castle Bromwich where Handley Page 0/400s and de Havilland D.H.10s were tested and delivered to the squadrons. Some ferry pilots had been killed through engine failure when flying the D.H.10 and Farnborough had been asked to investigate the circumstances. George delivered one of the machines and met Sqn Ldr Roderic Hill, brother of Geoffrey Hill, who had himself been a research pilot at Farnborough. Roderic was in command of experimental flying at Farnborough from 1917 to 1923 and was himself a first class test pilot. He introduced a totally clinical approach to data gathering and analysis, whilst his brother displayed an equal talent, carrying out much of the test flying, of his revolutionary Pterodactyl, later developed in association with Westland.

Roderic was articulate, and defined precisely the results he obtained in the air, so that the scientists investigating the phenomena he reported, saw no woolliness in his statements. His technical reports were masterpieces of their kind. He recognized in Bulman a kindred spirit of immense ability, and offered him a post in the engine flight. In October 1919 he took up his new responsibilities with enthusiasm. His work was not confined to engines, for at this time a number of fatalities were occurring when aeroplanes, particularly the Camel, suddenly went into an inverted spin during an aerobatic manoeuvre. George Bulman and Roderic Hill established a reputation for their work on this problem. When George first tried to simulate the condition he found it almost impossible to rotate the Camel on to its back. Once having achieved this, he practised inverted flying, and the conditions leading to an inverted spin. The arrival of a naval pilot named Gerrard in 1920 brought more expertise to bear upon the phenomenon. He had managed to recover from an inverted spin in 1917 by pulling the stick *back* and he also knew how to begin an inverted spin by using aileron and rudder oppositely. So, by teamwork and painstaking flying, the elements of the spin were slowly pieced together and the problem solved. All that remained was to brief the squadrons whose younger pilots were naturally uneasy about the circumstances of these unpredictable happenings.

In his five years at Farnborough George Bulman made an invaluable contribution to the development of the air cooled radial engine by 'getting the bugs out of it' as he put it. He also carried out work for Blackburn testing the cumbersome Cubaroo, the Beagle and the Airedale. A particularly

interesting experience was in flying the Brennan helicopter. As early as 1920, when there was little tangible information about Cierva's rotating wing experiments in Spain, the elderly Louis Brennan was building, in great secrecy, a helicopter in the old airship shed at Farnborough. Its 60 ft diameter twin blade rotor was powered through two propellers at the tips by a Bentley BR.2 rotary engine mounted above it. This location presented serious starting problems, so Brennan designed a pull-cord system, similar to the starter on an outboard motor for boats. It was most satisfactory. The machine embodied all the basic elements of the modern helicopter and was technically advanced for its time. By March 1922 it had achieved a tethered flight to a height of 20 ft. There were many frustrations and problems in translation from vertical to horizontal flight, so not until May 1924 did outdoor trials commence.

After 200 short tethered flights at Farnborough, mostly in the hands of Bob Graham, who held the distinction of being Britain's first helicopter test pilot, a minor control fault caused damage to the machine when it tilted, allowing the rotor tips to hit the ground. Like the Breguet brothers, Paul Cornu and Oehmichen in France, Marquis de Pescara in Argentine, Henry Berliner and de Bothegat in USA, Louis Brennan's hopes foundered on the problems of cyclic pitch control; an essential element which compensates for the fact that, in normal forward flight, the forward moving blade is travelling faster in relation to the airflow over the machine than is the rearward moving blade, so the pitch of the blades must be changing constantly to maintain level flight.

After the Brennan accident the helicopter could have been repaired at reasonable cost, but officialdom, in the guise of the Aeronautical Research Committee, recommended that no further work be carried out on this type of machine but that development should follow the Cierva type of autogiro, if indeed any further work was to be carried out on rotary wing aircraft. Here was one of the earliest examples of the many occasions when a promising British development has been cast aside by craven official inability to comprehend the potential. Not until May 1940 did Igor Sikorsky fly the first successful single rotor helicopter.

George Bulman had one of his worst test flying experiences in a Hurricane – not the famous Merlin engined fighter – but a tiny 30 hp monoplane built by members of the RAE Aero Club, of which he was chairman. En route to the Lympne light plane trials in 1923 his engine failed at 800 ft over

Redhill. He realized that the fuel cock, a primitive motorcycle type hidden under the dashboard, had shut due to vibration. Whilst trying to find it, he had to put the Hurricane into a steep dive to reach sufficient speed to turn the propeller over fast enough to start the engine. He managed it but had little height to spare.

George was rapidly building a reputation as one of the finest pilots in Britain and his superb skill led to many appearances at the Hendon RAF displays. He also carried out assignments for Hawkers, including the Woodcock, which first flew in 1924. The Hawker board were so impressed by his ability that they invited him to become assistant test pilot to Fred Raynham, who, it will be recalled, had the dubious distinction of landing the Handley Page HP.21 without a joystick when it came away in his hand! Bulman resigned his commission and joined Hawker in 1925.

The Horsley, named after Harry Hawker's old home, Horsley Towers, was under test; a day-bomber/torpedo carrier, it gave good service in the RAF. George was fully responsible for the Mark II Horsley, including the modifications to J8607 in preparation for a non-stop flight from Cranwell to India. The pilot was to be Flt Lt C. R. Carr, later Air Marshal Sir Roderick, with Flt Lt L. E. M. Gillman as his navigator. The aeroplane was so grossly overloaded for the flight that the tyres burst whilst it stood awaiting its crew at Cranwell. After 34½ hours in the air they were forced down at Jask on the Persian Gulf 3,420 miles away. Two hours later their unofficial record was beaten by Charles Lindbergh's flight from New York to Paris.

Starting with the Heron and Hornbill, George test flew all the Hawker prototypes, up to and including the Hurricane fighter, turning good designs into superb flying machines with high military potential. His handling of aeroplanes was meticulous and smooth, he was a great leader, working closely with the Hawker design team from Sydney Camm downwards to investigate and improve flight characteristics. All had complete faith in his judgement. He once said that 80 per cent of his work was done on the ground making certain that his findings in the air were properly understood and acted upon by the design and production staff. This thoroughness permeated his test team and infused their work upon engines as well. Unquestionably this attitude was responsible for the excellent handling qualities and high performance of most Hawker aeroplanes.

1924 saw the entry into the aircraft industry of another great test pilot who has also made a substantial contribution to the literature of aviation. Harald J. Penrose, also the possessor of a remarkable talent in marine architecture. In his autobiography, *Adventure with Fate* he tells of his training – at the suggestion of Mr Handley Page, to whom he wrote for a job – at the Northampton Engineering College, Clerkenwell in London, where HP taught before the war. As part of his 'sandwich course' he spent some time at the Cricklewood works of HP and was fascinated by the beautiful mahogany wind tunnel models in the design office. He would sit in the cockpit of an abandoned fighter built for the US Navy dreaming of flying and ridding himself of his pre-occupation with lift and drag co-efficients, hinge and pitching moments and all the other complex formulae. Drawings revealed to him that manufacturers might design ten aeroplanes for every prototype constructed.

Handley Page did not exactly encourage his young protégé to devote his life to aeronautical engineering. In an interview he said to Penrose, 'I hope you don't think there is a fortune in building aeroplanes.' To his question 'What made you take up aeronautics?' Harald said 'I just like aeroplanes.' HP paused, 'That's as good a reason as any,' he said. 'It's a gamble whether there are any material rewards, enthusiasm is everything.' At £1 per week the young man was not prepared to disagree with the philosophy. Penrose continued his studies and joined his first and only employer, Westland Aircraft Company, in 1926, as an assistant draughtsman.

Farnborough and Martlesham Heath were the catalysts for the development of test flying techniques on a scientific basis, rather than the ad hoc groping for information which, understandably, marked the early years of the second decade. Martlesham soon achieved such eminence in the world of aviation that a posting to A&AEE was a most coveted plum job in the Royal Air Force. To be known as a Martlesham pilot was the mark of an élite breed, only the best served there, and the tradition has continued to the present day, although the base is now Boscombe Down.

The aircraft industry was beginning to expand again. The RAF displays were measure of progress, firms were trying to show a new aeroplane in the New Types Park each year. Their test pilots were being recruited from Martlesham, so the test flight standards rose as the Service Establishments developed and perfected techniques appropriate to the more advanced aeroplanes which were appearing. A memorable innovation at Martlesham, which established the friendliest relationships between the Service and the constructors, was the Industry Annual Dinner, first held in 1923. This was often a riotous affair enlivened by superbly witty speeches by Frederick Handley Page, one of the finest raconteurs in the business. In an annual ceremony one of the most eminent guests was wrapped in a rug, to be transported thus around the Mess. Most took it in good part as the normal ritual; one, however, felt it as such a grave affront to his dignity that he wrote a letter of complaint to the Air Minister. These dinners were valuable in consolidating the splendid relationships between the industry and the RAF test pilots.

There was one occasion when this relationship endured strain. The tycoon who was rolled in the rug was leaving the Mess at Farnborough in his large and expensive car, followed by a Pilot Officer in his small Morris two seater. In through the gate came a co-director of the great man, who promptly slammed on his brakes so that he could intercept his colleague. The Pilot Officer's reflexes were obviously in low gear as he crashed into the back of the Rolls. He leapt out to confront the six-foot two-inch driver, 'What the hell do you think you are doing, you fool?' Drawing himself up to his full forbidding height the tycoon rasped 'Do you know who you are talking to? I am so and so, the aircraft constructor.' Far from being over-awed by his interlocutor, the P/O said with some asperity, 'You obviously don't know who you are talking to, I am P/O Blank and I am testing your latest bloody aeroplane!' To the credit of the culprit, who recognized his defeat, his works lorry was summoned to Farnborough to pick up the damaged car, which was returned a few days later in immaculate condition. History does not relate the outcome of the tests upon the aeroplane.

Service test pilots were among the first to be issued with the new Irvin parachute in 1925. This led them to look a little more tolerantly upon the terminal velocity dive as the ultimate test of structural integrity and immunity to flutter problems. The first machine to be tested in this way was the Gloster Grebe single seater fighter which had shown symptoms of flutter. Modified ailerons and a Vee strut outboard of the main interplane struts were fitted in an attempt to cure the trouble. Flt Lt D'Arcy Grieg, later to command the RAF High Speed Flight in the Schneider Trophy Races, dived the Grebe at the unprecedented speed of 240 mph and pulled out with no sign of flutter.

For years to come the TV dive was standard test procedure but was always hazardous at the pull-out

stage. With maximum altitudes not much above 20,000 ft, the aircraft would be down to 5,000 ft in under a minute, leaving little time for test data recording and even less time to abandon ship if structural failure should occur on pulling out.

The Air Ministry had established a policy whereby more than one firm should tender for an aeroplane to meet a particular specification. Martlesham spent a busy year in 1926 testing a multiplicity of machines, good, bad and indifferent. In April Handley Page launched his new W.10 airliner with twin Napier Lion engines. Developed from the Hyderabad bomber, it was flown by Hubert Broad in February and proved to be a considerable improvement upon the W.8. Publicity for the airliner happily coincided with Alan Cobham's epic flight to Cape Town; 8,000 miles in 94 flying hours in a D.H.50. Cobham sent regular reports to the newspapers and indefatigably preached the gospel of aviation wherever he went.

At Felixstowe, for tests in 1926, was an interesting little aeroplane called the Parnall Peto with an Armstrong Siddeley Mongoose radial engine. This two seat seaplane was designed for service aboard HM Submarine M2 and was stowed with folded wings in a hangar only eight feet wide, located forward of the conning tower. Flown by Sqn Ldr L. P. Coombes and F/O O. E. Worsley, one of the Schneider Trophy pilots, it performed well but was so light that it bounced badly on its take-off run from a calm sea. The float assembly was extremely strong as was proved when F/O Worsley made a heavy landing and bent the struts. In the Squadron Line Book appeared a cartoon depicting the incident with Worsley saying 'I'm the guy who put the bust in robust!'

The Peto was lost when the submarine sank with all hands off the Dorset coast.

Richard Fairey's Fox, with the in-line engine he planned to build, was causing great interest at Air Ministry who were convinced that an aircraft manufacturer could not produce aero engines. Rolls-Royce was asked to evaluate the Curtiss D.12 which was very light, and of far more advanced design than any of the contemporary Rolls products. As a result of these tests Sir Henry Royce decided to begin work on an entirely new design based upon the Curtiss. Thus was developed the Kestrel, unquestionably the most successful aero engine built between the wars. Later came the famous Merlin which gave the Allies superiority in the air through much of the Second World War.

Fairey's triumph with the Fox was a hollow one. He expected that it would give him a head start

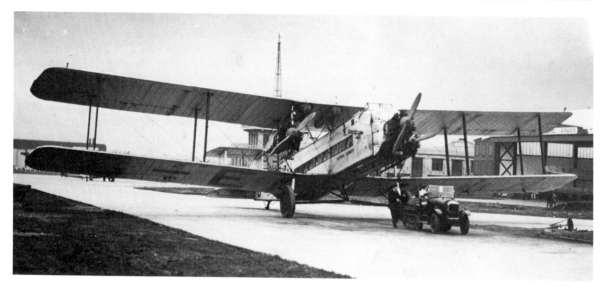

Armstrong Whitworth Argosy.

over his competitors in the light bomber project to spec 12/26. To his bitter disappointment, Hawker won the contract with the Hart, itself the forerunner of the superb range of Hawker single and two seat biplanes designed by Sydney Camm.

As the years passed the vital factor of engine reliability was being achieved. In March 1926 four Fairey IIID biplanes with Napier Lion 450 hp engines flew, without any mechanical trouble, to Cairo and Cape Town flying to a pre-determined schedule which, at every stop, was met within a few minutes. 10,578 miles were flown on the outward journey. The machines were fitted with floats and were flown back to Lee on Solent, the total round trip mileage being 14,400 miles flown in 150 airborne hours. Every stage was exactly to programme, a tremendous achievement by any standards. Bristol also gained valuable publicity by installing a sealed Jupiter engine in a Bloodhound, which F. L. Barnard and Lt Col F. F. Minchin flew continuously from Filton to Croydon, covering 25,000 miles in 226 flying hours without trouble. When the engine was bench tested afterwards it developed 440 bhp at maximum rpm compared with its normal 435 bhp.

Barnard made a significant first flight in the same month. Armstrong Whitworth had completed their Argosy airliner with three A.S. Jaguar radial engines, to meet Imperial Airways safety requirements for the continuation of a flight if one engine failed. It carried 20 passengers at 95 mph. Although of primitive design by comparison with the new Dutch Fokker FVII tri-motor high wing monoplane, built a year earlier, it set higher standards of comfort than hitherto, even if the haute cuisine on the prestigious 'Silver Wing' service to Paris was accompanied by an excruciating din from the engines and draughts through control and bracing wire apertures in the sides! One of the Argosy's minor triumphs was a race between G-EBLF and the *Flying Scotsman* express over the line from Kings Cross to Edinburgh. The aircraft won by 15 minutes, a saving which was not likely to persuade many would-be pasengers that London to Scotland was quicker by air. Seven machines went into service and were very reliable and safe.

English Electric closed down their aircraft department in response to the lack of interest in their designs, but Shorts were making good progress with their marine aircraft. John Lankester Parker flew the Short Mussel seaplane for the first time at Rochester in April. It was a very disappointing machine initially, with inadequate performance on take-off and climb. High drag appeared to be the reason rather than lack of engine power. The wing was connected to the base of the fuselage side with no fairing between the two. Interference drag at such intersections was imperfectly understood by designers at that time, but buffeting of the airflow at the stall indicated that a streamlined wing root fillet might help. Arthur Gouge, the designer, instructed that one be fitted. The result was a spectacular improvement in performance which enabled the Mussel to meet its specification.

Faireys followed the Fox with the Firefly biplane single seater fighter, powered with their version of the Curtiss engine, named the Felix. Norman Macmillan made the first flight, and was delighted with its performance. The Fox had galvanized the opposition into action, so the Firefly had competition from the Avro Avenger, flown by Bert Hinkler, and Sydney Camm's Hawker Hornbill, flown a few days after the Avenger by George Bulman. In the event, none of these machines was sufficiently attractive to the RAF to be ordered in quantity.

Juan de la Cierva had started his own autogiro company at Hanworth and appointed the ubiquitous Frank Courtney as test pilot and technical consultant. His path was a thorny one. Cierva was a brilliant man with a fierce pride in his theories, but the combination of his conviction that all his theories must be right, and the fact that he had no experience of piloting an aircraft, nearly cost Courtney his life. At a demonstration before VIPs at Villacoublay in France, it became clear that much more development work on the autogiro was needed. The weather was gusty and wet, and unfortunately Cierva had told the audience that his machine was unaffected by gusts which were absorbed by the hinged rotor blades. So Courtney came in to land, concerned by evidence from the nearby trees that a squall was imminent. He touched down on target, right in front of the distinguished spectators just as the squall arrived. As

German built Cierva Autogiro.

the principle of the autogiro depends upon the speed of the airflow over the rotors causing their rotation, the squall took over from forward speed, leaving the pilot in the unenviable position of having the rotor 'flying' and the fuselage on the ground with its tail down, an attitude which increased the rate of rotation. The machine bounced madly up and down for a few seconds, rose several feet, and then rolled to port, the blades hitting the sodden turf and distributing chunks of mud liberally over the visitors, before the rotor disintegrated and followed the mud. The top hatted gentlemen fled in disorder and showed no further interest in Cierva's helicopter, whilst Courtney emerged, dripping, from a large puddle into which he fell when he abandoned ship. Cierva agreed that more development work was necessary.

A second incident was much more serious, and a direct result of Cierva's obtuse attitude to logical engineering progress. In the rotor head design, he had included a hinge to permit the blades to flap through a small arc in the vertical plane. Courtney had totally failed to convince him that it was equally important that they must also be free to move in the horizontal plane, to withstand thrust and drag forces. During a demonstration in Germany the pilot discovered that the blade spars were bent sideways, proving his point. Cierva volubly disputed his conclusions, so Courtney prudently

decided to reduce his flying time until the designer saw sense.

During a demonstration at Hamble, flying at 1,000 ft, he heard a peculiar noise from the rotors; being, by this time, extremely sensitive to the possibilities of blade failure, he decided to descend as quickly as possible, heading for a line of trees which might cushion his fall if a blade failed and he dropped out of the sky. At 200 ft the worst happened, a blade broke away, leaving the machine vibrating madly as it fell on its side. Providentially a second blade, opposite to the first, also broke off, levelling the autogiro, which dived nose first to the ground. Courtney was extremely fortunate to escape with shock, concussion and a few broken ribs. Cierva was mortified. He agreed initially that Courtney was correct in his theory but then changed his mind. This was too much for the pilot, who decided to leave a man whose technical judgement was so seriously flawed.

Ironically, on 9 December 1936, Juan de la Cierva, who had spent his life developing an aeroplane which could not stall, died in one that did. A KLM Douglas DC-2 airliner made two attempts to take off in fog at Croydon. It crashed into houses in Purley Way; the Spaniard, with thirteen others, died in the blazing wreck.

Vickers' test pilot, Flt Lt E. R. C. 'Tiny' Scholefield, had a spectacular experience in a Vickers built French Wibault parasol monoplane. This large man had acquired the first Irvin parachute released to civilian pilots; during an aerobatic flight the machine went into an inverted spin from which it became impossible to recover. 'Tiny', quite unaccustomed to wearing a parachute, suddenly remembered it, and abandoned the machine, frantically trying to remember how to deploy the canopy. Grabbing at every buckle and strap within reach he suddenly found the correct ring, the parachute opened and deposited him, luckily, in a tree; at that height a landing on the ground would have resulted in serious injury. He climbed down and walked towards the wreck. A farmer who had seen the crash rushed over to the aeroplane, could not see the pilot, so turned away to summon help. Suddenly he came face to face with 'Tiny'. Convinced that the pilot must be dead and that this apparition must be his ghost the poor man collapsed in a faint! After this distressing introduction the farmer recovered, and the pilot strolled back to Brooklands with his parachute over his arm. He was killed later in an aircraft carrying out a test flight of such a routine nature that a parachute was not considered necessary.

D.H.66 Hercules.

Shorts' new Singapore flying boat was flown for the first time in August by John Lankester Parker. Leaks in the hull plating caused its immediate return to the shops.

In 1925 Imperial Airways was empowered to open up a service between Cairo and Karachi; de Havilland being commissioned to build an airliner with at least two engines to reduce the risk of forced landings and to have sufficient power for tropical operation. The D.H.66 was the outcome. Named Hercules by an Eton College boy, through a competition in *Meccano Magazine*, it was flown on 30 September at Stag Lane by Hubert Broad, watched by the whole of the factory workforce. Broad was pleased with it, and flew past on two engines, following this with a rather rash fly-past on one. Apart from sluggish lateral control due to the ailerons being only on the lower wings, the machine was very successful. Eleven were built and gave excellent service on the routes.

By the mid-1920s the pattern of the industry had become more stable. Armstrong Whitworth, Gloster and Hawker were primarily the 'fighter boys', Vickers and Handley Page the bomber experts; Avro and Westland specialized in general purpose machines whilst Short and Fairey built mainly marine machines. De Havilland concentrated upon the civil market. Blackburn tackled most types of aircraft.

The construction of private venture prototypes was becoming the popular practice, when the firm felt sufficiently strongly that the Air Ministry specification system was outdated by what the company designers could offer. Ministry support for this procedure was of immense benefit to Britain as, among other fine aeroplanes, it led to the Hurricane and Spitfire, both of which were PV submissions around which a specification was drawn.

4

THE QUEST FOR SPEED

Still the biplane remained supreme although a few interesting monoplanes appeared occasionally. The Westland Wizard was a smart and stylish newcomer, based upon the Widgeon light aircraft. Maj Openshaw made the first flight which ended in a forced landing when the fuel line airlocked on take-off. He skilfully avoided some houses at the boundary of the aerodrome but ran over soft ground where the Wizard turned over. The pilot was uninjured. The machine was rebuilt with a new metal framed fuselage and a 490 hp Rolls-Royce engine, being flown by Flt Lt L. G. Paget at Hendon. In spite of good performance and excellent handling qualities, the Ministry were still dedicated to biplanes, so the design languished into oblivion.

Sporting events, particularly air racing, were becoming increasingly popular and more dangerous as the number of competitors rose and aeroplanes flew faster. The Bournemouth meeting at Whitsun 1927 was marred by dire tragedy. Sqn Ldr W. H. Longton, a skilled pilot who in a practice flight had been shot at by an irate Bournemouth resident, was flying the prototype Blackburn Bluebird, hopefully the answer to the increasingly popular D.H. Moth. Maj Openshaw, of Westland, was flying the Widgeon which, rounding a turning point in a closely bunched pack, collided with the Bluebird; both crashed and burst into flames. Longton died immediately, Openshaw lingered on but eventually succumbed to his burns.

Westland appointed Louis Paget as test pilot, and Harald Penrose, although increasingly responsible for production of the big three engined Wessex, spent more time on flight test.

Frank Courtney made the first flight of the Westland Westbury, a very heavily armed twin engined fighter with two 37 mm COW guns and a .303 Lewis machine gun. The main armament was in no way connected with the ruminants of the field but was manufactured by the Coventry Ordnance Works. One of these guns was installed to fire forward and upward, anticipating by many years

one of the *Luftwaffe's* most formidable weapons first used in 1943 when twin 20 mm cannon were installed similarly in night fighters. Given the chilling code name *Schrage Musik* (oblique music or jazz), it fired non-tracer ammunition from below British bombers. Many were lost, their doomed crews having no idea what had caused their destruction. The Westbury was not developed.

Harald Penrose had supervised the construction of the Widgeon, and had joined the Reserve of Air Force Officers, learning to fly on a Bristol type 83 with a 100 hp Bristol Lucifer engine. His chief flying instructor was Cyril Uwins, Bristol's test pilot. Harald first heard the exhortation 'There are old pilots and bold pilots, but there are no old bold pilots' from 'Cy' Uwins. His ambition was to be an old one – an ambition which, happily, he achieved, so he decided that the right approach would be to extend his knowledge step by step. The philosophy served him well in his later career when he came face to face with some exceptionally dangerous situations. He soloed after only six hours dual and went on to fly a Bristol Fighter in which he beat up the aerodrome at Yeovil. The performance had been watched by most of the top management: expecting a reprimand he was agreeably surprised to receive an invitation to demonstrate the Widgeon at weekend flying meetings.

Only 30 were built but the type has always been Harald Penrose's favourite aeroplane: his delightful book *No Echo in the Sky* reflects the great pleasure his own Widgeon gave him over the years. It was the last of the breed to be built and, sadly, ended its life in flames against a hangar door after an unpiloted take-off. Of this episode he wrote, 'From the ashes no Phoenix arose – only ghosts of memories, and the haunting knowledge that there would be other days and other flights, using this aeroplane and that, but none so loved as the little Widgeon.'

A talented man of many parts, he showed such promise at Westlands that he was appointed manager of civil aircraft production and chief personal assistant to the managing director, Robert Bruce. He continued to demonstrate the Widgeon at airshows, his aerobatic and crazy flying displays delighting the spectators. During one of these events at Blackpool he had his first experience of near-disaster. In a low level loop he felt a jerk and found that the ailerons had ceased to operate. By dint of cautious turns on rudder alone he safely reached the airfield, to find that the wing folding rear hinge had failed and the wings had folded back, jamming the rear spar above the centre section in a position of very temporary security.

The Wessex three engined airliner was his next responsibility. This machine became very familiar to spectators and 'joyriders' at Alan Cobham's National Aviation Day displays, and was used by Imperial Airways, Sabena and Portsmouth, Southsea and Isle of Wight Aviation. Penrose flew the Wessex and the new Wapiti general purpose machine for the RAF. There was no opportunity for dual instruction as neither machine was fitted with dual controls. He recalled his astonishment when Louis Paget, the chief test pilot, bravely climbed into the passenger cabin of the Wessex for that first flight.

Harald Penrose (right) *with chief designer Arthur Davenport and the Westland Widgeon Mk 3 prototype (1930).*

Westland was working on a revolutionary design based upon experiments carried out by Capt G. T. R. Hill who, in 1914 had built a glider with his brother Roderic, later Air Chief Marshal Sir Roderic. The latter was awarded the AFC in 1918 when he was a test pilot at Farnborough investigating the effect of flying an aeroplane into a balloon cable. The Germans were beginning to use balloons to protect their factories and towns. An FE.2B had been converted to carry a 'bowsprit' at the nose, from which wires stretched to the wing tips in the hope that a balloon cable would be directed along the wire to disappear at the wing tip. At 3,000 ft he approached the cable at 55 mph, as planned; it slid smoothly to the tip where it caught a joint in the structure, the aircraft rotating two and a half turns round the cable until it disengaged, leaving a section of the wing behind. Hill regained control and staggered back to Orfordness.

Geoffrey Hill also flew fighters in the First World War and served at Farnborough. His new project was based upon the sweptwing tailless configuration with inherent stability pioneered by J. W. Dunne. Having built a successful prototype, Hill persuaded the Air Ministry to grant a development contract to Westland, whereupon he joined them to continue his work. Known as the Westland-Hill Pterodactyl, the subsequent Mk IA prototype was successfully flown by Louis Paget in 1928. The control system used pivoted wing tip 'controllers'

which operated differentially as ailerons or in unison as elevators.

The Schneider Trophy Races were continuing to arouse public interest and enthusiasm to a level inconceivable in these more blasé times. In the press, and on their rare public appearances, the pilots experienced adulation which would be reserved for pop stars today. For the 1927 event Shorts had built a handsome seaplane called Crusader, with a radial engine closely cowled with the cylinder heads under streamlined 'helmets' to reduce drag. Lankester Parker carried out taxying trials at Rochester but the Air Ministry decreed that flight tests be carried out at MAEE Felixstowe by Bert Hinkler who, as an RAF Reserve officer, took precedence over the vastly more experienced Short test pilot. The rudder design of Crusader proved to be unsatisfactory, and the machine was directionally unstable, as so often proved to be the case in those empirical days. Hinkler made a heavy landing as a wing dropped just before touch down, resulting in bent float struts.

The new Supermarine S.5 was flown by F/O Worsley of the High Speed Flight, and Flt Lt S. M. Kinkead, later to lose his life on a practice flight, flew the Gloster IV. Flown in the Race by Flt Lt S. N. Webster the S.5 won at Venice: it achieved a speed of 281.65 mph.

In 1927 Flt Lt H. J. T. Saint, a Farnborough test pilot, had joined Gloster's to succeed Larry Carter who had died.

All the important companies now had staff test pilots. Armstrong Whitworth had appointed Alan Campbell-Orde from their flying school to take responsibility for new projects approaching completion. These events had a serious effect upon Frank Courtney whose income from freelance test work was substantially reduced. The 'Man with the Magic Hands', as some of the newspapers called him – to the amusement of his flying contemporaries – decided that there was no future for him in Britain so he left for America in 1928, taking a post as aviation adviser to a New York firm of investment brokers, who specialized in aeronautical projects, upon which Courtney gave his opinion after studying the 'paper aeroplane', or flying it if completed. One such project led to the formation of the Curtiss-Wright Corporation, to become famous in American aviation. Courtney was invited to be technical assistant to the vice president engineering, Charles L. Lawrence.

In his book *Flight Path* he recalled a major problem of the early test pilots. Senior management had a propensity for treating a first flight as a social

spectacular for friends and associates, so as the planned date approached, delays inseparable from the development of a new aeroplane brought all sorts of pressures from high places, to ensure that the guests were not disappointed or incommoded in any way. He overcame the problem by being thoroughly evasive in giving the projected date for a first flight.

On one occasion he was to fly a Dutch Koolhoven FK.31 two seat fighter at Rotterdam. During the afternoon a procession of large limousines arrived to disgorge all the local civic and military dignitaries, together with the managing director of Koolhoven and the secretary of the Aero Club. He had no warning of this visitation and the wind was far too high for a first flight. After a totally unauthorized announcement by management that he would fly in half an hour, he drove his car back to the hotel to telephone the chief mechanic with instructions to have the aeroplane ready at daybreak next day, when the wind would have dropped. His assumption was correct, so Courtney took off. At 2,000 ft rudder control deteriorated to a point where it became non-existent. So there he was, in a new and untried aeroplane with only uncertain aileron control for a turn. He managed to return safely, to find that in the excitement of the previous day's VIP visit, a distracted inspector had failed to notice that nuts designed to secure the rudder cable cotter pins had not been fitted. The pins were subjected to vibration in flight and, as a result, fell out, disconnecting the rudder. If he had flown, as was announced, in the gusty air of the previous day a serious crash would have been inevitable.

Frederick Handley Page was still assiduously promoting his slots as a valuable means of improving safety in the air. Sqn Ldr Tom Harry England joined him in 1927 in a combined sales manager/test pilot role. An experienced Martlesham Heath pilot, he had been in command of Flight Test at the Establishment. HP had converted an HP.31 Harrow biplane from manually operated slots to the new automatic design, which deployed as soon as the speed of airflow over the wind dropped to a point where a stall was imminent. Until this stage, air pressure retained the slat, as the moving section was known, in the flush position. England's flight trial in this aeroplane were so convincing that Air Ministry officials were invited to a demonstration at Cricklewood. A number of very senior officers flew the type and were in full agreement that the slots enabled pilots to survive mistakes which would have probably been fatal without them.

D.H.71 Tiger Moth.

Cyril Uwins at Bristol was having trouble with the new Bagshot twin engine monoplane. When the ailerons were applied to bank the aeroplane it rolled the other way. The wing was found to be twisting as soon as aileron was applied, a phenomenon which bedevilled monoplane wing design for many years, later being given the exotic name of aero-elasticity. This defect initiated a major programme of wing redesign, and the resulting multi-spar concept, with several spars to take the load instead of one or two, was a major advance in structural integrity which benefitted the whole industry.

A major pre-occupation of the constructors was the competition for the very valuable RAF single seater fighter to specification F9/26. Boulton and Paul built the Partridge, Hawker submitted the Hawfinch, but the order went to Bristol, whose magnificent Bulldog served in the Royal Air Force until 1937 when the last of the 312 in service were replaced by Gloster Gladiators. Cyril Uwins made the first flight on 17 May 1927, and a number of modifications were made to the shape of the rudder and the length of the fuselage, which was increased due to a degree of directional instability – a totally unacceptable defect in a fighter. A number of foreign air forces were interested in the Bulldog and one was sent to America in 1929 for evaluation by the US Navy. Flutter and wing rib failure occurred during terminal velocity dives, so a further machine was sent out with strengthened ribs and balanced ailerons to prevent flutter. The Americans did not place an order.

The uncowled radial engine was a source of unacceptable drag and a number of attempts were made to overcome this difficulty. One was the helmeted cylinder heads seen on the Short Crusader Schneider entry, which introduced cooling problems on slower aeroplanes. Dr H. C. Townend developed the Townend ring cowling, a simple narrow chord cowl around the engine, which straightened out the airflow with no cooling problems. This soon became commonplace on radial engined aeroplanes as the speed increase was very useful. Surprisingly only the Mk IIIA Bulldog was fitted with the ring and this mark did not go into production.

The F9/26 competition highlighted the speculative nature of aircraft design. The Bulldog and the Partridge were designed to the same specification but were at opposite ends of the performance spectrum. The Bulldog handled superbly, as the Martlesham pilots confirmed. The Partridge was disliked for its heavy elevators, whilst directional and longitudinal stability left much to be desired. In spite of the most careful design by competent designers and thorough exploration in the wind tunnel, within the existing technical parameters, there were always questions over the design until the test pilot had flown it to find out how closely reality matched theory. The art lay in the interpretation of wind tunnel and theoretical data; some designers, Frank Barnwell of Bristols and Sydney Camm of Hawker, had a high level of ability in this art, and even they did not always get it right.

Geoffrey de Havilland was still absorbed in the civil market and decided to build a special racer for the Kings Cup Race. This was the D.H. 71

Tiger Moth. In 1927 de Havilland had tried to convince the Air Ministry that their ideas were archaic, as he did in 1939 with the Mosquito. He was convinced that the biplane fighter formula was outmoded and totally inadequate in terms of performance per horsepower, so he resolved to prove it with this little aeroplane powered by his associate, Frank H. Halford's new 100 hp in-line engine. When the design was under consideration the question arose, how slim could the fuselage be? 'Our test pilot, Hubert Broad, is not very big, design it around him!' was the answer.

Two Tiger Moths were built in great secrecy for the 1927 Kings Cup Race. Broad set up a world record in Class III (light aeroplane category) for the 100 km closed circuit with a speed of 186.47 mph; it also reached an altitude of 19,191 ft in 17 minutes, only oxygen starvation of the engine prevented it from beating the Class III height record of 22,251 ft. After the very encouraging performance of the D.H.71, Geoffrey de Havilland designed and built the D.H.77 all metal low wing fighter, with a Napier Rapier H type engine of 330 hp, also designed by Halford. This machine, with Broad at the controls, made its first flight; it handled well and achieved a speed of 182 mph, roughly the same as the Tiger Moth, but with two and a half times the weight for three times the power. It proved beyond doubt the validity of de Havilland's contention that the clean lined monoplane was the right answer for fighter aircraft, but the Ministry took no notice. Only the one prototype flew. Apart from the military conversion of the Dragon Rapide, D.H. did no more work on combat aircraft until the famous Mosquito in 1939.

In 1928 Handley Page recruited a debonair young RAF officer who had served in the trenches in the 1914 war and transferred to the RFC, much to the disgust of his colonel. He shot down two enemy aircraft, was posted to No 39 Sqn at North Weald, and spent the rest of the war flying Brisfits at night chasing Gotha bombers over London. He took an instructors course at Central Flying School and from 1923–28 served with No 5 FTS at Shotwick, later named Sealand. Maj James L. B. H Cordes joined HP as a research experimental pilot in charge of the flying department, under Sqn Ldr Tom Harry England, at Cricklewood.

The Clive airliner, Hinaidi military transport and Hyderabad bomber were in production at this time, the Hyderabad being the first big aeroplane to be fitted with wing slots, and the last airframe which HP built of wood. One of Cordes' early successes was to find the site for the company's new airfield at Radlett. He travelled to Woodford near Manchester to collect an Avro Avian which was to be used for experimental work on slots. As he flew south, the weather deteriorated, forcing him to follow the main St Pancras railway line, navigating 'by Bradshaw'. At St Albans the weather deteriorated seriously so he looked for a convenient field in which to land and wait for better conditions. Suddenly one appeared below him, alongside the railway line near Radlett. He landed, taxied around the hedge until he saw a farmhouse where he was entertained to dinner and allowed to stay the night. He quickly realized that this field might be the answer to HP's search for a new base, Cricklewood being too small and surrounded by housing estates. He phoned his chief who said 'Stay there and say nothing, I am coming right over.' By June 1929 flying operations had been transferred to the 154 acre site; the Cricklewood aerodrome sold for £100,000, but the factory complex retained.

Jim Cordes took a slotted Moth around Europe in 1928 to demonstrate the advantages of slots on light aircraft. At Thun, in Switzerland, he was asked to fly Hermann Goering, who was busy rebuilding the *Luftwaffe*. With this vast fleshy cargo the little Moth staggered into the air and climbed to 3,000 ft. As the pilot closed the throttle and moved towards a steep nose-up attitude to demonstrate the slots, he was amazed to hear this First World War hero shrieking in alarm, and demanding that the demonstration should cease immediately!

Handley Page decided to build an aeroplane to compete in the Daniel Guggenheim International Safe Aircraft Competition to be held at Mitchell Field, New York. The outcome was the Gugnunc with full span slots and flaps; its slow speed performance was shown by Jim Cordes to be remarkable. Flown in the Competition by two US Army pilots, the Gugnunc and the Curtiss Tanager, with manually operated flaps, were in competition at the final stage. The HP machine lost points in the slow glide and the Curtiss entrant with its markedly inferior slots, won the £20,000 prize. The Gugnunc is preserved in the Science Museum, London.

In May 1929 Tiny Scholefield was flying the Vickers Vanguard which had been undergoing route tests by Imperial Airways. It had been found that with one of its twin engines out of action it was difficult to trim directionally, so it was fitted with a Virginia tail which had no fins. Tiny took off from Brooklands with a flight observer, Frank Sharrett, to test the effect of the new tail. Suddenly, near Shepperton, it dived to the ground and caught fire, both men being killed. It was thought likely that Tiny pushed the rudders over to full lock at speed and overstressed the tail, which broke away. So died one of the most competent and experienced test pilots of his day.

Serving at A&AEE Martlesham was an exceptional young pilot, Flt Lt John Summers, for some strange reason known affectionately as 'Mutt'. At the age of 21 he was granted a short service commission in the RAF and learned to fly Avro 504s and Sopwith Snipes at Duxford. He passed out at Digby in 1924 and was posted to the crack No 24 (Fighter) Sqn flying Sopwith Snipes, soon to be replaced by Gloster Grebes. His exceptional talent for flying must have been evident in his earliest days with the squadron, for after only six months he was posted to Martlesham Heath as a test pilot, an unusual honour for a short-service officer. He began by testing the Gamecock, Bulldog, Hornbill and Avenger. The early instability problems with the prototype Bulldog almost caused Mutt to make his first parachute jump. He spun the machine, and nothing would induce it to come out of it. Grabbing the handholds in the centre section to haul himself out of the cockpit to bail out, he suddenly realized that the disturbance to the airflow caused by his body between fuselage and upper wing had so altered the flow over the tail that corrective action was beginning to work. He returned to his seat and abandoned spinning trials until the fuselage had been extended by eighteen inches. No further problems were found with the Bulldog.

Another unusual event concerned a terminal velocity test in a Hawker Hawfinch. Diving at top speed, almost vertically, the upper decking of the fuselage collapsed. It had the unfortunate side effect

Major James Cordes demonstrating the Handley Page Gugnunc at Cricklewood airfield (1929).

of overtightening the Sutton harness which passed through a slot at the rear of the pilot's seat, so 'Mutt' was jammed tightly in his seat hardly able to breathe. He decided never to use shoulder straps again, a decision which undoubtedly saved his life on another occasion.

Martlesham worked very closely with constructors and Summers was lent to Blackburn and Avro to test fly their aircraft and demonstrate them overseas. For Blackburn he tested seaplanes built at their factory in Greece, and he demonstrated the Avro Avenger in the Balkans.

After the death of Tiny Scholefield, 'Mutt' Summers was invited to join Vickers as chief test pilot.

The work of the Aeroplane and Armament Experimental Establishment at Martlesham had reached a stage where the methods of technical and operational appraisal of an aeroplane had been developed to a set pattern of logical sequential testing. To conform with normal Service procedures the Station accommodated two squadrons, No 15 and No 22. No 15 was concerned with the offensive and defensive capability of the aeroplane, testing guns, bombs and the sighting devices associated with them. No 22 was the authority responsible for Air Ministry Acceptance Trials of military machines and the issue of Certificates of Airworthiness for civil aircraft. The Squadron was set up in three flights. 'A' Flight concentrated upon testing fighter and light civil aeroplanes; 'B' Flight was responsible for bombers and heavier civil aircraft, whilst 'C' Flight dealt with those machines which did not come into the other categories.

The Olympia Aero Show and subsequent flying display showed the state of the art in Britain at the end of the 1920s. For military and larger civil aeroplanes, wood had almost disappeared as a main structural material. Armstrong Whitworth, Bristol, Boulton and Paul and Gloster used steel, Short Brothers and Vickers were using duralumin whilst Fairey, Blackburn and Hawker used either of these metals. The competition between radial air cooled and in-line liquid cooled engines was fierce, and it was clear that the whole industry was becoming much more professional. The test pilots were making a useful contribution to this situation as most of them were being recruited from Martlesham Heath. They would therefore carry out their test work in the full knowledge of what was required by the Service test pilots. This was the short cut to the standards of test flying set by George Bulman for Hawker and Cyril Uwins for Bristol.

The 1929 Schneider Trophy Contest again exposed to public adulation the group of Martlesham or Felixstowe test pilots who were members of the High Speed Flight. Commanded by Sqn Ldr A. H. Orlebar the team included Flt Lt D'Arcy Grieg who had the distinction of becoming the first RAF member of the Caterpillar Club, the exclusive membership roll of which includes only those airmen who have saved their lives by a parachute jump. F/O R. L. R. Atcherley, later, Air Vice Marshal Sir Richard, one of the greatest characters in the Royal Air Force, and Flt Lt H. R. D. Waghorn were in the team, the Contest being won by Waghorn in the Supermarine S.6 with the Rolls-Royce 'R' engine, at a speed of 328.63 mph. Blackburn had appointed Captain A. M. 'Dasher' Blake as their test pilot, although he was engaged in testing the rather prosaic Ripon and Dart naval aircraft.

One of the last designs to take to the air in the 1920s was the Hawker Hart prototype, a two seat day bomber to spec 12/26. From their study of the Curtiss D12 engine, and their experience with the Condor, Rolls-Royce developed their F10 and F12 series twelve cylinder in-line liquid cooled engine, later named Kestrel. The Hart was designed by Sydney Camm around this power unit. George Bulman flew the prototype in 1928, and fifteen development machines went into squadron service in 1930. Bulman was delighted with the first flight, and the machine was outstanding – a real 'pilot's aeroplane.' Dick Fairey was angry that the contract had not been placed with his firm after his pioneering work on clean entry in-line engined aeroplanes. He was not even invited to submit a design. Ultimately the Ministry relented, so he put forward a Fox Mk II. The Hart was the progenitor of the classic range of Hawker biplanes which were soon outclassed by designs overseas and, indeed, in Britain, but which served with distinction in noncombatant roles well into the Second World War. A Hind still flies from the Shuttleworth Collection at Old Warden. Immaculately restored to its original RAF livery it is a beautiful and evocative sight and sound in the air.

Avro's chief test pilot Capt H. A. Brown was seriously injured when an Avocet crashed at Woodford due to engine failure. Hubert Broad, at de Havilland, recruited Capt de Havilland's son Geoffrey to his flying staff just as the recession was beginning to show ominous signs for the industry, particularly with those firms concentrating upon civil aeroplanes.

An interesting and little known aspect of test flying developed directly from the Francis Mond Professorship of Aeronautical Engineering at the University of Cambridge, endowed in 1919 by Emile Mond, in memory of his son who was killed flying in the First World War.

The first Professor was Bennett Melvill Jones, later Sir Bennett Melvill Jones, CBE, AFC, FRS, Hon FRAeS, Hon FAIAA, one of Britain's most highly respected aeronautical scientists. Under his aegis, with support from the Air Ministry, aeroplanes were made available at RAF Duxford where the Cambridge University Air Squadron was based.

The Professor was primarily interested in aerodynamics rather than the structure of the aircraft. He wrote, in 1930: 'It ought to be realized that free flying experiment provides the essential cutting edge of aeronautical research.' He recognized the problem inherent in wind tunnel experiments – the difficulty in relating the results obtained from tests upon a small model to full scale production. It was clearly impossible to scale down turbulence, so the interpretation of model data was often misleading.

A major element in Jones's research at Cambridge concerned the stall which he recognized as the most serious hazard. Working with him as research pilot was J. A. G. Haslam who had served in the RFC and RAF during the war as an observer, learning to fly after the war.

In 1929 Melvill Jones, in a paper to the RAeS, discussed the streamlined aeroplane and his major research projects, which were directed towards drag reduction. He recognized the importance of being able to measure drag accurately, so he devised a pitot traverse method of analysis, with a comb of pitot tubes capable of mechanical traverse along the trailing edge of the wing. Haslam's scientific training was invaluable to Jones and they made a formidable combination of great value to the science of aviation.

The data presented in the 1929 paper established profile design parameters for aeroplanes and for the first time the designer was presented with an ideal at which to aim. The effect on the industry was quite dramatic; aircraft began to appear with the minimum of shapeless external protuberances. The days of the biplane were numbered, and the retractable undercarriage became a subject for serious consideration. In this way Professor Jones and Haslam – who later took holy orders – had a major effect upon designers throughout the world.

The decade ended in tragedy when two Martlesham pilots, Sqn Ldr A. G. Jones-Williams and Flt Lt N. H. Jenkins, in an attempt to set up a long distance record in the Fairey long range monoplane, flew into a hill near Tunis. Both were killed instantly. It was surmised that a defect in the cabin altimeter caused the accident.

5

THE BURGEONING CIVIL MARKET

Although the nation was stimulated by Britain's outright win of the Schneider Trophy on 13 September 1931, when Flt Lt J. N. Boothman flew the Supermarine S.6B round the Calshot Course at 340.08 mph, the aviation scene reflected deepening concern for the effects of the American recession.

It was considered by many experts that the great non-rigid airships R.100 and R.101, awaiting flight trials at Cardington, would revolutionize air travel, setting the highest standards of luxury and reliability. One sceptic, however, was E. F. Spanner, a talented and hard headed engineer, but without a background in aviation: in *This Airship Business* he was totally derisive of the project.

Lord Thomson, the Air Minister, demanded that R.101 fly him to India for an important Empire conference, ignoring the advice of those engineers and airmen who knew that the ship was totally unfit to fly. The disaster at Beauvais in the early morning of 5 October 1930, which resulted in the loss of 46 lives, including the Minister, Sir Sefton Brancker and most of Britain's airship experts, proved Spanner to be so tragically correct. R.100, in spite of her successful flight to Canada, was broken up, and development of large airships ceased in UK.

Two of the designers working on R.100 with Barnes Wallis at Howden, Yorkshire, A. Hessell Tiltman and Nevil Shute Norway (later to become famous as a novelist), decided to start their own aircraft company in York. With financial assistance from Lord Grimthorpe, a Yorkshire landowner, and Sir Alan Cobham the record breaking airman, they rented a bus garage in York and built a sailplane called the Tern, which was test flown for a mere pittance by a young German pilot, Carli Magesuppe, who impressed Norway with his modestly scientific approach to testing the machine.

Flying clubs were thriving and Geoffrey de Havilland's company was busy turning out Moths by the score at the modest price of £595. A metal framed Moth was produced which was chosen by the Prince of Wales for his personal transport, an event of immense benefit to de Havilland. By her flight to Australia in 19½ days the unknown Yorkshire typist, Amy Johnson, proved the reliability of the machine, and also the fact that record breaking flights were not the sole preserve of highly trained pilots.

Hubert Broad demonstrated the new steel tubular fuselage Moth to the high command of the RAF, making such an impression that a Service trainer version, the immortal Tiger Moth, was produced; Broad flying it for the first time in October 1931. The D.H.80 Puss Moth cabin monoplane was already established on the production line at Stag Lane and Geoffrey de Havilland demonstrated the machine at every opportunity.

The peak of RAF biplane fighter development in 1930 was the new Hawker Hornet, later re-named Fury. Designed by Sydney Camm, it went into production after uneventful flight testing by George Bulman, and trials at Martlesham Heath which demonstrated the potential of the design. One of the Martlesham pilots was F/O P. E. G. 'Gerry'

Hawker Fury II with steam-cooled Goshawk engine and spats. Note radiators on leading edge. Probably the most beautiful biplane ever built.

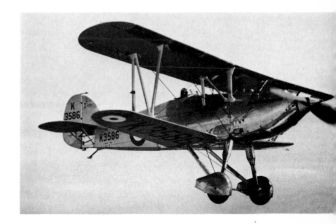

Sayer who soon joined George Bulman's test team and was the first pilot to fly the first British jet propelled aeroplane, the Gloster E28/39, in total secrecy at RAF Cranwell in 1941.

Among the bomber building fraternity Handley Page completed in 1930 the prototype HP.38 Heyford, J9130. The Heyford was a most unusual biplane, with the upper wing mounted on the top of the fuselage, the lower centre section being thickened to accommodate bombs. The position of the upper wing gave an unrivalled field of fire for the upper gunners, whilst the underside was protected by a gunner in a retractable 'dustbin' turret originated by Maj Cordes, who made the first two flights on 12 June 1930. Slight vibration of the fins, heavy elevators and minor trouble with the undercarriage was reported. The tailwheel collapsed as he turned on taxying. T. H. England made a flight later in the month and expressed himself well pleased with the machine which he said, 'was devoid of vice and had all the essential features required of a night bomber.' He criticized cockpit layout and the visibility of the instruments. Further flight development revealed cooling problems which necessitated larger radiators for the Kestrel engines. There was a fairly frantic rush to complete the modifications as Prince George was due to open the new Radlett aerodrome on 7 July, and, rather more importantly, the Vickers type 150 competitor for the bomber contract had already been shown in the New Types Park at Hendon and was under test at Martlesham. The Martlesham deadline for the B.19/27 competition submission was 1 September. It was impossible for the modifications to be made in time. The Vickers machine crashed after a double engine failure, so the date for submission was put back to February 1931. In November 1930 another contender had entered the field, Fairey's new monoplane, the Hendon. This, too, crashed in 1931 and was badly damaged. Repairs to the Vickers 150 were not completed until May 1931 so Handley Page had a further breathing space. All-up weight was increased from 12,000 lb to 14,760 lb and rose again to 15,270 lb. This introduced directional stability problems with one engine out, which necessitated a 25 per cent increase in rudder area and adjustments to the lower fins.

Tom Harry England was critical of the controls at low speed, so modifications were made which Cordes considered to be completely effective. England agreed after his flight, which terminated in brake failure as he taxied in. The hydraulic brakes were changed for pneumatic ones, which proved to be useless, and for several months flight trials were bedevilled with brake problems and then with propeller vibration. The Heyford was eventually cleared to go to Martlesham in October.

By February 1932 A&AEE had completed their tests, but disliked the position of the pilot's seat and the rudder pedals. The 'Rams horn' exhaust shrouds also ejected flames of sufficient volume to affect the night vision of the crew, so longer exhaust pipes were required. Nevertheless the aeroplane was generally well received and J9130 was subjected to a week of maintenance tests with No 15 Sqn. The Vickers 150 was still undergoing modifications at Weybridge and the Fairey Hendon was experiencing severe tail buffeting. After checks at Radlett the Heyford prototype was delivered to No 10 Sqn for further flight trials in the hands of five different pilots, all of whom liked the machine. The only vociferous complaint was by the armourers who were saturated when bombing up on wet grass. Handley Page could hardly do much about this problem so assumed that if this was the only real complaint their chances of an order were good. Investigations into drag reduction were initiated but no practical ideas emerged. In June the Heyford appeared at Hendon and then went to Upper Heyford for a demonstration before senior officers. During this display a fatigue failure in the end of the centre section front spar caused the starboard undercarriage to collapse. This was soon repaired on site and the machine then went to Radlett for new wheel spats to be fitted and on again to North Coates, Lincolnshire, for armament trials where it met its rival, the Fairey Hendon. The latter was designed to carry a larger bomb load than the Heyford, whose RAF crew decided that it should be bombed up to the same weight as the Hendon so that the trials could be directly comparable. As it took off the biplane was seen to be in serious trouble. It completed a slow circuit at full throttle

Handley Page Heyford.

Fairey Hendon.

and very low altitude, subsiding into the sand dunes where it was destroyed by fire. In spite of this inauspicious start, the Air Ministry ordered the type which entered service in 1933. 124 were built, the last survivor being struck off charge in 1941. One languished for a year or two, minus its outer wings, at Cardington where its propellers blew air at barrage balloons under development.

In March 1935 the Heyford had the distinction of being the first aeroplane in Britain to be detected by radar, or radio-location, as it was known in those days. Robert Watson-Watt, the 'father' of radar, established a 50 metre radio beam from the BBC transmitter at Daventry, Northants. A cathode ray oscilloscope connected to a suitable receiver displayed a deflection as soon as the bomber flew to within eight miles of the station, the deflection increasing as the Heyford approached. This was clearly a major break-through; transmitting towers were built at Orfordness, Suffolk, and formed the basis of the British radar network which was so crucial to the survival of the country in 1940. Later a Heyford was fitted with an aerial array between the wheel spats and, in company with an Avro Anson, carried out a major programme of flight test and radar development based on Martlesham Heath and Bawdsey Manor where the scientists worked.

Harald Penrose was creating a considerable reputation at Yeovil and was selected to take a Wapiti on a demonstration tour in South America. He tells, with relish, of his briefing by Sir Ernest Petter, the autocratic chairman of Westland. 'Do not forget, my boy,' said Sir Ernest, 'you represent a famous company; keep up appearances! Find the finest hotel in the place – but book a small room at the top – it will be cheaper!'

Soon after Penrose's return from South America, Louis Paget was seriously injured when his Wid-

geon failed to recover from a spin during an aerobatic display. Both legs were broken so he decided to retire. Harald was appointed chief test pilot at the age of 27. He immediately took over the flight trials of the Westland-Hill Pterodactyl.

Development had reached the stage of Mark 4 so the young pilot inherited the fascinating responsibility of testing an aeroplane for which there was little aerodynamic or structural precedent.

F/O F. J. Brunton, Louis Paget's assistant, did not like flying this machine with its tricky idiosyncracies, so he resigned, leaving all the work to Penrose who wrote, 'I found her a touchy little beast; I therefore regarded the new Pterodactyl with due caution as I strapped myself in the seat while Geoffrey Hill poured soothing words about the straightforwardness of its control . . . I went to the limit of the 600 yard airfield before turning into wind and gradually opening up. For a hundred yards we lurched, bucketed, yawed – the elevons initially ineffective. Suddenly ground roughness bounced her airborne, almost stalled; she touched only to be thrown up again, my instinctive control movements momentarily building up an increasing longitudinal oscillation coupled with yawing and lateral lurching that was almost beyond control. If this was Pterodactyl flying it seemed beyond me!'

Harald Penrose in the cockpit of a Westland Pterodactyl (1932).

Westland Pterodactyl Mk 5 showing the rear gunner's position.

Yet in a few seconds I found she could be kept straight because of increasing speed, and could hold a steady gentle climb. The worst was over. As soon as height was safe for a parachute escape I tried each control. Clearly she was very light and sensitive fore and aft and on the verge of instability, but laterally nearly as heavy as a Wapiti, and her single drag-plate rudders were sluggish, though easy to operate.'

'Within ten minutes I felt I knew the Pterodactyl reasonably well, though she was certainly not my ideal! I tried her at the stall before coming in to land, finding a gentle nod and lateral control giving excellent response.'

'I made two further take-offs, both fairly steady, but felt each time that there was a risk of a wing tip stall – and some months later this occurred after a premature bounce. Scarcely airborne, the machine turned through a right angle completely out of control, then continued climbing on this unpremeditated course. It seemed that testing new aircraft could have its moments!'

Preliminary spinning tests were carried out by Penrose and full trials were carried out at RAE Farnborough by Flt Lt G. H. Stainforth, who held the world speed record of 407.5 mph set up in 1931 in the S.6B, and who also flew the Pterodactyl at RAF displays when it was adorned with a shark mouth livery of unbelievable gaudiness.

The success of this machine inspired the Air Ministry to exploit the remarkable field of fire afforded by the tailless configuration, so Geoffrey Hill designed the Mark 5. This all metal version with the steam cooled Rolls-Royce Goshawk 600 hp engine had a top speed of 190 mph, considerably faster than the contemporary Hawker two seat biplanes. Harald Penrose commenced taxying trials, and was considerably dismayed when the whole wing structure collapsed due to an unsuspected off-set load in the struts which connected the rear wing spar to the outrigger balancer wheels.

After rectification, the test programme proceeded smoothly at the lower end of the speed range, but at high speed the wings twisted, nullifying the effect of the wing tip controllers. On the final flight a take-off bump raised the front wheel of the pivoted bogy undercarriage far enough to hit the radiator coolant cock and shut down the flow. In seconds the red warning lights were on to indicate that the notoriously hot Goshawk was in serious trouble. Penrose was low over Yeovil at the time but skilfully survived a potentially catastrophic situation by making a 180 degree turn, just managing to land at the aerodrome with the engine seized solid! The Mark 5 never flew again.

At Avro, H. A. 'Sam' Brown was busy with a range of Fokker monoplanes built under licence, whilst at Brough, 'Dasher' Blake was flying the Blackburn Bluebird, which, it was hoped, would offer serious competition to the D.H. Moth. It enjoyed limited success. In the military sphere their Iris flying boat for the RAF was in production. Glosters were in the doldrums with parts of the works being used for non-aviation activities.

In parallel with their work on the Heyford bomber Handley Page was building the famous HP.42 airliner for Imperial Airways. Also under construction was a three engine machine of similar configuration as a bomber transport to supersede the venerable HP Clive and Vickers Victoria. This design was known as the HP.43, but was not a success.

The airliner was to set new standards of luxurious comfort and cuisine on the airways of the world. The cabin was reminiscent of a Pullman

Handley Page HP.42 prototype. Note horizon bar over nose.

railway carriage. The type was named Hannibal. C. G. Grey suggested in *The Aeroplane* that it was chosen to assist in crossing the Alps.

The structure was built at Cricklewood and taken in sections to Radlett for final assembly and flight test. Frederick Handley Page was a frugal employer to whom spending money was anathema. He was approached by the works manager who explained the transport problems which continually arose. 'We must have a lorry, Sir,' said he. 'Rubbish!' said HP. 'Absolute rubbish! We cannot afford to buy a lorry, you will go out and buy a motorcycle and sidecar, and make do with that!' So the works made do until the size of components to be transported demanded that a proper vehicle be provided.

The HP.42 had four radial engines driving four bladed propellers, with two engines at the leading edge of the upper wing – a layout reminiscent of the ill-fated Tarrant Tabor, which killed its pilots at Farnborough in 1919, when the upper engines were opened up for take-off, driving the nose into the ground. So Tom Harry England paid particular attention to this possibility when he began taxying tests on 31 October 1930. There was no difficulty; although later, gates were fitted to the throttles, to ensure that it could not happen with the HP.42 loaded, to locate the centre of gravity too far forward. Flight tests were encouraging and posed few problems. England had only flown aeroplanes with long noses to provide an horizon datum, so he

fitted an horizon bar just in front of the windscreen which was right over the nose. Maj Cordes, who had experience of pusher aircraft and was accustomed to the absence of a datum, had it removed before he took responsibility for testing the HP.42. Other than problems with tailwheel collapse and visual distortion through the windscreen – soon overcome with optically flat glass – criticisms were few. The machine handled well and its ground manoeuvrability was remarkable, in that it could be turned easily in either direction with a pair of engines stopped on one side – a very valuable facility at the crowded Croydon terminal.

In June 1931 the HP.42 received its C of A and went into service on the Paris run where it was extremely popular. Its smoothness was indicated by a series of accelerometer readings taken on a full journey from London to Croydon by coach, flight to Le Bourget by 'Helena', and a French coach to the centre of Paris. The London coach recorded 2.75G, the actual flight 1.1G, and the French coach, predictably, 4.75G. The machine took off in nine seconds and landed at 50 mph. Top speed was a mere 127 mph. An amusing aspect of the cost effectiveness of these venerable aeroplanes was revealed by Sir Peter Masefield when he was chief executive of British European Airways. It is said that he was addressing a public meeting at a time when BEA was highly unprofitable. A member of the audience asked why Imperial Airways always managed to make a good profit when they operated these slow HP.42s, whilst BEA failed to do so with their modern aircraft. Sir Peter replied: 'That's easily explained, they were so slow that all the profits were made in the bar *en route*!'

Eight of these remarkable airliners were built, and not one of their passengers was injured in over five million miles of airline operation. In 1940 Hannibal was lost on war service over the Gulf of Oman, eight persons being killed.

The operation of the Hannibal class should, however, be seen in the context of what was happening in the United States. In February 1933 Boeing flew the first Model 247, a sleek all metal low wing monoplane with two radial engines, carrying ten passengers cruising at 155 mph. This was quickly overtaken by Donald Douglas's DC-1 all metal airliner, of similar configuration to the 247, but carrying twelve passengers in much greater comfort than in the cramped Boeing. The DC-1 was the precursor of the DC-2 and DC-3 Dakota. Over 10,000 DC-3s were produced and it was unquestionably a classic design upon which

Douglas DC-2 of Swissair at Croydon Airport terminal.

the immense success of the American commercial aircraft industry was based. Not until December 1938, when the de Havilland Flamingo flew, could Britain be seen to have an airliner remotely comparable with the American machines. The anti-cantilever monoplane lobby had left a formidable legacy of prejudice to be overcome.

By the beginning of the third decade Vickers had absorbed Supermarine, and the new company adopted the name Vickers Supermarine for its operations at Southampton. Vickers were busy on the Viastra, a high wing braced monoplane, which had the unusual facility of offering one, two or three engines. This undistinguished aeroplane was flown by Mutt Summers from Hamble in October 1930. It was chosen by the air-minded Prince of Wales as his personal transport.

At Brooklands, Barnes Wallis (who returned from Howden after the completion of design work on the R.100 airship) was busy designing the geodetic form of metal construction for large aircraft, which was to emerge in 1935 in the Wellesley bomber.

Edgar W. Percival, of Gull fame, was working at Cowes in 1931 on a joint project with Saunders-Roe. Alliott Verdon Roe had sold his interest in the company he founded, was knighted in 1929, and acquired an interest in the Cowes boat building firm of S. E. Saunders, who were building rudimentary flying boats.

With Percival in charge of the project, the Saro-Percival Mailplane was test flown by himself in 1932 and went to Martlesham for its C of A trials. Soon afterwards Percival sold out his interest and the Cruiser, as the machine became known, was handled by a separate company at Cowes called Spartan. The first flying boat built by Saunders-Roe was an attractive monoplane with two Cirrus Hermes engines. Flown initially by F/O Chilton it proved to be a satisfactory aircraft and was named Cutty Sark. More powerful Gipsy II engines were fitted, and in 1931 Capt S. D. Scott, who had joined Saunders-Roe as test pilot from RAF Calshot, carried out a 3,000 miles sales tour in a Cutty Sark to Dubrovnik, Belgrade, Budapest and Stockholm.

Saro test flying was a part-time occupation as the production rate was slow. Scott resigned from the firm, and the post was taken by Capt Leslie Ash, a one time RFC and RAF pilot who, on demobilization from service in No 70 Sqn in France, returned to the Sunbeam motor vehicle company where he had been an apprentice before he joined up. After a spell in India representing Sunbeam, he was attached in 1924 to their South Coast agent, Wadham and Company. From there he moved to the Isle of Wight in charge of a garage near Cowes. During the war he had delivered Camels and Pups (which he considered to be the most delightful aeroplanes he ever flew) from Cowes to France. In charge of the Cowes factory was S. E. Saunders, and if an aeroplane was not ready, he would entertain Capt Ash to lunch with the directors. To their mutual surprise they met at Ash's garage, Saunders being a regular customer. He tried to persuade Ash to join Saro. A year elapsed before he succumbed to the lure of aeroplanes, feeling that he was mad to relinquish a well paid job with commission for one offering a mere five pounds per week! So he joined the drawing office staff to work on the Medina, a wooden twin Bristol Jupiter engined flying boat, to carry ten passengers. Only one was built. Capt Scott felt that the Cowes aerodrome was too small for serious test flying so he resigned, leaving Leslie Ash as the only man with sufficient flying experience to test the aircraft. Whenever one was completed, Ash would leave his drawing board and carry out the trials. From the Cutty Sark was developed the Cloud, with Armstrong Siddeley Double Mongoose engines of 340 hp. This boat went into RAF service as an amphibian trainer for potential flying boat pilots. Throughout the 1930s, including the London flying boat period, Saro test flying remained a part-time job until the disastrous Lerwick was built in 1938. The company was subcontracted to build the Supermarine Walrus.

In 1932 York-based Airspeed completed the first Ferry, a three engined biplane mini-airliner for Sir Alan Cobham's National Aviation Day displays.

Airspeed Ferry prototype.

Cobham had joined the board of the new company at its inception and had suggested production of the Tern sailplane which had not been a commercial success, only four being built. So Sir Alan placed an order for two Ferrys and saved the struggling company.

The prototype was built in the cramped bus garage at York and was towed through the night to Sherburn in Elmet, the base of the Yorkshire Aero Club. At 2 am the convoy, with the Ferry reduced in width to sixteen feet by the removal of its outer wings, met the rudder of the liner Berengaria en route to the building yard on Clydebank. The air had to give way to the more senior service so the Ferry was manhandled into a side road whilst the liner-less rudder passed by.

The test flights were carried out by Capt H. V. Worrall, chief pilot of Yorkshire Flying Services, for a fee of £30. After satisfactory engine runs and taxying tests Worrall took off for a 19 minute flight. Hessell Tiltman recalled a newspaper reporter writing about the flight: 'He watched with intense interest the face of the designer (Tiltman) as an expression of acute anxiety gradually gave way to one of intense relief as the machine safely took to the air.'

After lunch workpeople were embarked and taken for a flight, a venture which, by modern licencing procedures, was reckless in the extreme. One of them was terrified. As he sat gazing at the brightly polished engine cowlings, the Ferry broke through the cloud and a flash of bright sunlight on the cowling convinced the nervous passenger that the aeroplane was on fire! Further flight trials revealed a longer take-off run than envisaged, but this was overcome with propellers of finer pitch.

To ensure closer control of structural integrity and handling characteristics, the designers 'bible', Air Publication A.P.970, was amended in 1932 by Design Memoranda defining procedures for fixing CG positions, speeds right through the range, effectiveness of cooling systems and other criteria which must be built into the design at its inception. Slowly the art of building aeroplanes was becoming more scientific.

The work of the best of the industry test pilots and their counterparts at Martlesham Heath and Farnborough, combined with the skill of the aerodynamicists and wind tunnel technicians was creating a much better correlation between theory, model testing and full scale testing. Structural innovation flourished. A new firm, General Aircraft of Hanworth, developed the twin-Pobjoy engined Monospar, with a patented form of pyramid wire bracing on a single wing spar to prevent it twisting. This unattractive looking aeroplane enjoyed limited success in a market totally dominated by de Havilland.

Glosters were advocating variable pitch propellers for high performance aircraft. They had an interest in the Hele Shaw Beecham design. Whereas the Air Ministry showed total indifference, the propeller was seen by the American builder, Tom Hamilton, who returned to his works and quickly developed it, and before the end of the decade de Havilland were building it under licence.

Cierva had moved his works to Hanworth Air Park and, by the end of 1933, Reggie Brie with his assistant Alan Marsh (sadly to be killed after the war in the Cierva Air Horse), were testing a new autogiro which had dispensed with the fixed wing. Every opportunity was taken to demonstrate the new machine at air shows throughout the country. Avro had abandoned work on autogiros so Cierva had the field almost to themselves with de Havilland toying with a project based on a Puss Moth fuselage.

General's prototype Monospar came to grief at Croydon on its fourth flight, when test pilot Fl Lt H. M. Schofield had an engine failure on take-off and ran into an iron fence; the nose and wing were damaged.

Gloster completed their TC.33 four engine bomber transport which was flown for the first time by their test pilot, Flt Lt H. J. Saint. The tandem engine installation had serious cooling problems and its controls left much to be desired. In an attempt to improve handling in the event of a double engine failure on one side, the rudders were so large that in a sideslip they were almost immovable. After many adjustments to overcome directional hunting and tail flutter, the TC.33 went to Martlesham, where it was rejected due to its hopelessly inadequate take-off performance.

Imperial Airways had issued in 1929 an outline specification for an airliner to operate their African services, carrying nine passengers, three crew and 1,000 lb of freight. The envisaged range was to be 400 miles at 9,000 ft with a cruising speed of 115 mph. John Lloyd, Armstrong Whitworth's chief designer, decided to flout the British biplane convention which was looking so dated by comparison with contemporary American and European practice. He designed a handsome high wing monoplane with four 260 hp Armstrong Siddeley Serval radial engines. It was of composite steel, plywood and fabric construction, with a very unusual streamlined undercarriage, taking advantage of the deep fuselage and high cantilever wing, to pivot a cantilever leg at the bottom curve of the fuselage with the shock absorbing strut inside. In spite of the ingenuity and clean line of the arrangement, it was found to contribute 20 per cent to the total drag of the aeroplane, a fact which constituted a strong argument in favour of the retractable undercarriage, not to be seen on a British commercial machine until the advent of the Airspeed Courier in 1933.

On 6 June 1932 Alan Campbell-Orde carried out taxying trials of the prototype AW.15 Atalanta, experiencing some problems with flat spots in engine response when the throttles were opened. Nevertheless, a fifteen minute flight was made. Campbell-Orde was satisfied with the machine but alarmed to hear, as he landed, a great clattering from behind. This turned out to be an unlatched lavatory door. A more serious problem arose next day on the third flight. As the Atalanta touched down, the locking device for the pilot's seat broke and slid to the rear of its travel. With the occupant gripping the control column, just at the point of touchdown, a heavy landing resulted, but fortunately there was no damage.

Flight tests proceeded without undue difficulty and the AW.15 was flown to Martlesham on 11 July for its C of A trials. During its eight days at the Heath, four Service pilots flew it and were impressed by its handling characteristics and performance. Some tailwheel vibration was experienced and a lateral oscillation of the rudder occurred when a turn to port was initiated. After minor modifications to clear these snags, Atalanta was flown to Croydon for acceptance trials by Imperial Airways. On 26 September a service to

Armstrong Whitworth Atalanta prototype.

Brussels and Cologne was flown by the prototype. Three and a half months from first flight to a route proving commercial flight was a creditable achievement.

In October Atalanta was back at the works for modifications to the fuel tank venting system, as it was afflicted with a minor problem which has affected many aeroplanes. The position of the vents on the wing surface was such as to induce an imbalance of pressure in the tank with consequent restriction of flow. Some new vents were fitted, and Alan Campbell-Orde took off with Donald Salisbury Green as co-pilot and Air Marshal Sir John Higgins, chairman of Armstrong Whitworth, in the passenger cabin. Just after take-off all four engines failed, so a forced landing had to be made on a hillock just outside the aerodrome. Atalanta was badly damaged, Campbell-Orde and Sir John were uninjured, but Salisbury Green, who was out of his seat trying to locate the cause of the engine failure, was seriously injured. His test flying career was terminated by this crash which proved to be due to the new fuel tank vents demonstrably inferior to the ones they replaced.

Imperial Airways were embarrassed by the occurrence which reflected no discredit upon the aeroplane as such, but the airline decided to re-name the third machine off the production line Atalanta, hoping that the change of registration letter would not be noticed!

Eight AW.15s were built. It was soon realized, however, that they were too small for the expanding routes so there was no commercial future for this reliable performer. In 1942 the three survivors were impressed into the Indian Air Force.

Tom Harry England and Jim Cordes at Handley Page had a rough time with two new prototypes in 1933–34. Resulting from strong competition between HP and Blackburn to achieve an order for a deck landing torpedo bomber for the Royal Navy, the Japanese Navy approached them and asked for design submissions. The two Navys' requirements were similar so a project was commenced on the HP.40 for Japan and the HP.41 for the Royal Navy. Blackburn's machine was chosen by the Japanese, so HP proceeded with the HP.41. RN specifications for aeroplanes were traditionally diabolical and this one was no exception. Invariably the 'fish-heads' asked for the utterly impossible so great compromises were called for; the usual outcome was that the aeroplane tried to do so many jobs that it did none of them properly. In addition the matelots treated them as though they were built of ship's plate. Intensive design work was carried out; when it was almost complete, the Admiralty changed the specification, so a new design was commenced, which appeared on the airfield for its first flight as the HP.46. It was a strange looking machine with an inverted gull lower wing, and a sophisticated system of slots and flaps. England made the first flight and landed after a few minutes with a large snag list. The worst being that when the slots were open the flaps, which were connected to them, dragged on the ground when taxying; furthermore the controls were generally sloppy. Endless modifications were made between the first flight in October 1932 and the sixth one in July 1933, still England and Cordes were dissatisfied. Frederick Handley Page realized that he was throwing good money after bad, and managed to persuade the Air Ministry to take the HP.46 to Farnborough as a research machine for high lift devices. To the relief of everyone concerned, the Ministry agreed, subject to a formal expression of the director of technical development's dissatisfaction. So it disappeared on a lorry in April 1935, having cost twice the contract price and flown for a mere 5½ hours. No other biplane was built by the company. It was considered that most of the troubles in the aerodynamic sense were due to the inability of the aerodynamicists at that time to interpret misleading data in the wind tunnel.

The Handley Page HP.47 was another aeroplane designed to a specification calling for it to perform more roles than could reasonably be expected. It was to replace the Vickers Vincent general purpose machine in the Middle East and India, act as a day and night bomber operating from rough air strips

Handley Page HP.47.

anywhere in the world, and serve as a land-based torpedo bomber in tropical areas.

The layout was ingenious, although the original model with a short tail boom showed undesirable flat spinning tendencies in the RAE vertical tunnel. Various modifications were made to the design and not until November 1933 was the Bristol Pegasus engined prototype ready for its first flight. Once again the snag list was a long and serious one. England and Jim Cordes shared the flying and were unanimous that the undercarriage oleo legs were too spongy, the elevators too heavy, the brakes generally unsatisfactory, and the tailplane incidence impossible to adjust. And, for good measure, they were also unhappy with the hood sliding arrangements which were difficult to operate against the slipstream.

By August 1934, when Tom Harry England retired, and Cordes was appointed chief test pilot, England had flown the HP.47 on twenty test sorties and Cordes had made forty flights in it with continual problems and modifications between flights. Westlands monoplane contender for this contract had crashed in 1933 and the specification was changed after the HP.47 had been flown by Martlesham test pilots, who criticized it on several counts.

Vickers were awarded the contract, which was ultimately written around their new Wellesley bomber. After Jim Cordes had flown the unhappy prototype 79 times, it went to RAE at Farnborough for investigation into low speed controllability problems and engine development work, before being struck off charge in 1937.

The crash of the Westland monoplane competitor of the HP.47 gave Harald Penrose the dubious distinction of being the first British test pilot to escape by parachute from an enclosed cockpit.

The PV.7 high wing braced monoplane suffered, as did the Pterodactyl, from wing torsional flexure at speed. Arthur Davenport, the chief designer, was sceptical when this was reported and rashly went up with Penrose to see for himself. The machine entered a gentle dive and aileron was applied. 'See the twist?' asked Penrose over the intercom. 'No twist,' said Davenport. 'Right, I'll show you!' Speed increased and full aileron was applied. 'Stop Harald!' yelled the discomfited designer. 'You'll have the wings off!' The aeroplane was suitably modified and went to Martlesham where the pilots were impressed with its performance. The Air Ministry decided that further tests should be carried out with the CG further aft. Westland engineers loaded the ballast whilst Harald Penrose adjusted his parachute. It was a windy day and he climbed to 14,000 ft where conditions seemed fairly stable. As he climbed, a telegram was received at Martlesham from Westland demanding that the flight be postponed as the strength requirements were not adequate at the new loading. It was too late and there was no radio link with the pilot.

Preliminary dives were made to ensure that instability had not been introduced by the altered CG. All was well, so the aeroplane nosed over into a dive. Penrose watched the speed rise, checking engine revs to avoid over-speeding. Suddenly the machine faltered and there was a loud bang as the port wing broke off, then a thud as it tore the tail off. Trapped in the cockpit by the enormous G forces as the wreck gyrated downwards, the pilot struggled to escape through the deep side window. The parachute deployed but his troubles were not yet over. After a heavy landing which damaged his ankles, the high wind dragged his parachute across a stubble field until it was arrested by a hedge. Casting off his harness he rose painfully to his feet, to be confronted by an attractive young lady on the other side of the hedge who breathlessly enquired after his health. Before he could answer he had to clutch at his falling trousers, every vital button of which had been torn off in his high speed transit across the field!

The wreck was spread over seven miles and proved that the port rear wing strut had failed in turbulence – although Harald Penrose suggested that a previous landing problem, when a wheel came off may have weakened the structure. PV.7 development ended on a sour note, with the Air Ministry repudiating all liability as the machine was being flown at an RAF station by a civilian

Westland PV.7 before cockpit cover fitted (1932).

pilot. By the time interminable arguments had persuaded them to pay a notional figure for the aeroplane, it was too late to build another. The PV.7 laid the foundations for another memorable high wing design, the famous Lysander.

In 1933 Shorts were building the R24/31 monoplane flying boat with two steam cooled Rolls-Royce Goshawk engines. This impressive but ugly boat, generally known as the 'Knuckleduster', was flown for the first time by John Lankester Parker whilst the Air Minister was at the Rochester works. Years later Parker commented to Tom Brooke-Smith, who succeeded him as chief test pilot, on one of the paradoxes of the test pilot's life. He said that on this occasion he was to fly the Minister back to the capital in a Calcutta flying boat, which would alight on the Thames so that the great man could be ferried straight to the steps of the House of Commons. During the morning he flew the 'Knuckleduster' for the first time. It was a frightening experience; the machine would not climb so he staggered back to put it down on the Medway. He commented to Brookie, 'On that trip I nearly killed myself for a paltry fee of £5, for the later flight to the House of Commons I was given a gold cigarette case with my initials in diamonds!' Flexing of the rear end was another problem which beset the R24/31, which had the usual Goshawk overheating characteristics as well. It was abandoned after trials at Felixstowe.

A more satisfactory contemporary was the Short Scion small airliner with two Pobjoy Niagara radial engines. A later model, built in 1935, was used as a trial horse for some of the high lift devices to be used in the great Short Empire Class flying boats which were in the works. On one test of a Scion without ailerons but with small flaps, which moved

out on one side or the other as the control column was moved across, the machine commenced a roll as soon as it left the ground. It was saved by Parker's quick thinking; he put the nose down, switched off the engines and landed, all in a matter of seconds.

Structural failure caused the loss of Vickers M1/30 torpedo bomber prototype when Mutt Summers and John Radcliffe, his observer, began TV dives at full load with a torpedo fitted. At speed in the dive both sets of wings broke away, Summers being thrown from the cockpit whilst Radcliffe had to free his parachute harness from the machine gun before he, too, floated safely to the ground. Further revisions to the stiffness requirements in the appropriate design memoranda were promulgated.

At Fairey Aviation, Chris Staniland was busy refining later Marks of the Fox which had found favour with the Belgian Air Force, whilst Mutt Summers, after his narrow escape in the M1/30 crash, had turned his attention to a new Vickers fighter, the low wing, radial engined Jockey and a new amphibian, the Seagull (later Walrus, or affectionately 'Shagbag'), which had been designed by Supermarine for the Australian Government and had been ordered for the RAF.

The Vickers Monoplane was first flown in 1930 with slots along the leading edge near the wing root. Buffeting was experienced and torsional rigidity of the rear fuselage left much to be desired. Soon after the crash of the Heyford prototype the Jockey was under test at Martlesham. For its time it seemed an advanced aeroplane, although some prejudice existed among the pilots who thought that the Hawker Fury was the most perfect fighter that could be built. The continuing problem of buffeting did not help its image; a Townend ring cowling around its Bristol Mercury engine made a slight improvement, but the one thing that probably would have solved the problem, a streamlined fillet between the wing and fuselage, was not known at that time. The spinning characteristics of the Jockey were also suspect. In 1931 the RAE had commissioned the first spinning tunnel in the world. Thirty feet high and twelve feet in diameter, it was used to test a dynamic model of the correct scale weight in the rising current of air. From the results of tests in this tunnel the Jockey was rebuilt, with a changed fuselage taper, a new rudder with greater chord and a longer tailplane.

Tests continued with Mutt Summers' assistant, F/O H. W. R. Banting in charge. To check the effect of the modifications on the flat spin propensity of the aeroplane, an RAF pilot climbed to 10,000 ft

and initiated a spin – the nose lifted, and it adopted the disastrous flat spin which the tunnel tests had indicated was now most unlikely. Recovery proved impossible, so the pilot took to his parachute at 5,000 ft. RAE decided that much more work should be done on flat spin research; the phenomenon was not fully understood, and it was clear that a number of otherwise inexplicable fatal accidents had resulted from it. It was thought that turbulence generated by the tailplane as the aeroplane rotated blanketed the rudder, causing it to be ineffectual. This proved to be the case after exhaustive tests in the spinning tunnel.

With rather unhappy memories of the Short Gurnard seaplane, with its badly overbalanced ailerons, and the problems of the 'Knuckleduster' in mind, John Lankester Parker was preparing to fly the great Sarafand six-engined flying boat with a wing span of 120 ft. The Gurnard had been the first Short machine to have Frise ailerons, designed by Leslie G. Frise, Bristol's chief designer. A portion of the aileron was forward of the hinge line to counteract air loads and lighten the controls. As soon as the Gurnard left the water it performed three 45 degree banks to each side with the control column thrashing from side-to-side, hammering the pilot's hands against the cockpit. Trapping the stick between his legs and using all his strength, Parker managed to alight again, about one minute after take-off.

Designed by the talented Arthur Gouge, the Sarafand had six Rolls-Royce Buzzards in tandem pairs. On the slipway, engine runs revealed a high level of vibration at low rpm. This was overcome by linking the engine nacelles with streamlined steel tubes. Sarafand was also fitted with Frise ailerons, so Lankester Parker was determined to wait for an absolutely calm day for the maiden flight, which was extremely successful. The big boat flew exceptionally well and was the fastest flying boat in the world with a top speed of 153 mph at sea-level. It was right in almost every detail from the start of its trials at Rochester, and at Felixstowe, where Parker flew it for the first few days. At MAEE an engine fire damaged one of the lower wings; this was replaced, and trials continued most satisfactorily, but no order was forthcoming. The prototype languished at Felixstowe until 1936 when it was broken up, or 'reduced to produce', to use the Service jargon.

The first half of the third decade saw a series of prototypes which were improved versions of machines, representative of the state of the art. An exception was the Airspeed Courier. A low wing cantilever wooden monoplane with an Armstrong Siddeley Lynx radial engine and a retractable undercarriage, it was designed by Hessell Tiltman for Sir Alan Cobham. The latter intended to use it for development work on in-flight re-fuelling, pioneered by the Hon Mrs Victor Bruce in August 1932, when she flew in a Saro Windhover amphibian with an RAF crew for 54 hours 13 minutes, being refuelled eight times by a converted Bristol Fighter tanker.

Cobham immediately recognized the potential value of the technique in extending the range of aircraft and placed an order for the Courier which he planned, originally, to fly non-stop to Australia.

Airspeed moved their works from York to Portsmouth whilst the Courier was being built in 1933 and were fortunate enough to obtain the services of an RAE test pilot, world speed record holder, Flt Lt G. H. Stainforth.

No other British commercial aeroplane had been fitted with a retractable undercarriage; the technical jeremiahs complaining that they were too costly, too heavy, too complicated, too unreliable and of only marginal value in improving performance. So Tiltman and Norway designed the 'Retractor' undercarriage from scratch. Intensive static tests proved its reliability but its in-flight performance was an unknown factor. George Stainforth spent hours in the cockpit of the prototype which was jacked up in flying position, checking and re-checking every aspect of the undercarriage until he had satisfied himself that it was as perfect as static testing could determine. The first flight was uneventful, the machine handled superbly and showed a top speed of 155 mph, 10 mph faster than Tiltman had predicted. It flew 37 mph faster with the undercarriage retracted than with it down – a convincing answer to the pessimists. On a later flight Stainforth saved the Courier – and Airspeed – from disaster. Taking off over Langstone Harbour the engine failed at 300 ft. Stainforth reacted brilliantly, pushing the nose down to maintain flying speed and lowering the landing gear as he made a gentle turn downwind to touchdown smoothly on the aerodrome.

Cobham's own flight refuelling tests were memorable. Using a Handley Page W.10 airliner as a tanker, he would formate behind and below it, with Sqn Ldr W. Helmore standing on the seat of the Courier, his body through the roof hatch, endeavouring to catch the line connected to the W.10's nose so that it could be drawn down, and the nozzle inserted in the collector tank filler tube. On one occasion the weight on the end of the line

Airspeed Courier being refuelled from the Handley Page W.10 tanker – early experiments which led to present techniques used by the RAF and others.

caught in the aileron gap, putting the aeroplane into a sideslip. Cobham attempted to centralize the stick, but this was unsuccessful with height being lost at an alarming rate. Six turns of a spin had been completed before he was able to extricate the line and regain control. Thereafter a child's balloon full of water was used as a weight.

Cobham completed his trials and began a flight to India. After a successful airborne refuelling near Ford, Sussex, he repeated the operation at Malta. Unfortunately, a failure of the throttle linkage, due to a split pin coming out of a joint fitting, caused the throttle to close and a forced landing with a grossly overloaded Courier was safely made at Malta. Cobham's work had been sufficiently convincing in proving the value of in-flight refuelling, to lead to the formation of his famous company, Flight Refuelling.

Charles Fairey had developed the Fox for service with the Belgian Air Force. His Belgian designer Marcel Lobelle conceived, as a private venture, one of the most elegant aeroplanes ever built, the Fantôme. Powered by a 925 hp Hispano-Suiza in-line engine with a 20 mm Oerlikon cannon firing through the propeller shaft and four .303 Browning machine guns, this exceptionally clean biplane had a top speed of 270 mph. It was demonstrated at the Evere Air Show in Belgium in July 1935 by test

Fairey Fantôme.

pilot S. G. H. Trower, but crashed, killing him. Three more were built, one going to A&AEE for armament trials. The type was not developed – the day of the biplane was drawing to an end.

After the 1931 Schneider Trophy contest, F/O Leonard S. Snaith and other members of the victorious team returned to Martlesham with the thought that a further challenge might be made. In a BBC broadcast several years after the war Sir Hugh Dowding, that great leader of Fighter Command in the Battle of Britain, recalled that during his service as Air Member for Supply and Research it was hinted that the Air Ministry would consider donating a further trophy. Dowding was emphatic. 'No!' said he. 'Many thousands of pounds have

Supermarine S.6B seaplane, which won the Schneider Trophy in 1931 at 340.08 mph.

been spent on these seaplanes, and they are no use to us at all, we must have a new fighter and it must be a monoplane.' At this time a replacement for the Bulldog was under consideration and Dowding expressed his dismay that after the success of the Schneider machines a biplane should be considered desirable. As usual, he was right, and managed to convince the Air Ministry. Consequently the momentous specification F7/30, which, indirectly, gave Britain the Hurricane and Spitfire, was issued on 1 October 1931. In the next three years eight designs were offered by various companies, five of them being biplanes.

Bristol's Type 123 biplane with its Goshawk engine was flown by Cy Uwins. It had endless cooling problems. Lateral instability and buffeting were evident, the project being abandoned as was the odd looking Blackburn F7/30. This was another aeroplane bedevilled with the Goshawk engine and the additional worry of instability on the ground. It never flew. Another Bristol contender was the private venture Type 133 monoplane. It was a clumsy looking aeroplane with rearward retracting undercarriage legs housed in large fairings on the wings. Cyril Uwins flew it and was favourably impressed. It achieved a speed of 260 mph at 15,000 ft and a rate of climb of 2,200 ft/min. Performance and most of the handling trials had been completed in only 18 flying hours, only diving and spinning tests remained to be carried out before the machine was to be flown to Martlesham. Uwins carried out the spinning trials and two dives to 310 mph IAS. Another test pilot, T. W. Campbell, took it up again and started a right hand spin at 14,000 ft. The landing gear however was still down, and the 133 developed a flat spin; centrifugal force

Bristol 133 monoplane after spinning problems.

caused fuel starvation which stopped the engine. Recovery was impossible and Campbell bailed out, the sole prototype being destroyed in the crash.

R. J. Mitchell designed the Supermarine 224, which was also fitted with the Goshawk, this installation being evaporatively cooled, a system which, on a low wing monoplane, required most complex and troublesome plumbing. This inverted gull wing design with a trousered undercarriage was not among Mitchell's most inspired designs. Its 45 ft span manoeuvrability was poor and the engine was continually overheating. As its top speed was only a few miles per hour faster than the Gloster Gauntlet biplane it was a disappointment to Mitchell, who immediately commenced work on an entirely new low wing monoplane with a retractable undercarriage, designed around the new Rolls-Royce PV VII engine, later named Merlin. Around this design was written the final spec. F37/34, which brought a private venture design into respectability. Contrary to legend, the Air Ministry was not antagonistic towards the low wing layout at this stage; the old prejudice was almost dead and it was realized that biplanes must go. Further convincing evidence of the trend was supplied by Rolls-Royce, who had equipped their test fleet with a very sleek Heinkel 70 monoplane powered with a Kestrel engine.

Sydney Camm, at Hawkers, was working on another low wing monoplane fighter to be powered by the Rolls-Royce PV VII, so the two Battle of Britain winners entered their gestation period as a new phase of aeronautical technology dawned.

A major breakaway from accepted practice was taking shape at Weybridge where Barnes Wallis's geodetic Wellesley single engine bomber was under construction, using a system of lattice members 'wound' helically round the fuselage with a similar lattice structure for wings and tail surfaces, the airframe being covered in fabric. Immensely strong and light, geodetic construction proved itself in the later Wellington to be able to withstand very serious battle damage and still fly home.

Armstrong Whitworth were planning their great Ensign airliner to an Imperial Airways specification. At their Rochester works Short Brothers were building the magnificent Empire flying boats for Imperial Airways whilst Handley Page was busy with the Harrow, soon to be superseded by the very advanced Hampden all metal twin engined bomber. In his Woodford drawing office Roy Chadwick was studying the general arrangement of the bomber to be known as the Manchester, later – rather by accident – to become the remarkable Lancaster.

Armstrong Whitworth was building the Whitley heavy bomber, whilst at Blackburn's Brough factory, the Skua dive bomber/fighter was taking shape for the Fleet Air Arm. Fairey's Great West Road factory near London was developing the shapely P4/34 which was turned into the excellent Merlin engined Fulmar fleet fighter. Of the major manufacturers only de Havilland was still building wooden aeroplanes.

So, at last, the monoplane had come into its own; engine development was almost keeping pace with aerodynamic design based upon the results of theoretical and wind tunnel research at Farnborough, the National Physical Laboratory at Teddington, and in the aircraft constructors own experimental and research departments. Flight test at Martlesham Heath was a valuable source of data but it was restricted in circulation to the manufacturer of the particular machine. It took a world war to achieve a level of cooperation which created a close interchange of information between A&AEE and all firms in the industry, to the great benefit of the industry and the nation.

An exciting new era was approaching for the test pilots who were to face major challenges with the new generation of military and civil aircraft soon to become their responsibility and, in the case of the military machines, make a vital contribution to the very survival of the United Kingdom, and indeed, the free world.

THE WAR CLOUDS GATHER

1935 and 1936 were vintage years for prototype aeroplanes. In 1935 signs from Nazi Germany were so ominous that re-armament on a massive scale became essential. Adolf Hitler had told Anthony Eden, the Foreign Secretary, and Sir John Simon, that the *Luftwaffe* was already 30 per cent larger than the Air Staff had predicted.

A watershed in the fortunes of the aircraft industry was reached in 1935; two years earlier there would have been little alternative to ordering biplanes and braced monoplanes of inferior performance, totally outclassed by the Messerschmitt Bf 109 which they would have to meet in combat. By the end of 1936 prototypes of Hurricane, Spitfire, Battle, Blenheim, Wellesley, Anson, Wellington, Whitley, Lysander and the famous Empire flying boats, from which the Sunderland was developed, had all made their first flights. A new breed of aeroplane had emerged.

The Government Shadow Factory scheme was under way. The importance of this to the successful outcome of the Second World War can hardly be overestimated. Huge factories were built by the Government to be managed by appropriate large companies to build war materiel on a very large scale.

The new military aeroplanes designed for front line service were of stressed skin metal construction; they were clean, very efficient, cantilever monoplanes with retractable undercarriages and flaps. The engines were supercharged and drove variable pitch propellers which were going into production at de Havilland's Stag Lane factory, and at Rotol, a company owned jointly by Rolls-Royce and Bristol. Engine power was dramatically increased by the introduction of high octane aromatic fuel, available in quantity for the first time.

So the pioneers of all these innovations triumphed at last and routed the pessimists. The nation, and particularly the Royal Air Force, was deeply in their debt as events during the next few years were to show. If the pioneers ruminated in their studies and said quietly to themselves 'I told you so', they could have been forgiven.

The industry had passed through its adolescence, and was becoming professional and scientific in its approach, albeit with much to learn, often the hard way. Professional, too, were the test pilots. 'Seat of the pants' flying of the early days had given way to carefully planned trials which owed much to the Farnborough and Martlesham pilots, a number of whom had joined, or were about to join, the firms. There were many unexpected hazards to face, and obscure problems to arise and overcome, but the principles had been established by which a predictably reasonable aeroplane could be built and refined by flight trials into a good one or, indeed, in the case of the Spitfire, a brilliant one.

The devoted and painstaking work of the engine test pilots, whose often boring job brought them no publicity unless they crashed and killed themselves, was directed towards improving engine reliability. Every move to extract more horse power from an engine inevitably increased the risk of engine failure and required hundreds of hours of test on the dynamometer and in flying test beds before the up-rated power unit could pass its Type Test.

The pilots proudly demonstrated their new aeroplanes, although a cloak of secrecy shrouded many of them. The New Types Park at the Hendon RAF Display, the Society of British Aircraft Constructors Show, the Royal Aeronautical Society Garden Party and air displays all over the country, and in Europe, were the constructors' shop windows although there were embarrassments. One company was said to have despatched to an Eastern European country a prototype small airliner which rejoiced in the name 'Avatar'. An official welcoming committee awaited its arrival at the airport of the capital city. As the pilot taxied towards the reception tent the British Chargé d'Affaires was shocked to see the name emblazoned on the nose in red paint; it was, apparently, a word never used in polite society in that country. A pot of aluminium

Major James Cordes boarding a Hampden bomber (1938).

dope quickly reduced the offending name to the inocuous 'Ava'!

The social scene was memorable. All the Service and civilian mandarins that mattered attended events, often with very attractive and elegant ladies. The test pilots had a slightly gladiatorial charisma about them; in *Flight* or *The Aeroplane* one might read, 'The immaculate Major Cordes put up a polished display in the Hampden/Harrow at the RAeS. Garden Party.' James Cordes always wore a smart white flying suit and a monocle – being a handsome man he was always noticed. The constructors' dinner at Martlesham Heath was the highlight of the social calendar, when, away from the public gaze, the letting down of whatever top level hair remained was accomplished with great gusto.

Membership of the Society of British Aircraft Constructors was a jealously guarded privilege. To be able to build good aeroplanes was certainly not the only qualification for entry to 'The Family', as the SBAC was known – rather sarcastically in some quarters.

Hessell Tiltman, of Airspeed, submitted a very advanced design for a bomber to specification B1/35. The 113 page brochure was ignored at Air

Ministry under circumstances of great discourtesy by the very senior civil servant responsible. The exclusivity of the Society is said to have originated with a Cabinet Minute promulgated in the 1920s when orders for military aircraft were few and Handley Page had demanded guarantees that only the well established manufacturers should be considered for future orders. So the newer firms, such as Airspeed, Philips and Powis – later, Miles, General Aircraft and Martin Baker, were seriously handicapped and the RAF probably deprived of very useful aeroplanes. This was certainly the case with Martin Baker if, indeed, this notorious minute was invoked to stifle their MB.2, MB.3 and MB.5 fighter designs during the Second World War, when the simple and effective MB.2 could have been developed to be of immense value in the Battle of Britain.

Two advanced civil aeroplanes made their first flights in 1935. Avro, by then in the Hawker Siddeley Group with Gloster, had built a pair of low wing monoplane airliners with a cruising speed of 165 mph, at that time a remarkable achievement on two 290 hp Cheetah VI radial engines. From these machines, delivered to Imperial Airways in March 1935, came the immortal Anson, remembered with affection by many thousands of aircrew under training, and in its coastal reconnaissance role. That affection was tempered, on the part of

Bill Thorne at the controls of an Avro Anson (1941).

those who operated its retractable undercarriage, by the recollection of 140 tedious turns of a handle driving a chain operated screw gear – it is hardly surprising that many Ansons were to be seen during the war with undercarriages down!

'Faithful Annie' was first flown by S. A. 'Bill' Thorn on 11 March 1935. De Havilland had produced a rival for the coastal reconnaissance function, the converted Dragon Rapide; both were soon under evaluation at the Coastal Defence Development Unit at Gosport where the Anson proved its superiority. It appeared in the New Types Park at the Hendon RAF Display and was flown to Martlesham immediately afterwards. Stability problems were experienced, and the tailplane was increased in span by 25 per cent and elevator area reduced. An order for 174 was placed immediately. Over 7,000 Ansons and derivatives were built for services throughout the world.

Hessell Tiltman and Nevil Norway, of Airspeed, had very limited commercial success with the Courier, although its advanced technical features had caused great interest. They decided to build a twin engined derivative, the Envoy. An extremely attractive low wing monoplane with two Wolseley radial engines, the prototype, G-ACMT, was flown on 26 June 1935 by Flt Lt C. H. A. Colman, a young RAF officer whom Norway had met when Colman was flying a D.H. Fox Moth for John Sword, of Scottish Motor Traction – a bus company diversifying its activities. Norway saw Colman pace out the length of the field in which he had landed to ensure that he could fly safely out of it. This seemed to indicate a responsible attitude not always manifest by young officers at that time, so Norway offered him the job of test pilot.

Also working for Airspeed at this time was George B. S. Errington, who, after engineering training at Sheffield University, worked in the Vickers and Avro design offices. He took a course in aeronautical engineering, joined the small Comper Company at Hooton in 1932 as an approved inspector, bought his own Avro Avian, and rebuilt a Comper Swift, joining Airspeed as an inspector in September 1934. He soon involved himself in the flying side of the business, assisting Cyril Colman in his work on the Courier and the new Envoy. Having acquired all his Ground Engineers Licences, his experience was of great value to the struggling small company at Portsmouth, where the works were then situated.

The Envoy appeared to be perfect from the beginning of its test flights, although at Martlesham some problems arose with the engine accessories.

Envoy prototype, minus port engine cowling, with RAF Furys and Virginias at Portsmouth in 1935.

A failed gasket in the hydraulic system caused the machine to land with one undercarriage leg half down, with consequent damage and delay. On 2 July it appeared at the SBAC show at Hendon, where its sleek lines revealed with stark clarity the total obsolescence of most of the RAF machines performing there.

De Havilland caused a major sensation in the industry when the abrupt departure of Hubert Broad, after twenty years with the company, was announced. No explanation was given at the time, but it later transpired that Capt de Havilland and his co-directors felt that Broad's great skill as a demonstration pilot had led him to be, perhaps unwittingly, insufficiently critical of undesirable characteristics in some types he had flown and pronounced satisfactory. This was particularly so in the case of the types with sharply tapered wings, Comet, Rapide, Express airliner and, most seriously, the new D.H.87 Hornet Moth three seat cabin machine. Designed to be flown by normal flying club pilots, the machine had been involved in several fatal accidents due to its vicious tip stalling tendency. De Havilland replaced most of the original wings with straight tapered, square tipped ones, calling the resulting design the D.H. 87b. The cost was unacceptably high to the firm.

Hubert Broad became a freelance test pilot, flew for the Air Registration Board and RAE Farnborough, joining Hawkers at Langley to take charge of production testing, a field in which he excelled. He retired after the war having flown aeroplanes with engine power ranging from a 35 hp Anzani to over 2,500 hp in the Centaurus-engined Tempest.

R. J. Waight, Broad's assistant, was appointed chief test pilot with young Geoffrey de Havilland as his second in command. Geoffrey received his baptism in flying at the age of six when his father took him up in a D.H.6, derisively known as the 'Clutching Hand'. At the age of 18 he joined the firm and spent four years as a premium apprentice, learning to fly on Moths. After two years in the drawing office he joined de Havilland, carrying out aerial survey work in South Africa. Six months later he returned to become an instructor at the de Havilland Aeronautical Technical School and took his commercial pilot's B Licence. By 1935 the company was well established at Hatfield, opened in the previous year, as Stag Lane became too congested with houses encroaching upon the airfield.

One of the most important events in British aviation took place on 12 April 1935; Cyril Uwins made the maiden flight of the Bristol 142 and new technology became a reality, embodied in one precious prototype.

Roy Fedden had produced the first of his sleeve valve radial engines, the Aquila, which had run for the first time in September 1934. Frank Barnwell, the Bristol chief designer, sketched out a twin engined high-speed six passenger transport, using the new engine. It was officially known as Type 135 and unofficially as 'The Captain's Gig'.

Lord Rothermere, the proprietor of the *Daily Mail*, heard about the new aeroplane, and placed

Cyril Uwins with a Blenheim Mk I in 1936.

Bristol Blenheim Mk I.

an order for it as his private transport in the hope that it would encourage businessmen and their firms to take an active part in civil aviation. He also hoped to prove to the Air Ministry that the current breed of biplane fighters would be hopelessly outclassed by a well designed light monoplane bomber. Type 135 was altered to carry eight passengers, and construction began under a new type number, 142, whilst a quasi-military prototype was commenced, the Type 143.

Uwins was delighted with the handling characteristics of the 142; within two months of first flight the test programme had been completed, furnishings and equipment installed and the original wooden propellers replaced by de Havilland variable-pitch metal units. In June he flew the machine to Martlesham Heath, where its outstanding performance created a sensation – it was 50 mph faster than the Gloster Gladiator. The Air Ministry asked if they could retain it for further evaluation. Lord Rothermere, a great patriot, whose newspaper had given much support to aviation, presented it to the nation and named it *Britain First*.

From it was developed the Blenheim I with Bristol Mercury engines, flown by Uwins in June 1936. Many variants served throughout the war, but in the day bombing role they were extremely vulnerable to determined fighter opposition. By 1941 the Blenheim was used as a stop-gap night fighter and pioneered airborne radar interception techniques.

Fred Miles, of Phillips and Powis, Woodley, near Reading, had launched his outstanding Miles range of high performance light aircraft, and his test pilot, the genial Tommy Rose, was to be found at all the air races, locked in deadly combat with the rival Percival Gulls and Mew Gulls often flown by their designer, Edgar W. Percival, whose trilby hat became legendary at these events. In moments of exasperation he would hurl the unfortunate hat across the hangar accepting the inevitable deterioration of his headgear. In 1982 he told the author, 'My aeroplanes would never fly unless I wore my hat!'

Two aeroplanes designed to meet specification C26/31 for a twin engined bomber transport were nearing completion. At Armstrong Whitworth, Alan Campbell-Orde and his assistant Charles Turner-Hughes were preparing to fly the cumbersome AW.23 whilst the Bristol Type 130, to be named Bombay, was almost ready, and looked a much more satisfactory machine. A third contender was the Handley Page HP.51, a monoplane conversion of an earlier HP.43 biplane which was completely unsatisfactory and had been abandoned in 1932.

Cumbersome though the AW.23 appeared, it was the most advanced of the trio, and was the only one with a retractable undercarriage. The first flight, on 4 June 1935, was entirely satisfactory and it handled well. Campbell-Orde later experienced an engine failure on take-off; the remaining Armstrong Siddeley Tiger VI at full throttle was able to maintain sufficient power to crawl round the circuit and land again. The hydraulics were driven by the dead engine and the undercarriage did not lock-down. The port leg collapsed just before the end of the landing run, damaging the wing tip.

Only the prototype was built, and this finished its days with Flight Refuelling, where it was used as a tanker to refuel the Short C Class flying boats operating an experimental service across the North Atlantic in 1938.

The HP.51 was ultimately developed into the Harrow bomber which was, in effect, an interim bomber/trainer, awaiting the arrival of the new generation of high performance bombers.

With Pegasus radial engines and a 96 ft wing span, the Bombay was Bristol's largest aeroplane to date. It carried 24 troops at a top speed of 189 mph. Cyril Uwins flew the prototype, K3583, on 23 June 1935. Few modifications were required before it went to Martlesham to be flown by Flt Lt A. J. Pegg, who later resigned his commission to join Cyril Uwins' test team.

After a successful career as a fighter pilot, and instructor at the Central Flying School, Pegg was commissioned and posted to Martlesham. He spent

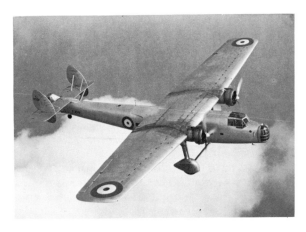

Bristol Bombay.

the next five years flying – mostly single engined machines – and viewed with some apprehension the next stage in his Service career which, conventionally, would require him to fly a desk. Having heard that Bristol was in the market for another test pilot he decided to talk to Cyril Uwins when he next visited Martlesham to discuss progress with the Bombay.

In collaboration with his flight commander it was arranged that, whilst Uwins was at the station Pegg would put in a few hours on the big monoplane. After the briefing – 'Level speed test, Pegg, two o'clock this afternoon, Bristol Bombay over at B Flight check the CG and loading with technical office' – Pegg prepared for a flight which he knew was crucial to his career, in front of a critical audience of fellow pilots and the great Cyril Uwins, who had an immense reputation as one of the finest test pilots of his day.

The flight was uneventful, and A. J. Pegg resigned his commission and an assured pensionable career for an uncertain future in the cold commercial world, where firms were not over-generous to their test pilots. In December 1935 Bill Pegg became Cyril Uwins assistant, although Uwins had, in his function as manager of the Bristol Flying School, access to the services of his instructors, who often carried out the routine engine test flying, which Pegg soon found extremely boring after the variety of work at Martlesham.

One of his first assignments was the Bristol 138 monoplane designed to attack the world height record held by Italy at 47,360 ft. Bill Pegg was intrigued to discover that it had a 'dead man's handle'. The pilot had to wear a special pressure suit designed by Siebe Gorman, the diving suit firm, in collaboration with RAE Farnborough, who have the original suit in their museum. Any failure of this highly experimental suit would cause the pilot to lose both consciousness and his grip on the control column. The device caused the throttle to close if a grip on the column was relaxed, and the aeroplane would then glide down to less hostile altitudes, whereupon it was hoped the pilot would recover. Fortunately for Sqn Ldr F. R. D. Swain, who climbed to 49,967 ft on 28 September, and for Sqn Ldr M. J. Adam, who flew to 53,937 ft in 1937, the dead man's handle was not put to the test. Paradoxically the height records obtained on Bristol engines did not produce a dividend in war-time Bristol powered aircraft. Rolls-Royce engines had superior altitude performance by virtue of multi-stage supercharging – later, with inter-coolers. Nevertheless the flights made by the Farnborough test pilots were of great value in research into high altitude problems affecting the pilot, the engine and the airframe.

On 19 June 1935 Mutt Summers flew the Vickers Wellesley bomber for the first time. This was the first of Barnes Wallis's geodetic structures derived from his work on the airship R.100. The Wellesley was so efficient that an immediate production order was placed for it. A problem inseparable from its construction was the impossibility of housing bombs in the wings. Containers were mounted below them to avoid the extra drag of externally located bombs. On 23 July Mutt Summers was landing when the port undercarriage leg collapsed; serious damage was done to the wing so the machine was in the shops for several months.

In the marine aircraft world Arthur Gouge, of Short Brothers, was busy with the Empire flying boats which were nearing completion. John Lankester Parker flew on 22 October the Short Scion Senior four Pobjoy engined seaplane. Coincidentally it had similar aerodynamic characteristics to the Empire boats; indeed, in 1939, one was converted to have a large single float which was a scale model of the planing bottom designed for the Sunderland.

Another interesting development under consideration at Rochester was the Short Mayo composite aircraft; where a four engined high performance seaplane was mounted on top of a specially converted Empire boat, thereby adding its engine power to that of the seaplane which could not lift its own fuel load from the water. The combination made its first flight early in 1938.

Few people present at Brooklands aerodrome on 6 November 1935 realized the crucial importance of the event they were about to witness. From the Experimental Flight Shed was wheeled the sleek silver doped Hurricane prototype K5038. After preliminary checks and taxying trials George Bulman took off and climbed away. He did not retract the wheels as there was slight doubt about the hand pumped hydraulic system. Bulman was very happy with the machine which handled well on that short flight. As he came in to land he experienced, for the first time, the powerful cushion of air underneath the Hurricane generated by the close proximity of the thick wing to the ground. The wide track undercarriage made landing very easy and proved to be of great benefit when squadron pilots were converted to the new fighter.

Relatively minor modifications were required; the cockpit canopy was re-designed, the tailplane bracing strut, and the small flaps closing the wheel wells were removed. The two blade wooden propeller was replaced with a three blade de Havilland two pitch unit, due, it is said, to George Bulman's ability to 'scrounge'. No official sanction could be obtained for fitting a variable pitch propeller; so he purloined a Hurricane off the production line, persuaded de Havillands to supply a suitable two pitch model and then approached the Hamilton Standard Corporation in the USA, borrowing from them a constant speed unit to control the propeller pitch automatically. A spectacular performance resulted in a major panic to fit VP propellers to all Hurricanes and Spitfires, and yet another one, later, to fit constant speed units.

The board of the Hawker Siddeley Group fully supported a decision by the Hawker board to proceed with plans to build 1,000 Hurricanes, although an order for 600 was not received until June 1936. This crucial decision, to commence production three months early, gave the RAF an extra 600 Hurricanes in time for the Battle of Britain in 1940. This remarkable example of commercial courage and foresight probably made the difference between victory and defeat.

In 1934 Flt Lt Gerry Sayer had left the famous triumvirate of Hawker test pilots, Bulman, Sayer and Philip Lucas, to join Glosters as their chief test pilot. So most of the Hurricane development flying was carried out by Lucas who had left Martlesham in 1931 to join Hawker.

Sayer had a very unpleasant experience when testing an early Hurricane. He flew to the rated altitude of 17,000 ft and then descended again to find that ground fog had developed. Trying to feel his way to establish his position, he took a large area of fabric off the underside of his wings on some trees near Kenley.

Prototype Hawker Hurricane (1936).

In April 1936 K5083 was delivered to Martlesham. One of the pilots who flew it was Sgt S. 'Sammy' Wroath, later to become a Group Captain and the first Commandant of the Empire Test Pilots School.

In 1925 Sammy took his course of training as an aircraft apprentice at No 1 School of Technical Training at Halton. Posted to No 58 Sqn at Worthy Down, he was encouraged to apply for flying training at a time when it was generally considered in the Service that only officers could fly aeroplanes. He was accepted for training at No 3 FTS at Grantham where a fellow member of the Course was Acting Pilot Officer (on probation) Jeffrey K. Quill whose later work on the development of the Spitfire made an immense contribution to its flying qualities. Sammy Wroath passed out with a distinction which qualified him for a posting to the prestigious No 1 (Fighter) Sqn at Tangmere, where he was chosen for the synchronized aerobatic team display at Hendon.

In 1935 a signal arrived at Tangmere posting him to Martlesham for performance testing duties. Returning to the Mess he was accosted by a Flt Lt who said, 'I hear you have been posted to Martlesham, Wroath, who the hell is your father?' Sammy was mystified, he had not heard of the job,

and had no idea, at that time, what a plum it was. He had volunteered to be a flying instructor. With 687 solo hours in his log book he joined 'A' Flight, Performance Testing under F/O A. J. Pegg.

Sgt Wroath had taken the trouble to obtain as many qualifications as possible by attending every course on offer. As a non-commissioned pilot he was one of the youngest members of the Sergeant's Mess, and when he was quickly promoted to Flt Sgt there was much sucking of teeth among the old stagers. They were even more shaken when he was rapidly promoted to Acting Pilot Officer. This was quite unheard of in the Royal Air Force; when men were promoted in this way they were invariably posted to a new station. Nevertheless, everyone became accustomed to Sammy in his new rank, and gave him the duller testing jobs to 'break him in gently'. His log book for this period is an interesting catalogue of contemporary military and civil aircraft: Bulldog, Hart, Fury, Hind, BA Eagle and the Demon for Australia (A1/1). Sammy recalled the comment of an Australian pilot on the 1943 Empire Test Pilots School Course when he learned from Wg Cdr Wroath – who was the CO – of the work he had done on the Demon. 'Christ!' said the Aussie, 'You must be damned old.' An American Northrop metal monoplane was used to train pilots in the use of flaps, whilst other interesting types there at that time were the Hornet Moth,

Percival Vega and Mew Gulls, Vickers Wildebeeste, Hawker Osprey, Miles Nighthawk and the two Airspeed machines, Courier and Envoy.

With the arrival of the Hurricane prototype a new era opened for the A&AEE. Sammy Wroath's first flight in it ended in a forced landing due to engine trouble. The early Merlins were unreliable and Sammy recalled that if anyone had suggested that the new engine would be a world-beater he would have been ridiculed; radial engines were considered to have the best development potential. Rolls-Royce was aware of the problems and took vigorous action.

In his book *Sent Flying*, A. J. 'Bill' Pegg, chief test pilot of the Bristol Aeroplane Company from 1947 to 1956, gave a diverting account of life at Martlesham, to which station he was posted as Acting Pilot Officer after a period instructing at Central Flying School, Wittering. He was paid fourteen shillings and tenpence (74p) per day, of which four shillings and sixpence (22½p) had to be paid to the Mess. This left him three pounds twelve shillings and fourpence (£3.62p) for upkeep, renewal of uniform including a very costly mess kit, payment of batman, cigarettes, beer and the running of a small car.

Surprisingly, in those halcyon days he was not financially embarrassed.

As a new P/O, he did have a few embarrassing moments, such as a meeting with his old Regimental Sgt Maj from Wittering who was at Martlesham. Old habits died hard and he found himself in the slightly ludicrous situation of them addressing each other as 'Sir'. To his surprise he was posted to 'B' Flight, the flight commander of which had a reputation for knocking the rough edges off the juniors. After his interview with this officer he left his presence only to be almost transfixed by a violent electric shock as he touched the metal door handle. He had received the traditional Martlesham welcome from an aircraft magneto connected to the door!

His first task was to fly a series of routine test flights in a large single engine torpedo bomber. Having been shown the various cockpit controls and become airborne, he discovered a large lever which had not been mentioned to him. He decided to operate it. Suddenly his seat dropped down far enough to put his eye level well below the cockpit coaming, whilst the aeroplane began a series of grotesque manoeuvres. With difficulty he managed to raise his seat and regain control. For six months he flew a number of different types which had already been tested fairly thoroughly, but it gave

him the confidence and experience to enable him to develop an objective judgement of any type.

The performance testing section, usually known as 'Per T', was responsible for every aspect of handling in the air; taxying characteristics on level and rough ground, engine temperatures during taxying and whilst waiting for take-off clearance. Length of take-off run, unstick speed, rate of climb through various height bands, maximum speed at these height bands with engine temperatures and boost pressures were carefully monitored. All flight tests were repeated with differing flying weights and centre of gravity positions; also efficiency of cockpit heating, and oxygen, if fitted, operation of variable pitch propellers with particular attention to actuation at height when hydraulic types might be sluggish due to oil chilling. The instrumentation was checked out, particularly the pressure head of the airspeed indicator, which often revealed position error due to its location in a high or low pressure area on the airframe. Investigating the operation of the retractable undercarriage, which appeared in 1934, was important, whilst ease of maintenance was studied in depth. In the air, spinning trials and the terminal velocity dive were tested towards the end of the programme. Early in his Martlesham career Bill Pegg had to abandon an Avro Cadet trainer when the upper wings broke away in a TV dive; at 3,000 ft, at 240 mph, there was a tremendous bang and the machine began to break up. Fortunately he was thrown out, and pulled the parachute rip cord immediately. The accident was attributed to flutter of the ailerons causing intolerable stresses in the wing structure. Pegg said that he could never get over the uneasy frightened feeling which came over him whenever he went into a steep, high speed dive; as the noise level rose to a crescendo he always held his breath waiting for the loud bang.

Martlesham Heath had a strong complement of some of the finest engineering officers in the RAF who worked with the constructors' engineers to establish maintenance procedures, and produce the various Air Publications for accepted aeroplanes, which formed the 'Bible', to which the maintenance sections of squadrons must work.

The armament testing section were responsible for the guns and bombing equipment which was often left out until 'Per T' had carried out their work, dummies and ballast being carried to simulate the armament.

Work on a particular aeroplane was generally the responsibility of one pilot, but others would fly it to give their expert view of its handling qualities.

An unfortunate occurrence was the crash of a Vickers Virginia on take-off. The occupant of the front cockpit was killed by an engine which fell on him as he jumped out. The station medical officer rushed to the wreck with his morphine syringe at the ready. On entering the remains of the fuselage, and heading for a loud moaning, he found a large backside into which he smartly jabbed his syringe. An NCO, who had reached the scene a few minutes before the Doc, slept for hours!

Towards the end of the second decade aeroplanes were capable of reaching altitudes where oxygen was essential, although the effect of an inadequate supply of it was not realized. On one occasion Bill Pegg flew a Siskin to 20,000 ft to test a new form of cockpit heating. The test schedule called for 1½ hours at that altitude, with temperature readings taken at intervals with the heating on and off. He flew at full throttle and he recalled some difficulty in reading the thermometers, not realizing that he was suffering from anoxia due to an inadequate supply of oxygen. This insidious phenomenon leaves its victim in a state of euphoria, thinking that he is in good form and certainly unaware that his physical and mental processes have been seriously affected. After two hours flying the engine stopped. Bill was not perturbed; he was quite clear in his mind that he should just quietly glide back to base. At 10,000 ft he realized that he had run out of fuel, was over 10/10ths cloud and had no idea where he was. At 2,000 ft he came out of cloud, to find himself over an unrecognizable length of coast. He made a successful forced landing in a field, and awaited the arrival of the usual crowd of spectators, but none appeared. He walked to the nearest road and caught an approaching bus asking to be dropped at the nearest garage. He was relieved to see from the bus destination indicator which read 'Brighton' that he was still in England. So, in full flying kit, watched by curious passengers, he went to the garage to buy sufficient petrol to fly to a nearby RAF station which happened to be Tangmere, where he had recently served. Saying very little about his experience he refuelled and flew back to Martlesham.

Flt Lt S. N. Webster of Schneider Trophy fame, had an alarming experience flying Westland's tri-motor Wessex at A&AEE. At full load he took off for fuel consumption tests; travelling at speed over the bumpy surface of the aerodrome there was a bang from the direction of the undercarriage which, on the port side, disappeared from the view of an observer in the cabin. Men on the ground held up a wheel from which it was deduced that one had

disappeared. After a number of circuits to hurl ballast out of the cabin and generally lighten ship, Webster made a very careful approach, to land as slowly as possible on the sound wheel and hold the other wing up as long as there was lift from it. As he touched down there was another bang and the aeroplane rolled smoothly to rest. The upper fitting of the oleo leg, where it joined the engine nacelle, had failed, and the wheel and oleo swung downwards, hinged upon the 'vee' strut which connected the axle to the underside of the fuselage. The initial landing impact had swung the assembly back into position to take the weight of the aircraft.

In January 1936 the man whose name will always be associated with R. J. Mitchell and Joe Smith in the development of the Spitfire joined Supermarines. F/O Jeffrey Kindersley Quill, fascinated by flying at an early age, took a Short Service Commission and learned to fly at No 3 FTS Grantham, going solo after only 5 hours 20 minutes. In the senior term he flew Siskins under Flt Lt H. L. P. 'Pingo' Lester and F/O Kenneth Knocker. Jeffrey, with characteristic modesty, has said, 'Any subsequent success that I achieved as a pilot, and indeed my very survival, I attribute primarily to the quality of the teaching and encouragement I received from those two men, and the solid horse sense about flying aeroplanes which they imparted.'

He passed-out at Grantham with the pilot rating 'Exceptional'. A period with the crack No 17 (Fighter) Sqn followed, flying Bulldogs. Aerobatic displays at the Hendon Pageant, air firing courses and the annual Air Exercises were interesting diversions. He heard a remark which stayed with him throughout his career: 'Aeroplanes are not inherently dangerous but they are very unforgiving.' A comment emphasized by the sight of one of his friends in a neighbouring squadron misjudge a stall turn, and dive vertically into the ground.

Jeffrey was posted to the meteorological flight at Duxford, due, he thought, to the reference in his Grantham Passing Out Report to his aptitude for flying in bad weather. The Met Flt had Siskin IIIa's with provision for an electrically heated suit, a dire necessity for a twice daily flight in an open cockpit between 18,000 to 25,000 ft.

In his first year he carried out 258 sorties, of which only 14 ended in diversion to other aerodromes or convenient fields.

In November 1934 F/O Quill took command of the Flight, and was joined by F/O R. C. Reynell, later to become a Hawker test pilot. In the first year under his command not one scheduled sortie was missed. There were no let-down aids, and a

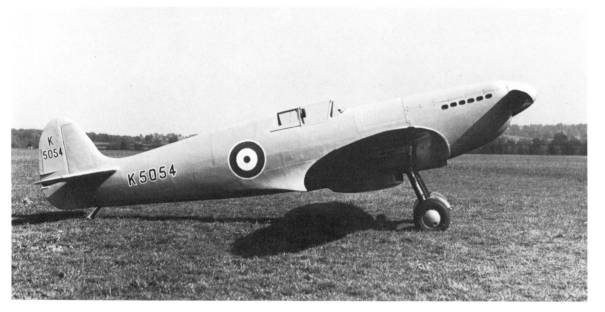

Prototype Supermarine Spitfire showing the coarse pitch of the wooden propeller blades (1936).

few aeroplanes were bent in the process. The CO gave Quill a pilot rating of 'Exceptional' and recommended him for an Air Force Cross.

In 1935 he chartered a Puss Moth, to tour Germany with friends, returning with the uneasy conviction that Britain was being left behind in a race which had no rules. Later in the year he heard that Mutt Summers was looking for a test pilot. He had a taste of test flying in a modest way when No 17 Sqn received some aeroplanes from Martlesham in continuation of their Service trials, so he was immediately interested, although his main ambition was a permanent commission. He met Summers, who needed help with an intensive flight test programme at Weybridge and Southampton, resulting from the Air Force Expansion Programme. Mutt also mentioned the new fighter which Mitchell had designed and which was nearing completion. With mixed feelings, Jeffrey Quill flew his last Met flight on 28 December 1935 and then joined Vickers.

At Weybridge, were two test pilots, 'Sonny' Banting and 'Ronnie' Louis, who concentrated on production testing whilst George Pickering flew flying boats at Southampton. As Summers' principal assistant, Jeffrey was active at both bases, flying Wildebeestes, Vincents, Hart Trainers and Valentias, although his main task would be the prototype Wellesley bomber, then approaching completion of repairs after its undercarriage failure.

On 5 March 1936 Jeffrey flew Mutt Summers in the company's new Miles Falcon from Martlesham to Eastleigh, where Mutt was to fly the new fighter, known only by its specification number F37/34. The maiden flight of fifteen minutes duration was encouraging. Jeffrey flew it for the first time on 26 March and thought 'Here is a real lady!'

No attempt to deal with the history of test flying the Spitfire will be made in this narrative. Readers are referred to Quill's own book, *Spitfire, a Test Pilot's Story*, in which he describes his work in fascinating detail. It is appropriate, however, to mention the highlights of the test programme which began most inauspiciously. Top speed was disappointing at only 335 mph at 17,000 ft, not much faster than the Hurricane, which was a fairly rudimentary aeroplane, potentially more attractive to the Air Staff for its simple, orthodox construction, easier production, and straightforward maintenance requirements. Mitchell knew that unless the F7/34 showed a major improvement in performance over the Hawker machine, Hawkers would receive the contract.

It was suspected that compressibility problems at the tips of the two bladed wooden propeller were being encountered. It was intended to fit a de Havilland/Hamilton Standard three blade variable-pitch propeller, but none had been delivered so a major propeller design study was set in hand. Supermarine's design office produced the answer, and an immediate and spectacular improvement allowed the aircraft, now named Spitfire, to go to Martlesham with a corrected top

Above *After the first flight of K.5054. Left to right: Mutt Summers, H. J. Payn, R. J. Mitchell, S. Scott-Hall, Jeffrey Quill.* Below left *Quill in a Spitfire 1, Eastleigh 1939.* Below right *The elegant Mk XIV flown by Frank Furlong.*

speed of 349 mph, one mile per hour below Mitchell's target. The designer's response when the name
was announced was terse: 'Just the sort of bloody
silly name they would give it!' For once his judgement was wide of the mark. Sammy Wroath first
flew the Spitfire at Martlesham on 8 June 1936. It
was thought by all at A&AEE to be a beautiful
aeroplane, but too much of a thoroughbred to be
satisfactory in service.

Soon after the first flight of the Supermarine
F7/34 Chris Staniland flew the Fairey Battle light
bomber. Its performance was good, and it appeared
to be a satisfactory replacement of the Hart and
Hind two seat day bombers. Martlesham were
quite satisfied with it, but the outbreak of war
revealed a different picture. With a top speed of
257 miles per hour and a defensive armament of
one Vickers K gun and a .303 Browning in the
wing, it was hopelessly outclassed and shot out of
the sky. It was rapidly relegated to training and
target towing, also doing sterling work as a flying
test bed for a wide range of engines, including the
Napier Sabre and Dagger, Rolls-Royce Exe, which
was abandoned, Bristol Taurus and Hercules, and
the Fairey Prince 24 cylinder engine which was also
abandoned.

June 1935 saw the first test flights of three of the
new designs. The Vickers twin engine geodetic
bomber to spec. B9/32 was flown from Brooklands
by Mutt Summers and the Westland Lysander
Army Co-operation machine flown from Yeovil by
Harald Penrose on the 15th.

Both the Handley Page Hampden and the Vickers Wellington were built to specification B9/32.
No two aircraft could be less alike; the flat, slab
sided angular Hampden and the smoothly streamlined Vickers prototype were both excellent machines. Later to be converted with turrets at nose
and tail in the Wellington version, the Vickers
prototype had smooth fairings at each end, soon
to be glazed. Mutt Summers was at the controls on
the first flight of K4049 and was satisfied with its
flying characteristics. Its performance was remarkable and fully justified Barnes Wallis's claims for
his geodetic construction, which was so strong and
light that the range was twice the 1,500 miles called
for, and it could carry twice the bomb load over
that range. After many months of test flying by
Summers the B9/32 was flown to Martlesham
Heath for Service evaluation. In April 1937 Flt
Lt Maurice Hare with LAC Smurthwaite as his
observer were carrying out diving tests. A sudden
violent flutter of the tail unit occurred, and the tail
of the machine broke off. The sudden nose down

Top *The Vickers prototype B9/32 bomber.*
Centre *Vickers Wellington bomber fuselages being
assembled in 1938.*
Bottom *Handley Page Hampden, also built to
specification B9/32.*

pitch caused Hare to be hurled out through the top
cockpit glazing, the unfortunate LAC losing his life
when the aircraft hit the ground. A major search
for wreckage was immediately made along the
flight path of K4049 to try to identify the cause of
the break-up. A lump of lead was found, which
turned out to be the mass balance of the elevator
system, fitted, of course, to prevent control surface

flutter. Most of the problems had been resolved as a result of earlier test flights, so production of the Wellington, which had already begun, was not affected by this crash.

Harald Penrose's first flight in the Lysander was uneventful – as first flights were now tending to be. So much research in the wind tunnel was carried out in the early stages of design that really traumatic first flights were few and far between. The Lysander had a strange beauty. The double tapered wings and enormous spatted cantilever undercarriage gave it a distinctive appearance, whilst the full span slots and extensive trailing edge flaps ensured an exceptional short field performance, put to good use in the most secret operations of the war, when those heroic Special Operations personnel made clandestine journeys into, and out of, tiny fields deep in enemy occupied territory, with only a hand torch to guide the pilot to a safe landing – if such a landing could ever be described as safe.

Harald Penrose enjoyed the 'Lizzie', describing it as 'noisy, smelly, heavy on the controls, but able to bump in and out of ridiculously small spaces whatever the load.' At Martlesham the second prototype lost most of its upper wing fabric in a dive. Sqn Ldr Collins brought it back to a safe landing and was awarded the Air Force Cross for his masterly flying. There were problems with downwash on the powerful tailplane assembly.

Prototype Westland Lysander.

If a pilot opened the throttle with full negative incidence on the tailplane, for example, in an overshoot, even a modest movement of the stick towards him would precipitate a stall.

Earlier in the year Jeffrey Quill continued tests on the Wellesley prototype which had been repaired after its landing accident. He carried out stalling tests with 'undercarriage up' and 'undercarriage down'. As he selected 'down', only one green light appeared. This looked like a repeat performance, so he decided to return from Martlesham to Brooklands where the bits could more easily be collected. At Staines, fog made it impossible to get into Brooklands, so, with his observer, Bob Handasyde, the course was re-traced. Three hours after the first attempt, the sticky leg came down, but did not appear to lock properly. Jeffrey thought it would probably hold in a careful landing and, to his relief, it did. A broken ballrace at the upper leg mounting was the cause.

On 5 July 1937 the Wellesley revealed a particularly nasty side of its character. Quill was testing a production machine at the stall and for general slow flying characteristics at 12,000 ft, over the southern outskirts of London. He was completely confident, after many hours of testing, that the machine was impeccable at the stall, so, as it waffled along at slow speed, he wrote his test notes on his knee pad. Suddenly it pitched into a spin to starboard; immediate recovery action was useless, and the spin developed into a dangerous flat, slow one. He tried everything but still the spin continued.

Vickers Venom.

At 3,000 ft he decided that discretion was the better part of valour and bailed out, horrified at the prospect of his machine crashing into a built-up area of London. Eventually it hit a house, but fortunately there was no fire, and the house was empty. In his book, Jeffrey tells of a strange coincidence 37 years later. His daughter Virginia, working at the BBC, met a girl who said, 'Was your father by any chance a test pilot?' 'Yes,' said Virginia. 'Well, he dropped a damned great aeroplane on my mother's house!'

There was, of course, a thorough investigation into the incident, but it produced few satisfactory conclusions. In October 1938 a Wellesley took off from Farnborough ostensibly to do stalling tests. It spun into the ground, the pilot, Flt Lt Salmon, being killed.

The type went into service with the RAF and was most successful, particularly in the Middle East, and popular with its crews.

As the Wellesley was the first production aeroplane for which Jeffrey Quill was responsible, he watched with keen interest the results of tests on production aircraft. He was struck by the almost casual approach of the production test pilots in contrast to the meticulous work of those testing prototypes. It seemed to be a 'circuit and bump' operation to check that the machine was not flying one wing low and had smooth controls, followed by a couple of loops for the benefit of the groundcrew.

Jeffrey resolved that every aeroplane coming off the line would be tested throughout its flight envelope – the flight envelope defines the handling and performance of the machine – within the limits set by the experimental test pilot, the envelope being verified by A&AEE test pilots. A further flight envelope, giving more tolerance for flying by less experienced squadron or civil pilots was also projected. In the case of civil aircraft this is now verified by the Air Registration Board test pilots.

So Quill and flight test observer Bob Handasyde sat down to develop a minimum test schedule for all production aeroplanes. Another step forward along the road to safe and reliable flying had been made.

In between flying the Wellesley and the Spitfire, Jeffrey flew a new single engined fighter, the Venom, descended from the ill-fated Jockey. The Aquila powered machine was intended to meet a demand for a simple fighter with a high performance in overseas commands. The Bristol Aquila engine was not fully developed and, on one flight to carry out consumption tests off the south coast, the engine stopped. He managed to pull off a 'dead-stick' landing at Gosport and discovered that the sleeve valve engine had seized up and the inertia of the metal propeller had sheared the reduction gearing. Another alarming engine failure on take-off from Brooklands, where the chances of a safe landing were nil, ended happily when the engine picked up again at the last minute and enabled him to reach Eastleigh. Work on the Venom was abandoned, Quill thought, prematurely, for it would have made a superb Fleet Fighter with a similar performance to the Hurricane, at a time when the Nimrod biplane and Sea Gladiator were being flown by the luckless Fleet Air Arm.

On 17 March 1936 Alan Campbell-Orde flew the Armstrong Whitworth Whitley, stablemate of the Wellington and Hampden. This massive and forcefully ugly aeroplane was originally designed without flaps, and to maintain a slow approach speed the wing was set at a large angle of incidence. This was the reason for its strange nose-down flight attitude. Later, flaps were fitted, but it was too late to alter the wing, except for an increase in dihedral, due to lateral instability revealed on the early flights. The Armstrong Siddeley Tiger radial engines left much to be desired in terms of reliability. Later marks had Merlin engines and gave good service in Bomber Command until the four engine 'heavies' were available. One cannot forget the courage of the Whitley crews who, night after night, flogged through the Alps, as they could not fly over them, to deliver leaflets, and later bombs, to the cities of Milan and Turin.

The Whitley was used as an engine test bed for the projected three row radial, 21 cylinder Armstrong Siddeley Deerhound. This came to grief when an RAF pilot was killed taking off with the tail trim right aft; the machine stalled and crashed. Deerhound development ceased. John Grierson, who was testing for AW, had a narrow escape at the end of a carburation test at 18,000 ft. To conserve his oxygen for a long flight, Grierson used it intermittently, and had reached a stage of mild annoxia without realizing it. This insidious, and often fatal, condition induces a false feeling of well-being in the victim, and with gay abandon, Grierson threw the Whitley into a stall turn; at that altitude the air was so thin that the stall was vicious and the heavy Whitley hurtled downwards at ever-increasing speed. At 240 mph the ASI needle went off the clock, the engines over-speeded, one of them breaking up in the process, the nose hatch blew in and fabric stripped off the starboard wing. Grierson, recovering his faculties at lower altitude, was able to regain control and landed safely.

Handley Page's submission to meet specification B9/32 differed from its competitors, the Whitley and Wellington, in having no power operated turrets, consequently it was faster and more manoeuvrable. No powered turret could be fitted into the narrow fuselage so the machine was vulnerable to enemy fighters. Another snag resulting from the narrowness of the Hampden was the great difficulty in helping or replacing the pilot if he was injured by enemy fire.

James Cordes flew the prototype on 21 June 1936 and caused a sensation by looping it at an early stage in the trials. With HP slots on the leading edge of the wing the speed range was remarkable, from 73 mph to 265 mph. In October Maj Cordes was flying with R. S. Stafford, later technical director of HP, as observer. As they returned to the hangar, after landing, the starboard undercarriage leg collapsed. Stafford, commenting from his position low in the nose, said to Cordes, 'There is a hell of a strong smell of grass in here!' The engine, propeller and wheel were replaced.

On a later flight the prototype was making its landing approach to Radlett when there was a violent bang from the replacement engine which had shed its propeller and reduction gear housing, fortunately there was no fire. James Cordes landed safely and asked the works manager to report to the police that the three bladed metal propeller had fallen into a field which he was able to describe fairly accurately. The police inspector, said, most helpfully, 'That's all right, Sir, I'll send one of my chaps out on a bike to fetch it in!' First prize for weight lifting at around 500 lb!

By the end of 1937, the foundations had been laid for the RAF which, two years later, was to bear an immense burden. In the meantime the design offices, encouraged by the evident high quality of most of their new designs were busy planning the aeroplanes to replace them; Typhoon, Tornado, Tempest, Stirling, Halifax, Manchester and

John Lankester Parker, one of the world's most experienced flying boat test pilots (1955).

Prototype Short Empire flying boat taking off from the River Medway at Rochester.

Lancaster. The Spitfire was never replaced, it was further developed right into the jet age.

On 2 July 1936 Short Brothers launched the flagship of the Empire flying boats, G-ADHL, *Canopus*. Far ahead of its time, it was a beautiful aircraft, elegant in every line, afloat or in the air, with standards of passenger accommodation which would be a joy to return to today. Twenty-eight were ordered off the drawing board by Imperial Airways. Their success was a tribute to the testing and planning which had been applied to every aspect of design – mechanical, aerodynamic and hydrodynamic. The hull had been developed in a series of tank tests, the Gouge flaps proved in flight tests upon a Short Scion monoplane, whilst general handling qualities were checked out with a four engine Scion Senior which, effectively, was a half scale model of the big flying boat.

John Lankester Parker's first flight on 3 July was flawless. The second prototype, G-ADHM, *Caledonia*, went to Felixstowe in September and was soon approved for operations, which *Canopus* inaugurated with a flight over the Mediterranean on 31 October. From one of the most famous and successful pre-war transport aircraft was developed the Sunderland, which became the backbone of Coastal Command on convoy protection duties.

After the war, a number of Sunderlands and derivatives were converted to the civil transport role, and continued to delight those to whom a leisurely air passage in comfort was a pleasure sadly unknown to us today – the antithesis of the mass-transit jet airliner.

In May 1936 H. M. Schofield had flown the General Aircraft Monospar ST.18 Croydon. It was thought that, at £14,000, this ten seater passenger aircraft would have wide appeal among the smaller airlines. Once again it can be said that flight trials were most satisfactory, only minor modifications being required. At a prestige luncheon in July it was announced that Lord Sempill was to finance a proving flight to Australia over the Empire air routes, the aeroplane being piloted by Tim Harold Wood, later to become chief test pilot of General Aircraft. The machine had, in the meantime, been purchased by Maj C. R. Anson who had consented to its loan. After an outward flight delayed at Karachi by tail wheel damage the machine was effectively demonstrated in Australia. On 6 October the Croydon left Melbourne for home.

The first part of the flight was bedevilled by compass problems and course was set for Koepang, 518 miles away across the shark infested Timor Sea. Prudently, Wood often checked his heading through Darwin radio and by the time he was out of range of the station he was fairly sure of his track. On his estimated time of arrival all that he

Monospar Croydon marooned on Seringapatam Reef, 6 October 1936.

could see was a reef. Assuming that land must be fairly close he tried a planned search, even throwing out a can with the inscription 'Which way is Koepang?' to a fishing boat north of the reef. There was no response.

The situation was desperate, with fuel for no more than an hour's flight. As they had no idea which way to go Wood decided to land on the reef and await rescue by local fishermen. If land was nearby they might then be able to obtain fuel and take-off before the reef and aeroplane were swallowed up by the sea. The tailwheel was damaged by the difficult landing so take-off was impossible. The crew paddled towards the fishermen, later being picked up by the steamer *Nimoda* en route to Durban. Their landing had been made on Seringapatam Reef, 225 miles from Koepang. The extent of their incredible good fortune was clear when they were told that the reef only appears during neap tides.

The great significance of the years 1935 and 1936 was that they were true vintage years and the crop was a good one, particularly in the vital military sphere. The industry had proved that it

had worked out the right sums, and the products had emerged from the shops capable of doing what they were expected to do, but requiring the refinements that the ever more competent and resourceful test pilots would work on with increasing urgency as Europe moved remorselessly towards war.

The question that had to be answered, and only service experience in war could answer it, was had the right requirements been called up on the specifications prepared so many years ago?

Considering the rate of technological advance of the industry in the intervening years it must be concluded that, once the Air Staff had buried the prejudice against monoplanes, they issued, in most cases, specifications which met the need of the period. The constructors made a major contribution in the design and mock-up stages, where bugs were ironed out in full scale wood and paper models, which showed where all the equipment could be fitted, and the test pilots refined the basic aeroplanes by the exercise of their expertise which was growing year by year. No longer was the test pilot a driver of aeroplanes who saw them for the first time when they were ready to fly. He was, in most firms, a full member of the design team and the value of the input from men like Uwins, Summers, Bulman and Quill was incalculable.

7

THE APPROACH OF WAR

In 1937 the industry was trying to digest the problems inherent in mass production of the crop of new designs which, in many cases, called for entirely new manufacturing techniques. The teething troubles of the new Shadow Factories conspired to handicap progress with some of the new aeroplanes.

Fairey and Hawker had built prototypes of light bombers intended as Battle replacements – although the first production Battle did not emerge from Austin at Longbridge until 1938. It was realized that, although its handling characteristics were excellent, its top speed of 257 mph was inadequate, the specification to which it was built having been issued in 1932. Fairey's P4/34 had a strong family resemblance to the Battle, but was 7 ft 6 in less in span, 12 ft less in length and 2,000 lb lighter. Hawker built the Henley. Based upon the Hurricane, it was short and squat but not unattractive in appearance.

First flown by Chris Staniland in 1936, the Battle was well received at Martlesham as a worthy successor to the Hart and Hind two seat day bombers. It was a gentlemanly aircraft and substantial orders had been placed. It was the first machine to be produced in one of the new Shadow Factories. By the time Staniland had flown the P.4 and discovered that its top speed of 283 mph was well below the required 300 mph, but superior to the Battle, it was too late to drop the Battle from the programme. Staniland reported favourably upon the P.4 and George Bulman was equally satisfied with the Henley when he flew it for the first time in March 1937. With a top speed near to that of the Hurricane and the advantage of component interchangeability with the fighter, the Henley was a prime candidate for an order. Neither was put into volume production. The P.4 was developed into the Fulmar naval fighter, the prototype being delivered to Farnborough for research purposes, particularly the hazardous duty of balloon cable cutter evaluation, whilst the Henley became a target towing machine. One was used as a flying test bed for the development of the Rolls-Royce Vulture engine.

Air Commodore Arthur E. Clouston recalled his work as a civilian test pilot at Farnborough where his work ranged from the investigation of icing phenomena to flying aeroplanes into balloon cables. He had learned to fly in New Zealand, where he was born, before coming to Britain to join the RAF. He was told that it would be months before there was a vacancy so he found a job as a student at Faireys at 30 shillings (£1.50) per week. He went through the works, and flew as ballast with Chris Staniland whenever the opportunity arose. Finally he achieved his ambition and entered the Service, omitting to mention that he could fly. To the astonishment of his instructors he went solo after two hours dual. He was a born pilot and joined the élite No 25 (Fighter) Sqn. After his four year Short Service Commission he was invited to join the RAE as a civilian test pilot. His commanding officer in Aerodynamics Flight was Flt Lt D'Arcy Grieg, the famous Schneider Trophy pilot. His briefing was crisp and to the point: 'Get to know our aircraft, fly everything we have got.' Grieg taught him to fly the Cierva C30 Rota autogiro. His description of the take-off was memorable: 'The rotor blades and propeller began to rotate faster and faster, the noise was so loud that I could not think, the vibration shaking me like a jelly. The heavy control column came down from the rotor hub above our heads like the branch of a tree. Apart from the throttle and brakes this was the only control, and it went round and round as if it was designed to stir porridge, whilst the machine rocked from side to side!' 'Clou', as he was affectionately known throughout his career, soon mastered the technique and carried out most of the rotary wing tests during his period at RAE. One of his contemporaries at Farnborough was Hugh J. Wilson, a civilian test pilot who made a major contribution to test flying at Farnborough and Boscombe, established a World Air Speed Record in a Meteor in 1945 and retired from the RAF in 1947, with the rank of Group Captain and a CBE, AFC and two bars.

Clou and Willie Wilson were jointly involved in an autogiro exercise with Raoul Hafner, a talented Austrian designer, working in Britain on a new rotary wing machine which, in some respects, was the forerunner of the modern helicopter. He had built it himself, with controllable pitch rotor blades, which he believed to have considerable advantages over all other autogiro blades and he was proved to be right. Hafner persuaded Clou to fly it. After a few flights he pronounced it superior to current designs, so RAE hired it for research purposes. It was to be demonstrated to Capt Lord Louis Mountbatten in the hope of creating naval interest.

Clouston flew it from Hanworth to Farnborough, landing outside the CO's office just as the naval brass arrived. The wind was gusty, and, as one wheel touched down, a violent gust caught the blades, capsizing the machine, to the dismay of poor Hafner. It was repaired and flown by another pilot six months later. Unfortunately, he managed to entangle his large feet with the small rudder bar and took off with both feet on one side. He turned smartly through 180 degrees and hit the roof of No 4 Sqn hangar, removing the pitot head and landing heavily. Again it languished in a hangar awaiting repair.

Willie Wilson, whose turn it was to fly the Hafner machine after repair, had taken his Short Service Commission in 1929. From 1930 to 1932 he served in the crack No 111 (Fighter) Sqn at Hornchurch flying Armstrong Siddeley Siskins, and later Bristol Bulldogs on night fighter development work. The squadron was one of the first to introduce synchronized aerobatics into display routines, later calling its team the Black Arrows. He learned to fly seaplanes at the School of Naval Co-operation, Lee on Solent and, at the end of his Commission, joined the RAF Reserve, converting to flying boats at Hamble, subsequently training at his own expense to become a flying instructor at Air Service Training, Hamble. He became interested in racing, and flew his tiny Gipsy engined Comper Swift very successfully in many events. Becoming bored with an interminable diet of instructional duties, Willie accepted an invitation from Blackburns to join them as test pilot and assistant sales manager. He flew the Shark, Roc and Skua, the latter two aircraft being in the development stage at Brough. In 1937 he was invited to become a civilian test pilot at RAE. Realizing that test flying for a manufacturer

Flt Lt, later Air Commodore, Arthur E. Clouston (1938).

was rather limited in scope he accepted the offer and joined the Electrical and Wireless Flight where he specialized in wireless – to use the terminology of the period – moving to radar as it left the embryo stage known as radio-location. He later joined Aerodynamics Flight, returning to the RAF in September 1939 on the outbreak of war.

When the repairs to the Hafner machine were near to completion, Willie Wilson decided that, as he had to fly it, he should in fairness to the designer, learn something about flying rotary wing aeroplanes. He consulted one of the Farnborough experts, who loaded him into a Cierva C.30 Rota. Much banging and juddering on take-off heralded the partial disintegration of the machine. Willie stepped out of the wreckage, thanked his mentor for the lesson, and took a course with Reggie Brie, Cierva's test pilot at Hanworth. He returned to the Hafner with considerable apprehension, wondering whether it would be better to lock himself in the loo until interest in this unlucky machine had waned. In the midst of his pre-flight reverie he saw Hafner walking towards him to request that he should fly it himself. Willie graciously acceded to the request but, true to form, Hafner's take-off was accompanied by juddering and bits falling off. This time it was the designer's turn to step uninjured from the machine, which was not repaired, as autogiro development was abandoned for the duration of the war. Nevertheless, RAE learned much from this unfortunate little aircraft, and Hafner made a major contribution to helicopter development as chief designer of the Bristol helicopters built after the war.

Arthur Clouston told the story of the enterprising boffin who, in common with some others of his breed in the 1930s, was not noted for confidence in the test pilot's judgement. He asked Clou to fly him in a machine and land it at a speed well below stalling speed. Clou said that this was a tall order as he was already landing it too slowly for safety. The scientist departed in high dudgeon to find a more gullible pilot. Clou watched the aeroplane fall out of the sky and go through the hedge with a shattered undercarriage. He had immense admiration for the scientists who flew as observers. One with whom he flew regularly was Gilbert Palmer, a man in his fifties, of great courage with little flying experience. An Airspeed Courier was used for research into ice formation, a phenomenon which had not been taken too seriously by scientists whilst pilots avoided any clouds which might create ice. With Palmer, Clou would fly into cumulo nimbus clouds; violent gusts with forked lightning, hail and ice accompanied their hair raising flight into extreme danger. Soon ice accretion would cause the engine to stop, sometimes resulting in a dead stick landing in a field. When the engineers arrived, they made no secret of their doubts of the pilot's ability to handle the Lynx engine which had started immediately although, on landing, water had poured out of the carburettor. Finally it was realized that ice was forming in the air intake itself and was melted by the heat of the engine after landing.

The tests continued in a Handley Page Heyford bomber which had heated carburettors. The aircraft would continue to stagger through the air with up to two inches of ice over the wings, struts and propellers. As it sank to earth under the load, the ice began to melt and a further hazard arose; the pilot was seated in the plane of the propellers and was bombarded with chunks of ice until the propellers were cleared. The rest of the test programme was carried out in an American Northrop all-metal monoplane.

Clouston had an embarrassing experience in the Courier when landing after a test flight with a scientist in the back. As he approached the aerodrome at lunch time, he noticed that his aeroplane was causing unusual interest on the part of the homeward bound staff. He realized the reason as the Courier flopped on its belly in a particularly muddy patch of aerodrome. He had disconnected the warning horn, the lights were not working, and he forgot to lower the wheels. As both men leapt out, the scientist, not realizing what had happened, fell flat on his face in the filth. When he had struggled to his feet he enquired 'Have we crashed?' The pilot was most impressed with his proper spirit of scientific curiosity.

Miles Aircraft at Reading had built for RAE a special version of their Falcon monoplane so that various thicknesses of wing could be tested on the same basic aeroplane. After a very bumpy flight, Clouston landed the Falcon and opened the throttle to taxi back to the hangar. He was shocked to see the port wing tip suddenly drop to the ground; a few more minutes in rough air would undoubtedly have removed the wing.

With war clouds gathering, Farnborough began an evaluation of barrage balloons as a means of defence against bombers. It was important to know what would happen if a bomber flew into the cable, so Flying Officer Clouston was instructed to find out. He began by flying a Miles Hawk two seater trainer into a fishing line suspended from a parachute thrown overboard at 5,000 ft. At the end was a fabric ball soaked in red paint to indicate the contact points of the line with the surface of the aircraft.

The first approach was uneventful, the line catching the wing in the right place with the aircraft skidding away slightly. Suddenly the line raced over the wing a few feet from the cockpit. The friction generated smoke, and with the line end whipping around the wing, the pull of the parachute made a cut several inches deep in the leading edge. The major hazard was soon found to be loss of control under these circumstances when the line caught the aileron. On one flight it became entangled with the propeller, whilst the parachute gyrated astern at the end of the line which had fouled the rudder and elevators. The machine was almost impossible to control, and a parachute jump seemed imperative. 'Jump!' yelled the pilot to his observer, a young scientist on his first flight. The terrified boffin averted his gaze, 'Jump, jump!' roared Clouston. The scientist, marvelling that anyone should wish to jump out of an aeroplane 5,000 ft above Farnborough just shook his head. With the aircraft becoming increasingly difficult to handle the pilot scribbled a note, 'Machine out of control YOU MUST JUMP,' and passed it to his passenger. Ashen faced, he read it, released his safety harness and had one leg over the side when the parachute tore away leaving the Hawk under control again. 'Sit down, SIT DOWN!' was the next instruction. The poor fellow, utterly bemused by this time, continued his exit, his parachute catching on the side of the cockpit. Finally Clouston persuaded him to return. When they landed Clou was not flattered to be told, 'I did not know what the problem was, I realized the aircraft was a bit frisky but thought it was your flying!'

As the tests developed it became necessary to use balloon cable to establish complete realism. It was thought that such material would take the wing off the Hawk, so the all metal Fairey P.4 prototype was brought into service in 1938. The cable was much more difficult to locate, it also swayed as it dropped with the parachute. Often the landing at RAE was made with hundreds of feet of cable trailing astern and creating havoc among telephone and high tension cables. Once Clouston hooked a group of painters on a scaffold as they were painting the RAE Mess. The cable attached itself to the scaffold and distributed the men and their paint all over the ground. Fortunately no serious injuries resulted but the men refused to work when the P.4 was in the air. On another memorable occasion the cable collected a bicycle rack at the RAE main gate. It swiftly became airborne and eight bicycles were distributed neatly along the airfield!

For all the levity and levitation associated with these two episodes, it was for Clouston, Willie Wilson, Johnnie Kent and their colleagues an extremely dangerous aspect of test flying. On another flight Clou hit the cable at 170 mph; it caught the propeller tip and whipped around the fuselage flailing the nose, cockpit and wings and leaving deep gashes in the metal – one of them alongside the cockpit, two inches from the pilot's head, whilst a small fire broke out behind the propeller. Clearly there was a major risk of decapitation, so a thick steel canopy was built to cover the cockpit. Before this was installed a cable jammed in the aileron and forced the trim tab to its maximum deflection. The P.4 began a flat spin; with both arms and one leg Clou managed to force the stick over to regain a measure of control and flew back to make a very high speed landing.

The scientists decided that two lives should not be risked in these extremely hazardous flights, so solo tests continued over derelict ground in Norfolk, with the P.4 flying into longer cables suspended from barrage balloons. Finally the length was such as to offer a grave risk of the main spar

being severed. The scientists concluded that an explosive charge attached to the cable would blow the aircraft to pieces when the wire was wrapped around the wing. Clou was rather relieved that they were prepared to leave this in the realms of hypothesis without an air test.

Another RAE pilot, Sqn Ldr Hawkings, had an incredible escape when he flew a Wellington into a balloon cable. The impact set up a violent yaw, the machine turning instantly through 90 degrees with enough side stress on the tail to break it right off. Air pressure and the nose-down pitch of the aircraft caused all the debris to hurtle forward to close off the escape hatch. The pilot escaped, miraculously, and almost unbelievably, through the direct vision window in the canopy.

Having proved the hazards of hitting the cables, work commenced on methods of protection. A steel sheath on the leading edge was a starting point; it was heavily abraded by the cable sliding off at the tip so cable cutters were fitted to the leading edges. These cutters came from the fertile brain of James Martin, later Sir James, of Martin Baker Aircraft, better known for his famous ejector seats. The major problem was the extreme hardness of the cable. Martin's cutter gathered the cable into a recess and held it there on an anvil. A hard steel cutter blade was then driven through it by an explosive charge detonated by the entry of the cable into the cutter.

From all those months of exceptionally dangerous test flying, the pilots of Bomber Command went into battle with adequate and effective protection against the hazards of balloon cables. Air Commodore Clouston told the author that his work on this project gave him more personal satisfaction than any other. He was awarded a well merited Air Force Cross for it.

D.H.88 Comet.

D.H.91 Albatross with Handley Page HP.42.

In the less stressful district of Hatfield, de Havilland was finishing an aeroplane which was conceived after the success of the D.H.88 Comet racer in the 1934 MacRobertson Air Race to Australia. Flown by C. W. A. Scott and Tom Campbell Black, this specially designed racing aeroplane flew from Mildenhall, Suffolk, to Melbourne in 70 hours 53 minutes. Second place went to a virtually standard Douglas DC-2 airliner, owned by KLM and flown by Captains Parmentier and Moll, which arrived 19 hours 19 minutes after the Comet. As Francis St Barbe, one of de Havilland's directors said afterwards, 'What an appalling thing to have to do – design a little racer to compete with production passenger airliners!'

Geoffrey de Havilland clearly saw this as a measure of the lead which the American industry had gained at a time when the venerable HP.42 was the mainstay of the Imperial Airways fleet. He wrote to the Air Ministry, pointing out the obsolescence of the national carrier's equipment and Britain's non-competitive position in the market. He proposed that his firm should build a large landplane which would acquit itself well against any competition. After 14½ months of frustration

and Ministerial prevarication, an order was placed in January 1936 for two aircraft, on terms which left the company to bear the major share of the financial risk.

Arthur Hagg designed what was undoubtedly one of the six most beautiful aeroplanes ever built anywhere in the world. Some people, including the author, consider it the most beautiful. The construction of the D.H.91 Albatross was unique: the fuselage was a plywood, balsa, plywood sandwich, moulded to a sleek double curvature under pressure. The mould had retractable sides to enable the completed fuselage to be removed in one piece by crane.

The wing was built in similar fashion to the Comet wing with a thick laminated timber skin which required little internal bracing, all the stresses being taken directly by the skin.

Four D.H. Gipsy Twelve air cooled engines, virtually two Gipsy Six cylinder blocks in an inverted vee on a new crankcase, gave 525 hp each, albeit with a rather poor power/weight ratio. In spite of this handicap, the ingenious system of cooling, in which air was ducted through two leading edge intakes to the rear of the engine, passed forward through the cylinder cooling fins and ejected through a controllable flap underneath, gave the machine a remarkable performance. Charles Walker, de Havilland's technical director, with his penchant for explaining complex technical matters in vivid and simple terms, said that if the wetted area of the Albatross was represented by a sheet of glass of negligible thickness, and drawn through the air by the power of the four engines, its speed would only be 49 mph faster. In other words the aerodynamic efficiency was 81 per cent – a remarkable achievement by any standards.

On 20 May 1937 chief test pilot R. J. 'Bob' Waight flew the prototype for the first time. It handled well, although the undercarriage failed to retract fully – the first of many problems with the undercarriage, which highlighted the difficulty of retraction into a thin wing. The take-off run was 385 yards in a 5 mph wind, and the landing run only 320 yards. Today such a performance would put the Albatross in the STOL class. There was a problem with inadequate rudder response in the climb. This was overcome by a modification which replaced the flat tailplane and inset rudders by a dihedralled tailplane with endplate rudders – incidentally improving considerably the appearance of the aeroplane.

The de Havilland Aeronautical Technical School had designed and built the fourth of a range of single engined racers, the diminutive TK.4. In October 1937 Bob Waight was flying it for photographic purposes when he flew into the ground and was killed. Group Captain John Cunningham, the distinguished night fighter pilot (later to become chief test pilot at Hatfield), was a pilot at the Tech School where he saw Waight positioning the TK.4 for a low level run towards the photographer. It appeared that he had trouble in completely retracting the undercarriage, and the slightly 'switchback' flight path indicated that he was using the hand pump to lower the wheels slightly and bring them up again. Presumably his concentration was disturbed, he came in too low and too slow, the aircraft disintegrating as it hit the ground in a level attitude.

Geoffrey de Havilland, the 27 year old son of the founder of the company, who had been assisting Bob Waight, took over as chief test pilot and, with George Gibbins, continued flight trials of the Albatross.

On 22 June, Capt Geoffrey flew for the first time the D.H.94 Moth Minor, a very attractive two seat open cockpit touring monoplane designed to sell at £575. The Moth Minor was the last aeroplane upon which de Havilland Senior carried out the major part of the test programme. John Cunning-

Peter, John and Geoffrey, the sons of Captain Geoffrey de Havilland. John and Geoffrey were to die in de Havilland aeroplanes (c 1943).

ham had joined the Auxiliary Air Force, and learned to fly in 1935 with the County of Middlesex Squadron at Hendon. By 1938 the first three prototypes of the D.H.94 had been tested very thoroughly. Spinning trials had been carried out with anti-spin parachutes in the tail; the spinning characteristics were impeccable. Capt Geoffrey asked John Cunningham, who was only 21 at the time, to complete the development flying of the type. The fourth aircraft off the line was the first production model, and it had a slightly modified rudder shape with altered travel. Geoffrey Junior and John Cunningham began spinning trials with the centre of gravity at its aft limit. The machine did not respond to recovery drill, and, at 3,000 ft there seemed no likelihood of success. Geoffrey instructed Cunningham to bail out and he quickly followed. It was ironic that, as the spinning trials on the earlier aeroplanes had been so successful, no anti-spin 'chute had been fitted to this one. John Cunningham recalled the doomed aeroplane hurtling past him and wishing he had a camera with him. The two pilots were picked up by senior D.H. men and driven to lunch at the local Chequers Inn where the incident was hardly commented upon. This problem taught de Havilland a great many lessons in spinning phenomena and the Moth Minor became a particularly safe aeroplane as a result of it. As with the Albatross and the later Flamingo, airliner development was terminated by the war. Some sets of Moth Minor parts were sent to de Havilland Australia for completion and there are still a few examples of the type to be seen around the world.

One of de Havilland's few failures also flew in the same month as the Albatross. This was the D.H.93 Don. Built to an Air Ministry specification for a trainer to be loaded with an impossible collection of equipment, including a turret, it rapidly outgrew its engine power and was abandoned, to the great relief of all concerned.

1937 saw the first flight of another elegant aeroplane, the Miles Kestrel Trainer. The introduction of the Hurricane and Spitfire had convinced Fred Miles that it was essential to produce a suitable trainer to replace the Hart biplane which was, clearly, quite useless for the advanced standards required of those who would fly these new machines. He studied the potential requirements and decided to submit to the Air Ministry a design for a low wing monoplane powered by a Kestrel engine. It would have a retractable undercarriage, flaps and a variable pitch propeller. The Kestrel engine was a shrewd move, as the withdrawal from service of all the Hawker biplanes would release a large number of these engines. Furthermore, Rolls-Royce had just taken a substantial financial interest in Miles's company, Phillips and Powis, and had agreed to design the engine installation.

Named Kestrel, the new design was submitted to the Ministry, who promptly rejected it on the grounds that there was no immediate requirement for an advanced trainer. Backed by Rolls-Royce, Miles decided to proceed with a prototype as a private venture. In the meantime the Ministry had second thoughts, deciding that, after all, they

Miles Kestrel Trainer.

Blackburn Skua short-nosed prototype.

would need an advanced trainer. Miles considered the specification which was issued, but reckoned that it was an impossible one. He continued with the Kestrel which would meet most of the specification, but not completely.

On 3 June, Fred Miles flew the prototype G-AEOC. The performance was superb and surpassed all expectations. With a top speed of 296 mph at 14,500 ft it was only about 15 mph slower than the Hurricane, with handling characteristics very similar to the two new fighters. Unfortunately the exigencies of production engineering modified the beautiful lines of the prototype and the production Master, as the type was called, looked rather different. It was a successful trainer and several variants emerged with radial engines. It was also used for glider and target towing.

Another significant aeroplane, the Blackburn Skua, was flown for the first time by 'Dasher' Blake on 9 February 1937. The first naval machine to be designed in the modern style, it was built as a two seat dive bomber fighter. Blake found the Skua to be seriously tail heavy, the engine having to be moved 2 ft 5 in forward to locate the CG in the correct position. Martlesham Heath gave the Skua a good report so production went ahead. A further development of it, the Roc two seater turret fighter, which flew in 1938, was a heavy, cumbersome aeroplane with an abysmal performance.

By the time the two Blackburn machines had entered squadron service in 1940 they were hopelessly outclassed, although the Skua carried out a number of successful operations in its dive bomber role. The Roc was originally conceived as a twin float seaplane, but was not flown as such until the end of 1939. Tests were carried out at the Marine Aircraft Experimental Establishment which had moved from Felixstowe to Helensburgh on the Clyde. Serious problems of directional instability were experienced, the prototype crashing on take-off. Increasing fin area under the tailplane failed to make an appreciable improvement. Together with the Skua this unlovely aeroplane was soon relegated to target towing.

In October 1937 Flt Lt A. M. Blake, who had been Blackburn's chief test pilot for ten years, was found dead in his garage, the doors closed and his car engine running. His assistant, Flt Lt Henry Bailey, succeeded him with Sqn Ldr J. L. N. Bennett-Baggs helping on the production side.

After repeated attempts to break into the military aircraft market, Airspeed at last succeeded in securing orders for their Oxford trainer, derived from their attractive Envoy airliner, which later received the accolade of purchase for service in the King's Flight. Flt Lt C. H. A. Colman, the chief test pilot, flew the prototype from Portsmouth on 18 June 1937 and the twin Armstrong Siddeley Cheetah engined machine was a winner from the start. It was shown in the New Types Park at Hendon and the flight test programme continued in the hands of Cyril Colman and George Errington. George

George Errington leaving the Airspeed Oxford prototype (1937).

had a distinctly hairy experience during spinning trials. These flights were to take place over Devon, and the spinning characteristics investigated with various loads and CG positions. With CG forward all was well; George allowed eight rotations and recovered quite satisfactorily, although the engine on the inside of the spin tended to cut out. The spin was stable and the pilot was able to photograph the instrument panel on the way down.

After about 100 turns in this loading pattern the technical department was satisfied, and tests commenced with the CG behind the theoretical aft limit. It was appreciated that this might cause difficulties so an anti-spin parachute was fitted in the tail, to be operated by a lever fixed to the cockpit roof and released by a similar lever alongside. As an added precaution, George had a rope fixed along the centre of the fuselage to help him reach the door if it should be necessary to leave the aircraft in the spin. So the nose of the 'Oxbox' was turned towards Devon, climbing to 16,000 ft. Errington checked his parachute and stopwatch and spun the machine with camera poised. After eight turns unsuccessful recovery action was taken. The time had come to deploy the tail parachute as only 8,000 ft was left before boring operations into the Devon soil commenced. The lever was pulled but the Oxford continued to spin. George decided to bail out smartly, released his harness and staggered aft to the door. Suddenly the spin ceased, the tail came up and a slow spiral dive developed. Errington rushed back to his seat and pulled the parachute jettison lever, assuming that the 'chute had suddenly deployed. Again nothing happened. Perhaps he hadn't pulled it hard enough. Another ferocious pull, as he said, 'Hard enough to shame a Scot at a fruit machine!'

This time the whole lever assembly parted company with the cabin roof and swung around dangerously on its cables. By now the distance to Devon was only 4,000 ft, the surface being shrouded in cloud for good measure. An immediate departure was vital so, once again, the pilot headed for the door. Again the machine began to recover, and again George rushed to the seat, with no time to do more than lean over the back of it to try to recover from the dive, as the altimeter unwound between one and two thousand feet, still in cloud. The Oxford emerged at high speed, missed the top of a hill by 200 ft, and continued straight and level with both aircraft and pilot trembling like jellies. The Oxford was notorious for its spinning habits, and much work was directed towards improving its characteristics, but not even a twin rudder tailplane solved it, and the machine always remained sensitive to the fit of the engine cowlings with the wing leading edge fairing. One of the great trainers of the Second World War, 8,586 were built.

Airspeed was invited, in 1935, to tender for a replacement of the de Havilland Queen Bee radio controlled target aeroplane. Based upon the Tiger Moth, it was a floatplane catapulted off ships with the controller on board the ship. Hessell Tiltman produced an attractive Cheetah engined biplane and two prototypes were built, K8887 on wheels, and the much better looking K8888 on floats. Cyril Colman and George Errington were extremely pleased with its performance. Hessell Tiltman recalled a strange incident during stalling trials. Errington asked him to fly with him so that he could demonstrate an unusual phenomenon. George said, 'I would like you to look over the side: we are at 2,000 ft heading into wind over the leeward side of the aerodrome. I shall now close the throttle and pull the stick back until the angle of incidence is on the other side of the stall.' Tiltman saw the air speed indicator reading drop to 45 mph and, gradually, to zero. 'In the meantime we were losing height rapidly. Errington assured me that we were under proper control which he demonstrated by applying full aileron. The machine responded by rocking gently as it would do under normal flying conditions. Errington had to apply full throttle to reach the aerodrome; we just skimmed the hedge!'

'Whilst we were in the super-stalled condition we must have descended vertically, indeed I think we were going astern in the ten knot wind. During the descent the attitude was normal, say, plus five to ten degrees, but the angle of attack must have been nearer eighty degrees. This confounded the theory that highly tapered wings are unstable in the stall and tend to drop sharply.' It was possible to reproduce the phenomenon on K8887, but not on K8888 or later production models, which attracted adverse comments from pilots who found that the stalling characteristics of the Wasp were, predictably, rather vicious.

It is sadly ironic that George Errington, who was deeply interested in the stall, and who, in this episode, was probably the first test pilot to encounter and identify the stabilized super-stall, should meet his death in 1966 as co-pilot of a de Havilland Trident airliner on a test flight, when the stall was being explored. Recovery was delayed, causing the machine to enter a super-stall in which the high tail was blanketed by the wing wash. Without a tail parachute, the test crew died when the machine crashed near Norwich.

2nd Prototype Airspeed Queen Wasp on floats; and after catapult take-off crash at Farnborough.

A Farnborough test pilot, Flt Lt McDougall, had a narrow escape in K8888 during catapult trials which followed flights from HMS *Pegasus*. The floats had been exchanged for wheels, and the ground based catapult was fired. Onlookers were surprised to see that the pilot had disappeared. The Wasp rose gracefully into the air, dived slightly, touched a wheel on the grass and bounced again to drop the other wheel. The wing tip hit and dug in, the aircraft rolling right over, disintegrating as it went. The onlookers, fearful of fire, rushed over to find the pilot shouting for release from the rear fuselage. He was quickly rescued, soaked in petrol, but otherwise almost uninjured. His rapid transit into the rear of the aeroplane had occurred when the acceleration forces of the catapult launch proved too much for the mild steel bolts of the seat anchorage. These bolts should have been replaced with high tensile steel ones when the catapult spools were fitted to the machine, but someone forgot this vital precaution. McDougall was an extremely lucky man.

The A&AEE Martlesham lost two of its most experienced officers in the Kings Cup Race on 10 September 1937. Flying a Miles Falcon, Wg Cdr Ted Hilton, Sammy Wroath's CO, and Wg Cdr Percy Sherren encountered heavy turbulence when negotiating the Scarborough Castle turning point. Hilton, piloting, was thrown upwards so violently that his harness broke, he hit the cabin roof and broke his neck; Sherren, a heavily built man, was thrown through the roof of the Falcon, which crashed into the sea.

Two major civil developments flew in January 1938, the Short Mayo Composite on the 21st and the Armstrong Whitworth Ensign on the 24th.

Regular Transatlantic services were the aim of Imperial Airways. Flight refuelling, which Sir Alan

Short Mayo Composite aircraft just after separation.

Cobham was energetically promoting, appeared to be the answer, but Maj R. H. Mayo persuaded the airline that an alternative would be to mount a heavily loaded seaplane, incapable of take-off under its own power, on the top of a lightly loaded Empire flying boat, the two aircraft separating at an appropriate height. Short Brothers converted the flying boat, to be called Maia, and built a seaplane powered by four Napier Rapier engines. John Lankester Parker had successfully flown both aircraft in 1937 so, on 1 January 1938 taxying trials of the complete assembly were carried out. Later, a brief hop was made with H. L. Piper at the controls of the seaplane, Mercury.

On 6 February the first separation in the air was made with complete success. On 21 July Maia, with Capt A. S. Wilcockson of Imperial Airways at the controls, and Mercury commanded by Capt D. C. T. Bennett (later, Air Marshal Don Bennett of the wartime Pathfinder Force), took off from Foynes on the River Shannon. After a flawless separation, Mercury flew non-stop to Montreal with 1,000 lb of freight, mail and newsreels in 20 hours 20 minutes, the first commercial flight across the Atlantic. In November the same crew set up a world distance record for seaplanes, when they

flew from Dundee to the mouth of the Orange River in South Africa, a distance of 6,045 miles flown nonstop.

The Air Ministry lost interest, saying that the idea was outdated – only suitable for mail, and unacceptable for passengers – so the project was abandoned. Clearly the right decision was made, but probably for the wrong reasons. Expensive and exclusive cranage and handling facilities were necessary at all ports of call. To use the current jargon, it could not be cost effective.

A significant military aeroplane to fly on 11 August 1937 in the hands of Cecil Feather was the Boulton Paul P.82 Defiant; built as a Merlin engined turret fighter to specification F9/35, as was the Hawker Hotspur. Like the Hotspur, it had a serious operational weakness. Although its four gun Boulton Paul powered turret could fire a powerful salvo in all directions but ahead, it had no armament firing forward. It proved to be an excellent aeroplane from the handling point of view, as did the Hotspur, which had a single gun firing forward. On operations the Defiant achieved initial success, the *Luftwaffe* pilots mistaking them for Hurricane fighters and attacking from astern, but as soon as the true nature of the aircraft was recognized, the tactics changed and attacks from ahead decimated the squadrons. The Defiant was soon withdrawn and relegated to the less hazardous role of target towing.

At Hatfield the flight test programme of the beautiful Albatross was running into difficulties. In March, Geoffrey de Havilland had been forced to belly-land the prototype, G-AEVV, when both electric and manual undercarriage actuators failed to work. Damage was slight and the machine was soon flying again. In July the second one G-AEVW, flew and quickly came to grief. Geoffrey was carrying out maximum overload tests and, to avoid the necessity of jettisoning fuel he landed at full overload.

In spite of the greatest possible care to make a smooth touchdown, the first two landings had evidently strained the rear fuselage. In the third it broke across the rear entry door. Fortunately the test crew were uninjured. De Havilland were very embarrassed by the incident and tried to avoid publicity. A newsagent, who owned a shop on the edge of the aerodrome, photographed the sad looking beauty from his bedroom window and sold the print to one of the national dailies. He was not popular with DH and, doubtless, his orders were reduced. It is not clear why this accident happened; it has been suggested that a vital longitudinal

D.H.91 Albatross prototype after fuselage failure.

strengthening member below the entry door had been left out – this is certainly a likely explanation. The broken halves were replaced upon the building jig, minor strengthening was introduced and, five weeks later, 'VW flew again. The first two machines were mail planes but not used as such. A further five went into service with Imperial Airways.

The Albatross was not an unqualified success, the undercarriage was a quite literal Achilles heel. In January 1939 the flagship *Frobisher* taxied over sodden grass at Croydon, the wheels meeting the edge of the tarmac at an angle in front of the Terminal Building. The leg immediately folded and the wing hit the hard standing; it broke outside the engines, and the other leg then collapsed, breaking the other wing. A most unseemly performance in front of would-be passengers.

Normal commercial services having ceased as war became imminent, the type was used on National Air Communications work, but continual exposure to the weather, as hangars were not available at dispersal aerodromes, took its toll of the wooden structure. After several crashes and a near disaster when *Fortuna* shed its flaps coming into Shannon airport the survivors were scrapped.

De Havilland had decided that a metal airliner was essential to meet the American competition, so the 20 seat D.H.95 Flamingo was built to the design of R. E. Bishop, who had succeeded Arthur Hagg as chief designer. Powered by two Bristol Perseus sleeve valve engines, Geoffrey de Havilland Junior and George Gibbins first flew the prototype, G-AFUE, from Hatfield, on 28 December 1938. There was, initially, some doubt of its directional stability so a central fin was added. Later flights proved it unnecessary. The machine handled extremely well and it seemed a very promising design. Jersey Airways operated AFUE successfully although the pre-delivery checks were rather fraught. Geoffrey de Havilland was to carry out a final air test. As he walked out to the machine the engines were being run up to full throttle against

D.H.95 Flamingo airliner.

the wheel chocks. As the test pilot approached the tail to enter the door on the port side, the port wheel rode over the chocks, and the machine, with the port engine at full throttle, pivoted violently about the starboard chock, almost hitting Geoffrey de Havilland, and breaking the tail off against the attendant fire engine which was rolled on to its side.

The unit construction which was a feature of the design permitted swift replacement of the tail and delivery of the aeroplane was made on time. The war terminated development of the Flamingo, although a number were used for communications duties and by British Overseas Airways Corporation in the Middle East.

The only other major pre-war civil project was the Armstrong Whitworth Ensign. The 90 ft 8 in span Armstrong Siddeley Tiger engined airliner first flew with Charles Turner-Hughes and Eric Greenwood at the controls in January 1938, already 18 months behind schedule. The rudder was found to be badly overbalanced, requiring the efforts of both pilots to return it to neutral. The rudder servo unit was modified, and checked on a delivery flight from Hamble, where the Ensign was built, to Armstrong Whitworth's base at Baginton near Coventry. An improvement was reported but other small problems were apparent. After further work on the rudder servo another flight was made on 3 March. After 1¾ hours in the air both starboard engines cut out, fortunately whilst the aircraft was near Baginton, a safe landing being made. Mishandling of the fuel tank controls by the flight crew had caused all the fuel in the starboard tanks to flow to the port tanks.

A flight later in the month was marked by the cutting of all four engines. This, too, was due to misuse of the fuel controls which had been carefully marked, unhappily in an ambiguous manner, to avoid further trouble. Very fortunately the aeroplane was near RAF Bicester where a successful dead-stick landing was made.

C of A trials at Martlesham Heath revealed a take-off performance below specification and some modifications were needed. Imperial Airways acceptance trials, with Turner-Hughes in charge of a flight to Paris from Croydon with two Imperial Airways pilots, caused some consternation when shortly after take-off from Baginton, the elevators were found to be locked. The machine returned immediately to Baginton, being landed with the aid of the elevator trimmers. It was found that two adjacent fork end fittings in the control system had jammed together.

The Ensign was a good aeroplane which was afflicted with engine problems for much of its life until 1941, when Pratt & Whitney Cyclones were installed. Its performance was well below the contemporary American Douglas DC-4 airliner and the war terminated development with the type being used in National Air Communication work. Due to the lack of a satisfactory alternative transport, BOAC were forced to consider the use of the survivors on the routes after the war. In the event they were worn out and fit only for the scrapyard.

November 1938 saw the first flights of two important military aircraft, the Bristol Beaufort and the Westland Whirlwind. The Beaufort was a torpedo bomber based upon the Blenheim and using many Blenheim components. It was designed, as indeed was the Blenheim, by Capt Frank Barnwell, Bristol's chief designer, who was considered to be one of the finest in the country at that time. He was a very mediocre pilot and was not permitted to fly the later Bristol high performance machines, so he built to his own design a small monoplane with a 25 hp Scott Squirrel motorcycle engine. He test flew it for the first time at the end of July 1938

Armstrong Whitworth Ensign.

and killed himself in it on the second flight on 2 August – a tragic loss of a first class engineer.

His last design, the Beaufort, was flown by Cyril Uwins and months were lost in overcoming cooling problems with the Perseus engines. In every other respect the machine was excellent and served with the RAF throughout the war, as did its sister machine, the Beaufighter.

It became clear in 1938 that the German Messerschmitt Me 110 would be a formidable adversary as a bomber interceptor, and the RAF had no twin engine fighter to counter its depredations. Leslie G. Frise, who had succeeded Frank Barnwell, realized that the Beaufort had a number of major assemblies which could be used to build what, at that time, was considered to be a stop-gap fighter. Wings, tail unit, engine nacelles and undercarriage only required a new fuselage and the installation of a pair of Bristol Hercules radial engines. The Air Staff liked the idea and instructed that work should commence.

The Westland Whirlwind twin-engined fighter flew four days before the Beaufort in the hands of Harald Penrose.

W. E. W. Petter, the son of the chairman of Westland, Sir Ernest Petter, was an exceptionally able designer with some slightly idiosyncratic ideas, such as the Whirlwind exhausts passing through the fuel tanks. His basic design concept was to achieve a single seat fighter to carry four cannon with minimum drag. This lean, handsome aeroplane certainly exuded an impression of speed and was nicknamed 'Crikey' after the famous Shell advertisement of the time, in which a two faced man looking at a high speed cloud of dust says, 'Crikey, that's Shell, that was!' Unfortunately the Rolls-Royce Peregrine engine, developed from the Kestrel, was a low altitude engine, and this severely restricted the potential of the new fighter which had a number of innovations, many of which caused development delays.

Harald Penrose flew the prototype from Boscombe Down. He found that rudder control was unsatisfactory, there being little effect on direction in the first five degrees of movement, and a rapidly developing heaviness as deflection increased. With rudder free there was snaking, a nose down trim change was observed, and the machine shuddered in a tight turn. Penrose decided that this was due to interference between the fin and tailplane – this was overcome by a bullet fairing between the two.

The chief test pilot's prediction about the effect of routeing the exhausts through the tank – supported also by his senior engineering colleagues –

Westland Whirlwind.

was proved to be sound when on one test flight an exhaust pipe burned through the tank. Incredibly the fuel did not catch fire, but incandescent gases burning at the hole melted the aileron control rod, and the Whirlwind rolled viciously to starboard as the aileron on that side moved to full lock. Harald Penrose fought to recover control, managing to fly back with the other aileron held at full lock to balance the machine whilst he gingerly returned on rudder only. Two squadrons of Whirlwinds were used most effectively for low level operations.

In September 1938 one of the most humiliating events in British history took place when Prime Minister Neville Chamberlain flew to Germany to meet the German dictator Hitler, returning with a declaration of goodwill which he waved at the steps of his aeroplane declaring 'I believe it is peace for our time.' The practical benefit of this visit was the extra year of preparation for war which it gave to the nation, a year in which a number of very important and advanced aeroplanes flew for the first time.

8

RAF EXPANSION

1939 was a year in which the aircraft industry was resolutely and urgently expanding its facilities and developing its technology to meet the desperate needs of the forthcoming war which, in the opinion of those in high places, was inevitable. Production of aircraft in Canada and Australia was under consideration, and the Shadow Factory scheme in Britain was beginning to show results. At Longbridge, near Birmingham, the plant controlled by the Austin Motor Company was building Battles, the management and workers quickly discovering that the construction of aeroplanes was very different from making cars. The Castle Bromwich factory managed by Nuffield was switching its tooling from the obsolescent Battle to the Spitfire, which was produced there in large numbers.

They were flown by a team of test pilots, led by Alex Henshaw, who had, in February 1939, made an amazing solo flight to Cape Town and back in his Percival Mew Gull G-AEXF, setting up a series of records which are still unbroken in 1984.

In the *London Gazette* there appeared the names of RAF officers to become famous wartime commanders: Air Vice Marshal C. F. A. Portal, Group Captain J. C. Slessor and Group Captain R. H. N. S. Saundby. The Auxiliary Air Force Reserve was formed to train ex-RAF men to be ready to return to active service at short notice.

Serious consideration was given to the purchase of American aircraft. The Lockheed 14 transport was investigated although its handling characteristics were said to be a bit vicious. Similarly, the North American Harvard trainer was of interest but was suspect for the same reason. Nevertheless the decision was taken to purchase both and they gave good service despite the piercing howl from the Harvard when the ungeared Pratt and Whitney Wasp drove the propeller tips at supersonic speed. Three inches off the tips lessened the noise.

The Air Minister, Sir Kingsley Wood, carried out a series of morale boosting visits to manufacturers, where he saw the latest aircraft in prototype form, or on the drawing board. At Parnall Aircraft in Tolworth, he was shown the new Fraser Nash powered gun turret, its precise controllability demonstrated by his name being written on a piece of card by a pencil in one of the gun muzzles. At Airspeed's Portsmouth factory the Minister saw Oxfords in production, the new Queen Wasp target biplane was flown, and George Errington demonstrated his aerobatic skill in the two seat Bristol Bulldog, in which the type tests of the new Alvis Leonides radial engine were being carried out. The power/weight ratio of this new 450 hp engine was so good that the engine bearers were extended about two feet to ensure that the centre of gravity of the aeroplane was in the right position.

In a rash moment George flew the Bulldog through a massive cumulo-nimbus cloud at 17,000 ft to demonstrate to John Marlow, the Alvis engineer, something which George himself had not experienced – the immense natural power which is unleashed in these clouds and which has been known to rip aeroplanes apart. He thought that the Bulldog, being stressed to fighter standards, would be quite secure. Icing was immediate; the struts, pitot head and the venturi driving the blind flying instruments became the first casualties. George was certain that he could fly this veteran by the seat of his pants so he just relaxed. Suddenly an alarmed shout from his observer alerted him to a tightening of his harness, and the spectacle of Marlow sitting white faced in his cockpit surrounded by leads apparently rising vertically from within. He suddenly realized that they were in a fast inverted dive heading for Chichester Cathedral which appeared to be almost overhead as they levelled out. Suitably chastened, George resumed level flight, concluding that if one flies an old crate by the seat of one's pants one should be sure that one's seat is in contact with old crate all the time!

The traditional rivalry between Hawker and Supermarine took an interesting turn in January 1940. Hawker had made capital out of the flight

Group Captain H. A. 'Bruin' Purvis (1946).

made in February 1938 when Sqn Ldr J. W. Gillan, OC of No 111 Sqn flew his Hurricane from Edinburgh to Northolt at 17,000 ft, averaging 308 mph. Little was said about the strong tail wind which he enjoyed.

A Spitfire was to be exhibited at the 1939 Paris Air Show so Jeffrey Quill flew it to Le Bourget, a distance of about 200 miles, in 42½ minutes. His flight home in a venerable Handley Page 42 of Imperial Airways took 2½ hours. The potential of the Spitfire as a world speed record breaker had been recognized in 1937, when Rolls-Royce had been asked to convert a standard Merlin into a special high power sprint engine. The redoubtable Rod Banks prepared a special fuel cocktail which enabled the engine to develop over 2,000 hp with 28.5 lb boost pressure.

A standard Spitfire was modified, the new version having short wings, a different cooling system, and sixteen coats of high gloss blue paint. Early trials were disappointing: the best speed that Jeffrey Quill could attain was 408 mph; not enough for a record breaker. As the Air Ministry was paying for this project they had nominated Sqn Ldr H. A. 'Bruin' Purvis to make the attempt on the record.

He worked closely with Jeffrey on the flight trials of the aircraft, and on one occasion, whilst making a high speed run at very low level along the unofficial speed course — the Farnborough to Basingstoke railway line — the engine stopped. Bruin had sufficient speed to climb high enough to be able to glide home and make a dead-stick landing at Farnborough.

Sqn Ldr Purvis was undoubtedly one of the finest of the RAF test pilots; there are many who say he was the top man of his generation. His test flying career began as a Flt Lt in 1932 when he was posted to the torpedo development flight at Gosport to fly Blackburn Darts, Ripons and Hawker Horsleys. He became a flight commander in 1936, soon being posted to RAE Farnborough where, in command of the engine flight was Flt Lt R. L. R. Atcherley, the immortal 'Batchie', whose exploits will be forever enshrined in the history of the RAF. Purvis flew hundreds of hours in the Hawker Horsley flying test bed used on Merlin development. Sharing this rather boring work were the Rolls-Royce chief test pilot, Capt R. T. Shepherd, and the Rolls-Royce test pilots, Harvey Heyworth and Ronnie Harker. In 1940 Bruin was awarded his first AFC for his engine development work.

Various modifications were made to the high speed Spitfire, N17. Finally the large external ducted radiator was removed altogether, and a scheme was devised to use the main fuel tank as a heat sink, condensing the steam and jettisoning the excess which could not be condensed. Jeffrey Quill's first flight with this arrangement was aborted when, as he taxied out for take-off, a coolant pipe burst, turning the cockpit into a passable imitation of a Turkish bath. He was extremely fortunate to avoid serious scalding.

Speed Spitfire.

The imminence of war caused the project to be abandoned. N17 was converted to a photographic reconnaissance aircraft which was used on several operations by Flt Lt John Boothman, later Air Marshal Sir John, before finally it became a communications hack.

The major significance of N17 was the proof it offered of the immense growth potential of the Merlin engine. From its original 1,000 hp it was already developing 2,000 hp at 3,200 rpm with the remarkable boost pressure of $28\frac{1}{2}$ lb per sq in. The message was loud and clear to Joe Smith, who had succeeded R. J. Mitchell as chief designer at Supermarines, when Mitchell tragically died of cancer in 1937. Smith was convinced that airframe and engine 'stretch' were compatible in the time and performance scale, and that it would be unnecessary to follow the Hawker competition, which was forced to produce an entirely new design to succeed the Hurricane, because of Sydney Camm's espousal of fabric covering. So Supermarines continued development of the basic Spitfire airframe up to the Mark 47 – first flown by Jeffrey Quill in 1946, ten years after the first flight of K5054.

Early in 1939 deliveries of the first American aircraft to serve in the RAF began, and a Hudson, developed from the Lockheed 14, was at Martlesham Heath with a North American Harvard trainer. Both had acquired a rather nasty reputation for unpleasant habits. There had been a number of accidents with the Lockheed 14, largely due to the inability of pilots to master the handling characteristics of aeroplanes with what, at that time, were high wing loadings. They needed to be flown precisely and with considerable skill. The Harvard, too, was looked upon initially as a tricky beast, particularly in the spin. The early models had built in slots near the tips. The Martlesham pilots decided that these were unnecessary but at low speed the wing drop phenomenon was pronounced, and dangerous. R. P. Alston, a scientific officer at RAE Farnborough went to Martlesham to observe the Harvard spinning trials.

On 16 February 1939, with Sqn Ldr Robert Cazalet as pilot, Alston's Harvard spun into the ground, killing both of them. The anti-spin parachute had been deployed and the machine had recovered. It appeared that the parachute had then torn away and a further spin developed. Bob Alston, and, later, his wife Gwen, flew many hours at RAE, and even this tragedy did not prevent her carrying on most courageously well into the war years. The memory of R. P. Alston is commemorated in the award of the Alston Medal for Test Flying, established by his wife and administered by the Royal Aeronautical Society.

The only one of the three famous British heavy bombers of the Second World War to be designed as a four engined machine, the Short Stirling, made its first flight on 14 May 1939. The Avro Manchester, later to become the Lancaster, was fitted with two Rolls-Royce Vulture engines and the Handley Page Halifax was originally conceived as a twin engined aeroplane. Profiting from their experience with the Short Scion Senior, which served as a flying scale model of the Empire flying boat, a half-scale Stirling, the S31M4, was built of wood and powered originally with 90 hp Pobjoy Niagara engines, later changed to 115 hp versions. John Lankester Parker had flown this delightful machine since mid-1938; he decided that the tailplane was not large enough so a new one was fitted, the bomber being modified similarly.

On 13 May, the great Stirling high on its complicated and stalky undercarriage, was towed from the hangar; Lankester Parker making a few very satisfactory runs across the airfield, on one occasion lifting off for about fifty yards, to 'feel' the elevator control and general trim. On the following day the chief test pilot, with Sqn Ldr Eric Morton (loaned to Shorts from the Marine Aircraft Experimental Establishment to assist with flight test of the new Sunderland flying boat), and with George Cotton as flight engineer, flew the Stirling for about twenty minutes. As it came in for a perfect touchdown, onlookers were horrified to see it suddenly swerve, the huge undercarriage collapsing beneath it as it subsided in a cloud of dust on its nose and wing tip. The crew escaped unscathed but the prototype was a write-off. The accident was caused by a seized brake.

The second prototype was nowhere near completion, and did not fly until 3 December. The Air Ministry had, however, sufficient experience of Short Brothers expertise, when the Empire flying boats were ordered off the drawing board, to permit production plans to go ahead. Parker was satisfied, from his observations on that one short flight, that no untoward handling problems were likely to arise. He was right; for generally it was well liked by its pilots once they had become accustomed to the powerful swing to starboard on take-off, before the rudder became effective. Captains soon learned to open the throttles with the starboard pair and lead three or four inches ahead of the port pair.

The major problem with the Stirling was its inability to cruise much above 12,000 ft. This

Short Stirling.

was due to the remarkable edict in the original specification that its wing span must not exceed 100 ft, so that it would fit into standard hangars – although many RAF stations had Type 'C' hangars designed in 1934 with an open span of 150 ft. So, sweating aircrews sat below Lancasters and Halifaxes well above them, as torrents of HE and incendiary bombs dropped towards German soil. Many Stirlings were hit and their crews returned to tell the tale. One shudders to think of those who met disaster from a 'friendly' bomb.

At the Avro works near Manchester the new Vulture engined heavy bomber named after that city was approaching completion. Many hours of ground running and air testing had been carried out by Rolls-Royce test pilots in Hawker Horsleys and a Henley, but the great 24-cylinder 'X' engine left much to be desired in terms of its power output of 1,760 hp and, vitally important in a twin, reliability (see chapter twelve).

Surprisingly, specification P13/36, to which it was built, called for it to be stressed for catapult launching to enable it to operate from relatively small airfields. The prototype spent many months at Farnborough developing launching and arresting techniques which were never used in service. It first flew without gun turrets on 25 July 1939 with the Avro chief test pilot, Capt H. A. Brown and

his assistant Flt Lt S. A. 'Bill' Thorne at the controls. The obvious imminence of war forced production to proceed without waiting for the results of flight test, so it was fortunate that few modifications were required. Directional instability was cured by fitting an additional fin above the rear fuselage, wing span was increased slightly, and the original metal covered elevators and ailerons were replaced with fabric covered ones.

The Manchester was exceptionally strong and light, it being said that Roy Chadwick, the chief designer, inspected every part of the structure of the prototype with a stress man. If he suspected that a particular member could be eliminated or lightened he would instruct the stress man to check it. In this way all surplus metal was removed. When it was decided to abandon the two Vulture engines in favour of four Merlins, the Lancaster inherited an airframe which had been refined to the highest degree and Bomber Command received what was undoubtedly the outstanding bomber of the war. No 207 Sqn at Waddington received the first Manchesters. The station commander, Group Captain J. N. Boothman, of Schneider Trophy fame, decided to check the effect upon the new central fin when the mid-upper turret was traversed through the beam position. He flew at gradually increasing airspeeds in the dive; in one of them the fin folded flat across the tail. Boscombe Down became involved at this stage and, as a result of other tests, the

Group Captain H. J. Wilson (1946).

central fin was deleted and the tailplane increased in span, larger fins and rudders being fitted.

Group Captain H. J. 'Willie' Wilson was a Flt Lt in Aerodynamics Flight at RAE. He tells the story of a Manchester arriving for assisted launch trials. At one stage the machine was fitted with rockets, two packs of twelve under the wings inboard of the engines, but designed to fire in pairs, one each side, in sequence. Some successful trials were made and a group of VIPs from Air Ministry and Bomber Command came to watch a demonstration. Willie taxied out to begin his take-off in front of the visitors. Sadly it had not been noticed that one of the brackets retaining the rocket pack on one side was fatigued, and, as the engines were opened up, and the rocket operating button pressed, all hell was let loose. The bracket failed and short circuited all the cables to the other rockets, the sequence control was by-passed, and all the rockets fired in a spectacular holocaust which shot them all through the propellers, where they were chopped into short lengths and distributed in the direction of the incredulous spectators!

Murphy's Law was also invoked on the occasion of another VIP visit when Flt Lt Wilson was to demonstrate bomber arrester gear, similar to that used on aircraft carriers, to stop the Manchester. Large concrete blocks had been sunk into the aerodrome on either side of the landing path, there being no runways at that time. The arrester gear was connected to these foundations. Willie brought

his aircraft in to catch the wires; unfortunately 'Works and Bricks' had made a mess of their sums and, as the load came upon the wires, all the blocks rose from the ground to be catapulted in all directions as the visitors fled for their lives. The pilot meanwhile had the utmost difficulty in maintaining a straight path with all the hardware hanging around his aeroplane. Needless to say neither scheme was adopted.

These incidents, potentially dangerous though they were, were the source of considerable merriment amid the serious and hazardous work in which the Farnborough and Boscombe Down pilots were involved.

At Bristol, Cyril Uwins flew the Beaufighter prototype for the first time on 17 July. Originally designed for Hercules VI, shortage of these powerful sleeve valve engines forced the use of the less powerful Mark III in early production. Nevertheless, Uwins was very satisfied with the aeroplane: handling was excellent, but some directional instability required an increase in fin area, and modifications to the undercarriage were made to accommodate inevitable weight increases and the strain of night landings which, it was suspected, would often be heavy ones.

By the time the formidable armament of four 20 mm cannon had been installed, and the Beaufighter brought up to operational status, the top speed of 335 mph achieved by the prototype had dropped to 309 mph at 15,000 ft, well below the speed of the Hurricane. After trials at Boscombe Down, to which aerodrome A&AEE had moved on the outbreak of war, various modifications were made to improve top speed. One test involved the filling and painting of all rivet holes and panel joints and sealing of all air leaks with tape. This labour intensive job produced an increase of only 10 mph at 16,000 ft.

As airborne radar development continued, it was soon realized that the Beaufighter was the ideal mount for the interception units, so its distinguished career as a night fighter began. Six machine guns were added to its armament, and the Mk II was powered with Merlin XX engines. Throughout its life the type was prone to a slight degree of longitudinal instability, particularly when climbing. A Mk I was fitted with a wide tailplane with twin fins and rudders at the ends. This was not sufficiently successful to warrant a change, so a further experiment was carried out with the original tailplane set at 12 degree dihedral. This was completely effective but it made the machine too stable as a night fighter. The modification was

Bristol Beaufighter Mk VI prototype.

however of considerable value in the anti-shipping role with Coastal Command; torpedo dropping requires a very accurate approach, with a high degree of directional stability.

The Beaufighter was a fine aircraft; 5,564 were built in Britain and 364 in Australia. As is so often the case with a new type, its introduction into service was marked by a number of crashes, often as a result of engine failure on take-off, which, if the correct drill was not carried out instantly, would result in a wing drop and a spin. A split second life or death decision had to be made by the pilot: had safety speed been reached? If it had, the machine would climb on the remaining engine, if not, a landing straight ahead gave the only chance of survival.

Bill Pegg told, in his book, the story of one of his Beaufighter test flights from Filton. Taking off from the shortest runway he selected 'undercarriage up' at 30 ft just as the starboard engine failed. His options were minimal. He thought he had safety speed, but there was a golf course between himself and the city of Bristol right ahead, so could he climb over the rising ground of the golf course and miss the built-up area in the event of trouble with the other engine, which had to remain at take-off power? He opted for the golf course, cut the port engine and, missing a bunker by a foot or so, arrived at the first tee accompanied by loud and expensive noises of metal tearing all around him.

Turning off the fuel and ignition, he leapt out of the cockpit to meet the astonished gaze of his managing director's wife who was about to drive off when this unseemly intrusion took place!

Delivering the prototype to Boscombe Down, Pegg completed the diving trials to 400 mph. There was a loud bang; gingerly he slowed down, peering out to try to locate the source of the noise. He found that a large piece of cowling had disappeared from the top of the starboard engine nacelle, so he returned to Filton. On his next diving test, as he arrived at Boscombe Down, there was another bang and yet another piece of cowling had disappeared; it landed on the aerodrome. The suction loads induced by high speed flight were beginning to become tiresome.

When he eventually landed at A&AEE he was asked why he thought it necessary that sample bits of the Beaufighter should be sent before delivery of the aeroplane; it was thought quite unnecessary to advertise as the Beaufighter was already known as a good machine! It certainly proved to be so. It was as fast as the Hurricane but rather heavy on the controls; various modifications were made to the control surfaces, slight improvements being achieved.

Saunders Roe were still desperately trying to turn the Lerwick twin Hercules boat into a satisfactory marine aircraft. In 1938 Frank Courtney had flown the prototype of another Saro boat, the A.33, with its wings mounted entirely on struts above the hull, and two massive sponsons which were substituted for wing tip floats. In a heavy landing he gave the hull such a jolt that the wing spar failed, and the whole assembly fell apart – leaving Courtney with only one major problem, the Lerwick. The design of the planing bottom was suspect, and threw masses of spray and bow wave up to the propellers as it rose upon the step for take-off. Porpoising was a built-in hazard and the Lerwick could not be held straight on the rudder, engine torque turning it to starboard. Even with up-rated engines its top speed was only 215 mph instead of the required 230.

For months the machine remained in the shops whilst a new planing bottom was fitted and three more prototypes built to speed the flight testing of the type. These were completed in 1939 and work continued under Courtney and Leslie Ash. Auxiliary fins were fitted and the tailplane raised in an attempt to improve stability, all to no avail; still the Lerwick wallowed through the sky. A taller fin and rudder represented a slight improvement but it was still almost impossible to trim for level flight with one engine or two. Longitudinal stability was so marginal that rotation of the upper gun turret to abeam caused the nose to drop.

Only twenty-one were built and the unfortunate No 209 Squadron at Oban was the only squadron to operate it at full strength, the Lerwick being withdrawn from service within a year. The superb Consolidated PBY5 Catalina replaced it, and, with its range of 4,000 miles and duration of 17.6 hours, became a formidable sister ship to the Sunderland as many U-boat crews discovered just before they were sunk.

On 13 August, Mutt Summers flew the Vickers Warwick heavy bomber for the first time. Developed from the Wellington and using Barnes Wallis's unique geodetic construction, the Warwick handled extremely well but shared with the Manchester the problems of the Vulture engines. Performance also suffered through engine deficiencies. The second prototype was fitted with 2,520 hp Bristol Centaurus radial engines, but this machine did not fly until April 1940, by which time it was obsolescent in the bombing role. It was converted to air/sea rescue work carrying an Uffa Fox designed moulded plywood lifeboat. Other marks were used for general reconnaissance and transport duties.

In lighter vein the de Havilland Technical School had designed an interesting little single seat canard powered by a Gipsy engine driving a pusher propeller. Geoffrey de Havilland made a number of fast runs across Hatfield aerodrome during the late

De Havilland Aeronautical Technical School TK.5.

summer but the TK.5, as it was known, showed a marked reluctance to leave the ground – one felt, much to Geoffrey's relief! More pressing matters concerning another de Havilland aeroplane, being built in very strict secrecy at nearby Salisbury Hall, diverted attention from TK.5, which languished in limbo until it was broken up later in the war.

Other very secret activities were taking place in Germany and in Britain. On 24 August the first ever flight of a true turbo jet propelled aircraft took place in Germany when Heinkel's test pilot Erich Warsitz flew the Heinkel He 178 powered by an engine developing 834 lb of thrust.

Prior to this flight the Italians had flown the Caproni Campini CC2; a curious hybrid with a 900 hp piston engine driving a three stage axial flow ducted fan in the nose and a vapourizing burner in the tail, whilst an adjustable 'bullet' controlled the size of tail orifice. Its rate of climb was 137 ft per min, and the maximum speed was said to be 256 mph, at a fuel consumption of 350 gallons per hour.

In Britain the brilliant F/O Frank Whittle, an instructor at Central Flying School, had conceived the idea of a turbojet with a single centrifugal compressor driven by a single stage turbine. In spite of the Air Ministry's view that his predictions of performance and efficiency were over optimistic, the RAF, to its eternal credit, recognized him as an outstandingly able engineer and, by 1934, he was at Cambridge University studying Mechanical Sciences. His work is described in more detail in chapter ten.

The Hawker Hurricane was in full production. The firm had worked hard upon the successor to

specification F18/37 issued in March 1938. Sydney Camm had the engine options of the Vulture or the equally new and undeveloped 'H' type 24 cylinder Napier Sabre of similar power output. He decided to play safe by designing the 'R' type to use the Vulture and the name Tornado, whilst the 'N' type was to be powered by the Sabre and called Typhoon. Both fighters would be armed with twelve .303 machine guns in the wings, firing outside the propeller arc. With a maximum speed approaching 400 mph it was out of the question to continue with the Hurricane technique of metal construction with fabric covering.

The forward part of the Tornado fuselage was a steel tubular frame covered with easily removable metal panels; aft of the cockpit was a metal monocoque shell. The wings were metal covered, as was the tailplane. On 6 October 1939, Philip G. Lucas flew the prototype from Langley. The Tornado was a very heavy aeroplane and the position of the ventral radiator caused severe airflow problems at high speed. It returned to the experimental department for two months whilst the radiator was mounted under the engine giving it that pugnacious brutal appearance characteristic of the breed. The second prototype with four 20 mm cannon flew over a year later, but the Tornado, which was to be built by Avro, was stillborn when development of the Vulture engine was abandoned. Effort was concentrated upon the Typhoon which was first flown on 24 February 1940. One of the Tornado prototypes was fitted with the Centaurus 2,210 hp engine but not flown until October 1941.

Joint air force exercises with the French Air Force took place over Britain in August. Later in the month the Emergency Powers (Defence) Bill was enacted and Reserves of the Royal Air Force, the Army and the Navy were called up. Hitler invaded Poland, and in conformity with its treaty obligations to that unfortunate country, Britain, on 3 September, declared war on Nazi Germany.

If only Churchill's warnings had been acted upon in the 1930s there is little doubt that British forces would have been powerful enough to have deterred Hitler from his aggressive intent, and, if he had persisted, could have moved into action with immediate success. Thanks to the respite accorded by the humiliating Berchtesgaden meetings between the German dictator and Prime Minister Chamberlain, we had in Britain, on the outbreak of war, an air force consisting of fairly modern aeroplanes; 347 Hurricanes, 187 Spitfires, 350 Blenheims, 169 Hampdens, 160 Wellingtons, 140 Whitleys, 530 Battles and 300 Ansons. Above all we still had the

enterprising pioneers, their designers, production engineers and test pilots with their opposite numbers in the aero engine business – an unbeatable combination as history was to prove.

The original Handley Page Halifax concept was for a twin Vulture or Sabre engined bomber with, surprisingly, dive bombing capability and no armament, as it was thought that its high top speed would protect it from fighter interception. This was rejected, although, presumably unknown to Handley Page and his designer George Volkert, Geoffrey de Havilland was pressing a similar case upon the Ministry, a case which, thanks to the foresight and tenacity of Air Marshal Sir Wilfrid Freeman, became the Mosquito.

The specification was finally amended to use four Merlin engines and a four gun powered turret in the tail. On 25 October Maj James Cordes flew the prototype from RAF station Bicester. This was chosen for two reasons: the maximum take-off run at Radlett was only 750 yards from east to west, and was also more vulnerable to enemy air attack. So the Halifax was transported in sections and built in a hangar used for training aircraft maintenance at No 13 Operational Training Unit. Cordes visited the site frequently in a Magister to disarm suspicion that important work was in progress.

Taxying trials were discouraging. The Lockheed hydraulic brakes were not sufficiently swift in response, so Cordes refused to fly until they had been changed to the well proven Dunlop pneumatic brakes. Working for three days and nights, a Dunlop team completed the work whilst Handley Page fumed and fretted – generally making himself very unpopular with the team who were already under considerable stress. Maj Cordes became distinctly out of favour with his managing director when he was given a lift across the aerodrome in the new Rolls-Royce, HP's pride and joy. On the door sills were some massive brass 'grab' handles – 'Looks like a bloody hearse!', commented the test pilot.

Auxiliary fuel tanks were required in the bomb bay, as the wing tanks with their jettison pipes were to be used for water ballast when full load and overload tests were to be carried out. As the aeroplane could not land at these weights, the jettison facility was essential. On 25 October, with E. A. 'Ginger' Wright as test observer, Cordes made a satisfactory first flight and completed the initial handling trials before returning to Radlett, where a second prototype with armament and other military equipment was being built.

The size and complexity of the new bomber called for a major test flying programme which was

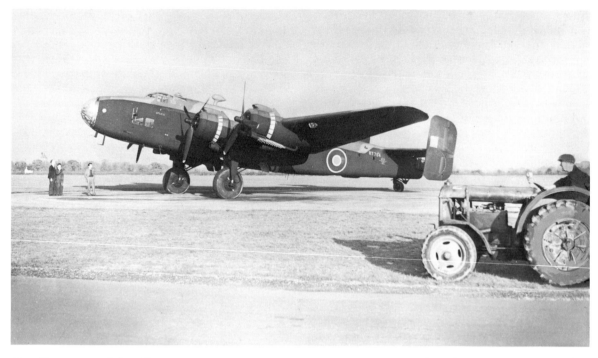

Handley Page Halifax III.

satisfactorily completed. An alarming incident was the cracking of the elevator skin along the line of the spar. Fortunately, with the CG in mid-range, Jim Cordes had sufficient control to make a safe landing. One major snag with the Halifax did not emerge during flight test; indeed it would have been thought inconceivable that such a large machine should be manoeuvred sufficiently violently to stall the rudders and lock them over to one side. A number were lost on operations before the problem was recognized and solved by a major re-design of the fins and rudders.

Some oscillation of the fuselage had been noticed on early flights, the trouble being attributed to the shedding of vortices from the inner engine nacelles. Here, too, experimental work was carried out to reduce drag levels, these being incorporated on the production line as convenient.

The major Halifax development was the Mk III with Bristol Hercules engines. This powerful machine was built in greater numbers than any other Mk, 2,127 being produced. A strange problem arose with some of the Mk IIIs in Six Group, Bomber Command. A number of aircraft returning from ops had been lost when an engine overspeeded, the pilot being unable to feather the propeller, which then broke away, usually starting a fire in the engine. The author was involved in the

investigations into this alarming situation. After many inconclusive air tests an aircraft of No 158 Sqn managed to reach RAF Coltishall, after a fire and the loss of a propeller over Holland. The propeller had climbed away from the aircraft and as its momentum diminished, returned to poke a blade through the back of the instrument panel, leaving the pilot with little instrumentation. It then rolled aft missing the tailplane in some miraculous manner, and disappeared – leaving F/O Marshall to navigate back from Holland with no instruments and no maps as they had been sucked out through one of the holes. He received a well deserved DFC for his courage and enterprise.

When the engine was inspected at Coltishall the reason was clear. The reduction gear housing was connected to the wheelcase of the engine by studs in the front of the engine, passing through holes in the gear housing flange. To provide a flat seating for the retaining nuts, recesses were trepanned on the front of the flange; washers being fitted under the nut. On some engines the recesses were fractionally too small in diameter, so the washer was located on the edge of the recess instead of the face of it. All was well until the aeroplane had flown a few hours, when the thrust of the propeller caused the washers to adopt a conical shape, allowing the reduction gear housing to part fractionally from the engine face. All the oil for gear lubrication, propeller pitch control and feathering passed through cored holes in the engine and reduction gear housing, so the increasing gap caused all the oil to go to atmosphere, and the propeller into fine pitch, causing the overspeed. Loss of lubrication oil caused failure of the reduction gear thrust races which, in turn, permitted the bevel gears to move outwards carving their way through the housing and causing the fire. It was typical of many unforeseen problems that production test pilots could hardly be expected to find before delivery.

A few days after this investigation was completed, a Halifax III crash landed near Market Weighton in Yorkshire, with all four propellers feathered without initiation by the pilot. All four constant speed unit (CSU) control valves were jammed in the up position by tiny aluminium crescents. These were the products of oil tank rivetting which became trapped under a flanged baffle. The usual swilling in solvent would not shift them, but engine vibration certainly did. Oil filters in the CSU lines quickly cured that difficulty before anyone was hurt.

On the day war broke out the A&AEE was swiftly moved from Martlesham Heath to an aerodrome on Salisbury Plain – Boscombe Down, near Amesbury. To some officers this was a most unwelcome move. There were no test facilities and pilots had lost their main navigational aid, the distinctive coastline near Martlesham, where the River Deben flows from the vicinity of the aerodrome to the sea, and the even more distinctive area near Harwich, where the rivers Stour and Orwell approach the sea. These navigational aids were just as valuable to German pilots, so no risks could be taken. Boscombe Down had no such distinguishing marks, so enemy pilots would have the utmost difficulty in finding this vitally important target.

Facilities were quickly installed, and work proceeded with great urgency to turn the new prototypes into operational aeroplanes, in close collaboration with the manufacturers. One of the first problem aircraft was the Manchester which arrived on 10 December during the coldest winter in living memory. The inadequate power of the Vulture engines gave the prototype totally unacceptable take-off performance, a run of over 1,000 yards being required to clear a twenty foot barrier. The elevators were heavy and the take-off swing intolerable.

On one take-off an engine failed, the machine landing in a cabbage field. The pilot cryptically reported that 'At 40,000 lb the aircraft would not maintain height on take-off.' The landing was so skilfully executed that the Manchester was repaired and flying again within a few months. To overcome the stability problems the tailplane was increased in span from 28ft to 32 ft.

The test flying staff at Boscombe Down was rapidly expanded by posting 'Above Average' rated bomber and fighter pilots to 'B' Flight and 'A' Flight. Untrained in the more subtle techniques of test flying, and in some cases having little aptitude for it, they learned the hard way as there was little time to train them. Some paid for the experience with their lives. Those who survived quickly built up a formidable expertise on which the Boscombe Down tradition was soon founded. The main cross borne by 'B' Flight was the Manchester, the Vulture always being suspect. A baulked landing was a hazardous affair even for a test pilot; for a relatively inexperienced squadron pilot it was often non-survivable, as many crews returning from ops found to their cost.

On some test flights it was found that the 32 ft tailplane vibrated violently with the mass balance of the rudders in rapid oscillation. Many flights were carried out to find the reason for this, and a number of different combinations of speed, attitude and flap angle were explored. It was finally found to be due to a fairing that had been fitted to improve airflow through an oil cooler extractor. Its effect on the aerodynamics of the aeroplane was quite disproportionate to its size, but it was in alignment with the fin/tailplane intersection.

The unfortunate operational squadrons using this very unsatisfactory bomber pressed on until January 1942, when all of them were withdrawn from operations, being replaced by the magnificent Lancaster, a hugely successful development of the Manchester, powered by four Rolls-Royce Merlin engines.

By the end of 1939 Europe was at war, even if it appeared to be a phoney war, with RAF bombers

Avro Lancaster.

dropping leaflets, not bombs, on German cities, taking great care to avoid killing civilians.

In the twenty years which had elapsed since the end of the First World War the aircraft industry had grown into a well organized, highly responsible, industry building aeroplanes which were, in the main, second to none. They were refined by the work of the test pilots, many of them being the world's best, and were to be flown by equally competent Service pilots.

The degree of technical mastery achieved is evident in the course of this narrative. Early chapters revealed the serious, and in some cases catastrophic difficulties in first flights. Later chapters are largely free from drama. There were, and always will be, problems, but most of them were identifiable and capable of solution without major design changes. It became clear, however, that engine designers were not keeping pace with airframe designers, perhaps understandably, as it is not possible to shorten the hundreds of hours of test running on static beds, and in flying time, to develop the increasingly complex and powerful engines to ensure their reliability in service.

It is appropriate at the end of this important period to reflect upon a major development of benefit to all aircraft, namely navigational and automatic piloting equipment. As far back as 1910 Elliott Brothers of London, forbears of Elliott Automation, and now within the Marconi Avionics Group, published a booklet written by Commander Robert A. Newton RN, entitled, *Aeronautical Navigation*. In his introduction the Commander said, 'There is no royal road to safe navigation, it requires a capacity for taking trouble, and unremitting attention . . .' a philosophy as true today as in 1910. He continued, 'Every aeroplane will eventually carry a compass, and this will be considered as much an integral part of it as its engines.'

Since those days navigational instruments and auto controls have been the subject of deep research at Farnborough and elsewhere. As early as 1894 Sir Hiram Maxim had produced an automatic stabilizer, which contradicted the theories of Lilienthal and his hang gliders and later J. W. Dunne, whose inherently stable tailless aeroplane was described in chapter one. Maxim, and indeed, the Wright brothers, were convinced that the aeroplane should be controlled by active pilot effort, not by inherent stability. Only in this way could manoeuvrability be achieved. History has proved them to have been correct.

In 1912 the Sperry Gyroscope Company of New York fitted a gyroscopic lateral stabilizer to a Glenn

Curtiss flying boat fitted with aircraft stabilisation system.

Curtiss floatplane which was test flown with Lawrence Sperry, the founder's son, as test engineer. A major advance was achieved in 1914 when, from the River Seine at Bezons, Lawrence Sperry flew a Curtiss flying boat fitted with a gyro stabilizer, which the company had spent several years developing. Its development costs were recovered when Sperrys won the first prize of 400,000 francs in a safety competition. Onlookers saw the boat flying steadily at low altitude, with Sperry standing in the cockpit with his hands above his head, whilst his French mechanic Emile Cachine walked along the wing.

In 1917 B. C. Hucks was drawing the attention of the Royal Aeronautical Society to the risks inherent in flying through cloud, and at the Royal Aircraft Factory, S. Keith Lucas was developing a highly damped magnetic compass which was designed to avoid disturbance due to manoeuvring forces. Hucks mentioned an artificial horizon with which Sperry was experimenting. The mid 1920s saw F. W. Meredith at RAE working on automatic landing schemes. After a mathematical study of the phugoid, or switchback motion of an aeroplane in marginal fore and aft stability, he proposed that a

Vickers Vimy should be trimmed tail heavy after an approach at a steady glide speed. At a predetermined height, an indicator line of specific length was to be paid out, and as the observer warned the pilot that the end of the line was in contact with the ground, the pilot would release the stick. The tail heaviness of the bomber would then flare it out into a three point landing. Tests proved the theory of it and by 1925 McKinnon Wood at the RAE was developing the principle into an entirely automatic flight control system from take-off to landing, including a 'radio fail' mode for radio controlled target aircraft. This was used experimentally in a Fairey III with extra dihedral to give it inherent lateral stability, and was later installed in de Havilland Queen Bees, converted Tiger Moths, and the smart Airspeed Queen Wasp, which looked far too good to be shot down. When Hessell Tiltman of Airspeed was designing the Wasp he was lunching with the directors of de Havilland and discussing the Queen Bee. He told them of a story he had heard at Martlesham of one Bee pilot who had gone up to monitor a radio controlled flight on the clear understanding that transmission would cease at 12.00 in time for lunch in the Mess. At noon the character of the transmission changed markedly; the aeroplane was gyrating about the sky in a most unpleasant fashion with the unfortunate pilot feeling less and less interested in lunch. After twenty minutes of this he decided that he had no wish to scrub out the cockpit so he switched off and landed, ashen faced. He hurried to the Mess to find the control officer at the end of his second pint, having switched off the transmission at the agreed hour. Further tests were carried out and it was found that as the control transmission ceased, the radio picked up a dance band programme from Radio Paris, converting the signal into aerobatic commands quite unknown to Central Flying School. The de Havilland men had not heard of this, but a Group Captain at the table said, 'Yes, I can confirm it, I was the pilot!'

From these early experiments came the Autopilot developed commercially by Smiths Instruments.

Eastern Airlines, in USA, fitted a Sperry Autopilot in a Curtiss Condor airliner in the early 1930s, and in 1933 the potential of the system was clearly demonstrated when Wiley Post flew solo round the world in his Lockheed Vega *Winnie Mae* in 7 days 18 hours 49 minutes. In the same month Floyd Bennett flew 25,596 miles in the same time. Both aircraft were fitted with the Sperry A2 Gyropilot.

At Farnborough F. W. Meredith led the team which developed the RAE Mk IV autopilot, a pneu-matic system installed in many multi-engine Second World War aircraft, and known affectionately as 'George'.

In parallel with these aids, radio communication received high priority as a system of the highest importance in fighter control, where limited endurance required close surveillance of sorties. The team at Farnborough, under Dr F. C. Bartlett included Dr Robert Cockburn, J. C. Stewart, J. E. Clegg and C. H. Smith. Between them they produced a reliable very short wave fighter communications system working on 100–150 megacycles which could also be used to provide a radio direction finding facility. As Fighter Command went to war it was put into production by private industry and permitted the fighter squadrons to become highly efficient flexible and potent weapons guided to their targets by radar via the radio channels.

All these developments increased the complexity of aeroplanes requiring high levels of electric power to drive them and substantially increasing the work load of the Boscombe Down and Farnborough test pilots who carried out most of the development work.

9

THE PRESSURES OF TOTAL WAR

Life at Boscombe Down in 1940 was frustrating, in that the influx of nearly fifty experimental aeroplanes imposed great strains upon the organization; there was no runway, no firing butts, and no range facilities. Firing trials could only be carried out using local Army facilities when these were available. An additional hazard in the first winter was the presence of No 58 Sqn's Whitleys.

Stop butts were constructed whilst land and sea ranges were established at Crichel Down in Dorset, in the New Forest, and in Lyme Bay. Further land was requisitioned to extend the grass runway and form dispersals. The scope of the Establishment was extended and new sections formed. To the Performance Testing Squadron – Per T, was added 'C' Flight to test multi-seat single engine aeroplanes. Armament Testing Squadron – Arm T, remained a separate unit, but to Per T a blind approach training and development unit was added, and, in 1941, a High Altitude Flight to investigate flight problems above 30,000 ft.

A Navigation Section was formed, with a staff of one, Sqn Ldr Waghorn, whose brother piloted the Schneider Trophy winner in 1929. An important stage in the development of A&AEE was the recruitment of a number of university graduates who made a contribution to the solution of many aerodynamic, physical and engineering problems of ever increasing complexity.

A similar expansion was taking place at RAE Farnborough, where, in addition to orthodox aeronautical research (including the development of an automatic bomb sight which had gone into service with Bomber Command in 1939), an utterly bizarre project was under active consideration. Project 'Razzle' was based upon a strong conviction in certain official circles that the best method of defeating Hitler's regime was to lower civilian morale by creating a multitude of fires, burning the population and destroying their homes, whilst agricultural produce would also be a target. A start was to be made in the Black Forest.

The bomb development section had already produced a satisfactory 4 lb incendiary bomb which could be, and was, successfully dropped in clusters but this was too heavy and expensive for 'Razzle'. So small incendiary packets of matchbox size were made. Two small rectangles of celluloid with a hole in the middle enclosed a phosphorus soaked pad of cotton wool. So long as these were kept damp in tins, all was well in the aircraft from which they were to be dropped through a 4-inch diameter tube leading from a chute into the bomb bay. So, as the bomber flew over its target, the bomb doors were opened and the devices poured out in thousands.

The first test scenario would have done credit to the script writers of 'Dad's Army'; Wellingtons from Mildenhall carried out experimental drops, and returned with frantic crews fighting fires which had broken out all over the aircraft, due to the incendiaries having drifted in the turbulence when the bomb doors were opened. One, with a major fire on board, crashed, killing the crew. Ultimately a large number of the devices were dropped over Germany with negligible results. It seemed that the only casualties were small boys who put them in their trouser pockets and received burns when their body heat dried out the moisture.

Lindemann, with the backing of Prime Minister Churchill, was the instigator of a number of strange devices which diverted effort from more valuable projects. The Parachute and Cable Unit was one of them. A bomb was attached by a long wire to a parachute, and on the approach of an enemy aircraft, they were launched into its path by means of a rocket. The enemy was supposed to fly into the wire which would then wrap itself around the machine and the bomb would blow it apart.

The sausage bomb was another masterpiece of ingenuity. This consisted of large sacks of wood shavings, paraffin wax and suitable igniters which were intended to be dropped over forests, where they would ignite and set the timber alight. The first air test was farcical; a Whitley was used to drop the device from a hole in the bomb bay, several of the sacks being lashed together as a 'sausage'. The first two were locked underneath by air pressure, with the igniters burning merrily in the slipstream, whilst the despatcher was trying to unload the rest of the ungainly packages. The pilot wisely decided to return to Farnborough post haste before the aircraft began to blaze. As he reduced speed, to land, the 'bomb' fell away, dropping on a barrack block where troops were able to put the fire out.

Bomber interception was a key aspect of research. Radar was in such an early stage of development that it was unable to guide the fighter within firing range of the target. Douglas Boston bombers were fitted with a powerful searchlight in the nose, but the scheme was not very successful, so was soon dropped. Another interception aid which was tested consisted of 250,000 candlepower reconnaissance flares ignited under the wings of a Hampden. On a test flight over North West England during a raid the pilot ignited the flares – a move which left him feeling utterly exposed to the mercy of any marauding German, and gave the raiders first class target illumination for a very successful attack.

At Supermarines, Jeffrey Quill had been busy developing the Mk II Spitfire to take advantage of the increased power of the Merlin XII. By the beginning of 1940 the Mk III was flying and the Admiralty was showing interest in it for carrier borne operations. Chris Staniland had successfully flown the prototype Fairey Fulmar fleet fighter (developed from the P.4 light bomber), and the Air Ministry hoped that its success would deflect Naval interest from the Spitfire as the Air Force needed all they could get. To their dismay an order for 50 seaborne Spitfires was placed!

When France fell in June 1940, Quill felt that he must quit test flying and rejoin a squadron. So he returned to the Service, being posted to No 65 Sqn flying Spitfires from Rochford, near Southend. His operational flying, in the thick of the Battle of Britain, was a very valuable experience for him, and enabled a number of improvements to be made to the aircraft as a result of the problems he recognized during the sorties. The heaviness of aileron control at speed was of considerable concern to him. The Spitfire had always suffered from this, but as it was originally conceived as a bomber destroyer, not for dogfighting, he was not unduly worried about it. When the Germans began to base Messerschmitt Bf 109 fighters in the Low Countries

Sqn Ldr, later Wg Cdr, C. G. B. McClure (1948).

the difficulty took on an entirely different character and action had to be taken immediately. Visibility from the cockpit was another problem area and the weakness of a normally carburated engine which cuts out under negative G forces left Spitfires and Hurricanes at a disadvantage when fighting the Bf 109, whose direct injection system kept its DB601 engine firing – a spin-off from the Germans' pre-war domination of Grand Prix motor-racing.

Wg Cdr Charles McClure was involved, as OC of Engine Flight at Farnborough, in the remarkable story of Miss Shilling, the legendary 'carburettor queen' at RAE. She was called in to advise, and suggested that it was important to know whether the engine cut in rich or weak mixture – too much or too little fuel. She suggested that a Hurricane should be put into a half roll and, when upside down, the fuel turned off, the pilot checking with his stop watch how long the engine continued to run. The test should be repeated without turning off the fuel. It was found to run about five times as long with the fuel turned off as it did with it turned on, so it was a rich cut not a weak cut – obvious when one thought about it! She said that with 20 lb/sq in pressure from the fuel pump, the displacement of the cork carburettor float would inject neat fuel causing an inevitable engine failure. She returned home and, in her workshop, machined metering orifices of suitable size to permit the flow of 110 per cent of the full fuel requirement at full throttle. The device was fitted to the fuel line and was proved to work. Charles McClure flew around No 11 Group Stations distributing 'Miss Shilling's Orifices' to incredulous and sceptical engineer officers who were amazed to find that a substantial improvement resulted from their use.

At the end of August Jeffrey Quill was instructed to return to Supermarines, in the hope that, once he had completed the test programme of the Spitfire III he would be able to return to his squadron.

Many attempts were made to solve the problem of heavy ailerons; Jeffrey Quill, Alex Henshaw and George Pickering, with Joe Smith, the chief designer, burned the midnight oil for weeks. Variations in aileron entry profiles, the inclusion of geared tabs on the trailing edge of them, and all-metal skinning were tried. The metal skinning with its very thin trailing edge achieved a spectacular improvement. Henshaw and Pickering flew the modified aircraft and agreed that the problem had been solved. Jeffrey flew it to Farnborough where Wg Cdr H. J. 'Willie' Wilson, OC of Aero Flight, and Sqn Ldr Roly Falk flew it. They were delighted and recommended that all Spitfires be modified as quickly as possible. Quill was encouraged to find, when he flew a captured Bf 109 at Farnborough, that its ailerons were also very heavy at speed so the modifications could only improve the Spitfire pilot's chances in combat with this machine.

On 24 February 1940 Philip Lucas flew the prototype Hawker Typhoon with the 2,100 hp Napier Sabre engine. The machine performed well and control forces were reasonable for an aeroplane with an all up weight of over six tons. The Sabre engine, however, had not been fully developed and failures were frequent. Lucas had an alarming experience on 9 May when the joint between the rear fuselage and the centre section of the aircraft failed at speed. He courageously stayed with the machine and landed safely at Langley. He was awarded a George Medal.

Performance at altitude and rate of climb were poor, so the Typhoon, although designed as an intercepter fighter, was never a success in that role. Severe criticism was levelled at the poor rearward view from the cockpit, and later in its career a bubble type canopy was fitted.

Some of the problems associated with the Sabre engine were due to the inability of the de Havilland constant speed unit to control the pitch of the large four blade propeller fast enough to avoid dangerous overspeeding, and, as a result, engine disintegration was a familiar problem. Surprisingly, the Sabre would continue to run on six or seven cylinders, emitting clouds of black smoke accompanied by expensive noises.

At Luton, later in the programme, test pilot E. W. 'Jock' Bonar put a Typhoon through a series of high speed dives to investigate engine oil scavenging problems. On one flight he rolled into a dive at 35,000 ft, the Tiffie accelerating vertically at a rapid rate. Suddenly all control had gone, elevators, rudder and ailerons were completely ineffective. The thought crossed his mind that six tons of aeroplane hitting the ground at 600 miles per hour would not cause too much trouble as the crater could easily be smoothed over with a small bulldozer!

Recalling the Typhoon's reputation for shedding its tail on a pull-out, he centralized the controls. Using elevator trimmers and a steady pull on the stick against the enormous aerodynamic forces, assisted by the fact that compressibility effects from which the aeroplane was suffering were lower as he descended to warmer air, the machine began to recover rapidly, as Jock blacked out under the G forces. When he could see again he saw that he was flying at high speed, at low altitude, near Royston. He was shocked to see that the wing skin was shuddering and flapping with a large number of rivets missing. He landed safely at Luton to find that the Typhoon was a complete write-off. The skin was buckled everywhere as a result of this unexpected encounter with compressibility effects, which left the thick wing of this aircraft at a great disadvantage.

Fortunately an automatic observer was recording all the instrument readings, so valuable data was obtained and put to good use in the development of the Tempest with its thin wing and superior control characteristics at high, sub-sonic speeds. Later, another Napier test pilot continued the high speed dive programme, and died when the tail came off in the pull-out.

Michael Daunt became chief test pilot of Glosters in 1942. He had served in No 25 (Fighter) Sqn in the early 1930s, when it was the crack aerobatic

Hawker Typhoon Ib.

team, performing tied together manoeuvres in Hawker Furies. Meeting at the Hendon Displays, the squadron pilots knew the Hawker pilots, George Bulman, Gerry Sayer and Philip Lucas. In 1935, on the termination of his Short Service Commission, he left the RAF and became an instructor at the de Havilland Flying School at Hatfield. In 1946 George Bulman telephoned him and invited him to join the Hawker test team. As Mike said, 'I just went through the ruddy ceiling! It was exactly what I wanted to do.' In 1937 he joined the Gloster Aircraft Company under Gerry Sayer with Maurice Summers, brother of the famous 'Mutt', as Gerry's number two. After a year Summers left, so Mike became assistant to Gerry.

Mike's comments on the Typhoon are memorable as indeed were most of this genial and witty Irishman's comments during an entertaining meeting with the author. 'As an aeroplane, one of the most bloody ever! The things that went wrong with it before it went to the RAF were appalling. The tail dropped off, and pilots suffered from carbon monoxide poisoning due to exhaust gases being sucked into the cockpit. By the time we had fitted a gas analyser in the cockpit to measure the concentration several pilots had been killed. The instrument was christened the Oxometer which, for the benefit of the uninitiated, was a wartime invention to measure a commodity dispensed in bulk at Initial Training Wings – "bull"!'

This caused some hilarity at the expense of a Ministry official visiting the factory in connection with another problem. He reported that 'The aircraft I investigated, with the assistance of Mr Daunt, contained an Oxometer!'

Happily, the preoccupation of this gentleman with the natural functions of the bull ceased when cowling modifications prevented exhaust gases from entering the cockpit. The installation of the Oxometer was no longer necessary.

'The Typhoon vibrated as it went round corners – it was said to rattle the eyebrows, indeed it was so bad that the pilot's seat had to be mounted on springs to isolate him from the effects of it.' Mike saw a camera gun film of an encounter with a Spitfire in which the Spitfire appeared to be a biplane. Bill Humble, one of the Hawker test pilots had a very dry sense of humour, and suggested that too much exposure to Typhoon vibration would cause impotence! Somehow this joke found its way to a Typhoon squadron. A certain pilot officer, probably Prune by name, approached his commanding officer with an official request to be posted away from Typhoons as his marriage was suffering! It required a letter from Farnborough to set the poor fellow's fears at rest!

The oil scavenge pump, which had also been a serious worry to Jock Bonar at Luton, caused many forced landings at Brockworth. Gerry Sayer and Mike Daunt had for some years followed the practice of treating every landing as a forced landing, aiming to stop at a certain spot. The skill which Mike had acquired served him well on one occasion when his engine lost its oil and blew up. He was able to make a potentially perfect belly landing in a small field but the 14 ft propeller was bent into a passable imitation of a pair of skis and the Typhoon shot across the field, heading at high speed for a sunken road with a high bank on the other side.

Mike was convinced that this would mean 'the chop' for him. He had not noticed a pair of trees ahead until the machine hurtled between them, neatly removing the wings and fuel tanks and allowing the fuselage to coast on until it reached the road, positioned conveniently for the salvage crew.

One of Michael Daunt's worst experiences was in a large monoplane built by Follands at Hamble for use as a flying engine test bed. Folland was too small to employ a test pilot so Gloster assisted whenever possible.

Folland F4/37, dubbed the 'Frightful'.

Neither Gerry nor Mike liked the 'Frightful' as they dubbed it so they tossed up as to who should do the diving trials, Mike lost.

In one dive the tail came off, the aeroplane pitching violently downwards. In conformity with the First Law of Newton which states that a body will continue in its path of motion until acted upon by an external force, Michael hurtled out through the canopy under an acceleration calculated to be minus 8G. He was almost strangled by his parachute harness straps, a few of which remained to support him. He landed very heavily, severely injured. The first person to arrive at the scene was a local vicar who, poor man, was assaulted on his errand of mercy.

Mike's story of this encounter should for ever be enshrined in aviation's funny stories. 'The vicar was very kind and had a voice just like Robertson Hare (a famous actor with a magnificently plummy voice). The doctors told me that if you are slightly strangled, you tend, when you come to, to be violent, and, although I had a broken collar bone on one side and a broken wrist on the other, I clocked this poor little man who had been doing this good Samaritan act! Despite that he visited me in hospital and made a remark I have never

forgotten. "When I picked you up you were muttering something like 'Oh, shee! Oh shee!' which seemed to me like a Rugger cry!" I had to explain to him that when you have a very badly damaged mouth your pronunciation of the letter T is rather affected!'

Michael Daunt spent six months convalescing from this very narrow escape.

On 20 March 1940 the Armstrong Whitworth Albemarle made its first flight from Hamble with Charles Turner-Hughes at the controls. Designed to meet an Air Ministry specification, which reflected concern that the RAF expansion would lead to a serious shortage of light alloys, it was built of steel and wood in a simple structure which could be put out to sub-contractors who had little experience of aircraft.

A quite revolutionary feature was the tricycle undercarriage, the first one to appear on a British military aircraft. The first flight was fairly satisfactory, so the prototype was flown to Baginton for the rest of the test programme, which resulted in the wings being increased in span from 67 to 77ft. An A&AEE pilot disgraced himself by force landing in a field when he became lost, but little damage was done to the Albemarle. In November it was flown to Boscombe Down, after the fins and rudders had been increased in area to overcome slight directional instability. On 4 February 1941 part of the plywood skin of the port wing broke away, the noise being such that the pilot diagnosed engine trouble. He cut the suspect engine, and immediately entered a spin from which recovery appeared impossible. The two flight observers were ordered to bail out; one of the men found himself suspended by his harness underneath the aeroplane, and when his parachute deployed, it wrapped itself around the tail where it acted as an anti-spin 'chute. The pilot managed to pull out but was unaware of the drama behind him! He realized that the Albemarle had to be landed at high-speed due to the loss of lift on the damaged wing, so he elected to belly land it.

The unfortunate observer tried to climb the rigging lines but was too cold to do so. As the aircraft descended to about ten feet from the ground he released himself from the harness and fell into some bushes on snow covered ground, miraculously surviving, but with severe injuries. The prototype was burned out, the pilot escaping with cuts and bruises.

There were many delays to the production programme. By mid 1942, when deliveries reached fourteen a month, the Albemarle was obsolete in its intended bombing role, so it was relegated to glider towing.

In the spring of 1940 Flt Lt Bailey flew the Blackburn B.20 for the first time. This unusual reconnaissance flying boat had a very ingenious device for reducing the drag inherent in deep hulls, which were necessary with monoplanes to raise the propellers out of the way of spray. The planing bottom was retractable, being linked by hydraulic rams, which also gave the precise angle of wing incidence required for take-off and low cruise drag. The wing tip floats were retractable, to lie at the tips. The B.20 had the misfortune to be powered by two Rolls-Royce Vulture 1,720 hp engines.

Built at the Blackburn Dumbarton plant the formula proved to be successful, both on the water and in the air. However, aileron control was unsatisfactory and, during a high speed run over the Clyde on 7 April 1940, flutter developed, the B.20 crashing into the sea. Bailey was killed, having stayed at the controls long enough to see his crew of two escape by parachute. No further work was done on this promising project.

On 7 December 1940 Chris Staniland flew the Fairey Barracuda torpedo/dive bomber from Great West Road aerodrome. Loved by few pilots, hated by many, and the subject of a bawdy Fleet Air Arm wardroom song, this curious flying machine had a chequered career. As with most naval specifications the requirements were almost impossible to meet. It was a fast, heavy aeroplane supposed to be sufficiently docile to be operated from carriers by pilots who were accustomed to the Fulmar and the amiable Swordfish. It was fitted with Youngman flaps mounted separately below and behind the wing. For dive bombing or torpedo attack, they could be inclined, trailing edge up, to 30 degrees

Fairey Barracuda.

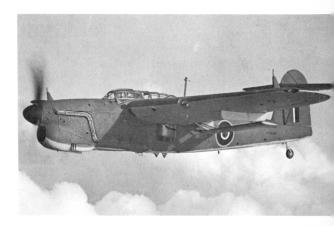

to act as dive brakes; otherwise they acted as normal high lift devices.

Staniland found that the flaps in the dive brake mode created severe buffeting of the tailplane which, initially, was conventionally mounted at the top of the fuselage. Heavy vibration and elevator control degradation occurred.

The tailplane was finally raised four feet to a position near the top of the fin which, of course, needed substantial stiffening with a consequent weight increase, to accept the heavier loads. So it entered service with the Royal Navy. One of the outstanding Service test pilots, Capt Eric M. 'Winkle' Brown, first encountered the Barracuda at the Service Trials Unit Arbroath in 1942. He had joined his University Air Squadron in 1936 after an initiation into flying in Germany, where he met Ernst Udet, the First World War fighter ace, who had become a Major General in the newly formed *Luftwaffe*. Udet took him up in a Bucker Jüngmann trainer, and gave him a disconcerting taste of aerobatics, coming in to land in an inverted position and rolling out at the last minute!

Eric was hooked on flying. On the outbreak of war he expected to be called up immediately, but there was a waiting period due to the 'Phoney War', during which there was inaction on most fronts, so he joined the Fleet Air Arm to be retrained to fly. One day over Wiltshire, in a Hawker Hart trainer, he was shocked to see his companion Hart shot down by a marauding Messerschmitt Me 110. Revenge was sweet, however, when later, flying a Gladiator in company with another, he saw a pair of Heinkel IIIs in close formation. Just as they approached and opened fire one of the bombers blew up, the other immediately following suit – flak had hit a bomb on one, the other was too close to survive the explosion.

Brown served in No 802 Sqn at Donibristle, flying Blackburn Skuas, later re-equipping with the American Grumman Martlet. He dived one into the sea upside-down when the engine seized during a low-level demonstration flight before Winston Churchill. He survived almost unscathed to receive a message of sympathy from the PM. Allied convoys were being decimated in the Atlantic by U-boats, and the long range Focke-Wulf Condor, a converted civil airliner. Merchant ships were hurriedly converted to become aircraft carriers of a most rudimentary nature. There was no room to strike the aircraft below for maintenance, so servicing personnel worked on the open deck in all weathers. In 1941 Lt Brown was posted to the *Empire Audacity*, operating six Martlets. In Sep-

tember two of the aircraft shot the tail off a Condor which had managed to damage the convoy's hospital ship, *Walmer Castle*. At the end of 1941 (in which two voyages had resulted in five victories over the raiders), *Empire Audacity* was sunk in a night torpedo attack which blew the bow off. The ship sank swiftly by the bow as Martlets, ranged at the stern, broke their lashings and hurtled down the deck, killing many who had survived the torpedo explosions. Two-thirds of the ship's company perished. Eric Brown was picked up, with the few who were left, by a corvette soon after daybreak. He was awarded a DSC for his gallantry.

'Winkle' went to Arbroath and to his astonishment, met the Barracuda, expecting to see, from the drawing board of Fairey's Marcel Lobelle, a more elegant descendant of the Fantôme, Battle and Fulmar. He was appalled as one of them 'turned on the approach and disgorged a mass of ironmongery from wings and fuselage transforming the pedestrian and unappealing into what could only be described as an airborne disaster.' He concluded, 'There were events that I could await with rather more pleasure than taking this quaint contraption into the air.'

Having carried out, with Jeffrey Quill, deck landing trials of the Seafire on Fleet and Escort carriers, he commented: 'Nobody would pretend that it was an ideal carrier fighter but I had probably deck landed it more than any other pilot and never felt anything but exhilaration at the challenge it presented . . . it is true that it was a lousy ditcher and I witnessed a number of fatal accidents resulting from its emulation of the diving characteristics of a submarine, but it had been designed for fighting, not ditching.'

By the end of 1943 'Winkle' was a Lt Cdr, with 1,500 deck landings on 22 carriers noted in his log book, and a formidable reputation as a test pilot. When, in 1944, he was posted to RAE Farnborough as chief naval test pilot, his main task was to investigate the feasibility of landing the de Havilland Mosquito on a carrier. By this time five Barracudas had crashed in mysterious circumstances, mostly on torpedo dropping exercises. As the pilot dropped his torpedo and pulled out, turning hard, the Barracuda rolled over and followed the torpedo into the sea. The trouble appeared to be associated with the use of the Youngman flaps, and 'Winkle' recalled his impression of his first flight in the aircraft when he felt that the rudder was overbalanced. With flight observer Mrs Gwen Alston, he took off to simulate at altitude the exact circumstances of pull-out from a torpedo dropping exercise. He checked sideslip performance at various speeds, deliberately stalling the rudder. As soon as it overbalanced the nose dropped, as it did when the flaps were set to neutral at the bottom of a high speed dive. Instrument recording camera switched on, he then simulated the precise sequence of a torpedo attack. At the limiting speed for flap retraction he set them to the cruise position and kicked on full rudder to starboard. Instantly the aircraft began an inverted dive. Suitable procedures were developed and the spate of crashes ceased. Later versions of this undistinguished aeroplane were fitted with a larger rudder and fin to avoid a recurrence of the problem.

To revert to the year in which the Barracuda first flew, the great event in 1940 was the first flight of the de Havilland D.H.98 Mosquito. The story of this remarkable aeroplane has been so well documented that little needs to be said about it.

Conceived by Geoffrey de Havilland, C. C. Walker, the chief engineer, and R. E. Bishop, the chief designer, this revolutionary concept began with the success of the D.H.88 Comet in the Mac-Robertson Air Race to Australia in 1934. This aeroplane was the aerodynamic progenitor of the Mosquito, whilst its carapace construction of a moulded ply/balsa/ply sandwich for the fuselage was also used on the D.H.91 Albatross airliner. An Air Ministry specification for a high speed bomber

with twin engines and heavy defensive armament was issued in 1936. Geoffrey de Havilland, in spite of his abhorrence of war, and his reluctance to deal with the Ministry, decided to submit a design. A military Albatross was considered, and then a twin Merlin engine version of it. There was no prospect, however, of combining high speed, good payload and heavy armament so the idea of an unarmed high speed twin-Merlin powered machine took shape. In 1938 D.H. and Walker submitted to the Ministry a design for a wooden aeroplane to economize on metal and to tap reserves of wood working labour which was not being used in the industry. The Ministry showed no interest, suggesting that de Havillands would be better employed in building wings for other bombers. Another specification, B18/38, was issued; this was of no interest to D.H. and was ultimately met by the Albemarle.

When war broke out D.H. approached the Ministry again. They showed slight interest, but required a turret for defence. This would have had a serious effect upon performance, range and payload, so it was rejected by the firm. Their one and only supporter was Air Marshal Sir Wilfrid Freeman, the Air Member for Development. He saw clearly the potential of the proposals, and without his dedicated enthusiasm the design would never have reached the prototype stage.

Built, for reasons of security, at Salisbury Hall, an historic country house near London Colney,

D.H.98 Mosquito prototype, W4050.

the prototype Mosquito, W4050, was ready for taxying trials on 24 November 1940. During these tests Geoffrey de Havilland Junior made a short hop. Next day, eleven months after design work had begun, W4050 flew for thirty minutes.

The author was present at Hatfield on this historic occasion and will never forget the sight of this beautiful aeroplane in its chrome yellow colour scheme with RAF roundels, taking off with John Walker as flight observer to Geoffrey de Havilland. 'Freeman's Folly', as it had been dubbed, handled beautifully and showed promise of being an exceptionally fast aeroplane. Manoeuvrability was good, but some flutter of the tailplane was apparent. A dihedralled tailplane was fitted, but the final solution was an increase in the length of the engine nacelles to a point beyond the trailing edge of the wing, a modification which improved the already superb appearance of the aircraft.

The top surfaces of W4050 were camouflaged before it was flown, on 19 February 1941, to Boscombe Down for acceptance trials. The de Havilland team became irritated by the apparent lack of urgency in commencing the trials, but once the Mosquito had been flown by Wg Cdr Allen Wheeler, the OC Performance Testing Squadron, there was great enthusiasm to proceed. Wheeler was impressed and a mere five weeks of trials established that, in the bomber role, it was 30 mph faster than the fastest known German fighter and 100 mph faster than any comparable bomber.

On 24 February, the last day of the trials, Sqn Ldr Charles Slee landed the prototype on a rough patch of the airfield, but after a bounce, the controls tightened up. This was reported to the engineering officer who ordered a thorough inspection. There was no apparent reason for the tightness. Suddenly an airman on the starboard side shouted, 'It's all right, Sir, it ain't the controls at all, she's broken 'er bleedin' back!' And so she had. Tail wheel shimmy had caused a failure of the castering device, and the strain on the wheel, caused by the rough surface, had forced the shell of the fuselage to crack near an access door. A simple hardwood strake along the fuselage underneath the access door was fitted, and W4050 was flown again three weeks later. The shimmy was cured by fitting a Marstrand tailwheel which had two tracks moulded on the outside faces of the tyre, leaving a deep groove between them.

The Mosquito was undoubtedly one of the outstanding aeroplanes in the history of aviation. Its development potential was immense with no less than 38 different versions put into service. The total production was 7,781, and the prototype is preserved at Salisbury Hall, which has become a de Havilland Museum.

The Mosquito was the instrument of Sir Geoffrey de Havilland's greatest triumph, but also of the first of his great tragedies. On 23 August 1943 his youngest son John, with his observer Nick Carter, the flight shed superintendent, collided in cloud with another Mosquito flown by George Gibbins and John Scrope, an aerodynamicist. Both machines crashed near Hatfield, killing their crews.

Another wooden aeroplane, vastly different from the Mosquito, flew on 18 October 1940. This was the Airspeed Fleet Shadower, a remarkable structure designed at the behest of the Admiralty who required an aircraft to shadow and maintain contact with enemy ships. General Aircraft and Airspeed submitted almost identical designs, fitted with four 130 hp Pobjoy Niagara radial engines spread along the wings, to pass slipstream over as much of the span as possible and maintain lift and control at speeds as low as 35 mph. This ungainly and unattractive machine was flown by George Errington, who found that rate of climb was hardly noticeable and elevator control left much to be desired. Drag was excessive, and when the throttles were closed a large nose-down change of trim occurred, due to the areas of airflow instability behind the engines, accentuated by the sudden loss of slipstream, which left the wing aft of the engines in a stalled condition. The wing was set at a high angle of incidence, and on take-off, the rear wheel strut was extended to bring the wing to a minimum drag angle of attack.

Airspeed Fleet Shadower with wings folded.

Both the Airspeed and the General Aircraft prototypes were abandoned, although the advanced principles of high lift devices embodied in the Airspeed machine were of value when Hessell Tiltman began design work on the Horsa military glider.

On 19 February 1941 George Errington flew the prototype of the A.S.45 Cambridge single engine trainer – not one of Tiltman's more inspired designs. George carried out most of the development flying and had an alarming experience. Due to excessive drag, difficulty was experienced in achieving the maximum specified diving speed. On one flight he entered a vertical dive. As he began to pull out at 270 mph, there was a tremendous bang and a large section of the upper surface of the starboard wing disappeared. He carefully reduced power, expecting the wing to fold. To his amazement there was no change in trim down to 100 mph so he managed to land it – at a higher speed than usual.

On another test flight, when REMB 'Bob' Milne selected undercarriage down, the starboard green warning light flickered. He landed carefully and taxied back to the flight line, turning in a series of circles to ensure that the suspect leg was always loaded outwards. Milne filled in the snag sheet and mentioned the trouble to colleague Ron Clear, just as George Errington, who was to take the A.S.45 up again, entered the office. Milne told him of the trouble and warned him not to fly until the leg locks had been checked. 'Oh!' said George, 'that's all right, it has flickered with me before.'

He boarded the machine, started the engine and taxied towards the downwind end of the field, as the two pilots watched apprehensively. As the Cambridge turned to starboard their worst fears were realized, and the leg collapsed. A disconsolate Errington awaited the arrival of the crash crew, no doubt regretting his folly. It was a surprising lapse on the part of a pilot who was normally so meticulous.

The Cambridge was abandoned, and Ron Clear flew the prototype to Farnborough where it was used to fan the flames in fire fighting equipment trials. He wondered whether the many hours of flight testing to achieve satisfactory control responses and drag reduction had been worthwhile.

The success of German gliders in the 1940 *Blitzkrieg* on the Low Countries proved to Winston Churchill the value of such aircraft. At the end of 1941 he instructed that the 1st Airborne Division be formed. Work was carried out at Farnborough to determine the maximum practical size for a troop carrying glider. A Vickers Wellesley bomber

Airspeed Horsa glider.

was converted, its engine being replaced by a large block of concrete and towed trials were carried out. Its high aspect ratio wing, 74 ft in span, was suitable for a glider, so relevant parameters were drawn up for a troop carrier to accommodate between 24 and 36 men. In December 1940, specification X26/40 was delivered to the Airspeed design office. The production of the Horsa glider was a triumph of organization and improvization, using a labour force which was not heavily committed to wartime needs. The furniture trade, rail workshops, shopfitters and even gramophone cabinet manufacturers made sub-assemblies which were planned for erection at RAF Maintenance Units. On 12 September 1941 George Errington made the first flight, towed behind a Whitley, from Fairey's Great West Road aerodrome, now part of Heathrow Airport.

Flight trials were extremely satisfactory although occasionally they were punctuated with drama. For example, on one occasion the tug and glider unexpectedly entered the cloud base and Nick Carter (the tug pilot), found that the Horsa was far below the Whitley, George Errington being quite disorientated in the cloud. Nick said afterwards that he thought that Errington had forsaken the controls for the Elsan. Fortunately the loss of height which these antics achieved brought the two machines below the cloud base again. The Horsa had an undercarriage which could be jettisoned for operational landings to be made on a skid. Occasionally one or both legs would hang up; one failed to release until the glider was approaching a house where a wedding party was engaged in a photographic sortie in the garden. Suddenly one leg of the Horsa undercarriage hurtled to the ground between the photographer and the nuptial group. The expressions on the faces of the members would probably have been worth preserving for posterity! Another leg fell into an Army camp whilst the Army, thinking it might be a new type of weapon, wired it off pending the arrival of the bomb disposal squad!

A violent storm at Christchurch gusted up to 92 mph and created havoc among the parked Horsas. One flew past the pilots' office dangling its anchors of five gallon oil drums, full of concrete, only inches from the windows. Another executed a half loop on to its back, landing on fir trees, stripping the branches and leaving the trunks sticking through the wings and fuselage. A few days later a photograph of it appeared on the wall of the pilots' office with the caption, 'It's all right, old boy, she really can do steep turns at the stall, the designer said so!' The Horsa was a worthy mount for the airborne forces which included some of the finest fighting men the world has ever seen. Over 3,600 were built and many saw service at Arnhem and in the Normandy landings, in addition to other operations.

Another pilot involved in glider testing was Charles F. Hughesdon, chief test pilot of General Aircraft from 1939 to 1943. He learned to fly in 1932 and was commissioned in the Reserve of Air Force Officers in 1934, by which time he had an instructor's endorsement to his private licence. In 1936, he became a part time instructor to the RAFVR and on the outbreak of war he was posted, rather reluctantly, to Desford as a full-time instructor. After three months the Ministry appointed him

chief test pilot of G.A. at Hanworth where early marks of Spitfire were being repaired.

Under construction was a half scale model of the 110 ft span Hamilcar tank carrying glider. The first flight was uneventful and satisfactory. The glider had an undercarriage capable of being jettisoned so that, on the full scale machine, the landing could be made on a skid, the nose then opened and the 7-ton tank driven out. During the jettison trials on the full size glider, first flown by Hughesdon at RAF Snaith on 27 March 1942, Hollis Williams, the designer, asked for the undercarriage to be dropped nearer the ground as too many expensive assemblies were likely to be smashed as they dropped from the Hamilcar.

On the next flight the release was operated at a height of 10 ft; nothing happened, a further pull released the wheels and struts which bounced off the ground to hit the glider, ripping a hole in the fuselage and smashing one of the four longerons. In the confusion one of the RAE observers on board released a parachute which whipped around inside in the gale of wind created by the hole. The tug pilot gingerly towed the damaged Hamilcar around the circuit and a safe landing was made.

After a spell with the British Air Commission in Washington he returned to Britain to terminate his test flying career. He was awarded an AFC in 1944 and, after the war, built up a very substantial aviation insurance company.

At RAE Farnborough the redoubtable Wg Cdr T. R. 'Tam' Morrison was involved in glider testing after service in Bomber Command. A forceful Scot, always spoiling for a fight, Tam flew all the military

General Aircraft Hamilcar tank-carrying glider.

gliders between 1942 and 1944 and contributed greatly to the success of the airborne forces.

Leaving the RAF after the war, he flew with Sabena, training their pilots, afterwards joining a charter company owned by Geoffrey Alington, who had himself been chief test pilot at the Longbridge Shadow Factory. When Stirling production commenced there, the aircraft were transported to Castle Bromwich for assembly and air-test.

In 1946–47 Alington bought ten Stirlings for £2,000 and formed the company to operate out of Belgium. Tam Morrison was chief pilot.

On 22 December 1947 he was flying a Stirling out of a Chinese aerodrome at an altitude of 5,000 ft, with a full load of 29 monks and nuns. He was uneasy about taking-off at this height but seems to have been persuaded against his better judgement. As the aircraft became airborne, the engines overheated, actuating the fire extinguishers which stopped all four Hercules. Tam had no alternative but to put the machine down in a cemetery with 4 ft high burial mounds which tore the Stirling apart, hurling the Belgian co-pilot, who always refused to wear a harness, to his death through the windscreen. The other occupants escaped, miraculously, with minor injuries. Tam's skill in dropping the tail to take the first impact probably saved all their lives.

He recalled them on their knees giving thanks to God – and to him – for their preservation. By a sad irony, a short time later they were all massacred by Communist guerrillas.

On 9 January 1941 Capt H. A. Brown had flown the four Merlin engine Manchester for the first time. The Lancaster, as it was named, was almost right from the commencement of its trials. The central fin was later deleted and larger fins fitted at the extremity of the tailplane. An A&AEE pilot went to Woodford for preliminary handling trials before the prototype was submitted to Boscombe Down, still with its three fins. The rudders were found to be insufficiently powerful, but generally the controls were well harmonized. Various minor modifications to the cockpit layout were made and production went ahead as fast as possible. Later a version with Bristol Hercules engines was built. Diving tests on this one at Boscombe Down were distinctly alarming. Control forces were so heavy at 370 mph that recovery had to be made on the elevator trimmer. Serious aileron overbalance was also experienced. Only 300 of this Mk II were built with 6,464 Mk Is and Mk IIIs. During the war the type dropped over 600,000 tons of bombs in 156,000 sorties, whilst it was adapted to carry ever

heavier bombs culminating in the 22,000 lb 'Grand Slam'. It was an outstanding design which remained in Bomber Command service until 1953.

Fairey developed from the Fulmar a new fleet fighter, the Firefly, which was successful in a number of naval roles. On 4 June 1942 the second prototype was being flown by Chris Staniland in a high speed low-level run. Increasing speed caused the elevator to overbalance and the tail collapsed. This superb chief test pilot died in the wreck.

1941 saw the first flight of the Gloster E28/39, Britain's first jet propelled aeroplane. This historic event and its consequences form the subject of the next chapter.

During the years of the Second World War few new British prototypes appeared, maximum effort being directed towards high volume production of existing types which had proved their worth in battle, and had development potential, which could be exploited with the minimum expenditure in manpower.

One interesting project was the conversion of a Wellington for high altitude operation. Known as the Mk VI, it had a pressure cabin to simulate the conditions appropriate to flight at 11,000 ft at an altitude of 40,000 ft. The structure of the Wimpy was quite unsuitable for total pressurization, so a capsule to contain the crew was built, the pilot peering through a hemispherical blister on top of it. It was fairly satisfactory, but claustrophobic for the crew.

One of the prototypes was involved in a mysterious crash in July 1942. Taking off from Boscombe Down, with Sqn Ldr C. C. Colman at the controls, plus a crew of four, the machine was seen to dive from high altitude into the ground in Derbyshire. Examination of the wreckage revealed no explanation of the crash, as under security rules, radio silence had been maintained. The accident therefore remained a mystery.

A few Wellington VIs flew over enemy territory in the course of development trials of the new 'Oboe' precision navigational aid, and provided valuable data on operations at high altitude.

At Boscombe Down, in B Per T, were Sqn Ldrs Huxtable and Slee, Flt Lt Carr and Wg Cdr Jack McGuire, all ex-Martlesham hands with great experience. The methodical step-by-step progression followed by peacetime test pilots was impracticable in wartime, and McGuire was required to test a Wellington with greatly increased engine power and all-up weight. There was no time to build up slowly to overload conditions; the requirement was, simply, to prove it as fast as possible. It was desperately needed in service. So McGuire taxied out with the aircraft at full load, turned into what little wind there was to help him on the 1,000 yard run available, and opened the throttles to full boost, holding the bomber on its brakes until the tail came up to the minimum drag position – then it lumbered forward. At that weight every bump caused the tips of the wings to flex about a foot. McGuire calmly judged the rate of acceleration in relation to the distance left, little though it was, and achieved a clean take-off only a few yards from the boundary. An engine failure would have been utterly disastrous as the machine would probably have crashed into new prototypes parked in the C Flt dispersal area. Looked at in retrospect it may be concluded that such flying was reckless in the extreme, but it represented an essential philosophy which helped to save this country when our backs were 'up against the wall'. It was a philosophy followed by professionals of the highest calibre, analysing the risks and deciding that there was a strong chance that their judgement would be vindicated. Usually it was, as in the case of McGuire's Wellington, when weeks of work were saved. Tragically, in too many cases, luck deserted them, engine failure or some other utterly unpredictable fault costing them their lives.

McGuire was appointed OC of Per T, and he took under his wing a young New Zealander, F/O Fleming, who was required to test an American Liberator bomber. It was sensed that Fleming was not too keen on this aeroplane and he found various instrument malfunctions which were not unusual in the all-electric Liberator. He correctly reported the faults but Jack McGuire decided they were not sufficiently serious to warrant postponement of the flight, so he took over command himself, with Fleming in the second pilot's seat and a crew of seven observers.

After one and a half hours flying a fire broke out in one of the engines, the extinguishers were inadequate, and the pilot ordered 'abandon aircraft'. He remained at the controls until the crew had found their parachutes, clipped them on and jumped to safety. As the last man left, the fire burned through the wing which broke off, the Liberator taking a great test pilot to his death.

An interesting development designed to increase the payload of such machines as the Boston bomber with its small bomb bay was the Malinowsky trailer wing. It was also considered for the Spitfire. Initially a flying test rig was built with a Magister as the 'prime mover'. The 'wing', which looked like the tailplane of a twin rudder bomber, was attached to the Magister wing in such a way that it could float through a few degrees upward or downward in relation to the aircraft; it had its own tail wheels. Wg Cdr H. J. Wilson, OC of Aerodynamics Flight at RAE flew it, but found that, as the weight was loaded upon the trailer wing, the aircraft became almost uncontrollable – a case of the tail wagging the dog! The scheme was abandoned.

Jeffrey Quill and his Supermarine team were busy developing various marks of Spitfire. The Air Staff had decided that two types of day fighter were required – a high altitude aircraft with a pressurized cabin, and an unpressurized version for combat at lower levels. Rolls-Royce developed the Merlin 61 with a two-stage supercharger which was flown initially in a Spitfire Mk Vc. The Focke-Wulf Fw 190 was appearing in large numbers, its spectacular performance and heavy armament causing much concern in Fighter Command, so the high altitude Mk IX Spitfire was rapidly put into production. It was found that the Mk IX and the Fw 190 were so evenly matched that only the skill of the pilot determined the outcome of a combat.

Quill was close to becoming involved in a cloak and dagger operation to purloin an Fw 190 from an aerodrome in occupied France. Plans were under consideration when, in June 1942, *Luftwaffe* Oberleutnant Arnim Faber lost himself after a battle over the Channel, and landed by mistake at Pembrey in Wales. Much to the relief of most of the potential participants the hijacking was called off.

The Fw 190 was taken to Farnborough for evaluation by Wg Cdr Wilson. A trial was carried out, in front of a group of VIPs, to discover the relative speeds of three fighters; the Fw 190, flown by Willie Wilson, a Hawker Typhoon flown by a Hawker test pilot, Ken Seth Smith, and a Spitfire which represented 'the average fighter'. Jeffrey Quill decided to fly the Griffon engined prototype, which later became the Mk XII.

On a full throttle run at low altitude the Spitfire had a handsome lead over the other two although the German aircraft was suffering from engine problems. This exercise served to focus high level attention upon the potential of the Griffon engined Spitfire and an order for one hundred of the Mk XII was placed.

Wg Cdr Wilson was becoming an experienced pilot of the German aeroplanes against which he had fought during a posting to No 74 Sqn, when he arranged to obtain first hand experience of the Spitfire in combat. In 1940 this was a novel experience for a test pilot, and the scheme was developed to a point at which it became of great benefit to RAE and A&AEE whose pilots, almost without exception, served a period of posting to an operational squadron to see for themselves the problems which arose. Wg Cdr Allen Wheeler, at that time OC of the Performance Testing Squadron, told of one of the exceptions who announced that he considered that test pilots were too valuable to be sent on ops! He was rapidly posted to an operational squadron!

Willie Wilson had an alarming experience in a fully loaded Junkers Ju 88 when an engine failed on take-off. Previous interrogation of German prisoners of war had indicated that one of only two alternatives was possible – a forced landing straight ahead, or a crash. As neither was acceptable, he opened the remaining engine to full throttle and staggered into the air with everything white hot. He completed a circuit and brought the priceless aeroplane back to a safe landing.

Another of his responsibilities was the development of the CAM ship concept. Early in the war the German Focke-Wulf Condor was the scourge of the Allied convoys in the North Atlantic. Aircraft carriers were scarce and the land based patrol aircraft on both sides of the Atlantic had insufficient range to meet in the middle.

The suggestion, attributed to Winston Churchill, that a Hurricane fighter should be mounted on a catapult at the bow of certain merchant ships in a convoy, and launched when the Condor was approaching, was well received by the Chief of Air Staff, Sir Charles Portal. So the Catapult Aircraft Merchant ships came into being with a clapped-out Hurricane Mk I (or 'Hurricat') on the bow.

Wg Cdr Wilson developed the operating techniques and trained the pilots who, in some cases, were fighter pilots withdrawn from their operational squadrons 'for a rest'. For up to 10 hours they sat in their cockpits in freezing North Atlantic weather, in the certain knowledge that if they were launched they could only return to land at the beginning and end of the voyage, and that the only alternative was a ditching or parachute jump in the hope that a ship might pick them up before the icy sea killed them – only a matter of a few minutes in winter.

One of the CAM ship pilots was Sub Lt Peter Twiss RNVR who, in 1946, became a Fairey test pilot and, in 1956, as chief test pilot, established a world speed record of 1,132 mph. He said that his service with the CAM ships was the most tedious period of his career. On the occasions when he was launched he was, fortunately, within range of Belfast or Gibraltar.

The first to shoot down a Condor was Lt Bob Everett, who, in peacetime, had been a well known steeple chase rider, winning the Grand National in 1929. He was awarded the DSO. Ironically he was killed in a Hurricane in 1942 whilst delivering it from Belfast to Tern Hill in Shropshire. The aircraft was seen to crash into the sea.

The CAM ships, whilst achieving few victories, acted as a powerful deterrent to the Condors which had serious structural problems arising from their civil airliner origins. *Luftwaffe* pilots were not keen to indulge in evasive action with these huge machines, so the shipborne Hurricanes held the fort effectively until the Escort Carriers came into service in numbers in 1943.

Throughout its life the Spitfire was plagued with critical fore and aft stability problems. As the high altitude versions came into service oxygen bottles had to be installed, and these could only be accommodated in the rear fuselage. As any rearward shift of the CG had a de-stabilizing effect upon the aeroplane, a major programme of investigation was set up by Supermarines and A&AEE. Some experimental work had already been carried out in 1940 on the provision of a lever with a weight upon the end of it, with connection to the elevator control linkage, so that G forces applied to the weight could create a corrective movement of the elevator. RAE and A&AEE had tested the device and proved it to be satisfactory on a range of different aircraft, so the bobweight was introduced upon production Spitfires. Later, the development of the oxygen economizer valve reduced the number of bottles required in high altitude fighters.

On 27 February 1942 Flt Lt Arthur Thompson flew the Blackburn Firebrand for the first time. This massive single seat shipboard torpedo fighter, powered with a 2,305 hp Napier Sabre engine, was built like a battleship – some said it flew like one – but with the pilot nearer the tail than the huge nose it was severely handicapped as a carrier based aeroplane. In any case its fighter role had been usurped unexpectedly by the Seafire.

Not until 1944 was the second prototype flown by Arthur Thompson. This suffered an oil pipe fracture and engine failure on the approach to Brough. Whilst attempting a wheels-up landing with his windscreen obscured by oil, he flew into the heavy cable of the telpher at a cement works. The Firebrand was violently 'arrested' by the cable, which broke and whipped back through the fuselage, narrowly missing the pilot.

Lt Cdr Eric Brown was serving at Farnborough during the trials of the Centaurus engined Fire-

Lt Cdr Eric Brown discussing the Blackburn Firebrand with Lt Peter Lawrence, later to become chief test pilot to Blackburn and who was killed in a Gloster Javelin.

brand, which had torpedo dropping capability. View from the cockpit was even worse with the big radial, and although manoeuvrability was improved and the rate of climb was better, it had an unpleasant habit of dropping a wing at the stall. For carrier operations, power had to be used right down to the deck. Although design work had commenced in 1940 it was not until 1945 that the Firebrand embarked in a carrier.

The Blackburn chief test pilot, Peter G. Lawrence, investigated aileron flutter on one of the prototypes. It appeared to be worse as altitude was gained. At 20,000 ft a certain speed would damp out the flutter, but at 25,000 ft, at the same speed, the phenomenon would re-appear at an ever increasing magnitude, the wings flapping through three feet. Skin fractures in wings and fuselage occurred and the cockpit side window broke. Lawrence slowed down to 100 knots, preparatory to bailing out. At that speed the flutter ceased, so he was able to land the machine at Brough for further investigation. He had another unpleasant experience when he initiated a spin to port at 22,000 ft but could not recover after the customary three turns. After the 22nd rotation he streamed the tail parachute and levelled out at 5,000 ft.

At Woodford, Avro had developed from the Lancaster bomber the Lancastrian transport and the York. The York was a capacious slab sided

fuselage attached to Lancaster wings and tail unit, with a third fin fitted later to compensate for the greatly increased side area of the new fuselage. Flown for the first time by Capt H. A. 'Sam' Brown on 5 July 1942, the major problem with an early one (which was destined to be Winston Churchill's personal aircraft, later named *Ascalon*), was that when the wash basin plug was removed in the PM's cabin the contents of the basin were distributed upwards in a fine spray! A&AEE dealt with the difficulty in their unusual inimitable style!

The York performed yeoman service in RAF Transport Command, and in the post-war airlines for many years, whilst the Lancastrian noisily flew VIPs across the Atlantic during the war and opened up long distance civil routes when hostilities ceased.

The name of Martin Baker is associated with the development of the ejector seat which, by the end of 1984, had saved the lives of 5,288 aircrew members. Not so well known is the range of single engine fighters which James Martin, designed during the early part of the war, when the shortage of Hurricanes and Spitfires was so serious. The MB.2 with a Napier Dagger engine and a fixed undercarriage, had flown in 1938, but had serious problems in handling although the simplicity of its construction impressed everyone. If the effort had been made to overcome its defects there is little doubt that it would have made a valuable contribution to the war effort, particularly in the dire days of the Battle of Britain.

The MB.3, with its 2,000 hp Sabre engine, was a handsome aeroplane using the simplest constructional techniques, highly manoeuvrable and fast. It had a top speed of 415 mph at 20,000 ft. On 12 September 1942, James Martin's partner, Capt Val Baker, experienced a sleeve drive crank failure on take-off. In the attempt to make a forced landing he hit a tree stump and was killed as the aircraft caught fire. The project was abandoned as Martin Baker concentrated upon various other forms of military hardware, notably the cartridge operated leading edge cable cutter which had been tested at Farnborough by Arthur Clouston and his colleagues. 250,000 of these were made during the war, 80,000 of them by Martin Baker.

Shaken by the tragic death of Baker, which, it is said, led Martin to give serious thought to aircrew survival in the event of a take-off or landing accident, the company nevertheless decided to build another fighter based upon the MB.3. The MB.4 followed and was abandoned at the design stage in favour of the MB.5, a superb fighter with a 2,340 hp Rolls-Royce Griffon engine. Still Martin

Martin Baker MB.5.

continued with his simple steel tubular fuselage clad with light alloy detachable panels. There was little official encouragement and Martin Baker provided the finance themselves. In spite of lacking the facility of a wind tunnel, the MB.5 was acknowledged to be an outstanding fighter, as much for its handling qualities as for its simple construction, the merit of which was proved on 3 May 1944 when it arrived at RAF Harwell on a Queen Mary. Reaching its hangar before lunch, it was assembled in an hour or so and flown for the first time by Bryan Greensted, the test pilot of Rotol, who built the contra-rotating propeller fitted to it. Initially its directional stability was poor – a congenital weakness from the MB.2, perhaps – but a modified fin and rudder cured the problem. Flight test proceeded most satisfactorily apart from a nasty experience when giving a demonstration before a group of top brass, including Churchill. Greensted had flown the machine for 40 hours with virtually no problems. Suddenly, on the run-in at Farnborough, the Griffon stopped. He raised his arm to release the canopy and nearly lost the arm in the process. The canopy hit the tail, but fortunately the damage was not serious so he made a safe dead-stick landing.

Sent to Boscombe Down at the beginning of 1946, the MB.5 had an almost unique report, being favourably commented upon in every respect. In June 1946 the famous Czech test pilot Jan Zurakowski showed it off in a breathtaking demonstration at Farnborough. Due to what appears to have been undue prevarication and delay on the part of the Ministry of Aircraft Production, the MB.5 was overtaken by jet propelled aircraft. If its great merits had been officially recognized early enough it could have been in service well before the end of hostilities and Britain would have had a world beater. One of the A&AEE pilots thought it a cross between a Mustang and a V2 rocket!

The Hawker Typhoon had proved itself to be a useful low-level weapon, if a noisy and rough one. Compressibility problems were being experienced, frequently at the high speeds being attained by a number of fighters, both British and American, so Hawker had redesigned the 'Tiffie', with radiators in the leading edge of a new thin wing, and a Sabre IV engine. This version became known as the Tempest, and six prototypes were ordered; one had a Bristol Centaurus engine, another a Griffon. All had a bubble type canopy to overcome the serious visibility problems of the Typhoon.

Philip Lucas flew the first prototype, a Mk V with a Sabre 2 engine, on 2 September 1942. It

Hawker Tempest.

was a vast improvement on its predecessors. As it approached 500 mph its handling was impeccable, free from any tendency to buffet, it was crisp and responsive to the controls, and generally a superb aeroplane and a stable gun platform.

Flt Lt Roland P. Beamont, a fighter pilot, had completed a 200 hour tour of ops in December 1941 and had been posted to Hawkers at Langley for a 'rest'. After many hours of Hurricane production testing he flew the Typhoon. On his first cross-country flight to deliver one to Glosters, oil poured over his windscreen and goggles as black smoke poured from the engine. An immediate landing was imperative, the only possible site being a small airfield infested with Tiger Moths. With his oil pressure falling fast he managed to side slip in, missing all the Tigers by a hairsbreadth and stopping only yards from the far hedge. The worst was to come, however. As he left the cockpit he slipped on the oil covered wing and fell heavily to the ground – only to be summoned to an immediate interview with the chief flying instructor who was furious with this irresponsible pilot who had cut right across the approach path of his flying school!

After six months of flight testing Beamont returned to his unit and was soon posted to No 609 Sqn, where he became a flight commander after seeing his predecessor killed in a ground collision between two Typhoons.

On 1 November 1942 Harald Penrose flew the Westland Welkin for the first time. Designed by the brilliant W. E. W. 'Teddy' Petter, it was built to an Air Ministry specification for a high altitude single-seat fighter, and was the largest ever built – with a wing span of 70 ft. Fitted with Merlin engines and superficially similar to the Whirlwind it lacked the racy elegance of its predecessor. The second prototype went to Boscombe Down in October 1943, but was criticized for its poor roll performance, a full one at 10,000 ft taking 12–15 seconds, the aileron effectiveness becoming worse still at higher altitudes.

Mock combat trials against a Mosquito revealed that its limiting Mach number, at which compressibility effects became very noticeable, was lower than that of the Mosquito, so an adversary could easily escape by diving away. It became clear that the Welkin must be considered a bomber interceptor only. A total of 67 production machines were built. None saw active service, although a number of flights were made into the stratosphere to evaluate the machine's performance should it be called upon to intercept bombers flying at those heights.

The RAE was interested in the idea of injecting liquid oxygen into Merlin engines to increase speeds at high altitudes. The second prototype was converted to test the scheme with a large tank for the oxygen. It was abandoned due to the difficulty in handling liquid oxygen – although the principle was proved to be sound.

In 1943 the main events were the first flights of the Gloster Meteor and the de Havilland Vampire, described in chapter ten, and the further development of the Spitfire as a fully fledged naval carrier-borne fighter. In February two Mk XIIs were fitted with arrester gear and delivered to the Fleet Air Arm service trials unit at Arbroath for evaluation and ADDLS (aerodrome dummy deck landings). Experience with carrier-borne Seafires during the Allied invasion of North Africa had been disastrous, and in the Salerno landings of September 1943 the absence of sufficient wind over the decks in hot weather had, in 713 sorties, resulted in 73 deck landing accidents, which wrote off 32 Seafires.

A discussion between Jeffrey Quill and Rear Admiral Sir Denis Boyd, the Fifth Sea Lord, led to Jeffrey being commissioned as a Lt Cdr RNVR in the Fleet Air Arm to investigate the handling problems of Seafires aboard carriers. Quill carried out many deck landing trials and was able to recommend operating techniques which achieved a substantial reduction in the casualty rate. By the time he reported to Admiral Boyd on 29 February 1944, Lt Cdr Eric Brown had been appointed chief naval test pilot at RAE Farnborough, his predecessor having been killed landing a Seafire on a carrier. He became involved in a work programme resulting from Jeffrey Quill's recommendation and in tests of rocket take-off gear for the Spitfire. During catapult launch trials he left the catapult with the carriage still attached to his Seafire, fortunately it fell away before he had to land! Another

Eric Brown's Seafire taking off with a catapult cradle attached.

remarkable incident occurred at the launching of an American Avenger from one of the Farnborough catapults. A heavy carrier-borne torpedo bomber with folding wings, it left the catapult in good order, but almost immediately the astonished 'Winkle' saw the wings slowly folding upwards. He closed the throttle and the Avenger just hit the ground and trundled along until the brakes brought it to rest – leaving the pilot feeling distinctly foolish!

On 26 March 1944 he landed the prototype Griffon engined Seafire Mk XV on HMS *Indefatigable* for the first time, and on the same day, made the first landing of a twin engined aeroplane on a carrier when he brought the Mosquito aboard. Careful preliminary work had been carried out at Farnborough and RNAS Yeovilton with the converted Mk VI to establish a technique for minimum take-off distance, and to determine precise stalling speeds at different all-up weights. The take-off and landings were most successful although, due to the span of the aircraft, the port wheel was too near the edge of the deck for comfort. Swing on take-off had to be avoided; fortunately the speed of the ship ensured that the rudder was fairly effective from the beginning of take-off. Brown and his observer, Bill Stewart, an RAE Aero Flight technician, had a tricky experience next day when the arrester hook fixing bolt sheared as it caught the wire. Fortunately the pilot instantly realized what had happened. He opened the throttles to full boost and tore over the port side of the deck, the Mosquito dropping to within a few feet of the sea en route to Machrihanish.

At the other end of the spectrum of service aircraft, the Handley Page Halifax bomber was caus-

ing concern through a number of inexplicable accidents which resulted in the machine going out of control in violent manoeuvres when trying to escape the night fighters.

The early test reports from Boscombe Down had referred to a tendency for the rudder to overbalance and there were a number of differences between the prototype and the much heavier machines in squadron service. In February 1943 a test programme was begun to confirm earlier tests carried out by Sqn Ldr Bill Carr and a civilian scientist J. J. Unwin in a Halifax Mk I. On 4 February Flt Lt S. Reiss took off in a Halifax II with Unwin, and Sgt J. Fielding as flight engineer. At 12,000 ft the aircraft was seen to go into a dive, pull out and enter a flat spin from which it did not recover. It hit the ground, caught fire and all on board died.

It was found that the top half of one of the rudders had broken away, suggesting that violent overbalance had occurred, causing the Halifax to become completely uncontrollable. This crash proved beyond doubt that the problem was of major proportions, and further trials indicated that it was most likely to arise at approach speeds on landings. If it happened in a slight cross wind the outcome would be fatal. Asymmetric flight with one or even two engines out – by no mean unusual on ops – would achieve the fatal combination, especially when corkscrewing to avoid night fighters. Two solutions were suggested. One was to make the rudder heavy with cords along each side of the trailing edge, so the pilot could not deflect it to the danger point. This was found to be ineffective, but the other solution, restriction of rudder bar travel by a stop, proved to be a reasonable temporary expedient, until the introduction of the much larger fins and rudders of almost rectangular shape on Halifax IIIs and subsequent versions.

A&AEE was involved in the evaluation of American land planes considered for purchase by the British Forces. In Washington the British Joint Services Commission had been charged with the task of selecting and testing likely American types, and also of trying to achieve a common standard of test flying procedures in the USA and in the UK. It had been found that the standards at some American aircraft works were perfunctory in the extreme. Among the members of this Commission were Wg Cdrs J. F. X. McKenna and Leonard S. Snaith, the latter having been a member of the 1931 Schneider Trophy team. George Bulman, Hawker's chief test pilot, was also a member. He had been working closely with American companies in investigating compressibility problems which were beginning to

be serious in aircraft such as the Lockheed Lightning and the Republic Thunderbolt. George circulated a paper to all British and American test pilots analysing what, in his opinion, were the basic elements of this dangerous phenomenon, which, in a dive, caused controls to go solid or reverse their operation. His advice, which saved many test pilots' lives, was based on the fact that Mach number is variable with temperature, and therefore, with altitude. At 40,000 ft the speed of sound is approximately 650 mph, at sea level it is 720 mph, so if a pilot reaches his limiting Mach number at altitude, by riding it down to warmer air he is likely to regain control as the speed of sound rises at that level.

In some cases – the Thunderbolt was an example – a machine would 'tuck under' in the dive, a nose down pitch developing so fast that recovery was sometimes impossible. If height was available the machine would perform an outside loop, if not it would dive into the ground or break up as the luckless pilot overstressed the airframe in an attempt to pull out.

One of the outstanding fighters of the Second World War was the North American Mustang. In 1940 the Curtiss P-40 Tomahawk, which was on order for the French Air Force, was diverted, on the fall of France, for service in the RAF. Its unsupercharged Allison engine gave it a totally inadequate performance although it was a useful aeroplane in the Middle East. North American Aviation were building Harvard trainers for Britain, and the company was considered as a possible subcontractor to build the P-40, inadequate though it was.

James 'Dutch' Kindelberger, an experienced aeronautical engineer who was President of North American Aviation, suggested to the British Purchasing Commission that his company should build a fighter to a British specification. Outline sketches were discussed and an order placed for 320 aircraft. In view of the desperate British position in 1940 it was stipulated that the prototype must be flying within 120 days. North American, who had never built a fighter before, met this demand with three days to spare. On 26 October Vance Breeze, the NA test pilot, made a twenty minute flight which proved that the care taken in minimizing drag had paid off handsomely. The aeroplane was outstanding, but with its Allison engine it was no match for a Spitfire at altitude, although its top speed of 375 mph was 35 mph faster than the British fighter at 15,000 ft. Its handling characteristics were superb. The Mk I was used as an Army co-operation aeroplane, a role for which its low-level performance was well suited.

Ronnie Harker, a Rolls-Royce test pilot, was sent to the Air Fighting Development Unit at Duxford in April 1942 to evaluate Allied and enemy aeroplanes. He flew a Mustang, and as recorded in chapter twelve, set in train the momentous decision to fit a Merlin 61 engine into the American airframe, turning the Mustang into one of the outstanding fighters of all time.

During the flight trials of this aeroplane at Boscombe Down A&AEE lost one of their finest pilots, Wg Cdr J. F. X. McKenna, who died when a wing came off the Mustang he was flying.

The Merlin engined Mustang with long range tanks was able to escort American and British bombers on daylight raids deep into Germany, reducing substantially the appalling losses suffered, particularly by the Fortresses and Liberators, in these operations.

An attempt was made in 1943 to extend the ferrying range of Spitfires by towing them behind bombers. Sir Alan Cobham's Flight Refuelling firm devised an ingenious bridle system, which had a cable outboard of the guns on each wing attached to the main tow cable at a point which, for take-off, was clipped to the underside of the rear fuselage to avoid entanglement with the propeller. At cruising altitude the fighter engine was stopped and the tow established. Wg Cdr Wilson decided that, whilst the scheme was certainly feasible, the concentration demanded of the pilot was not acceptable in the case of young, inexperienced men, so he reported accordingly. Sir Alan Cobham was extremely annoyed, and telephoned Lord Beaverbrook demanding that further tests be carried out. The Wg Cdr pointed out that his conclusions would not change, so the project was dropped.

1943 was the year in which the whole technique of aircraft armament began to change. The 'weapon system' philosophy developed almost unnoticed and stores began to be seen on the undersides of wings. Rockets, bombs and long range tanks appeared on Hurricanes, Spitfires, Mustangs and Mosquitoes, whilst the Barracuda even appeared with a pannier under each wing to carry paratroops. Happily for the airborne troops this development was abandoned.

The effect upon the handling of aircraft resulting from the installation of large and often 'draggy' appendages under the airframe, increased substantially the work load upon the Performance Testing Squadron at Boscombe Down. Wg Cdr Sammy Wroath's 'A' Sqn was mainly affected as the single

engine aircraft were those which were experiencing major changes. Another innovation which was of immense benefit to the services and the aircraft industry, was the manner in which technical information about aircraft under test was given to all the manufacturers of that type of aeroplane. Indeed, test pilots would be invited to fly their competitors' machines – a practice quite unheard of before the war.

Sammy Wroath was probably the most experienced test pilot in the RAF at that time and he attracted a highly competent team to his squadron – Flt Lt Brunner, Flt Lt Kulczyski, a Polish officer and Lt Don Robertson, a Fleet Air Arm pilot. Much of their work was concerned with the problems of the notorious Typhoon and its Sabre engine, so hairy experiences were too frequent for much comment.

With increasing pressure on all British test flying establishments it became clear that some means of training pilots in standard test procedures was becoming vitally necessary. Many senior officers were convinced that it was not possible to train men in such an arcane occupation and that good test pilots were born not made. It was left to Wg Cdr Allen Wheeler, OC of Per T, to bring the controversy down to earth. He suggested that one of the most important requirements in a test pilot was a good sense of smell – so he could detect if the aeroplane was on fire! In 1943, the unit was formed which became the Empire Test Pilots School. Its evolution is described in chapter eleven.

10

BRITAIN ENTERS THE JET AGE

Reaction propulsion was used in the 16th century by the Chinese Army which was equipped with war rockets. It was also embodied in the principle of the ducted radiator used in a number of fighters from the mid-1930s and in the form of ejector exhausts used on Merlin engines: both devices gave a useful speed increment.

In the early years of the 20th century American and French engineers were working on a gas turbine, comprising a compressor to provide high pressure air in a combustion chamber into which fuel was continuously fed. The mixture being burned created expansion energy which then passed through a rotor driven at high speed, and which itself drove the compressor. Efficiencies were so low that all the power from the turbine was required to drive the compressor.

It was left to Brown-Boveri of Switzerland to transform the idea into a practical reality and by the late 1930s power was generated commercially, a B-B turbine being used in a railway locomotive.

The use of such a power plant in aircraft had been investigated by A. A. Griffith of the Royal Aircraft Establishment, who had not been deterred by a critical Air Ministry appraisal of the potentialities, published in 1920. He started work on a design for a turbine engine driving a propeller, and took out a patent in 1926.

It was recognized by engineers in several countries that the principle of compression, combustion and exhaust simultaneously and continuously was a desirable feature, and one which would not have the limitations of the orthodox piston engine/propeller combination at altitude.

In 1928, a young RAF flying instructor at the Central Flying School, Flt Lt Frank Whittle, worked on a thesis concerning future developments in aircraft design, and became aware of the work already done by Griffith. Whittle soon became convinced of the feasibility of the concept, and began to design a simple unit with a single stage centrifugal compressor and single stage turbine.

As was required of a serving officer, Whittle reported his work to the Air Ministry, who decided that his calculated performance and efficiency figures were far too optimistic. Whittle had taken out a patent in 1932 but the Ministry showed as little interest in this as in the case of Griffith's patent of 1926. Neither was considered of sufficient importance to be classified.

The RAF recognized the talent of this brilliant young engineer, and in 1934 he went to Cambridge to study Mechanical Sciences, whilst he continued his work on the gas turbine. He was able to obtain limited financial support from private sources and, in 1936, formed Power Jets to build an experimental engine. The pessimism of the Air Ministry abated slightly and he was permitted to continue with his work at Power Jets whilst he remained in the Service. By July 1937 private finance was at an end but the Air Ministry, by this time, had realized that the project might be a valuable one and so continued to finance it.

In Germany Hans von Ohain, a student at the University of Gottingen, designed in 1933 a gas turbine which was built in a car repair workshop owned by Max Hahn. Von Ohain observed that 'It behaved more like a flame thrower than an engine.' He approached Ernst Heinkel who was known to be involved in high speed flight research. Heinkel was interested, and employed the two men to develop Ohain's idea into an engine which first flew under a Heinkel bomber in 1939 and powered the first pure jet propelled aircraft, the Heinkel He 178, on its first flight on 27 August 1939.

By the end of 1938 Whittle had overcome many fearful and frustrating problems, and had run the WU (Whittle Unit) engine at 16,500 rpm for thirty minutes. David Pye, the Air Ministry Director of Scientific Research, saw it on test and was sufficiently impressed to recommend the production of an engine for flight trials, and an airframe in which to test this revolutionary powerplant.

Whittle visited Gloster's factory at Brockworth, near Gloucester, to discuss the project with George W. Carter, the chief designer. Carter showed him the mock-up of a twin tail boom Sabre engined fighter which was being developed. The pusher propeller design attracted Whittle, who considered it an ideal layout for jet propulsion. Some weeks later the designer was called to Air Ministry and asked if he would collaborate with Frank Whittle in designing an aircraft to be powered by the new engine. He was invited to visit Power Jets factory at Lutterworth, Leicestershire, where he saw the engine on test. He was so impressed that he agreed immediately to begin work on the project.

Right through the critical period of the Battle of Britain, when the fate of the nation was in the balance, work proceeded to complete the new prototype. With similar urgency Whittle and his team were trying to squeeze more and more thrust from the engine which was to power it. (There were people in high places who thought that it was a criminal waste of valuable resources to work on this speculative venture at such a time.) Fortunately their gloomy views were not heeded and the airframe took shape in the Gloster experimental shop at Bentham. A second prototype was also commenced. As far as was humanly possible knowledge of the existence of these aircraft was restricted to those working on them.

Brockworth aerodrome was too small to accommodate initial flight tests so the decision was made to fly from the longest runway in the country at RAF Cranwell.

On 7 April 1941 Flt Lt P. E. G. Sayer, Gloster's chief test pilot, reported upon the first taxying trials. The engine had been restricted to a maximum rpm of 13,000 instead of the designed 17,500, and Sayer was surprised to find that the machine did not move until 10,000 rpm had been reached. It had not been realized that thrust generated by a gas turbine built up slowly to a peak in the last few thousand revs. Up to the permitted maximum rpm, acceleration was poor, but controllability on the ground was excellent and the steerable nosewheel very effective. On the following day engine revs were allowed to rise to 15,000 per minute, Sayer achieving a ground speed of 60 mph. The elevators were not powerful enough to lift the nosewheel at this speed although, to compensate for the absence of propeller slipstream, the tail unit was larger than would have been considered appropriate to a conventional aeroplane.

The permissible rpm was increased to 16,000 and the machine lifted off for three short hops of about 150 yards six feet above the ground. Gerry Sayer was delighted with the smoothness of the engine which ran well, although the fact that most of the effective thrust was achieved over a small range of throttle movement created a sensation of throttle coarseness. During the hops the elevator control problem did not appear to be serious.

Various modifications were made and the E28/39, now officially named 'Pioneer', and unofficially at Glosters, 'The Squirt', was taken by road to Cranwell. On 14 May, Sayer carried out tests to check modifications to the undercarriage and throttle linkage and announced that he was ready for the first flight.

Gloster Whittle E28/39 Pioneer, Britain's first successful gas turbine, jet propelled aircraft, before its maiden flight on 15 May 1941; and Frank Whittle congratulating 'Gerry' Sayer on a safe landing.

The weather on the historic day, 15 May 1941, was poor and not until evening were the conditions suitable for a short flight. The tension which Frank Whittle and George Carter suffered is best left to the imagination, but Gerry was as urbane and calm as ever in spite of the comment of a VIP who had been quoted as saying earlier in the programme, 'Much as I admire the equanimity of Gerry in agreeing to carry out these flight tests, I cannot compliment him on his discretion!'

The Air Ministry was represented, as were Gloster and Power Jets, but it is quite incredible that, in spite of the need for absolute secrecy, no good film footage exists of this unique event, and only a few indifferent still photographs remain to remind posterity of this great British achievement. At 7.35 pm Gerry ran the engine up to 16,500 rpm and took off, lifting the machine by the feel of the elevators in 5–600 yards. Steering was easy and acceleration rapid; fore and aft control was, however, highly sensitive.

Frank Whittle relieved his feelings when one of the visitors rushed over to him exclaiming, 'It flies, Frank, it flies!' 'It was bloody well meant to wasn't it?' retorted Whittle with some asperity! For seventeen minutes Sayer explored the behaviour of the aircraft. The only area of criticism was that of fore and aft instability (probably resulting from the over-sensitive elevators), and there was a tendency to turn to the left – the jet pipe was found to be directed slightly in this direction. Approach and landing seemed straightforward, and generally the pilot was delighted with the results of the flight. The party adjourned to the Mess for a celebratory conference.

Michael Daunt, Sayer's assistant, who became chief test pilot after Gerry's tragic death, told the author that it was interesting to see the changed attitude of some of the official sceptics who had been vociferous in disparagement. 'Congratulations, old chap!' 'Always knew you'd got the right idea!' Frank B. Halford, de Havilland's talented design engineer also came over, 'Sincere congratulations, Frank, you were right and I was wrong!' To his assistant, E. S. Moult, he said, 'Come on, Eric, we have work to do.' They returned to their offices to begin work on the de Havilland H.1 turbine. Thus was conceived the Goblin which, because of delays in delivery of the Whittle engines, powered the prototype of the successor to the E28/39, the Gloster F9/40 Meteor.

Gerry Sayer handled the flight testing of the E28/39 himself, although he ensured that Michael Daunt was fully aware of the results, which sur-

passed expectations. In thirteen days fifteen flights were made in ten hours flying, without any attention to the engine.

Michael Daunt rightly feels that insufficient credit has been given to Henry Wiggin of Hereford, who developed the Nimonic range of alloys which withstood the high operating temperatures in the hot end of the turbine and, in the case of the rotor blades, withstood the temperature without 'creep' – a state in which the metal extends slightly under high centrifugal forces, causing the tip of the rotor blade to foul the inside of the housing. There is no doubt that the outcome of the test programme reflected great credit upon all the technicians responsible for the E28/39.

Not until 4 February 1942 did the E28/39 fly again. Its new up-rated Whittle W1A engine had barostatic control of the throttle to reduce the fuel flow as altitude increased. Sayer reported that the new engine was smoother than the original one, but a problem of turbine blade clearance arose and the exhaust cone was wrinkled due to excessive heat. When climbing to 30,000 ft on the eighth flight, Gerry noticed a change in engine note followed by severe vibration. He reduced revs to 10,000 and returned to base where it was found that a turbine blade had failed, damaging adjacent ones – the first of many such problems in the history of jet propulsion.

On 6 June the engine flamed out after a short period of rough running, a bearing in the gearbox having failed due to congealed oil in the feed pipe. With piston engined aircraft the problem was to keep the oil cool. In jets the problem was to be quite different. A modified ring main lubrication system was fitted, but this held up test flying for over three months. On 27 September Gerry Sayer made his last flight in the E28/39, in the presence of some American VIPs. Immediately after take-off oil pressure problems arose again so he had to return to the aerodrome. As he landed the port wing tip touched the ground, buckling the bottom skin. The lubrication systems were redesigned and modifications made whilst the aircraft was being repaired.

Test pilots attached to constructors are not normally involved in weapon trials, but Michael Daunt and Gerry Sayer had been invited to visit a Typhoon squadron at Acklington in Northumberland to fire the guns at targets off-shore. Gerry decided to take advantage of the lull in the test programme to go to Acklington.

In company with another Typhoon, he was to carry out dummy attacks, and climbed up through the overcast skies heading for clear air above. Neither machine was seen again although a report was received from someone who had seen an aeroplane diving into the sea trailing a cloud of smoke. It was assumed that the two fighters had collided in cloud – a tragic end to a superb test pilot of great charm and modesty, who had been awarded an OBE in the 1942 New Years Honours List for 'Services to Aviation.'

Michael Daunt had himself been out of action for six months recovering from the accident to the Folland 'Frightful' (see chapter nine).

To celebrate the return of his flying licence he had joined friends for lunch at a London restaurant. During that lunch he heard, to his deep sorrow, of Gerry Sayer's death. After his appointment as chief test pilot he completed the trials of the modified lubrication system and delivered the E28/39 to RAE Farnborough.

Mike had immense respect and affection for Sayer and liked the way in which he always expected his subordinates to share all aspects of the testing of new aeroplanes. He would not discuss the test flights until a report had been written and he had carried out a flight himself and written his own report. In this way an absolutely objective judgement was achieved during the subsequent discussion. Michael Daunt followed this example.

At Farnborough engine tests were carried out on the E28/39 and senior officers flew it. Wg Cdr H. J. Wilson, OC of Aerodynamics Flight quipped, 'It was the first aeroplane I have ever flown where you could see the fuel gauge needle moving the whole time the engine was running!' Sqn Ldr Charles G. B. McClure, OC of Engine Flight, was also involved in this phase of testing. As there were few aerodromes in the country where aviation kerosene fuel was available, a Lancaster was fitted with a large belly tank and flown to wherever the jet landed.

Not until March 1943 was the second prototype flown by John Grierson. In the meantime, Sqn Ldr W. D. B. S. Davie, Willie Wilson's assistant, had carried out a major test programme on the first one. Wilson considers that Davie made a major contribution to the success of British jet propulsion and was one of the finest test pilots at RAE.

The new jet was well liked by the pilots in spite of the unreliability of the early Whittle engine. The second machine had a Power Jets W2B engine, and on 17 April, Grierson made the first British cross country jet flight when he flew to Hatfield with an escort of Spitfires. At Hatfield Mike Daunt was to demonstrate the aircraft before Winston Churchill

for whom a show of new prototypes had been arranged. He carefully considered the form of his demonstration, and decided that as the only facility the E28/39 offered was speed this must be the substance of the flight, and that it must not be achieved in a dive as was pointed out to the PM by one of the Gloster team.

A spectacular high speed run was made at low altitude along the rows of new aircraft; the VIPs were duly impressed, and Daunt was received by Churchill who congratulated him on his demonstration.

In June 1943 Sqn Ldr McClure began flying the second prototype. The engine had been cleared for G loads so that aerobatics and exposure to negative G were possible. A switch to achieve an engine re-light in the air and a negative G trap-tank designed to ensure continuity of fuel supply during aerobatics had been fitted. From a study of the drawings McClure commented that he thought that under negative G the scheme would work, but when it returned to positive G the engine would stop. He carried out his aerobatics successfully, climbed and pushed the control column forward to create negative G. As he suspected, the engine flamed out, the jet pipe temperature gauge quickly recording a drop. He pressed the re-light switch and the engine started instantly. At 5–6,000 ft he continued his aerobatics ending with a stall turn, finding, to his dismay, that he had fin stall and the rudder locked over to one side. To add to the confusion the engine flamed out as the aircraft slid sideways with the nose tending to tuck down.

Pushing hard upon the rudder pedal, Charles suddenly found that the rudder went full over to the other side, causing a 50 degree yaw; by this time the nose was well down and speed increasing rapidly. Suddenly the rudder responded and a pull-out was achieved at about 1,000 ft, albeit with no engine and with ailerons which had suddenly stiffened up. In conformity with Murphy's Law the re-light switch failed to start the engine; coming round into the circuit, the switch having been left on, the engine suddenly started. McClure landed, somewhat shaken after a distinctly hair-raising twenty minutes. The control problem was found to be due to the freezing of condensed moisture around the aileron push rods, locking them in the fairleads. The inadequate fin area was overcome by fitting small end plates on the extremities of the tailplane.

Sqn Ldr Davie returned from leave a day or so later, and decided that he would carry out further trials on the ailerons. He planned to climb to

35,000 ft, but on the way up a degree of backlash developed. At 37,000 ft, his ceiling, the column would only move about half its normal travel and a further movement locked it solidly half way to starboard. Suddenly the aeroplane went violently out of control, the pilot being hurled out through the canopy at 33,000 ft without oxygen mask or goggles, and with only one glove. He had the presence of mind to put his emergency oxygen tube in his mouth and landed, shaken and frostbitten, near Guildford. The trouble was believed to be due to the difference in contraction rates between duralumin and steel. In the intense cold at that altitude the wing had contracted faster and further than the steel pushrods and chains, so the chains came off the sprockets.

The test flight programme now depended upon the hard worked first prototype. Jet propulsion opened the way to increasing operational altitudes and the RAF doctors at the physiological laboratory at Farnborough, who were also pilots, joined the test team. Pilots were tested in the decompression chamber where high altitude conditions could be simulated on the ground to ensure that they were not prone to the dreaded 'bends', which are due to the inclusion of nitrogen bubbles in the bloodstream as the pressure on the body is reduced.

Flights over 35,000 ft were carried out by Michael Daunt and John Grierson with assistance from John Crosby Warren who, somehow, managed to squeeze his six feet eight inches into the tiny cockpit. There were many turbine failures and rotor disintegrations; vibration and resonance were potentially extremely serious in an assembly rotating at 17,000 rpm.

Nevertheless the work done on this tiny aeroplane by these teams of test pilots at Glosters and at RAE, paved the way to such superb achievements as the Comet, Hunter, VC10, Victor, Concorde and Tornado, to name but a few of the aircraft which reflect such credit upon the British aircraft industry. The first prototype E28/39 occupies a place of honour in London's Science Museum.

Whilst the E28/39 was under construction the Air Ministry issued specification F9/40 for a twin turbine fighter. W. G. Carter produced a design which showed considerable promise in wind tunnel tests and, in 1941, a contract was placed for the construction of twelve of the new machines to be powered by Rover WB Series 3 engines of 1,500 lb thrust each. In practice only six were built and they were powered by a variety of engines.

The de Havilland Engine Company was developing Frank Halford's H.1 turbine, which differed from the Whittle design in having a single sided impeller, the air entering only at the front. Whittle drew in air for his double sided impeller at front and rear of it via the nacelle shell.

A deal had been struck between the various Ministries, Rovers and Rolls-Royce, whereby Rolls took over the gas turbine project, to take advantage of their vast experience in aero engines whilst, in exchange, Rovers took over the tank engine which Rolls had designed, and which was better suited to Rover technology. There had been many delays in the development of the flight engines for the W9/40. Instead of the designed thrust of 1,800 lb they only gave 1,000 lb at 15,000 rpm, so it was considered too risky to attempt flight with them. The official engine limitations sheet for the initial trials carried out at Newmarket stated, under 'Altitude Restrictions', 'The engines must not leave the ground.' So they were used only for taxying trials which began on 10 July 1942.

Since the first flight of the E28/39, Frank Halford and his team had been busy on the development of the de Havilland H.1 engine. Although heavily involved in the serious problems of his Sabre engine, which was giving so much trouble in the Typhoon, and the new de Havilland constant speed propellers, for which he had recently accepted responsibility, Halford and his team overcame all the new problems regarding thermodynamics, metallurgy and production. A prototype of the H.1 engine was run on 13 April 1942, 248 days after the issue of the first drawings, a truly remarkable achievement.

On 5 May the air intake ducts were sucked flat, and on 2 June the engine ran at full speed for the first time, giving its designed thrust within two months of its first test. A twenty-five hour flight approval test was completed at the end of 200 hours test bed running on two prototypes.

The continuing delay in satisfactorily developing the Whittle engines for the Meteor led the Ministry of Aircraft Production to instruct that the first flights should be made with the de Havilland H.1 installation. Alterations were necessary to the nacelles to accommodate the single sided impeller design of the engine.

During engine runs at Bentham, Michael Daunt had an alarming experience which could have been fatal. He was sucked into a turbine intake during ground running. In his own words, 'I was the third thing to be sucked into it, the other two were a hat and a tea tray! We were able, on the E28/39, to go up close to the engine to inspect the banjo joints of the fuel system for leaks – paraffin was a difficult

*Michael Daunt about to fly the Gloster F9/40
Meteor prototype.*

fuel to seal in. I happened to be wearing a large
leather flying coat, and the flap blew up in the wind
whilst I was at the side of the intake. I was sucked
in head first. The dividing fairing between the top
and bottom of the intake received a slight dent
from the impact with my ribs which, presumably
being well protected with fat, did not crack. I
can assure you, it was very noisy! My immediate
reaction was "keep your mouth closed, Daunt,
because you don't want a collapsed lung!" Luckily
the chap in the cockpit was very quick and closed
the throttles whilst I held my breath. I was quickly
hauled out, but it was a major shock to the system!'

Thereafter steel guards were placed over the
intakes of turbines during ground running, known
as Daunt stoppers! Suitable warnings were issued
to all personnel involved with jet aircraft, but sadly,
such accidents still happen occasionally.

On 5 March Mike made the first flight. A letter
had been received from RAE Farnborough drawing
attention to the possibility of fore and aft instability
due to the effect of the jet streams upon the elevator,

so it was decided to use 8,000 rpm, giving less than
1,500 lb of thrust, for the first take-off. The first
unstick is a vital stage in the test programme. From
it the feel of the controls is assessed and the landing
speed, which, obviously, must be in excess of take-
off speed becomes clear. The take-off was impeccable but, as speed rose to 180 mph a violent
yawing occurred which caused the rudder bar to
oscillate with such force that the pilot could not
hold it, so an immediate landing was made. John
Grierson, in his book *Jet Flight*, refers to Mike's
report on this first flight, 'Quite a lot had happened
– a successful take-off had been made, an out of
balance nosewheel detected, seriously unpleasant
directional instability had been encountered and
experimented with in an effort to trace its origin,
a safe landing had been effected, and a fault had
been detected in the undercarriage shock absorption. All this information was obtained as the result
of a flight with a duration of just three and a half
minutes! This is real test flying, when the pilot
notes everything that is happening and is able to
render a story, not only coherent but constructive,
on landing.' In discussion of this particular flight
Daunt made the interesting observation, 'A test

pilot's job at that time was that of a diagnostician, later it changed into being a very, very intelligent monitor.' This reflected the changes which had occurred in the twenty-five years from the George Bulman/Gerry Sayer era with knee pads and no radio, to the modern concept of data gathered automatically within the aircraft, and transmitted back to a ground station for analysis.

It was realized that a suitable aerodrome near to Brockworth would be required for the main test programme of the Meteor. Six miles south of Gloucester was RAF Moreton Valence, which already had a runway which could be extended to 2,000 yards. The Ministry authorized Glosters to use it, and on completion of the runway extension, the flight test department moved there.

The yawing experienced with the prototype had been cured by the simple and time honoured expedient of taping a length of cord to each side of the trailing edge of the rudder. Single engine handling was checked by Daunt and found to be satisfactory, although the performance was inadequate. A further prototype, fitted with Metropolitan Vickers F2 axial flow turbines was delivered. Two Meteors, and the E28/39 fitted with the Whittle W2/500, enabled good progress to be made.

Two serious problems emerged, with the Meteor; engine surging and aileron instability. Surging would usually commence on the climb at 14,000 ft and the violent 'hiccupping' could result in structural failure in the engine. On one flight Daunt's port engine began to surge at 25,000 ft. He descended to 20,000 ft in a shallow dive at 320 mph; at this speed the ailerons became heavily overbalanced. Between 20,000 and 15,000 ft they were satisfactory again although speed had increased to 360 mph.

Many modifications were carried out in attempting to overcome this problem. Most of them were effective at either high or low altitude but not at both; directional instability also appeared again. At high speed in the dive aileron flutter was apparent. Internal mass balancing of the ailerons cured this.

An attempt was made to cure the directional problems by fitting a streamlined bullet shaped fairing around the tailplane/rudder intersection, a slight improvement resulting.

The Ministry of Aircraft Production, being responsible for all aircraft development in Britain, created a new secret department within the Engine Department called 'special projects'. Dr Roxbee Cox, now Lord Kings Norton, an eminent aeronautical engineer, was appointed its director whilst

H. J. 'Willie' Wilson, then a Wg Cdr, was called back from a flight test assignment in America, to be assistant director in charge of all jet flying which was to be concentrated within a new unit called 'T' Flight. This new unit evaluated the E28/39, early variants and engine combinations of the Meteor, the Bell Airacomet and the de Havilland Vampire. The Air Ministry was extremely perturbed by intelligence reports that the Germans were about to put the Messerschmitt Me 262 into service as a fighter and were putting great pressure upon MAP to speed up development of the Meteor, to ensure that Fighter Command had an adequate response to the new German machine.

From that time major effort was made to bring the Meteor up to full operational status. Turbine failures were numerous, from the silly, such as the Metro-Vick Beryl engined prototype at Farnborough, when a tea tray was sucked into one of the intakes, wrecking the engine, to the potentially and actually catastrophic. On one occasion Michael Daunt was just commencing his take-off run when the compressor disintegrated with a tremendous bang, the debris being fortunately ejected through the upper cowling. On another occasion an impeller disintegrated at 5,000 ft. The debris again emerged through the upper cowling. Damage to the nacelle and the tail resulted, and the aircraft became laterally unstable. Michael jettisoned his canopy and, as the aircraft slowed down, he decided that there was a chance of bringing it back safely with the limited control available. He managed to make a belly landing in a potato field. In his dry, humorous way he commented, 'This is how we tried out for the first time the Whittle-Daunt potato-lifter chipper cooker!' Both of these engine failures were caused by resonance problems.

A test pilot who entered the Meteor programme in 1944 was Peter Cadbury, better known, perhaps, as the founder of Tyne Tees and Westward Television. The son of the famous First World War fighter pilot, Sir Egbert Cadbury, DSC, DFC, who shot down two Zeppelins, one of which was the flagship L70, Peter learned to fly at the age of 15 and, through his membership of the Bristol Aero Club, knew John Grierson. After Gerry Sayer's death it was necessary to recruit another test pilot. By this time Cadbury was an experienced naval test pilot. He was released from the Navy and spent a period at Langley with Bill Humble and Philip Lucas to learn the Hawker test techniques.

Cadbury had his share of problems with the Typhoon, not least of which was the loss of throttle control as he came in to land. He had to control speed by switching the engine on and off, feasible in the Typhoon's illustrious ancestor, the Sopwith Camel, but distinctly dangerous in a 2,000 hp fighter. From the Langley base he joined the Meteor team. He recalled the day when Mike Daunt told him that he would fly the new jet. His only instruction was to be shown the throttle, flap and undercarriage levers and an injunction to watch the jet pipe temperatures. Mike then slammed the canopy shut and held up two fingers! Cadbury was delighted with the experience and landed safely, elated to think that he was now a member of the most exclusive club in aviation – the jet club!

One of his worst days was the one on which his close friend John Crosby-Warren was killed. Peter had flown a Meteor on stability and fuel consumption tests at low-level. He handed the aeroplane over to John in the afternoon and went home. An hour or so later the police phoned to ask him to go to Minchinhampton Common where 'there had been a nasty accident'. He arrived to find the Meteor spread over most of the golf course in tiny pieces. There was hardly enough wreckage intact to give much hope of finding the reason for the crash and the test pilots were naturally very anxious. The bits were taken to RAE at Farnborough who carried out their usual remarkable investigation. They told Glosters to look for an aileron tab, a small piece of metal a few inches wide. It was found in a wood, broken off, making the aeroplane laterally uncontrollable. It had turned on its back and dived in.

In the Metro-Vick F2 engined Meteor RAE lost one of their most able young test pilots, Sqn Ldr Douglas Davie, on 4 June 1944. High speed runs were required at 5,000 ft and 20,000 ft. Davie was to carry out the 5,000 ft run in the morning with his superior doing the high level one in the afternoon. Davie returned after a particularly successful flight. Reporting to Willie Wilson, who had a bad cold, he said, 'A piece of cake, Sir, you have a lousy cold, would you like me to do the high level one as well?' Wilson gratefully accepted the offer.

At full speed one of the F2s disintegrated. Davie managed to escape from the aircraft, but died of his injuries.

Compressibility problems did not arise with the Meteor until Michael Daunt began diving trials. He was acutely aware of the good advice George Bulman had given in his 1943 paper on compressibility and was pleased when George came to discuss the phenomenon with him.

Aileron control was the first to be affected and, after a particularly alarming experience, when rivets were popping out all over the aeroplane as he pulled out, Mike exercised his wit and sent a memo to George Carter, the chief designer:

> Sing a song of shock stall
> words by Ernst Mach,
> four and twenty slide rules
> are shuffling in the dark.
> Be gone, oh doubting fancies
> our George will fill the bill,
> but George, please make the Meteor
> a wee bit meatier still!

The diving trials established beyond doubt that the Meteor, in its configuration at that time, had a limiting Mach number of 0.76 to 0.77.

Another poetic, if slightly macabre, masterpiece, dating from the days of test flying the Typhoon, was prompted by the proximity of a wood to the end of the runway. Daunt had made repeated requests to MAP through McKenna, the general manager, for some of the trees to be cut down to provide a landing path in the event of engine failure on take-off. In despair at the inaction of the Ministry he wrote:

> I wish to God that I could see a gap
> where now doth stand a tree,
> a tree that now is bearing nuts
> may, one day, bear some pilot's guts.
> Please Mac don't wait for MAP,
> just give us space and not a tree!

Another of Mike's artistic talents lay in playing jazz on a trumpet. He described the end of this hobby: 'As you get older you blow in sweet and it comes out rotten! A friend of mine wanted my trumpet, which was a good one, and gave me a Kenwood mixer, so my trumpet is now making excellent bread!'

Michael Daunt retired from test flying in 1944 and embarked upon a new career in farming. He quotes his colleagues' valedictory comments, 'Oh yes, Mike – he's now spreading it as well as talking it!'

So this entertaining and modest man left the industry he served so well. With Gerry Sayer and the Gloster team he made a major contribution in the realm of high speed flight. He was once described as a fussily accurate test pilot – surely high praise in a very exacting profession. For his services to aviation he was awarded the OBE.

The new chief test pilot was Eric Greenwood, who had joined the Hawker Siddeley Group in

1936 and was assistant to Charles Turner-Hughes from 1937 to 1941, when he became chief test pilot to Air Service Training at Hamble.

Wg Cdr Willie Wilson was instructed, in 1944, to concentrate upon the immediate introduction of the Meteor into squadron service. It became the only Allied jet aircraft to see operational service, and one was sent to the USA in exchange for a Bell P-59 Airacomet, America's first jet aircraft, which was flown at Moreton Valence in September 1943. Not until 12 July 1944 were the first two Meteor Mk 1s delivered to No 616 Sqn at Culmhead. At the end of the month the squadron moved to Manston where the first sortie against the V1 flying bombs was made by F/O Dean. He spotted the 'buzz bomb' heading for London and dived at 450 mph to intercept. The guns jammed, so this resourceful officer, realizing that he was, for a brief period, over open country, pulled alongside and gently placed his wing tip under the wing of the V1. The aerodynamic interaction caused the bomb to go into a spin, and it exploded in a wood near Tonbridge.

Space precludes a detailed account of the development of this historic design, but one of the highlights was the development of reheat. The acceleration of the Meteor was greatly inferior to contemporary piston engined fighters and it was thought that the injection of neat fuel into the jet pipe would substantially increase the thrust of the engines.

Trent Meteor prototype.

To test the validity of the idea the starboard engine of one of the prototypes was fitted with a crude afterburner. In 11½ hours of flying there were several weld failures in the jet pipe, due, it was thought, to a resonant vibration when reheat was selected. This was overcome but performance was still suspect. A gain in speed of 46 mph was achieved, and rate of climb increased by as much as 40 per cent, but the 46 mph was lost in normal flight without reheat due to the increased drag at the rear end of the jet pipe. Problems of surging and flame-out were also experienced.

An interesting variant of the Meteor was the world's first prop-jet aeroplane: a standard machine was fitted with Rolls-Royce Derwent II engines, driving five-bladed Rotol propellers. The engines, named Trent, each developed 750 shp with 1,000 lb of residual thrust from the tail pipe.

Eric Greenwood flew it for the first time on 20 September 1945. He experienced serious directional instability due to the increased lateral area and torque of the propellers. Two fins were added to the tailplane. Instability remained a problem so the propeller diameter was decreased from 7 ft 11 in to 4 ft 10½ in to absorb only 350 hp, the residual thrust increasing to 1,400 lb. A total of 47 hours flying was achieved before the Trent experiments terminated. A number of well known test pilots flew it to gain experience of prop-jets, which were considered to have a bright future for medium range subsonic aircraft. The potential economy of the straight jet turbine was not appreciated at that time. Neville Duke and Frank Bullen of Hawkers

flew it, Bill Else and Eric Franklin of Armstrong Whitworth, Dick Martin and J. S. Fifield of Glosters, Geoffrey Tyson of Saunders-Roe, whilst Farnborough pilots Sqn Ldr Johnnie Kent and Wg Cdr A. McDowell, one time CO of No 616 Sqn, also put it through its paces.

A major triumph for the Meteor which confirmed the pre-eminent position of the British aircraft industry was the establishment of a new world air speed record in 1945. It will be recalled that the ill-fated Heston Nuffield Hagg racer and the Speed Spitfire, N.17, had been destined to attack the record set up in 1939 by Fritz Wendel in a Messerschmitt 209 with a speed of 469.22 mph. Britain held the world land and water speed records so the development of the Meteor stimulated an ambition to achieve the hat-trick using this new and promising aircraft which, however, had proved to have aerodynamic limitations.

At the end of 1944 the aerodynamics section at RAE had carried out wind tunnel experiments in an attempt to increase the limiting Mach number of the Meteor, and it was found that lengthened nacelles would probably achieve a considerable improvement. A standard Meteor I was modified by, initially, extending the front of the nacelle. This was flown in November 1944, with encouraging results, so the rear ends were also extended, whilst the opportunity was taken to fit more powerful W2/700 engines of 2,000 lb thrust. This power was insufficient to achieve a high Mach number in level flight, so all the research work was done in dives, a dangerous business carried out partly by RAE pilots, but mainly by Flt Lt Philip Stanbury, a 27-year-old veteran of the Battle of Britain who had been posted to Glosters, presumably for a 'rest', to carry out work being done by that fine test pilot John Crosby-Warren until his untimely death.

Stanbury found the handling of the aircraft to be excellent at a Mach number as high as 0.84, although the nose began to pitch up as speed rose towards this figure. Normally the nose was expected to drop so this was a bonus as the speed record attempt, if it were made, would take place under *Federation Aéronautique Internationale* rules which called for a maximum height of 246 ft, a very hazardous operation requiring extremely accurate flying. The nose-up pitch was thought to be excessive so the tailplane incidence was increased by one degree. This appeared to be satisfactory.

Philip Stanbury had a very alarming experience in another Meteor which had been fitted with a pressure cabin. At 40,000 ft a windscreen panel blew out and the stabilized cockpit condition of 24,000 ft instantly changed to one of 40,000 ft. He began to pass out and instinctively closed the throttles. Starting to recover consciousness at 28,000 ft, he discovered that the aircraft, which had a smaller rudder than usual, was in a violent and very uneven spin with his head being jerked from side to side by the motion. He was badly disorientated, and the small rudder was totally inadequate for spin recovery. Only by bursts of power on the inner engine was he able to pull out to find himself at 3,000 ft feeling extremely ill. He decided to delay an attempt to land until he felt better. When, eventually, he brought the aircraft in, he felt as if he was landing on a runway which was rocking from side to side. He dropped the machine from twenty feet, but fortunately the sturdy undercarriage withstood the shock. After this horrifying experience Stanbury spent several months in hospital whilst John Grierson took over the trials of the high speed Meteor. Stanbury never fully recovered from his ordeal.

Grierson was diving at high Mach number when the machine began to pitch violently fore and aft, building up to an unpleasant 3.6G in the cockpit. This was attributed to an excessive alteration to the tailplane incidence so the alteration was decreased from minus 1 degree to minus ½ degree. This appeared to solve the problem.

Later Stanbury returned to the programme and experienced fore and aft instability and rudder buffeting at high speed. Taping cords to the trailing edges of rudder and elevators was the final solution and he was the first pilot to achieve 600 mph in level flight when, on 19 October 1944, he flew the high speed Meteor at 610 mph. Before this speed could be achieved various airframe modifications were carried out to enable it to withstand the enormous stresses caused by gusts at low-level.

Group Captain H. J. Wilson, who had taken over as Commandant of the Empire Test Pilots School on the death of Group Captain J. F. X. McKenna in a flying accident in 1945, formed a new RAF High Speed Flight, the first since the 1931 Schneider Trophy race, to make the record attempt over a course off the Kent coast between Manston, its base, and the Isle of Sheppey. The two aircraft prepared for the attempt were standard fighters with various modifications, including lengthened nacelles to delay the onset of compressibility problems, the strengthening of wing spars and alterations to control gearing.

Willie Wilson was to fly one aircraft painted in a high gloss camouflage finish and named *Britannia*, whilst Sqn Ldr Eric Greenwood, the Gloster chief test pilot, was to fly the other one which was finished in yellow.

Bad weather delayed the flights. The press at Manston became restive and in the absence of other news, concentrated upon the suspension of the Group Captain's trousers, focussing upon his red braces visible during the press briefing! He was irritated by their attitude, feeling that the technical aspect was largely ignored and that the tabloid press was not interested in the scientific value of the project but only keen to have something spectacular, if not catastrophic, to write about.

However, on 7 November 1945, both pilots flew the course in dull weather, the Group Captain setting a new record of 606.262 mph. He was awarded the Britannia Trophy for the outstanding contribution to aviation in 1946, given an OBE and, in the same year, was awarded a permanent commission in the RAF.

On 7 September 1946 Group Captain E. M. Donaldson and Sqn Ldr W. A. Waterton, who joined Glosters as chief test pilot in October, set up a new record of 616 mph in the Meteor flown by the Group Captain.

In 1945 the legendary Jan Zurakowski had joined Glosters. He managed to escape from Poland on the outbreak of war and joined the RAF. In the Polish tradition, he was a relentless and successful fighter pilot with many victories to his credit. He was selected for No 2 Course at ETPS in 1944 and, in 1945 began a very brief period at A&AEE, from where Eric Greenwood persuaded him to move.

Fred Sanders, who was head of the Gloster flight test department, recalls his superb character and his great strength in spite of his slight build. He was a very competent engineer. Jim Heyworth, the Rolls-Royce chief test pilot, was in Zura's office at Hucclecote when the subject of aerobatics and display flying arose. Zura said that he had discovered a new aerobatic manoeuvre and demonstrated the theory of it on paper – he had worked the whole procedure out mathematically and proceeded to blind Jim with complex formulae which lost him completely. Zura was convinced that this spectacular 'cartwheel', as he called it, would be a show-stopper at air displays, but he would require more power before it was feasible. Rolls-Royce gave him more thrust and the result delighted audiences for several years afterwards. He would dive at high speed, climb vertically and, as the Meteor lost speed towards the top of the climb, would close the throttle on one side and open it full on the other: the aeroplane would then rotate sideways like a catherine wheel. Jim considered him to be a quite outstanding pilot and a rare one at that time with such a deep knowledge of science and engineering. He made a substantial contribution to the success of the Meteor and Javelin, leaving, in 1951, to join Avro Canada where he was responsible, as chief test pilot, for the flight trials of the CF-100 fighter.

The Meteor was converted for carrier borne operations with an 'A' frame arrestor hook and strengthened undercarriage. Two F.3s were converted and simulated carrier landing trials carried out at Boscombe Down. On 8 June 1948 Lt Cdr Eric 'Winkle' Brown carried out the first ever landing of a British twin-jet aeroplane upon a carrier when he commenced trials aboard HMS *Implacable*. The RN liked the Meteor which proved to be a tractable machine for shipboard operation, but it did not go into naval service on a carrier as it was not specifically designed for that environment.

When in 1944 the provision of assisted pilot ejection was becoming vitally important, a primi-

Bernard Lynch on the first test tower ready for firing.

Sqn Ldr J. S. Fifield carrying out the world's first live runway-level ejection test, 3 September 1955.

tive swinging arm design was under consideration for the contemporary piston engine fighters. The arm was hinged forward of the fin and lay flush with the top of the fuselage, the forward end being hooked to the pilot's harness. A powerful spring was to be used to lift the pilot out, the aerodynamic forces on the rising beam then lifting him well away from the tail. This was quite unsuitable for the Meteor.

The Martin Baker ejection seat was developed and tested for the first time at Wittering on 11 May 1945 in a Defiant flown by Bryan Greensted, Rotol's chief test pilot. A dummy was used for the first seven tests, the other six being flown at Beaulieu. After a series of trials in which Bernard Lynch, a Martin Baker experimental fitter, courageously volunteered to 'ride' the static test rig, a seat was fitted into a Meteor III and after a number of dummy tests Lynch was ejected at 320 mph from an altitude of 8,000 ft on 24 July 1946. His memorable contribution to the development of the

'bang' seat was recognized in 1948 by the award of the BEM.

A further interesting development of the Meteor was the prone pilot conversion. In an attempt to permit the pilot to accept a higher G level in manoeuvring, a Meteor 8 was converted to have a prone pilot's position in the extended forward fuselage, the standard cockpit remaining for a check pilot. The forward pilot lay on a foam rubber couch with re-arranged flying controls. The proximity of the pilot's nose to the runway was disconcerting and visibility was poor. Trials of the aircraft ceased when the Bristol rocket powered interceptor fighter project, envisaged for a prone pilot, was cancelled. One of the pilots who flew it was Bill Else, of Armstrong Whitworth. To the question, 'What was it like?' he answered derisively, 'There is only one thing a pilot can do in that position and it has nothing to do with flying!'

The Meteor survived in service for a quarter of the century. In 1947 Sqn Ldr D. V. 'Digger' Cotes-Preedy, a Gloster test pilot, completed the first of a series of overseas demonstration flights. The type was purchased by a number of foreign governments, including Argentine, Australia,

Prone-pilot Meteor.

Belgium, Brazil, Canada, Denmark, Ecuador, Egypt, France, the Netherlands (where it was built under licence by Fokker), Sweden, Syria and Israel. Its success was a tribute to those who developed it.

The Meteor was outclassed by its contemporary, the Messerschmitt Me 262 which it never met in battle, but it gave many RAF pilots their first taste of jet flying, albeit in an aeroplane which had to be treated with respect; an engine cut on take-off could be dangerous in the early low-powered aircraft. The 'Meatbox', however, was well liked by its pilots and this early fighter gave good service.

In 1982 Peter Cadbury sponsored a dinner to mark the 40th anniversary of the first flight of the Meteor. Nostalgically, he told the author, 'Everyone concerned is now very old but it was 40 years ago and the only survivors of the flight test team are Mike Daunt and myself.' Group Captain Wilson, and others who were involved, came to the function, which was honoured by the presence of Prince Charles. Sir Frank Whittle was flown over by British Airways, appropriately in Concorde.

Other test pilots whose contribution to the Meteor programme should be recorded are Rodney Dryland who was killed when a PR version broke up in the air, Dave Dredge and a pilot named Moss, both of whom were killed in structural failure accidents, Jim Cooksey, Johnnie Towell and Mike Kilburn.

The third very important aeroplane in the saga of British jet aircraft development was the de Havilland D.H.100 Vampire.

After the successful flight of the E28/39, the D.H. Company's natural reaction was to follow the remarkably successful Mosquito with a jet propelled unarmed bomber, but this was not acceptable to the Ministry of Aircraft Production, as the major need appeared to be for a high speed interceptor fighter. Geoffrey de Havilland, Charles Walker, the

technical director, R. E. Bishop, chief designer, and R. M. Clarkson, the chief aerodynamicist, designed a twin tail boom single Halford H.1 engined fighter originally to be known by the unfortunate name of 'Spider Crab'.

On 4 April 1942 – the day after the H.1 engine had been run for the first time – an order was placed for three prototype D.H.100s. Sixteen months later, on 19 September 1943, Geoffrey de Havilland junior made the first taxying runs at Hatfield, then flew it on the following day.

The engine had already been flying for seven months in the Meteor so this was a useful safeguard in the case of a single engine prototype. There was also plenty of room at Hatfield with the advantage that all the back-up facilities for engine and airframe were at the flight test base. Geoffrey de Havilland and his assistant, Geoffrey Pike, were responsible for the test programme. Similar problems to those of the Meteor were experienced with the Vampire snaking at high speed. At first one side of a rudder was modified to give a directional bias, but this was ineffective. Clarkson suspected that the area of the fins and rudders were too great and suggested an ingenious experiment to prove his theory without modification to the tail. He fixed a fin to the front fuselage so that the relative effect of the tail surfaces was reduced. No snaking was experienced, and modifications to the rudder and elevators were carried out with complete success. The ailerons were too sensitive; they had convex surfaces which were changed to flat faced ones which improved the control at low-level but, as with the Meteor, it was not satisfactory at altitude. The trailing edges of the ailerons were subsequently thickened to give a totally satisfactory result. The Vampire's performance was well above predictions due, largely, to the elimination of propeller slipstream. By the spring of 1944 it was flying at speeds in excess of 500 mph.

Geoffrey de Havilland had an embarrassing experience when he flew the prototype to West Raynham to demonstrate it to a group of senior officers. After a spectacular demonstration he landed and taxied to his parking place. As he came to a halt the Vampire subsided gracefully upon its belly; Geoffrey, livid with rage at his stupidity, stepped out of the cockpit cursing the designers who had fitted the undercarriage lever next to the flap lever! He became rather unpopular when he insisted that the aeroplane must not be moved until a party from Hatfield arrived to carry out the work.

Geoffrey Pike had joined de Havilland as an apprentice in 1934 and learned to fly two years

De Havilland Vampire prototype before first flight. In the background, Geoffrey de Havilland Jnr (left) and Major Frank Halford (right).

later in the RAFVR. By 1943 he had become involved in the Mosquito programme and by the end of the war he had flown 500 of them. Pike had a remarkable escape in the prototype Vampire when the turbine flamed out on take-off. The machine was wrecked, the whole of the nose section right back to the pilot's seat being torn apart, but he was only slightly injured.

On 3 December 1945, Lt Cdr Eric 'Winkle' Brown, the naval chief test pilot, landed the third prototype, fitted with an arrestor hook, on the deck of HMS *Ocean*, the first time that a jet aircraft had landed on a carrier. The trials, which were carried out over two days, were completely successful and the Sea Vampire went into limited production for the Fleet Air Arm.

The Vampire just missed active service in the war, but equipped front line fighter squadrons until the mid 1950s. It was armed with four 20 mm cannon and could carry 2,000 lb of bombs or rockets under the wings. After front line service the type was widely used for training.

From the Vampire came the Venom. Its thin wing had moderate sweepback to take advantage of the performance improvement which could be achieved by replacing the de Havilland Goblin 35

of 3,500 lb thrust with the de Havilland Ghost 103 developing 4,850 lb.

The Venom remained in service until it was replaced by the Hawker Hunter in 1962, the Hunter having first flown in 1951.

So Britain's great teams of designers, engineers and test pilots at Glosters, Farnborough, Power Jets, Boscombe Down, Rolls-Royce and de Havillands saw, in the Meteor and the Vampire, together with their derivatives, the fulfilment of their dream of high speed flight. From 15 May 1941, when Gerry Sayer flew the E28/39 for the first time, to 7 November 1945, when Group Captain Wilson established the new world speed record of 606 mph, a mere four and a half years had elapsed – an incredible performance by any standards. It was an achievement accompanied by fearful risks for the test pilots. Indeed it is probable that the risks were not fully appreciated until the tragic accidents of the 1950s and '60s revealed the price to be paid to enter the new era of transonic and supersonic flight, an era in which Britain held a commanding lead until it was frittered away by the utter lack of comprehension and enterprise by successive Governments, but that is another story.

11

'LEARN TO TEST, TEST TO LEARN'

A watershed in Britain's aviation history was the winning outright, in 1931, of the Schneider Trophy by the RAF High Speed Flight. Flt Lt John Boothman flew to victory in the Supermarine S.6B seaplane, designed by R. J. Mitchell, at a speed of 340.08 mph. Powered by the Rolls-Royce 'R' engine, finally boosted to 2,550 hp, it was the progenitor of the Spitfire in all its 47 variants and created such a quantum leap in engine and airframe design that Britain was able to progress in military aircraft development to a stage which, without the stimulus of the Schneider contest, may well have taken a further seven years to achieve. From the experience gained on the 'R' engine the Merlin and the Griffon emerged.

In command of the 1931 High Speed Flight was Wg Cdr D'Arcy Grieg who had himself achieved third place in the 1929 contest. His distinguished Service career led him later to command the A&AEE, which moved from Martlesham Heath, Suffolk, to Boscombe Down at the beginning of the Second World War, when the rate of technical progress in the British aircraft industry, plus acquisition of American aircraft unsuited to the vagaries of European theatre combat, led to serious problems. There were simply insufficient test pilots to carry out the development flying necessary to improve their operational performance.

An expedient was devised by posting squadron pilots 'resting from operations' to the experimental establishments and aircraft manufacturers to assist the hard pressed resident pilots. This introduced its own problems, as pilots experienced on one type of fighter or bomber, naturally tended to use this as the yardstick of their judgement upon the type being tested. So a dispassionate view was almost impossible to achieve in the relatively short time before they returned to ops or other duties. Indeed, up to a year of intensive experience and practice was often required before a Service pilot was able to make his full contribution to the test programme. American test pilots who had passed US machines before their delivery to UK, under the initial direct purchase and later Lease-Lend arrangements, had little experience of the criteria directed to their aircraft at our experimental establishments, so much valuable time was wasted.

At the end of 1942 it became clear that some action must be taken to overcome these problems. Although, at that time, there was an element of doubt over the feasibility of satisfactorily training a test pilot, Air Commodore D'Arcy Grieg as Commandant of A&AEE, was instructed to establish a test pilots school under his overall command at Boscombe Down.

In command of 'A' Flight, Performance Testing, was Sqn Ldr S. 'Sammy' Wroath, a widely experienced and extremely able test pilot, who had joined the RAF in 1925 as a Halton apprentice, and became one of the first NCO pilots to be selected for test flying at Martlesham Heath. He was summoned to the Commandant's office, informed of the new school and a proposal was made that he should command it. Whilst he was strongly in favour of the scheme, he was very happy in 'A Per T', as his flight was known, and was most reluctant to leave it. He recalled saying to the Air Commodore, 'If you want me to volunteer, Sir, I won't. If you order me to do it, I will!' So he was ordered to do it. A promotion to Wg Cdr followed.

One of the senior civilian technical officers at Boscombe Down, G. MacLaren Humphreys, was appointed chief ground instructor and together they sat down to prepare a syllabus. The terms of reference were that the training should be of a standard to ensure that the student pilots were effective as soon as the course was completed, and that standardization of methods and continuity of ideas would be achieved. Number One Course started in April 1943 and took six months to complete, proving beyond doubt that the formula was sound. A report was prepared by Wg Cdr Wroath on the progress of this pioneer course, with proposals for a second one. This was submitted to

Above *ETPS No 1 Course, 1943, at the Bristol Aeroplane Company. Left to right: back row, Flt Lt K. J. Sewell, Wg Cdr G. V. Fryer, E. A. Swiss (test pilot, Bristols), Sqn Ldr M. W. Hartford, Sqn Ldr D. W. Weightman; middle row, I. Llewellyn Owen (Bristols), Sqn Ldr A. K. Cook, Sqn Ldr J. C. Nelson, Flt Lt R. V. Muspratt (Eagle Sqn), Flt Lt J. C. S. Turner; front row, Lt G. P. L. Shea-Simmonds RNVR, Wg Cdr P. H. A. Simmons, Wg Cdr S. Wroath (Commandant), A. J. Pegg (test pilot, Bristols), Lt Cdr G. R. Callingham RN, G. MacLaren Humphreys (CTI), Sqn Ldr H. G. Hazelden. Absent Wg Cdr P. F. Webster.*
Right *Group Captain J. F. X. 'Sam' McKenna.*

Air Marshal Sir Ralph Sorley, then Controller of Aircraft at the Ministry of Supply. Sir Stafford Cripps, the Minister, wrote on the report, 'A good idea, go ahead.'

In 1944 'Sammy' Wroath was posted to USA as chief test pilot of the British Joint Services Mission (BJSM) and Group Captain J. F. X. 'Sam' McKenna, who returned from the BJSM at Washington was appointed Commandant of what became known as the Empire Test Pilots School. A few months later they suffered a serious loss when the Mustang IV being flown by McKenna experienced a major wing failure, which resulted in his death. His memory is perpetuated by the coveted McKenna Trophy, presented annually to the outstanding pupil on each course.

Space at Boscombe Down was becoming a serious problem as the volume and tempo of development flying increased. In October 1945, the school was moved to RAF Cranfield. On 25 February 1946, *The Times*, under the heading 'University of Flying' reported upon the school, at that time under the command of Group Captain H. J. 'Willie' Wilson. *The Times* quoted as the school's objective, 'The provision of the most highly qualified test pilots in the world, men who are not only superb flyers but are capable of analysing scientifically the performance and construction of the aircraft they handle. To this university of flying are sent the most skilful pilots in the RAF, the Fleet Air Arm and the air forces of the Commonwealth and NATO countries. Test pilots employed by British aircraft firms also take the course which includes about thirty-five pilots, 11 from the RAF, 7 from the FAA, 4 for civilian test pilots and the remaining 6 for others. To date some 57 "super" test pilots, as they may well be described, have graduated.'

In 1947 ETPS moved from Cranfield to Farnborough and began its long and mutually profitable association with the RAE. In 1949 the school received its armorial bearings at (with the legend

Presentation of Armorial Bearings of ETPS at the 1950 McKenna dinner. Left to right: Marshal of the RAF Lord Tedder, Lt Cdr (later Admiral) Joe Smith, Group Captain Leonard S. Snaith (Commandant), Air Marshal Sir Alec Coryton, Sqn Ldr Jim Rowlands.

'Learn to Test, Test to Learn') a presentation in London's Horse Guards Parade, being addressed by Marshal of the Royal Air Force Lord Tedder.

With increasing urban development and the need for longer runways for high performance aeroplanes, a move from Farnborough became necessary, particularly as London Airport Control Zone was spreading over a much larger area with airways to North and South restricting airspace for flying exercises. So, on 29 January 1968, ETPS took up residence again at Boscombe Down, with its long runways in open country, its closer proximity to the Channel supersonic corridors, and the major advantage that it was the home of the A&AEE, one which it shares with the test pilots schools in USA and France, both of which have comprehensive technical support of similar character. As most British test pilots graduating from ETPS carry out their mandatory three year test flying tour at A&AEE the interchange of experience and cross-fertilization of ideas is of value to both.

On 11 June 1983 the ETPS celebrated its 40th anniversary by acting as host to a large number of graduates and guests at an 'open day' and flying display at Boscombe Down. The substance of that *Times* report, which also described training techniques at the ETPS, varies little from a similar report which could be written today. This says much for the wisdom and foresight of those distinguished officers and technicians who were responsible for the original and progressive planning of the syllabus, which has changed in content with the pattern of air warfare, moving towards the weapon system concept with its almost total reliance upon avionics.

The development of the helicopter in the civil and military spheres has now conferred upon it an equal significance with the fixed-wing aeroplane. In 1963 a rotary wing course was added to the syllabus and, by 1974, the increasing complexity of modern weapon systems, and the flight trials necessary for their proper testing, made it necessary to set up a course to train selected civilian scientific officers as flight test engineers.

The number of aircraft operated by the school, and the number of students taking the courses, has reduced with the number of new aircraft being built. During its life the ETPS has operated 11 different helicopter types, 6 different gliders and 53 different types of fixed wing aircraft, ranging in size from the Auster to the Hercules and, in speed, from the Twin Pioneer to the Lightning. By its 40th anniversary some 930 pilots and test engineers had graduated, 374 of them from overseas.

The 1983 course had a complement of eighteen students with eighteen members of staff, a ratio which emphasizes the high degree of knowledge and skill required to evaluate a modern military aeroplane, such as the Tornado, which has the capability of terrain hugging flight below the radar screen at Mach 1. This aeroplane could only be evaluated by a test pilot with high skills in the application of solid state electronics to communications, data gathering, navigation and aircraft control as well as superior flying ability.

As may be expected, the senior officers at Boscombe Down are some of the most highly qualified airmen in the RAF. On the occasion of the author's visit to ETPS during the 40th anniversary year the Commandant of the A&AEE was Air Commodore R. J. Spiers OBE, FRAeS, who was a Cranwell cadet in 1947. Commissioned in 1949, he flew Vampires and Meteors with No 247 Sqn at Odiham, then commanded 'B' Flight in No 64 Sqn at Duxford. He graduated from No 14 ETPS course at Farnborough, and was a test pilot at A&AEE from 1955 to 1959.

Having commanded No 4 Sqn in Germany, after various staff and flying postings, he became Commandant at Boscombe Down in 1979.

Second in command, as Superintendent of Flying, was Group Captain David Bywater MRAeS, MBIM. Graduating at Cranwell in 1958, he spent three years as a co-pilot on the new Victor bomber before becoming the youngest captain on the type at the age of 24. He graduated at ETPS in 1964 and won the Patuxent Shield as the runner-up to the best student.

Most of his flying tours have been at Farnborough or Boscombe Down. The Group Captain rated his job as one of the most interesting in the RAF, covering a large spectrum of technical interest in a quite different context fron normal Service life where the rules are quite specific. At A&AEE the rules are constantly changing as technology advances, with few guidelines to follow. He emphasized that the job of the test pilot at A&AEE is a projection of the establishment's scientific function, and the service to the scientists is provided in the closest rapport with them. ETPS must, therefore, produce the right sort of pilot for this environment.

The CO of ETPS was Wg Cdr Robin Hargreaves, BSc(Eng) MRAeS, a very experienced fighter pilot with 4,000 hours on thirty different types in his log book. Having a good command of French he welcomed an invitation to take the test pilot course at the French School at Istres. He graduated in 1966, and spent three years at A&AEE in 'A'

Above *Group Captain David Bywater (1984).*
Below *Wg Cdr Robin Hargreaves (1984).*

Squadron, initially testing the Hunter, but moving to the Jaguar programme in 1968. He was the first RAF pilot to fly it.

After service with No 74 Sqn at Singapore, and a three year staff posting in London, he spent two years as a tutor at ETPS, an essential prerequisite for command.

The flying tutors must be graduates of the British, American or French schools, have current ratings on eight types of aircraft and must have completed a three year test flying tour at Boscombe Down, Farnborough or Bedford – this tour is obligatory for all graduates of the school. The tutors will be specialists in systems and control, avionics or aircraft operation. The intangibles are more difficult to identify. The ability to be articulate and teach is clearly essential and personal judgements at the selection stage are made by the CO, the Superintendent of Flying, and the Commandant. This procedure ensures that ETPS tutors are the finest that can be found anywhere in the RAF, and it is axiomatic that training is of a similar order.

Sqn Ldr M. C. 'Mike' Brooke MRAeS, the principal tutor, fixed wing, trained on Jet Provosts and Vampires and, in 1983, had flown 5,000 hours on 22 different types. He graduated as a qualified flying instructor (QFI) at Central Flying School. On completion of his ETPS course in 1975 he spent three years at Experimental Flying Squadron, Farnborough, concerned, mainly, with weapon aiming, weapon delivery and associated trials. From 1978 to January 1981, when he joined the staff at ETPS, he commanded the Radar Research Squadron at RAE Bedford.

Mike Brooke commented that the wide variety of background experience in the tutorial staff is a major advantage of ETPS, which would inhibit any form of standardized instruction, even if this appeared to be desirable.

Sqn Ldr Dave Reid, the principal rotary wing tutor, is a dedicated helicopter man who believes that the independence of the rotary wing pilot, who is capable of making his own decisions operating solo away from a command structure, gives a higher level of personal involvement with soldiers on the ground, and a satisfaction unknown to the high speed jet pilot who is, necessarily, remote from the participants in the action. Sqn Ldr Reid has 4,000 hours on 25 different types of rotary wing aircraft and is qualified as first pilot on thirteen of them.

The all-important ground school is also staffed by highly qualified officers. On the occasion of the author's visit, Sqn Ldr A. W. Debuse BSc, MSc, CEng, MIMechE, MRAeS, taught performance and control on the rotary wing course, whilst Sqn Ldr A. A. Mattick BSc, MSc was his opposite number on the fixed wing course. They also teach other subjects, such as aerodynamics. Sqn Ldr M. J. Grange AE, the aerosystems specialist, is a graduate of the aero systems course at the RAF College at Manby and has wide experience in the testing and development of avionic systems.

The technical services department maintain the aircraft, giving that special quality of service born of pride in being a member of a superior and happy unit. This quality of pride in the job is very obvious in ETPS and indeed, throughout the Establishment, leadership is clearly seen to be of the highest possible order. Personnel are an élite group as their function demands, and they are well aware of it, although never obtrusively. The air of quiet efficiency at all levels is most marked and extremely impressive.

Forty years of growth have seen changes, but certain factors have remained constant. The objective of providing training appropriate to the current state of aeronautical and air warfare development, the keenness of the students and the exceptional qualifications of the tutorial staff are crucial elements in its success.

Students are chosen with a view to their future employment on fighter type, heavy or rotary wing aircraft. Applicants for a place are required to show a wide general knowledge of, and interest in, aviation generally, and in future trends. They must have a sound knowledge of their current or recent operational role and a full understanding of the characteristics of aircraft flown by them. In this sense the type of student has changed from one with many hours on different types, to pilots with flying time on, perhaps, only one machine. This is the result of the high cost of flying training which results in a man leaving his flying training school to join a squadron, flying a particular type, and remaining with that aircraft throughout its Service life.

A candidate must have capacity for technical understanding at a very advanced level and the ability to express himself clearly both orally and in writing. Enthusiasm and aptitude for test flying is obviously essential, and he must have a pilot rating of 'exceptional' or 'above average' in fixed or rotary wing flying. A recent operational tour, a high level of mathematical ability, and a further four years in the RAF from the commencement of the next course, ensure consideration for a place; provided that he is in current flying practice, holds, or has held recently, an instrument rating and has flown a minimum of 750 hours as pilot in command. The normal age limit for pilots is 32, and a full flying medical category is required.

British candidates apply to the MoD by May of each year for admission to the course commencing in February of the following year. Overseas students are recommended by their own Government. In July a selection board sits at ETPS. Written exams in mathematics and flying subjects are followed by informal interviews with an interview board. Standards are high, and there is emphasis upon personal qualities, flying ability and motivation.

With so few places available, competition is intense and only the finest candidates achieve the place, which will be followed, in the case of successful RAF officers, by a three year tour at one of the British flight test centres.

Having passed and received their graduation certificates, all RAF, RN and Army Air Corps pilots are entitled to use the symbol 'tp' which will appear after their names in the appropriate Service list.

Student exchanges between ETPS and the US Navy test pilot school at Patuxent River in Maryland, the US Air Force test pilot school at Edwards Air Force Base in California, and *L'Ecole du Personnel Navigant d'Essais et de Reception* at Istres in France are a common feature. In addition there are regular visits of staff and students from ETPS to the American Schools, EPNER, *Pratica di Mare*, the Italian flight test centre at Rome, and *Erprobungstelle 61*, the German flight test centre at Manching. Staffs and students of the two American schools make 'field trips' abroad and always include a liaison visit to ETPS, which has had a substantial influence on the American, and indeed, all other Western world schools and test centres. The first American student to win the McKenna Trophy later became director of the US Navy school and, in that capacity, introduced many ETPS techniques into the curriculum leading to a marked similarity in training. This close cooperation ensures that visits lead to an exchange of ideas and comparison of techniques. Trophies have been given by one school to another to be awarded to the students who achieve the best results in various aspects of training.

It is clearly quite impossible to train a test pilot fully. The most experienced is continually learning new techniques to solve unexpected problems, which may require modification of existing theory. His professional life will be devoted to exploring new fields of knowledge, so the ETPS course is a period of transition, broadening his experience of aircraft types, and conditioning him to the mental attitudes essential to success. The operational pilot, familiar with the strengths and weaknesses of his aeroplane, flies it within the limits of its specified performance envelope. The test pilot has set those limits for him. The school trains pilots to 'unlearn'

the skills of compensation for the deficiencies of an aircraft, in order to try to identify clearly the true nature of those deficiencies, so that they can be eliminated. It is stressed that the test pilot must be totally objective, completely honest and have the courage to withstand all pressures to modify his judgement of the aeroplane, which may require large sums of money to be spent on modifications. The machine may be in service for many years, flown by pilots of varying skills, but sooner or later a deficiency will emerge which could have fatal consequences.

In one respect the test pilot's job has become easier, as he no longer has to rely upon the knee pad to record data, although ETPS still teaches and uses this method. On-board recorders will accept information from as many sources as may be required, in some cases running into hundreds. The data may be transmitted to a ground station for analysis, but ultimately, it is the pilot who will make the qualitative assessment of the handling characteristics of the machine. He will decide if it is pleasant to fly, with well harmonized controls. From that point its value as a weapons system may be assessed.

Students are grouped into syndicates under one of the flying tutors, the tutor being changed for each of the three terms so that the maximum benefit is gained from the wide experience of each officer. The first three weeks are spent entirely in ground school on revision and introductory lessons, to ensure an adequate standard in mathematics, mechanics, aerodynamics, thermodynamics and other basic subjects. From the fourth week, ground school study until 10.00 or 10.30 hours, is followed by flying experience in various aircraft of the fleet which comprises seven types of fixed wing machine and five rotary wing types. The composition of the fleet is regularly changed to reflect types and classes in operational service. Long term plans include the acquisition of a Tornado and a variable stability Hawk to replace the Basset presently being used to demonstrate this condition. The students have an unrivalled opportunity to broaden and diversify their flying experience.

Early handling and performance exercises are designed to be straightforward in theory and execution. As students gain experience the exercises become progressively more demanding of their technical expertise and flying skill. They steadily develop their powers of observation and original thought and practise accurate and convincing reporting. Although the accent is predominantly on assessing military aircraft, civil test techniques are also taught and some evaluations made against British civil airworthiness requirements.

In the second term, both fixed and rotary wing students carry out a practical assessment of a typical airborne navigation/attack system, beginning with a ground rig evaluation of the components of it, and continue with an airborne assessment of it in the Jaguar or Sea King. The advanced stability and control exercise of the third term starts a progression through to a single flight assessment of an unfamiliar aircraft type, and on to the final and most demanding exercise, 'Preview'.

One of the most useful aircraft in the fleet is one of the last three Beagle Basset CC.1s still flying. Delivered in 1973, it has been equipped with an analogue computer and autopilot actuators capable of simulating a wide variety of stability and control characteristics. It is used to demonstrate in practice aspects of dynamic stability less easily assimilated in formulae on the blackboard. Dutch roll is a case in point: the tutor, in checking roll to yaw ratio, draws the student's attention to the motion of the wing tip which appears to be describing a circle.

A Hunter T.7 is used for stalling and spinning exercises. This classic aeroplane can be persuaded to perform with certainty an extremely unpleasant manoeuvre outside normal operating limits – the inverted spin. The student's briefing states that investigation of the spin will be outside the aircraft manual limits for the Hunter but will be within ETPS limits. The objectives will be: (a) to provide front line pilots with the knowledge to recognize, prevent and/or recover from out of control flight; (b) to evaluate the aircraft against requirements, bearing in mind its suitability for solo pilots.

The inverted oscillatory spin in this aeroplane is not a classic spin, and the test pilot must consider its effect upon the average squadron pilot, who may inadvertently find himself in this attitude after a badly executed combat manoeuvre. It may be so totally disorientating that he may be unable to judge the direction of rotation. The Hunter is an excellent mount upon which to demonstrate this phenomenon as it is predictable, and capable of recovery by correct control action.

An equivalent test in rotary wing aircraft is the establishment of auto-rotational flight with engine off, a manoeuvre which, at certain combinations of height and altitude, is fraught with potential risk, and requires for its execution the high degree of skill taught at ETPS.

A particularly valuable element of the course is the opportunity for students to visit leading manufacturers of aircraft, engines and components, and Government establishments in the United Kingdom and Europe. During these visits, students meet aircraft design teams and test pilots for discussions which are of value to both parties. A diversion from the norm is a parachute jump into the sea from an Argosy, probably one of the least attractive aspects of the syllabus!

The culmination of these months of intensive study is Preview, an even more intensive four weeks which brings together all the tests carried out during the year into an overall evaluation of performance, handling and role suitability. It requires ten hours flying by the syndicates in an aircraft which has not been flown by any of the members before, and it takes place away from base, normally at the Operational Conversion Unit for the type. The results are formally presented in a written report, and orally to an audience drawn from Boscombe Down personnel and from other Service units.

Preview enables the student to prove to himself, and to his tutor, that he is capable of making completely accurate quantitative and qualitative judgements of an aircraft with which he is not familiar. Students are encouraged to compare reports made earlier on the course with their Preview report to appreciate the improvements that have been made.

In addition to its primary function ETPS carries out a number of other tasks for which it is particularly fitted and which are set by the Procurement Executive of the MoD; these include instrument ratings and conversion to other types of aircraft. The facilities are available to approved civilian test pilots who may fly Ministry aeroplanes.

Social and recreational activities are of a high order at the school; staff and students are full members of the Officers Mess at Boscombe Down and enjoy its excellent social programme. In the first week a supper party allows staff and students' wives to meet, and visits by staff and students from overseas are always splendid excuses for a party. In this respect the RAF never changes!

The McKenna Dinner held every year at the end of the course is the occasion for the award of graduation certificates and trophies; a review, by the Superintendent of Flying of the year's work, and an opportunity to repay some of the hospitality shown by friends in industry and in Ministry establishments. The different nationalities represented by the students give a colourful flavour to the social occasions which emphasize and stimulate the close links between test pilots throughout the world.

The awards made each year are:

McKenna Trophy. In memory of the second Commandant of the School, Group Captain J. F. X. McKenna, killed in a flying accident. Presented by his friends to be awarded to the best student of each course. The winner's name is engraved on it and on a plaque in the school building.

Edwards Award. Presented by Edwards Air Force Base, California, for the student who most impresses the tutorial staff by his attitude and performance throughout the course.

Hawker Hunter Trophy. Model of the Hunter presented by Hawker Aircraft. To be awarded to the syndicate writing the best Preview report.

Patuxent Shield. Presented by the United States Naval Air Test Center, Patuxent River, Maryland. To be awarded to the fixed-wing runner-up to the winner of the McKenna Trophy.

Westland Trophy. Presented by Westland Aircraft. To be awarded to the rotary wing runner-up to the McKenna Trophy.

The Sir Alan Cobham Award. For the fixed wing student who demonstrates consistently the highest standard of flying in all aspects of the course.

The Dunlop Trophy. For the best Flight Test Engineer student.

ETPS graduates have circled the moon, served in Skylab and played major roles in developing significant aircraft including Concorde and Tornado. Their contribution to the unsurpassed efficiency of the RAF is immense. Future courses are unlikely to be any less demanding and their completion will always require hard work and dedication. Graduates will inevitably be involved in the world's most exciting aerospace projects and their work will add additional lustre to the proud reputation of the ETPS.

Over the years, the accountants have tried hard and unsuccessfully to cast doubts upon the value of ETPS. It is impossible to equate in financial terms the value of the first hand and advanced technology practised and acquired there, and the international aspects of its work, by the interchange of ideas and information, to say nothing of the immensely valuable personal friendships established between the school and pilots throughout the world.

It is fitting that Group Captain S. 'Sammy' Wroath CBE, AFC,* RAF Retd, who attended the 40th anniversary open day on 10 June 1983 should have the last word:

'It was a great pleasure for me to return to Boscombe Down to celebrate this special occasion.

Group Captain S. Wroath, Wg Cdr 'Pingo' Lester and Jeffrey Quill at author's home (1984).

It seems such a short time ago that the school was started in a Nissen hut on the far side of what was a grass airfield. An extensive network of runways now covers the site and the ETPS is housed in a permanent building in a style and manner befitting its importance and well earned international reputation.'

'Over the years the training syllabus has progressively changed to meet the requirements of military aircraft, now looked upon as integrated weapon systems. Human beings, however, have changed little so I would expect that the present day student test pilots start the course with the same excitement, enthusiasm and the same degree of apprehension as students before them.'

'The student test pilot will, I am sure, find much of interest and satisfaction in this period of his flying career, not only because of the knowledge and experience to be acquired, but because of his awareness of the great bond of friendship which exists between test pilots, bonds which have grown up over the years, and are so noticeable when test pilots of many nations meet on occasions such as this.'

'This camaraderie which the ETPS has done so much to inspire can only be to the benefit of test flying in this country and in all others whose students have been fortunate enough to have graduated from the school. I wish it long and continued success.'

12

THE ENGINE COMPANY TEST PILOTS

The work of the test pilots employed by engine manufacturers has not attracted the publicity accorded to their airframe colleagues, but their contribution has been equally important in matching the power plant to the airframe, whether it be driven by a piston/propeller, gas turbine/propeller or pure jet engine.

The early pioneers were deeply frustrated by the problem of finding an engine sufficiently light and powerful to lift their aeroplanes from the ground. The true efficiency of the engine was not of great interest, and test beds were few and far between. S. F. Cody measured the thrust of his engine by attaching a butcher's spring balance to the tail of his machine and lashing the other end of the balance to the famous tree at Farnborough.

Rolls-Royce, as the company later became, was early in the field. The Honourable Charles Stewart Rolls, son of the wealthy Lord Llangattock, was a brilliant, courageous and enterprising young man who met the Wright brothers in 1906 and was immediately attracted to flying. He was the first private owner of an aeroplane in Britain, and held the Aero Club Pilots Certificate No 2. No 1 was awarded to his friend, Colonel J. T. C. Moore-Brabazon, that great pioneering aviator, later to become Lord Brabazon of Tara, whose name was borne by the giant Bristol airliner, 230 ft in span, which flew in 1949 but was doomed to failure.

In 1906, with Henry Royce, a talented engineer from a very humble background, who was developing and building motor cars, Rolls formed Rolls-Royce Limited with a capital of £60,000. On 12 July 1910, at a flying meeting at Bournemouth, Rolls was tragically killed in an attempt to win a spot landing competition. His aeroplane was caught in a down draught as it passed low over a hangar and it dived into the ground. It was a shattering blow to Royce and the company, which was, however, sufficiently well established to survive under the wise leadership of Royce and Claude Johnson, one of his earlier collaborators.

When the First World War broke out in 1914, aviation in Britain, particularly military aviation, was in its infancy. The French Renault engine was being used in a number of machines and Rolls-Royce, with other manufacturers, was invited to build this V8 engine and its British derivative, the RAF.1A. In those days 'RAF' was the Royal Aircraft Factory at Farnborough. Desperate for work, Royce agreed, although he had no high regard for the engine. He decided to design his own. By February 1915 the 225 hp Eagle was running on the test bed and, later in that year, some of the twenty-five engines ordered by the Admiralty had been delivered – an astonishing achievement in design, development and production. So began the aero engine activities of this great company which has been right in the forefront of its industry to the present day. The 75 hp Hawk was developed from the Eagle and produced in limited numbers for the non-rigid airships known as blimps, and for trainers. The Eagle was too heavy for contemporary fighters, so it was scaled down to become the 200 hp Falcon which emerged in 1916, and, in its Series III form, powered the famous Bristol F2B fighter, the 'Brisfit'. The last and largest Rolls-Royce engine produced before the Armistice was the 650 hp Condor developed from the Eagle. Both Falcon and Eagle remained in service well into the 1930s, the Condor powering the rigid airship R.100. The oldest Rolls-Royce engine still flying is a Falcon, in the 'Brisfit' preserved by the Shuttleworth Trust at Old Warden.

Charles Fairey, as was recorded in chapter three, built the Felix in-line engine, in essence the Curtiss D.12 built under licence. He designed the Fox two-seat light bomber around it, the sleek biplane making such an impression on the Air Ministry mandarins that Rolls was invited to study the engine and submit a tender for a similar one. From this study emerged the famous Kestrel, possibly the finest liquid-cooled aero engine built between the two wars.

One of the greatest of the Rolls-Royce development engineers was Cyril Lovesey. It is said that he was the main protagonist of comparative flight testing and did, in fact, establish the Hucknall facility. Lovesey began to take an interest in flight test in the late 1920s when problems arose with aircraft builders who received their engines in a packing case with a book of instructions and a starting handle! It was obviously so much easier to make a mistake in a liquid-cooled engine installation, with the complexity of radiators and plumbing, than with the air-cooled engines of the period. Lovesey wanted to be able to advise customers on the basis of practical experience. The project was delayed for several years partly because of the pressure of the Schneider Trophy races, and also because there were proposals for a national aircraft, motor car and speedboat test establishment to be set up in the vicinity of the Wash. The years of the great depression caused this project to be abandoned so Rolls-Royce decided to set up their own test centre.

In 1931 Capt R. T. Shepherd was an instructor in charge of flying training at the Nottingham Flying Club at Tollerton. He had learned to fly in 1916 and served with the Royal Flying Corps in France. Rolls-Royce asked 'Shep' whether he would help them by carrying out occasional test flying work. In October 1931 he flew his first sortie for the company in a Kestrel engined Fairey III. This arrangement continued until 1934 when he was appointed chief test pilot. He was joined by an RAF officer, Flt Lt Harvey Heyworth and Ronnie Harker, both of whom were serving in No 504 (City of Nottingham) Sqn of the RAFVR.

Ronnie Harker had joined Rolls-Royce as a premium apprentice in 1925. The recession of 1930 left him without a job so he spent his idle months in learning to fly. He was invited to return to the company when work began on the engines for the Schneider Trophy seaplanes being built by Supermarine. From the Kestrel had been developed the Buzzard, which, in turn, was developed into the famous 'R' engine. There is an interesting story of the initial design of the 'R'. Royce had his drawing office in West Wittering, Sussex. When R. J. Mitchell decided, in 1928, that he must have a more powerful engine for the S.6 machines to fly in the 1929 contest, E. W. Hives, then head of the experimental department, with Cyril Lovesey and A. J. Rowledge from the design office, walked the beach at Wittering discussing the new engine. When Royce was tired they sat on a groyne whilst he sketched out his ideas in sand with his walking stick, smoothing out the sand design when alterations were suggested!

Harker flew the Hawker biplanes, most of which were Kestrel powered, so his background of engineering and flying was particularly valuable later, when he began liaison duties with the RAF.

The usual pattern of engine development was to build a single cylinder unit and test it on a dynamometer rig, establishing maximum power output, adjusting combustion chamber profiles, valve design, timing and other important details. When this single cylinder was up to specification the complete engine would be built and rig tested to establish its power output and handling characteristics: for example, whether the engine tended to stall if the throttle was opened or closed too quickly. After the satisfactory completion of a full throttle endurance test the engine would be installed in a flying test bed – an existing airframe compatible with the new engine, avoiding if possible a new engine in a new and untried aeroplane. There were too many variables and unknown factors as was discovered on the occasions when there was no alternative.

Harker's first project was the 'R' engine, which spent many an hour on the test bed with a lot of frustrating failures. The single cylinder built for this twelve cylinder engine finally gave 200 hp on the bed. On one run of the complete engine in the one hour endurance schedule, the crankshaft failed after 58 minutes. Ultimately an output of 2,700 hp was achieved, although airframe and propeller limitations caused a reduction in installed power to 2,530 hp. A record speed of 407.5 mph was recorded by Flt Lt G. H. Stainforth on 29 September 1931, the Trophy having already been won outright by Flt Lt J. N. Boothman at an average speed of 340.08 mph.

Tribute should also be paid to F. R. 'Rod' Banks (later Air Commodore), a fuel technologist with the Anglo American Oil Company, who produced a special 'fuel cocktail' to achieve this remarkable power and subsequently made a major contribution to the development of aero engines.

RAE Farnborough and A&AEE Martlesham Heath soon became involved in engine development flying but the main centre of Rolls-Royce activity was at Tollerton aerodrome near Nottingham. Ronnie Harker was soon approved by the Air Ministry to fly Service test aircraft, and was appointed as a test pilot at the handsome stipend of £4.50 per week. Ernest Hives, his manager, later to become Lord Hives, marked the occasion by commenting that Rolls-Royce was only a sophisticated garage, and that test pilots were only flying testers, not the knights of the air which the aircraft companies considered them to be!

In an attempt to reduce the drag inseparable from the use of radiators, Rolls were developing a system of evaporative steam cooling with wing leading edge condensers and a small retractable radiator underneath the fuselage. This required a number of extra coolant pumps so the Kestrel engine, when converted to this principle, became known as the Goshawk. It was initially installed in a Gloster Gnatsnapper fighter in 1931, but Ronnie Harker's first flight in it ended prematurely when a pump failure caused overheating. Major development work was carried out in Hawker Harts, Furys, a Vickers bomber and the Short R24/31 'Knuckle-duster' flying boat, but the system was never entirely satisfactory and was superseded by the pressurized water/glycol system which became standard practice for many years.

An interesting addition to the R-R test fleet in 1935, was a Heinkel He 70. The new engines under development were destined for the new monoplane fighters being designed by Hawker and Supermarine. It was essential to be able to measure drag reduction achieved by cowling and radiator modifications, data which had been impossible to obtain with the 'draggy' and slow biplanes in use hitherto. The new sleek German monoplane was ideal for the purpose, so a Kestrel was sent to the Heinkel factory at Rostock to be fitted instead of the standard BMW powerplant. The Kestrel was also initially used in a Messerschmitt Bf 109 and Junkers Ju 87 for trials.

When the Heinkel was delivered to the new R-R test base at Hucknall, it was found to have a top speed of 258.5 mph at 1,5000 ft, the engine developing 675 hp. It was almost 60 mph faster than contemporary British fighters.

Initial flight tests were devoted to performance investigations and calibration of various types of propeller. Measurement of airflow characteristics through the radiator cowling also took place. This was a major contribution to the development of the highly efficient cowling designs used in later years on in-line engined aeroplanes.

The Heinkel was a valuable engine test bed and ultimately achieved a speed of 300 mph at 16,000 ft, the available horse power having been increased to 870.

The first Merlins were installed in Hawker Horsleys. As the first flight of the Hurricane was imminent, a concentrated test programme was essential. Shepherd, Heyworth and Harker flew 100

hours in 6½ days, revealing a high level of reliability at this early stage of development. Nevertheless there is no substitute for prolonged flying under service conditions. The Merlin developed internal coolant leaks, more apparent than dangerous as it would require a serious loss of coolant before engine seizure would occur. A partial cure was effected by fitting a special thermostat, but a completely new design of cylinder later in the war was the only way to overcome the problem entirely.

When the Second World War broke out in September 1939, the flight test staff consisted of Ronnie Shepherd and Harvey Heyworth, who was recalled to the RAF (he fought in the Battle of Britain), Wilfred Sutcliffe and Jock Bonar, both flying club instructors. Jock was an experienced pilot, and had the unique distinction of being cashiered from the Army at the tender age of 16 when his true age was discovered just before a posting to Gallipoli. He served in the RN and the RAF and was appointed to the civil division of the OBE,

'Les pilots de Rolls-Royce'! 'Mac' is Wg Cdr C. McDowell (1954).

later changed to a George Cross, for attempting to rescue the pilot from a blazing fighter which crashed at Barton aerodrome near Manchester. Jock also flew with the Hospitals Air Pageant Circus – giving this author his first experience of flying in a D.H. Fox Moth at Sywell in 1936.

Harvey Heyworth later returned to Hucknall, following Capt Shepherd as chief test pilot when the latter required in 1952. His brother Jim, twelve years his junior, a Sqn Ldr in Bomber Command, and decorated with a DFC and bar, was seconded to Rolls-Royce for test flying duties, succeeding Harvey as chief test pilot in 1953, Harry Bailey having had a nine month spell in the job before Jim took over.

Until the Battle of Britain most Spitfires and Hurricanes had fixed-pitch two bladed wooden propellers. In 1940 many were fitted with two position de Havilland bracket type propellers, coarse or fine pitch – coarse for maximum power absorption and speed and fine for maximum thrust at take-off. In a dive, however, it was all too easy for the engine to overspeed, with disastrous effects. De Havillands provided a conversion kit consisting of a constant speed unit which fitted on the front of the Merlin, being driven by a short quill shaft from the accessory drive of the engine. Pitch was therefore controlled automatically within limits set by the pilot, and overspeeding was largely overcome. De Havilland's installation team, under Sergei Bentley, rushed indefatigably around the fighter stations, working all hours to make this vital modification.

Even this apparently simple project had its problems. There were a number of occasions when the quill shaft broke, leaving the propeller in coarse pitch. This was overcome by increasing the diameter of the quill shaft. There were many other more serious difficulties; engine surging with backfires through the supercharger, exhaust flames affecting night vision of night fighter and bomber pilots. So the test pilots were in the forefront of the effort to ensure that RAF crews always had the best equipment available in their battle with the enemy.

One wonders what the outcome of the air war, and in particular the Battle of Britain, would have been if Rolls-Royce had not developed the 'R' type engine for the Schneider Races. It should not be forgotten that the last contest would not have been won but for the generosity of that great patriot, Lady Lucie Houston, who came to the rescue and committed £100,000 of her own money when a parsimonious and short-sighted Government decided that it could not afford to sponsor the 1931

contest. Britain won the Trophy outright, and the 'R' type was finally confirmed as one of the greatest engines of all time.

In 1937 a brilliant mathematician, Dr S. G. Hooker, later knighted for his aero engine work, joined Rolls-Royce and turned his talents to improvements in supercharger design. Within a few months the output of the Merlin was increased by 30 per cent. Mostly the Battle of Britain participants in Fighter Command had Merlin III, pre-Hooker, engines, but the performance of these was improved considerably by the introduction of 100 octane aromatic fuel.

These developments kept Ronnie Shepherd's test team busy in proving the mechanical integrity of the more powerful engines. A major step forward was the introduction of the Merlin 61, with a two-stage supercharger and intercooler to cool the charge before it entered the carburettor. This was first flown in a Spitfire by Shepherd at Hucknall in September 1941 whilst Jeffrey Quill flew another prototype at Worthy Down in January 1942. The test results showed a spectacular improvement over the current Mk V aircraft. A&AEE at Boscombe Down recorded a maximum speed of 422 mph at 27,000 ft, and an operational ceiling of nearly 43,000 ft. Jeffrey Quill was so impressed with his tests that he flew the machine to Hornchurch where Group Captain Harry Broadhurst, an experienced Spitfire pilot, was the Station Commander. After lunch in the mess Broadhurst flew it, and to Jeffrey's dismay, he immediately joined the Hornchurch Wing who were taking off for a sortie over enemy territory, so the prototype of this outstanding and highly secret aeroplane and engine went to war, albeit with no ammunition. Fortunately it returned safely with an enthusiastic pilot whose enthusiasm soon permeated the upper echelons of command. The Spitfire Mk IX which emerged proved to be a worthy opponent for the Fw 190. The Merlin 61 developed, at 40,000 ft, double the power of the Merlin II of 1939–40. Even at 23,500 ft it developed 1,390 hp. This engine was also fitted by de Havillands to the prototype Mosquito. A substantial improvement in performance resulted, and the first of the many Mosquito variants to use the new Merlin was the photographic reconnaissance Mk VIII.

A major headache for the Rolls-Royce pilots had been the development of the Vulture 2,000 hp 24 cylinder 'X' type engine planned for installation in the Hawker Tornado fighter and the Avro Manchester heavy bomber. Four Kestrel cylinder blocks were fitted to a new crankcase with the appropriate

Hawker Henley flying test bed for the Vulture engine.

supercharger and carburettor modifications. A prototype was first flown in a Hawker Henley light bomber designed in 1937 to take the 1,000 hp Merlin I. Jock Bonar often flew it and thought it a complete menace. It had large ballast weights in the tail and the huge air intake and exhausts obstructed the view forward and downward. Twice Jock had to force land it in a field as the engine failed. He told the author that he used to lay awake at nights just before he was due to fly it! A violent torque swing was inevitable, so he had to begin his take-off run almost 90 degrees out of wind to compensate, and build up sufficient speed for the rudder to become effective, and for the elevators to be capable of lifting the tail. It landed at 120 mph, a fearsome speed at that time. After Ronnie Shepherd's maiden flight in it, the tailplane had been increased in size but it still remained a dangerous aeroplane.

Before the war the Rolls-Royce development flight had tested many interesting aircraft; one of them was the attractive Kestrel engined Miles Trainer. 'Shep' had a slightly embarrassing experience when the engine cut on take-off. He went through the hedge and across a field and stopped almost at the door of the hostelry used by the pilots. The landlord, recognizing the driver of the slightly unusual vehicle outside his pub, rushed into the cellar and drew a pint of beer. As he gave it to Ronnie the police arrived. Shep was not amused by the interruption, saying with some asperity, 'Even if I crash an aeroplane into a pub I still can't drink a bloody pint in peace!'

One of the flying test-beds was a Fairey Battle being used to fly one of the new de Havilland/Hamilton Standard fully feathering hydromatic propellers. Shepherd took it to 2,000 ft and satisfactorily feathered and unfeathered the propeller. To demonstrate how good the system was he flew low over the aerodrome and feathered again. In conformity with Murphy's Law, the fuse blew as he pressed the button to start the pump for the unfeathering cycle: there he was in a single engined aeroplane with a stationary propeller. The low drag of the Battle was legendary, and in the absence of a windmilling propeller to give some retardation, it seemed reasonable that he could glide round the circuit and 'grease' the aeroplane in, low over the hedge. The Battle smoothly swished in with the wheels lowered on the manual pump, but there was no time to lower the flaps fully. 850 yards away, at the end of the field, was a road two or three feet above the level of the aerodrome. The more prudent of the drivers watching the flying moved their cars as they saw the Battle hurtling towards them. The undercarriage was left on the roadside as it hit the bank, the Battle hurtling relentlessly on through two hedges until it came to rest astride a third one. Ronnie Shepherd, not one of the most patient of souls, was swearing volubly. He threw off his parachute pack and harness and stepped out of the cockpit on to the wing, only to slip and break two ribs as he fell against the fuselage. Jock Bonar said that he could be heard swearing all the way to Nottingham hospital, nine miles away!

Test sorties were not always so light-heartedly catastrophic. Late in 1940 Reg Kirlew was flying the prototype Vickers Warwick with Vulture engines. He had a cooling system failure which resulted in almost total loss of power. With superb skill he managed to make a perfect landing at the small Burnaston aerodrome near Derby.

In 1941 he had a similar experience in a Manchester. He tried to land at RAF Tern Hill, but touched down in a field just outside the boundary, hitting a tree which tore the wing off. Ronnie Harker, who was at Tern Hill to lecture to a Hurricane squadron, saw the aircraft burst into flames immediately. The flight engineer, Derek Brown, and the test crew of five staggered away from the wreck, but sadly Reg Kirlew was trapped and he died.

Engine company test pilots have to resign themselves to long periods of aerial boredom, routine flights at altitude with high speed runs checking every aspect of the behaviour of the installation right through the flight envelope. The Merlin was a classic example of the value of these flights as its power was increased from the 1,030 hp of the Merlin III in 1939, to the 2,050 hp of the Merlin 66 in 1944. Boost pressure rose from plus 6¼ lb to plus 25 lb. The operating altitude rose from sea level to 32,000 ft to sea level to 47,000 ft. One of the most significant developments was the maximum altitude at which the engine would develop 1,000 hp at full throttle and 3,000 rpm. This was 16,000 ft in the case of the Merlin III and 36,000 ft for the Merlin 113/114. These remarkable achievements had to be proven by unremitting toil on the test beds and by the pilots in the air.

Tests were carried out to determine the longest period of high power running which was feasible. The target was set at 100 hours at 3,000 rpm and plus 18 lb boost. It was achieved on two occasions.

The Spitfire was developed right through the war as new marks of the engine permitted even better performance; the Mosquito was also a beneficiary of these developments. The later Griffon engine, developed from the Kestrel, but embodying features of the Merlin, allowed a further quantum leap in Spitfire performance. It is however, interesting to recall a remark made to the author by Group Captain Sammy Wroath who was a test pilot at Martlesham Heath when the first Hurricane arrived there. He said, 'If someone had told us that the Merlin would be a world-beater we could not have believed it – it was one mass of trouble.' The early Merlin Is fitted to Hurricanes and Battles had the so-called ramp head combustion chamber which did not give the anticipated performance and was prone to cracking. Additionally the two piece Kestrel type cylinder block designed to eliminate coolant leaks was not a success. In the Merlin IIs and IIIs, a single piece block and symmetrical combustion chamber was fitted. Thereafter the Merlin became one of the most reliable engines ever built, enjoying the complete confidence of the aircrews whose lives depended upon it.

The wartime team of Ronnie Shepherd, Harvey and Jim Heyworth, Peter Birch from Bomber Command, Harry Bailey, an ex-apprentice Battle of Britain fighter pilot, Tony Martindale from RAE, and Rendell Stokes from Bomber Command, augmented by Service pilots posted to Hucknall to assist with the immense workload, did a first class job in ensuring that Roll-Royce engined aeroplanes were as reliable as it was humanly possible to make them; whilst the liaison pilots, with Ronnie Harker and Jock Bonar, ensured that the closest possible co-operation existed with the service to achieve a rapid and effective solution of any problems which arose.

To Ronnie Harker goes the credit for the conversion of the North American Mustang fighter, of limited use to RAF Fighter Command because of its poor performance at altitude, into one of the world's finest fighter aircraft. He was impressed with its handling and suggested that the replacement of the Allison engine with the Merlin 61

Prototype Merlin-engined Mustang.

would turn it into a formidable adversary for the Messerschmitt Bf 109 and Focke Wulf Fw 190. A performance study was carried out; it indicated that an extra 40 mph could be expected at 25,000 ft with a substantial improvement in rate of climb. After the inevitable frustrations that assail people who have good ideas in large companies, the wisdom of the proposal became apparent and work commenced. Within three weeks a prototype was available and the results were dramatic.

The American Eighth Air Force was suffering appalling losses in its daylight raids over Europe. The second raid on the Schweinfurt ball bearing factory, on 27 September 1943, was a disaster. Of 281 B-17 bombers despatched, 60 failed to return, 17 were severely damaged, and 121 received minor damage. The P-47 Thunderbolts could only escort them as far as Aachen, little more than 200 miles from base. Thereafter they were alone.

The Mustang was developed to have a range of 1,800 miles with a fuel consumption of 8.85 air miles per gallon – a remarkable achievement on the part of the Rolls team, and in particular the liaison pilots who visited all the Allied squadrons using Merlins, to ensure that aircrew had mastered the engine handling techniques necessary to obtain this phenomenal range, by extracting the last percentage point of efficiency. A major contribution was made by Rolls test pilot Michael Royce.

The involvement of Rolls-Royce in the development of the jet engine has been described in chapter ten, and it is the saga of the Welland and Derwent from which were developed other powerful turbines which concerns us.

It is surprising how little interest was shown in the new engine by designers of the calibre of Sydney Camm and Joe Smith. They were deeply involved in 'stretching' the Typhoon, Tempest and Spitfire, and paid little attention to the new development. Stanley Hooker, in his autobiography, *Not Much of an Engineer* tells how Sir Roy Fedden, the talented designer of the Bristol range of radial engines, wrote to Air Chief Marshal Sir Wilfrid Freeman to say that a 400 mph fighter could more easily be built with a large piston engine. Freeman passed a copy of the letter to Ernest Hives, who consulted Hooker who proved that such a speed at sea level would require an engine of more than 4,000 hp, double the size of any existing engine, and one which would require years of development, as the cooling problems inherent in it would necessitate 36-cylinders. He proved to Hives that the development of the Whittle engine from its design thrust of 1,600 lb to 2,000 lb would give the new Meteor

a sea-level top speed approaching 500 mph. So major redesign of the Whittle engine began. The first Meteors were fitted with the Welland, as the Rolls-Royce Whittle engine was known. Drawings were commenced in April 1943 and a test engine ran in July – an incredible achievement which, nevertheless, indicates the basic simplicity of those early gas turbines with their single stage centrifugal compressors. Hives's comment on the simple design was memorable: 'We'll soon design the simplicity out of them!' An inspection of a modern multi-stage, axial flow gas turbine with re-heat and thrust reversers will confirm the accuracy of the prediction.

In November 1943 the Derwent passed its 100 hour type-test at the full 2,000 lb rating and was first flown in a Meteor in April 1944.

Wg Cdr Harvey Heyworth was made responsible for flight testing this new powerplant and was almost certainly the first man in the world to achieve 1,000 hours of jet flight. He was awarded the AFC for his contribution to test flying.

When, in 1944, his brother Jim joined the team, the 24-cylinder Exe engine was being flown in a Fairey Battle. This combination had originally been tested in 1938, but the high priority given to the Merlin caused the project to be shelved. His first experience of the jet engine, which made the Exe and, indeed, all other powerful piston engines obsolete, was in a Wellington Mk II with Merlin engines and a Whittle W2B turbine in the tail. The flight engineer spent a miserable time in the rear muffled up in thick and cumbersome clothing which still left him frozen. He was a combustion expert named Clarke, usually known as Gassy. When the engine flamed out, the fuselage was filled with dense kerosene smoke until 'Gassy' cut off the fuel. Jim judged when this had been done by the cessation of gasping and choking noises in his intercom! Later, the turbine was fitted to a Mk II Wellington with Merlin X engines. This enabled it to be flown to 38,000 ft. The W2B was also flown by Rolls-Royce in a Meteor prototype. On a hot day so much power was lost that every foot of the 6,000 ft at Church Broughton was used to coax the Meteor over a low fence alongside the Uttoxeter road, all the traffic having been halted! All Meteor flying was carried out from this aerodrome as Hucknall was too small.

The problem of testing single-engined aeroplanes were highlighted when the V1 buzz bomb attacks commenced in 1944. 'Winkle' Brown's experience with a heavily boosted Tempest has been recorded in chapter thirteen. Both the Spitfire and Mustang

Wellington II with Whittle W2B jet engine in tail.

were modified and fitted with Merlins boosted to 25 lb – the RAF asked for a maximum of 32 lb for a five minute sprint period. Testing a Mustang, Jim Heyworth flew at 32 lb for eight minutes, after which there was a loud bang, with grinding and groaning noises as the engine failed, flooding oil all over the windscreen. With some difficulty he force-landed at an airfield in Lincolnshire. A few days later the experience was repeated, so the project was temporarily abandoned. During the following year the Merlin 100 series appeared with 30 lb of boost available.

In 1944 there were 48 piston and jet engined aircraft of 14 different types at Hucknall and Church Broughton, so test pilots had to be versatile. There were no altitude test facilities available and the operation of engines at low pressure and temperature had to be carried out the hard way – at altitude. Few aeroplanes, other than photographic reconnaissance Spitfires, had flown regularly to 35,000 ft, and even fewer to 45,000 ft. The multi-engine test beds eliminated the potentially dangerous consequences of engine failure in a single-engined machine whilst the Merlin/Whittle powered Wellington could fly at 38,000 ft and stay there for long periods. Such flights without a pressure cabin were extremely unpleasant. It was bitterly cold and the test crews were susceptible to the 'bends', a condition which can be eased by violent flexing and bending of the limbs. In a lecture

to the Rolls-Royce Heritage Trust in January 1984, Jim Heyworth said, 'To the little gremlins watching through the cockpit windows it must have looked hilarious with these humans throwing their arms about and then scribbling the test results on paper as the aeroplane tried to fly itself!'

In practice it was anything but hilarious. Time scale entered into it as well as altitude; sometimes as long as 30 minutes of high altitude flying could be experienced before the onset of bends. When the first crew member began to suffer he would try to continue the test until a companion began to feel the effects, then they would descend. On one occasion a flight engineer succumbed to a bubble in the blood supply to his brain, and was unconscious for 24 hours.

Distention of the stomach due to expanding gases was another hazard of high altitude flying at that time, so the diets of crews had to be carefully watched.

An interesting, and hitherto unrecorded, phenomenon was discovered by the Rolls-Royce test pilots – turbulence in clear air. It had always been accepted that turbulent conditions could only occur in the proximity of clouds. On one sortie a pilot reported, 'The effect of the rough air was such that it was impossible to write any results on a knee-pad at 37,000 ft.' The statement was received with polite disbelief, the meteorological experts being particularly sceptical. Further discussion with Spitfire and Mosquito pilots proved beyond doubt that they, too, had experienced high speed winds at high altitude. Some of these jet-streams, as they became known, are measured at speeds up to 150 mph, and the turbulence they generate is similar to the sensation of driving over cobbles, as many airline passengers will testify.

From the Derwent was developed the Nene engine with an ultimate thrust of 5,000 lb. The design of this engine was completed in a record 5½ months, and the prototype first ran on the test-bed in October 1944. On the second day of its tests it achieved the designed power. No British aeroplane was available, or even planned, to accept this powerful engine, so it was initially installed in a Lockheed P-80 Shooting Star fighter. This first flew from Hucknall in July 1945. Harvey Heyworth and Michael Royce continued the test programme at Church Broughton. In the following year Ronnie Shepherd flew for the first time a Lancastrian with two Nenes in the outboard engine positions.

Lack of interest in the Nene in official British circles persuaded Rolls-Royce to develop a slightly smaller version to fit the Meteor nacelles. This became known as the Derwent V and developed twice the thrust of the Derwent I. The only British installation of the Nene was a rather unsatisfactory one in a de Havilland Vampire, normally powered by a 3,000 lb thrust Goblin. It was naturally assumed that a substantial increase in speed would result. Astonishingly, there was no improvement although climb performance was extremely good.

It was concluded that the air intakes, which had been designed for the Goblin's single-sided impeller, were choking, so large 'donkey ears', or scoops, were fitted on top of the engine and the intakes enlarged. This introduced an entirely unexpected hazard: at Mach 0.72 at 10,000 ft the pilot experienced elevator reversal – as he pulled the control column back the aircraft dived. At 4,000 ft it began to pull out and control was regained at 2,000 ft as compressibility effects diminished at the lower altitude. It was considered that the elevators were partly blanketed by the effect of louvres installed to bleed air from part of the intake. Various new designs were tried, the problem being solved by trial and error.

In 1946 Sqn Ldr Cliff Rogers joined the Rolls-Royce test team. Having served with Bomber Command, where he was awarded a DFC, and in Transport Command, he was well acquainted with the Merlin. One of his first tasks was to fly the Eagle-engined Westland Wyvern. The Eagle was another engine which had suffered from inadequate development and although it was a superbly smooth power unit it was very unreliable. For five months

Cliff Rogers carried out various test assignments. He was then asked to carry out a full throttle level run in the Wyvern at 25,000 ft, but at this height, a sudden rapid rise in oil and coolant temperature, accompanied by steam, called for an immediate shut-down and a quick identification of a landing site. Looking down, he recognized, as an ex-No 5 Group Bomber Command pilot, Lincoln cathedral and the Saracen's Head, so he decided to head for the disused airfield at Skellingthorpe, to the west of the city. He recalled that the wind at take-off had been 25 knots and gusting. With a need for 125 knots over the fence with this heavy aeroplane, the landing was not likely to be an easy one, with no power and massive contra-rotating propellers which could not be feathered, and which acted as a massive air brake. He also recalled that a Westland test pilot, Mike Graves, had recently been killed under identical circumstances when belly landing a Wyvern. As the propellers dug in, the engine came back and had crushed him. Cliff's first thought was to abandon the aircraft, but there were problems, not the least of which was the feeling that he ought to bring the evidence back for investigation. So he lowered the undercarriage and headed for the totally inadequate 1,400 yard runway with a wood and a lake obstructing the approach path. Diving to maintain flying speed he made a perfect touch-down and stopped. Suddenly he saw the control column moving across the cockpit for no apparent reason. He looked out to see a gentleman in rustic garb thumping the wing with a heavy stick and waggling the aileron. Cliff was extremely annoyed to think that his Wyvern, so far unmarked, should be assaulted in this way. He opened the canopy to be informed by the visitor,

Rolls-Royce Eagle-engined Westland Wyvern.

who turned out to be the local farmer, that under no circumstances would the Lincoln Flying Club operate from Skellingthorpe; he had bought it and was going to farm it without interruption! When Cliff informed him that the Wyvern was not an elementary trainer and that it was an emergency landing, the farmer took him home for a splendid lunch and allowed him to shoot over his land for the next three years.

Four months later he was flying the Wyvern over the Derbyshire hills when the engine blew up. This time he again invoked his episcopal navigation system and found Lichfield cathedral, heading for another disused airfield. This time the situation was even less encouraging, as ominous noises were coming from the engine which then caught fire. Down went the undercarriage as he headed for one of the runways; this time he missed it and landed on the grass where the local football team was playing. He went from corner flag to corner flag and missed all 22 players. Cliff still has a vivid recollection of green and red shirts lying prone on the grass! The RAF fire engine moved off smartly as the Wyvern approached and chased it, putting

Part of the Rolls-Royce test fleet, from the era of the piston engine to the jet. Hornet (foreground), Trent Meteor, jet Lancastrian, Avon Meteor and Nene Vampire.

the fire out and undoubtedly saving the aircraft. Cliff was extremely angry to discover that the corporal in charge of it was to receive a reprimand for leaving the Fire Station without permission! Cliff saw the CO and ensured that justice would prevail!

After two rather dicey experiences in this lethal flying machine Cliff pondered upon whether he would have been better advised to take up chicken farming! Later, the Clyde propeller turbine was installed in the Wyvern, and finally the Python turbine. With this engine it went into naval service.

Cliff recalls vividly his first flight in a jet propelled aircraft in 1948. This was a Derwent-engined Meteor, and he found it so easy after the powerful piston-engined machines; the lack of take-off swing and the smoothness of the flight was memorable. He recalls the period from 1948 to 1950 as an exceptionally interesting one with a number of advanced and interesting aeroplanes on the tarmac at Hucknall.

One was the Nene engined Vampire which was being flown with a fuel mixture of petrol and oil. Great care had to be taken in starting this engine, otherwise it emulated a giant blow-lamp, emitting a tongue of flame 20 ft long! The fuel capacity was only 96 gallons, and it was found that its consumption was greater than with kerosene. On Cliff's first flight in it he checked the weather to

find that, at the 25–35,000 ft level, where he was to do a full throttle level run, there was a prevailing westerly wind of 50–60 knots. For such a run it was customary to check isobar charts so that the course could follow one of the isobars, and the same air pressure would be experienced throughout the flight. So he took-off and headed in a north easterly direction for four minutes. Having recorded the data on his knee-pad he looked down to see white caps on the ocean indicating that he was well out over the North Sea. A fuel check showed an alarming 25 gallons, or the amount he would normally expect to have when the Vampire was safely back in its hangar. This time there was no cathedral in sight! He turned back, and soon recognized the Lincolnshire terrain, making an emergency landing at the nearest airfield. As he rolled down the runway the engine stopped. 'Just another little incident on the way', as he commented upon the pattern of test pilot training at that time. One either had ten months at the Empire Test Pilots School or two years apprenticeship learning the trade. He felt that he was learning it a bit too fast for his peace of mind but he had been very lucky. It might be said that he had also shown a high degree of skill in coping with the emergencies.

Jim Heyworth discussed with the author the high casualty rate in test flying after the war when many Service pilots entered the profession, some because they just wanted to do a flying job, others because they had experience of being posted to test flying duties and were prepared to think logically and calmly about the potential emergencies they might experience, and the action to be taken. Generally, most of the casualties occurred in the former category, and many accidents were due to pilot misjudgement or error, understandable though some of them were. He quoted the case of one pilot flying a Lancaster equipped with a pair of Avon turbojets. For the purpose of a special test, one had been adjusted to give a slow throttle response. He overshot the runway with both turbines at idle and opened both throttles simultaneously. One engine spooled up to full power immediately and the aeroplane dived straight in, all aboard being killed.

A particularly tragic accident occurred at an air show held at Syerston in Leicestershire. The prototype Vulcan with Conway engines made a low-level pass in front of the spectators, when suddenly it reared up and all four engines broke away. The rest of the airframe came down tail first, crashing on top of the airfield control van. It was concluded that the aircraft was flying at the maximum permitted speed when the leading edge

Vulcan prototype disintegrating at Syerston.

of the wing opened up, ripping the wing apart. When production Vulcans were inspected some of the wing ribs were found to be cracked and reduced airspeed limitation was temporarily imposed.

Jim Heyworth had many discussions with John Derry on the subject of sensible flight testing of aeroplanes which were becoming hugely expensive. Derry was an extremely thoughtful and analytical test pilot and believed in the theory of the calculated risk – carefully evaluate the level of hazard in a particular situation, and only when you cannot calculate further is the risk justified. Jim was fully in agreement with this philosophy, but both had to be circumspect in discussing it openly as, in the mood of the period, it would have been considered 'chickening out' by some pilots.

It was a tragic irony that John Derry was killed in the Farnborough Air Show crash of the de Havilland D.H.110, which disintegrated due to a massive structural failure.

As the power of gas turbines increased the long take-off run was reduced considerably and a 6,000 yard runway was no longer necessary. Flight development moved back from Church Broughton to the grass surface of Hucknall in 1946.

The Meteor was a particularly useful test aircraft. With the nacelles tucked well inboard, assymetric effects of an engine failure on take-off were fairly easily controlled. With a standard production engine installed on the other side there was no problem in returning to base.

An interesting test was carried out during the development of reheat. Take-off was, of course, from grass, and it was necessary for the efflux nozzle of the test engine to be wide open for a full reheat thrust and climb until the reheat was cancelled. The other engine was at normal power so the take-off run was in the form of a curve due to the absence of rudder control below a speed of 30 knots. This became known as the banana take-off! A certain senior Rolls engineer who did not appreciate that the technique was quite safe, thought that such antics should be stopped!

A major problem in the design of a gas turbine is the phenomenon known as surging. If the airflow through the compressor is disturbed in any way the pressure distribution is seriously affected and the airflow in the combustion chambers becomes totally unstable. On a test rig this will result in flames shooting out through the air intake as the air flow reverses; this combustion of the mixture momentarily stabilizes the flow pattern. The cycle is then repeated until the engine is turned off. A series of loud explosions and a rapid and dangerous increase in turbine temperature accompanies the performance. Initially it caused tremendous problems, although the effects were not as bad on the simple Derwent centrifugal flow turbine as with the much more complex axial flow Avons. In the air a couple of thumps announced that the Derwent was surging but when the Avon – with the unprecedented power to weight ratios of almost one to one and phenomenal performance – was flown in a Meteor, jet pipe temperatures would quickly rise 30 degrees above maximum when the surging commenced. However this aeroplane could climb to 40,000 ft in 2½ minutes.

Meteor test flights had their hazardous moments and at one period the aircraft had a propensity for shedding the cockpit canopy. In 1945 one of the pilots lost his at over 500 mph, flying at 1,000 ft. 'Bone domes' had not been introduced at that time so the edge of the canopy hit his head, ripping the top off his leather helmet and giving him a serious gash and a headache. In 1947 another pilot lost his canopy at 25,000 ft. He was luckier: bone domes were in service, so he escaped injury. He had a rather disturbing experience, nevertheless. The canopy caught the ejector seat handle as it departed.

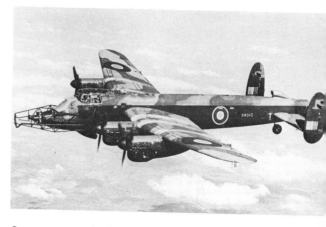

Lancaster test bed with four Merlins and Armstrong Siddeley Mamba prop-jet in nose with propeller blades sawn off. The frame is to reproduce icing conditions. In the tail is an AS Screamer rocket motor.

The handle was withdrawn from its housing and flapped about outside the machine just behind the cockpit. The pilot had two alternatives as the seat was now in an extremely critical condition – the slightest jar could project him into space. He could release his seat and parachute harness and lean out to try to retrieve the handle, in the certainty that if the seat fired, he would go out without a parachute, or, he could descend very carefully and make a feather-light landing – fully aware that if the seat fired below 1,000 ft the parachute could not deploy in time to save him. He chose the latter course and landed safely.

The Lancaster test-bed was used to quantify the problem of intake icing on gas turbines. A spray grid was mounted forward of the air intake, and valuable data was obtained from it.

Another useful test aeroplane was the English Electric Canberra which was used for most of the Avon development programme. It was a flexible aeroplane with good handling characteristics, even on one engine.

The installation of the Dart propeller turbine (destined for the new Vickers Viscount) into a Dakota was a valuable exercise in the evolution of this classic engine. Cliff Rogers had an amusing experience when flying it at 36,000 ft near Grantham. Cabin icing at such a height, unheard of for a Dak, was a problem. Cliff looked out through a gap in the ice covering the side windows to see a Canadian F-86 Sabre fighter flying alongside – a RCAF squadron was based at North Luffenham. When he returned to his base the air traffic

The most powerful Meteor ever built, with two 7,600 lb thrust AS Sapphire engines.

controller asked him to ring North Luffenham as one of their pilots could hardly believe that he had seen a Dakota at 36,000 ft. So Cliff spoke to a squadron leader at the Canadian base, who told him that they had an idiot on the station who reckoned he had seen a 'Gooney-bird' – as the Dak was known across the Atlantic – at 36,000 ft and was actually betting money on it and had about thirty dollars at stake! The Gooney-bird was reported to come from Rolls-Royce. Could Cliff confirm this? He did and spoke to the pilot, asking that four dollars should be put on for him! Later, a splendid party was held in the Canadian Mess to exonerate the fighter pilot from the charge of idiocy!

The development of the Avon during the 1950s and its installation in the Hawker Hunter fighter created nightmares for Rolls-Royce. Originally designed to produce 6,500 lb thrust, the A.J.65 (AJ for axial jet), was also destined for the Supermarine Swift and the English Electric Canberra. Sydney Camm decided that, as a safeguard against shortage of Avons, the new Hunter should also be capable of accepting the Armstrong Siddeley Sapphire. This was a direct descendant of the first axial flow turbine, the Metro-Vick Beryl, which had been taken over by the company when Metropolitan Vickers withdrew from aero engine work.

Three Hunter prototypes were built, and Neville Duke flew the first one in July 1948. The trials of the Hunter are described in more detail in chapter fifteen. Gun firing exercises are not part of the test programme carried out by the contractor's test pilots, so it was not until the Hunter arrived at Boscombe Down that the problem of engine flame-out when the Aden guns were fired was recognized. This was a serious matter as production was well advanced, with aircraft allocated for early delivery to the Central Fighter Establishment and to the first squadron scheduled to be re-equipped with the type. Rolls-Royce immediately took over responsibility for the investigation of this entirely unexpected phenomenon which, it was learned, was also being experienced with the Supermarine Swift.

The Avon was proving to be a tricky engine to handle in the air. The installation of an Armstrong Siddeley Sapphire compressor appeared to offer hope of a solution of this problem so a deal was concluded between the two companies. Armstrongs would permit Rolls to build the Sapphire compressor into the Avon, in exchange for know-how which Rolls possessed in retaining compressor blades in position – a problem which was a considerable worry to Armstrongs. The handling difficulty was eventually overcome. After many hours of flight and firing tests in the Hunter, it was decided that the gun problem could be beaten by introducing a solenoid into the gun button circuit, to actuate a valve and reduce the flow of fuel when the weapons were fired. As they only fired a few rounds at a time the 'fuel dip', as it became known, had little effect upon speed. So a difficult problem was neatly solved, and Hunters which were already in service were quickly modified. The fuel dip was also installed in the BAC One-Eleven airliner, to reduce power quickly should the aeroplane reach a high angle of incidence which was known to disturb flow through the rear mounted engines and which caused them to overheat.

Government pressure in the late 1950s forced mergers in the airframe and engine industry to achieve groups large enough to create the immense sums of money needed for modern developments. Bristol Siddeley had been formed when Bristol Aero Engines and Armstrong Siddeley engines merged. In turn, that group bought the de Havilland Engine Company and Blackburn Engines from Hawker Siddeley Group, so the industry looked healthy with the very advanced new projects such as TSR.2, the HS.681 short landing and take-off transport, the Hawker Siddeley P.1154 supersonic VTOL fighter, and the remarkable Saunders Roe SR.177 mixed powerplant fighter.

Vulcan test bed with Olympus 593 engine for Concorde under test. Water spray rig operating.

In 1964 the incoming Labour Government cancelled all these projects, and almost ruined both engine and airframe industries, losing in one stroke the technological lead which had been won by Britain.

Concorde remained in the programme only because the contractual penalties which would have been exacted by the French would have been higher than the cost of continuing development.

The great Olympus engines for Concorde were developed originally for the Vulcan bomber which required four engines of 10,000 lb of thrust each. In a Canberra test-bed, Bristol Siddeley's chief test pilot Walter Gibb established a world altitude record of 63,668 ft and later flew the machine to 66,000 ft. The Air Ministry suddenly decided that Britain only required one large engine, and chose the Rolls-Royce Conway, instructing that the Vulcan should be re-designed to take this powerplant. In the event, wiser counsels prevailed, and the Olympus remained in the Vulcan, giving valuable experience which enabled it to be increased in thrust to 38,000 lb with 17 per cent afterburning for Concorde.

The problems faced by the Concorde engineers were immense. At Mach 2.0 the air is approaching the air intake at the speed of a rifle bullet, approximately 2,000 ft per sec. By the time it reaches the inlet duct to the compressor it has to be slowed to about 500 ft per sec. Shockwaves at the inlet are used for the initial deceleration to 1,000 ft per sec. During this process (which takes about 100th of a second) a tremendous pressure increase occurs to give the necessary efficiency and thrust. At take-off

the conditions are entirely different. The full volume of the intakes is required to ingest the vast volume of air which does not have the benefit of high forward speed producing ram effect. As the aeroplane accelerates the conditions progressively change to the supersonic cruise condition, and to achieve this infinitely variable control, a complex system of ramps, flaps and doors is required in the nacelles, controlled by a computer. As may be imagined, the development of such an installation was a major undertaking, brilliantly carried out by using a Vulcan with the engine in a representative nacelle mounted underneath, the final adjustments being made as part of the Concorde flight test programme.

Similarly the development of the RB.211 engine for the wide-body airliner, was an immense task and an exceptionally costly one. Originally it was intended to make the blades of the 7ft diameter intake fan of carbon fibre, a new material offering high strength and low weight, with innovations which appeared to give the RB.211 a considerable weight advantage over its American competitors in

Cliff Rogers and Hank Dees, Director of Flight Test, Lockheed, USA, with VC10 test bed for Rolls-Royce RB.211.

the 42,000 lb thrust category. It was to power the Lockheed TriStar, which was well into prototype construction, when it was discovered that the carbon fibre blades would not withstand the mandatory bird-strike test of firing a 4 lb chicken at high speed into the intake, when the engine was running at take-off power. As with a number of aspects of this complex engine, the technique was beyond the state-of-the-art in 1970, so the fan reverted to orthodox titanium blades, losing the valuable weight advantage. There were other technical problems which caused concern to the Board.

So disastrous was the effect on Rolls-Royce that the Heath Government stepped in and bought the assets of this great company in 1971.

It was a salutary and tragic lesson in the economics of development in the aviation industry in the era of high speed, high technology. Even the principles of engine test flying had undertaken a radical change. It was no longer possible for an aircraft manufacturer to allocate a prototype to the engine company with aeroplanes such as Tornado costing £13m apiece. In the case of the Olympus 593 engines in Concorde, over 5,000 hours of test-bed operation and 500 hours of flight test under the Vulcan had been carried out before the French prototype 001 first flew in March 1969.

Modern practice is for the engine manufacturer to buy time from the aircraft manufacturer. When the RB.211 was flight tested, it was found that the huge beam carrying the four tail mounted engines of the Vickers VC10 was suitable for the installation of one RB.211 in place of two Conways. So a VC10 was hired from the Ministry at vast expense. Immediately the trials were completed this VC10 was returned to the RAE.

One of the most important modern gas turbine engines is the Pegasus, used in the remarkable Harrier. As this is so totally integrated with the aircraft itself engine development will be discussed in chapter sixteen.

13

LOOKING FORWARD TO PEACE

From the end of 1943 to the conclusion of the war in Europe few new prototypes emerged from British factories. One was the Avro Lincoln (originally designated Lancaster Mk IV), the last piston-engined heavy bomber to serve in the RAF. Capt H. A. Brown flew it for the first time on 9 June 1944 from Ringway and reported favourably upon it. A&AEE at Boscombe Down generally confirmed his opinion and the type entered service in 1946, too late for active service in Europe.

One of the most handsome piston-engined bombers was the Vickers Windsor, an unusual design with four Merlin engines and an undercarriage leg retracting into each nacelle. The Air Ministry was interested in remotely controlled defensive armament and specified that barbettes should be fitted at the rear of the outboard nacelles to be sighted from the normal tail gunner's position. Structurally the Windsor followed Barnes Wallis's well proven geodetic construction.

The prototype was first flown on 23 October 1943 by Mutt Summers from Farnborough where it had been assembled. It handled well but was badly damaged in a forced landing five months

Vickers Windsor prototype.

later. Three prototypes were flown and a fourth partially completed when the project was abandoned in 1946. The second prototype was flown by Wg Cdr Maurice Summers, Mutt's brother.

On 28 July 1944 Geoffrey de Havilland Junior flew for the first time the de Havilland D.H.103 Hornet twin-Merlin fighter, one of the most beautiful aeroplanes ever built – with performance and handling characteristics to match. Derived from the Mosquito but of composite wood and metal construction, its engines rotated in opposite directions ('handed') to eliminate take-off swing caused by the 2,030 hp engines. The Hornet was the fastest piston-engined fighter to enter service with the RAF although the top speed of 485 mph attained by the prototype dropped to 472 mph when No 64 Sqn took delivery of the production aircraft in 1946. Geoffrey de Havilland and Pat Fillingham completed the contractors test programme, but A&AEE test pilots were critical of its engine out performance with a strong tendency for the rudder to move over to full travel in a sideslip. Longitudinal stability was also considered to be marginal. A larger tailplane and a long dorsal fin appeared on production aircraft. Later the type was developed into the folding wing Sea Hornet for service with

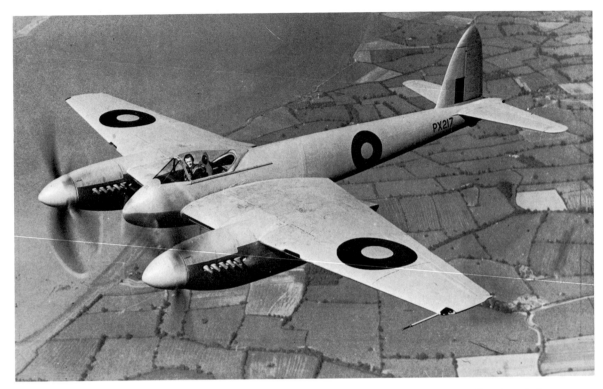

D. H. 103 Hornet flown by Pat Fillingham.

the Royal Navy. Sadly, not one of these superb aeroplanes was preserved when the type was withdrawn from service.

A trio of Bristol twins appeared in 1943–44. Planned in 1942 as a tactical day bomber to supersede the Blenheim, the twin Centaurus-engined Buckingham was flown by Cyril Uwins on 4 February 1944. By this time the Mosquito had proved itself to be capable of carrying the same bomb load as the Buckingham on 66 per cent of the power, so the contract was changed to reduce the number of bombers and convert the remainder to transport duties and to a trainer version – the Buckmaster, which Uwins flew for the first time from Filton on 27 October.

On 4 December the third version, the Brigand, made its first flight. Originally conceived as a torpedo bomber it reverted to the original Buckingham concept as a light bomber and saw service in Malaysia on anti-terrorist operations from 1950 to 1954.

At an early stage in the Second World War a successor to the Sunderland flying boat was considered. Based on the dubious philosophy that bigger was better, Shorts commenced the design of a massive boat to be powered with four 2,500 hp

Bristol Centaurus engines. Following their successful practice with the Stirling they decided to build a scale model to half the dimensional size. Shorts and Saunders Roe worked closely on the project, Arthur Gouge being vice-chairman of Saro and chief designer of Shorts. So Saro built the Shrimp, an attractive, four Pobjoy-engined boat which John Lankester Parker had flown in 1940. In reality the Shetland, as the big one was named, bore little resemblance to the Shrimp, having a deep, slab sided hull.

Two prototypes were built. When Lankester Parker and Geoffrey Tyson flew the first one on 14 December 1944 Coastal Command had already lost interest in it although it was thought, in high places, that the type had a commercial future.

Handling in the air and on the water was excellent. In 1945 representative passenger accommodation was installed and the Shetland was flown to the Marine Aircraft Experimental Establishment, which had returned to Felixstowe, for evaluation. One of the unusual features of this huge flying boat was a built-in power station with two 20 kVA generating plants. On 28 June 1946 a crew member on watch started one of the generators to enable him to cook his breakfast. He forgot to open an engine cooling shutter so the engine caught fire and the boat burned right down to the water line.

Short Shetland.

On 17 September 1947 Harold Piper and Tom Brooke-Smith, who became chief test pilot in 1948, flew the second prototype with civil registration G-AGUD. It was to be a representative passenger aircraft. A radical innovation was the first installation of powered controls in a British aeroplane. It, too, flew well but after only 180 hours flying it was dismantled at Belfast in 1951; yet another example of Britain's propensity for rushing into the construction of an expensive aeroplane for which there is no need, demand, or justification. The Shetland, Princess flying boat, and Brabazon airliner were classic examples of appalling waste of money in projects which were not researched in terms of market potential.

In the field of fighter aircraft Hawker had continued to develop the Tempest. Later marks had the 2,520 hp Centaurus engine driving a 12 ft 9 in diameter four-blade Rotol propeller. 'Winkle' Brown had a memorable experience in a Mk V during the period in 1944 when Britain was being attacked in daylight by V1s. Fortunately this weapon was slower than its designed speed so our fastest fighters could *just* catch it. However, to give pilots more time, RAE carried out trials on Mustangs, Spitfire XIVs and Tempests stripped of

armour and with heavily boosted engines using 130 octane aromatic fuel. 'Winkle' Brown was flying a Tempest at 400 mph when, at around 2,000 ft, there was a tremendous bang. The propeller stopped and oil poured over the windscreen. As he descended through light cloud there were obvious signs of fire with the cowling beginning to glow. When his flying boots became uncomfortably warm he decided to part company with the aeroplane, leaving it at 1,000 ft. He scored a bullseye in the middle of a farm pond. Unhappily, as he wiped mud and dirty water from his eyes, he saw a huge bull glaring malevolently at him from the side of the pond. Whichever piece of dry land he turned to, the bull was there first! Feeling the unfairness of salvation from a blazing Tempest degenerating into a goring by a bull he decided to wait until succour arrived in the shape of a farmhand 15 minutes later!

As chief naval test pilot at Farnborough he flew the Gloster E28/39 and thought it a lovely little aeroplane. Among other interesting machines was the Miles Libellula canard design which was to be developed for the navy. Unfortunately the induced drag levels were found to be too high so the project was abandoned.

The Supermarine S24/37, nicknamed 'Dumbo', was also on test at Farnborough. This interesting design had a variable incidence wing to assist in meeting a very exacting specification for shipboard operation and a requirement for dive bombing at an angle of 70 degrees. The Fairey Barracuda won the contract but Dumbo provided valuable data on variable geometry and high lift wings, the principle being embodied in the later Supermarine S12/40 Seagull amphibian.

One of many dangerous aircraft flown by 'Winkle' Brown was the General Aircraft GA.56 tail-less glider. In common with many tail-less designs longitudinal stability was poor and it had unpleasant self-stalling characteristics. As high angles of attack were reached it would rear up to a steep inclination and fall out of the sky. Eric Brown finally delivered it to Lasham airfield and briefed Robert Kronfeld on its handling tricks. Kronfeld, one of the world's most experienced glider pilots, was killed on his first flight in the machine.

Fred and George Miles of Miles Aircraft were working on an exciting project intended to achieve supersonic flight. Eric Brown was closely associated in the research programme of the M.52. The wing was unswept and bi-convex with a very sharp leading edge, a maximum thickness at 50 per cent back from the leading edge, and a remarkable thickness/chord ratio tapering from 7.5 per cent at the root to 4.9 per cent at the tip. A wing of this design was a totally unknown quantity in 1943, so it was decided to build a flying mock-up of the wing and fit it to the Miles Falcon, which had been used at Farnborough for a series of tests with different wing designs since 1938. The razor-edged wing caused it to be nicknamed the 'Gillette Falcon'. Eric Brown carried out a series of flights in it and proved that the design of the wing was certainly reasonably satisfactory at low speed although the landing speed was high at 70 mph. The projected landing speed for the 1,000 mph M.52 was 160 mph. There were problem areas such as the pilots view; he was located in a tiny conical cockpit in the centre of the air intake to the engine. The M.52 was almost complete when the Air Ministry cancelled the project. There has been controversy about the reasons for the cancellation, to say the least. It seems fairly conclusive that the main reason for it was the realization that the Power Jets W2/700 engine, a special version of the Whittle engine, was not likely to be sufficiently powerful to propel the machine at Mach 1 even if reheat was possible, and there was little room for any extra fuel. By this time it was becoming clear that a sweptwing was desirable, some thought essential, for supersonic

flight. Although the Bell X-1, the first aircraft to fly at supersonic speed, had an unswept wing, the brute force of its rocket powerplant and brilliant piloting by Chuck Yeager nudged the aircraft past Mach 1.

There was also the suggestion that Sir Ben Lockspeiser, the scientist in charge of the project, considered that the risk to test pilots was excessive. Whatever the reason for cancellation, which Eric Brown considers today to have been a serious error of judgement, it effectively deprived this country of the honour of being the first to fly an aeroplane at supersonic speed – albeit in a dive.

Research continued with models and Britain gave up the race towards Mach 1. It is interesting to realize that a scale model of the M.52 launched at 36,000 ft from a Mosquito in October 1948, recorded a speed of Mach 1.38 in level flight, proving that the aerodynamic shape of the machine was right.

In 1944 a radical project emerged in the form of a flexible deck upon which jet aircraft could land without undercarriages. Eric Brown carried out trials on an experimental deck, constructed of fire hoses overlaid with rubber, at Farnborough. The first landing was rather fraught when the deck arrester hook of his Sea Vampire bounced off the ground causing damage to the aircraft, which resulted in it diving into the flexible deck and penetrating it. In spite of this discouraging start over 200 landings were made by pilots with varying skills, some of whom had never before flown a jet. With the end of the war the urgency of the project faded and momentum was lost. VTOL with Harriers and helicopters became the way ahead for the Royal Navy.

At the end of the war in Europe, Eric Brown, being a fluent linguist in German, was posted to Germany to join a team investigating aeronautical research. 'That was a fascinating experience. I met people who had only been names throughout the war: Hermann Goering, Dr Heinkel, Hanna Reitsch, the fanatical Nazi woman pilot who flew the Messerschmitt Me 163 rocket fighter and a V1 flying bomb fitted with a rudimentary cockpit. I also met Kurt Tank who designed and flew his Fw 190 fighter; a fascinating character, he really knew his stuff!' Brown flew many German machines from the Arado 234 *Blitz*, the world's first jet bomber, to the giant Blohm and Voss Bv 222 six-diesel-engined flying boat which he flew from Trondjheim.

During his familiarization flight a *Luftwaffe* major attempted to wreck the Bv 222, whilst an engine failure during the delivery flight necessitated a landing on five at his destination! His first attempt at take-off in the Arado 234 was aborted as a turbine disintegrated when he opened the throttle at the beginning of the runway.

Another German aeroplane which he found particularly interesting was the unorthodox Dornier Do 335 twin tandem-engined fighter, the fastest piston-engined machine in the world and the second to be equipped with an ejector seat. In his book, *Wings of the Luftwaffe*, which tells the story of his test flights in *Luftwaffe* aircraft, Brown tells the macabre story of two prototypes which crashed, the pilots failing to eject. Their bodies were found without arms. The canopy jettison lever was attached directly to the canopy so, when it went overboard so did the pilot's arms. The trials of a Do 335 at Farnborough ended tragically in January 1946, when Group Captain Hards, OC Experimental Flying, recently back from a German POW camp, was in the circuit with the rear engine on fire, probably unknown to him. The fire burned through the controls and the aeroplane dived to the ground.

'A sensational aeroplane' was Eric Brown's description of the Messerschmitt Me 163 Komet rocket-propelled fighter which he flew in Germany and at Farnborough. It was of unusual design, had outstanding performance and was efficient in its interceptor role. A high standard of flying skill was required to survive the appalling hazards associated with the two chemical fuels which powered the Walter rocket motor. They were so unstable that a mismatch of volume in the two parts could lead to a devastating explosion as, indeed, could a heavy landing with fuel in the tanks. If the pilot escaped this hazard he could literally be dissolved in his seat if one of the tanks ruptured in the landing. Of the many casualties sustained in *Luftwaffe* units operating this machine only 5 per cent occurred in actual combat. For this reason it was decided that Brown's flight trials at Bad Zwischenahn should commence on tow behind a Messerschmitt Me 110, and at Farnborough behind a Spitfire, no powered flight being carried out. The RAE trials associated with a project for a Mach 1.24 aeroplane were cut short when the skid collapsed during a high speed landing at RAF Wittering. Brown, miraculously, escaped serious injury although the Me 163 was written off.

On 2 July 1965 Brown was a guest at the Munich Aviation Museum when a re-furbished Komet, for which a rocket motor had been supplied by RAE, was unveiled in the presence of its designers Dr

Captain E. M. Brown talking to Fritz Wendel, former Messerschmitt chief test pilot, in 1965. Half hidden behind Brown is 'Little' Spitz, the Me 163 test pilot at Peenemunde research centre.

Alexander Lippisch and Dr Willy Messerschmitt. Also present were the designer of the rocket motor, Dr Helmut Walter and two leading German test pilots, Fritz Wendel and Rudolf Opitz, who carried out many of the exceptionally hazardous flight tests on this remarkable aeroplane.

To return to less exotic projects of the period, the Supermarine flight test team under Jeffrey Quill had lost Don Robertson who had returned to the Naval Test Squadron after completing 400 hours of test flying in nine months. He was replaced by Lt Frank Furlong RNVR, a well known rider who had won the Grand National in 1935 on his father Noel's horse Reynoldstown. George Errington, considering himself under-employed as chief test pilot of Airspeed, joined the team on loan leaving Jeffrey Quill free to take a commission in the Fleet Air Arm to study and report upon the problems in operating Seafires from carriers. (See chapter nine.)

Worthy Down was an inadequate airfield for test flying, particularly as the Navy shared it. Jeffrey Quill himself had an unpleasant experience when he landed a Spitfire. As he came over the hill in the middle of the aerodrome, a Proctor was on the ground right in front of him. He hit it head on and the Proctor was wrecked. Fortunately injuries were slight but the incident added emphasis to the necessity of finding a more suitable base. In March 1944 the team moved to High Post, near Boscombe Down.

Lieutenant Pat Shea-Simmonds RNVR joined them from the first ETPS course and was the first test pilot with a formal training to join Supermarine. During a short period of attachment to Faireys immediately after leaving ETPS, he had the diverting experience of seeing the engine drop out of the Albacore he was flying. With great difficulty and skill he managed to land the tail-heavy 'glider' in a field where a working party from the factory fitted a new engine and propeller so that he could fly it home! Another well known test pilot who joined the team at this time was Flt Lt Les Colquhoun who stayed with the firm after the war.

In common with most test flying bases High Post saw its share of tragedies. The pressure on test pilots, both experimental and production, was remorseless. Seven day weeks, flying from sunrise to dusk was the norm. Flt Lt Frank Banner, attached for test flying duties, was practising simulated deck landings when he stalled his Seafire and died after being hauled from the blazing wreck.

The next ETPS graduate was Lt Cdr Mike Lithgow. During his service aboard HMS *Formidable* his life was saved by the remarkable ability of the carrier's navigating officers. Operating an Albacore at night he flew into the sea under circumstances which gave to the ship's crew no warning of the mishap. When his aircraft failed to appear for a landing it was obvious that he was in trouble.

Lithgow and his two crew members in their Mae Wests were 800 miles from land and their chances of survival seemed negligible. Five hours after their crash they saw *Formidable* zig-zagging towards them in the bright moonlight. They were spotted and taken aboard. Certainly this was one of the most remarkable escapes in naval aviation.

In 1942 Mike Lithgow was posted to A&AEE at Boscombe Down to familiarize himself with the Fairey Barracuda, with the probability that he would take command of a carrier based Barracuda squadron. Mike soon caught the test flying bug and remained a test pilot until he was killed in a tragic deep stall crash in a BAC One-Eleven in October 1963. Lithgow was posted to the US Navy Test Centre at Patuxent River to demonstrate the Barracuda to the Americans. A senior officer, seeing

it for the first time, suggested that only an aeroplane could possibly improve upon it! A better impression was created by the Firefly and the Seafire which was flown by Christopher Clarkson, in charge of the Flight Test Section of the British Air Commission.

Group Captain Sam McKenna was in Washington prior to taking command of the ETPS in succession to Group Captain Sammy Wroath. Mike Lithgow asked him for a nomination to the second course. After graduation and two months with Supermarine, he was again sent to Patuxent River as naval test pilot to the British Air Commission. After the war he returned to rejoin Jeffrey Quill and finally succeeded him as chief test pilot.

Quill had a disconcerting experience in a Spitfire Mk IX fitted, experimentally, with contra-rotating propellers. He climbed to carry out performance tests; suddenly there was a bang and the airspeed indicator needle began to unwind to 140 miles per hour with full boost indicated at the appropriate rpm. Quill was utterly baffled as the speed dropped even further. He suddenly recalled having flown near a gaggle of Dakotas towing Horsa gliders. The bizarre thought crossed his mind that he may have collected a towline on his tailwheel. He weaved sharply. Looking astern, there was no Horsa to be seen, but there was now a strong possibility of a full power landing on rough ground. Middle Wallop airfield was nearby so he entertained the onlookers with the remarkable sight of a Spitfire making a normal landing at full throttle! It was found that the translation unit which links the pitch change mechanism of the two oppositely rotating propellers had failed, causing the rear propeller to revert to full fine pitch and create a powerful airbrake.

At Castle Bromwich, near Birmingham, Alex Henshaw and his team were busy testing Spitfires, Seafires, and Lancasters in all weathers, with no radio or navigational aids other than the plume of steam rising from the cooling towers of a nearby power station. In the early days at Castle Bromwich Merlin engine failure was frequent as Henshaw recalls in his book, *Sigh for a Merlin*. He counted 127 forced landings by his pilots for various reasons during his six years there. He was extremely fortunate to survive a crash landing in a garden between two rows of houses in Willenhall, Staffordshire. His Spitfire was a total wreck. One of the test pilots at Castle Bromwich was Wg Cdr George Lowdell who began his testing career at Martlesham Heath in 1927 and continued until 1953. In February 1942, when he was 41 years

Above *Alex Henshaw with Prime Minister Churchill at Castle Bromwich.*
Below *Alex Henshaw's Spitfire after his crash at Willenhall.*

old, he tested and passed 21 Spitfire Mk Vs in one day, taking each one to 16,000 ft and diving at 450 mph to check the control alignment. For this particular series he carried out 50 such dives in the day.

At the end of the war Lowdell was involved in prototype trials of the Viking airliner under Mutt Summers, later working on the Viscount.

Compressibility effects were causing concern in the USA and in Britain. Briefly, the problem arises as air flowing over the surfaces of the aeroplane approaches the speed of sound which, as explained in chapter nine, is lower at altitude due to the decrease in air temperature. At subsonic speeds the air molecules in front of the leading edges of wings and control surfaces have time to 'warn' the molecules ahead that the aeroplane is approaching, thus a pressure pulse is set up. The human ear receives pressure pulses every time it perceives music, speech or noise. At Mach 1.0 pressure pulses generated can travel no faster than the speed of sound so the molecules are compressed to a point where a high degree of drag is generated and shock waves formed. At the same time the centre of pressure, which is the spanwise line along which the lift of the wing is concentrated, moves rearward; the aeroplane becomes unbalanced and a nose down pitch is generated. To complicate matters further the air does not flow at the same speed over all the surfaces; the wings, having a curvature on the top surfaces to create lift, have an airflow much faster than that over other parts.

An associated, and dangerous phenomenon, is the rate at which flutter can develop in control surfaces. Flutter had been a problem since the early days of aviation as this narrative has indicated. At lower speeds the pilot had a slight chance of reducing power and moving out of the flutter area. At the high subsonic speeds now being achieved the onset of flutter was usually immediate and catastrophic.

There was clearly a crucial area of research to be studied in evaluating these phenomena and the control design necessary to minimize the risk of flutter. Some remarkable rumours had originated in America that the Republic Thunderbolt had achieved high subsonic speeds in a dive but it seemed highly improbable that this bulky fighter could compare, for example, with the slim Spitfire, which had consistently proved to have outstanding high speed handling characteristics to Mach numbers well over 0.8.

Wind tunnel tests had been carried out at RAE in 1942, and in the following year the Aerodynamics

Flight commenced one of the most dangerous series of test flights ever carried out. A Spitfire Mk XI photographic reconnaissance aircraft was selected. It was decided to dive it from 40,000 ft at full throttle, reaching the maximum Mach number at about 25,000 ft.

At the end of 1943 Sqn Ldr J. R. Tobin reached Mach 0.92. In 1944 Sqn Ldr A. F. Martindale dived from 40,000 ft reaching Mach 0.89 – a true airspeed of 606 mph. At 27,000 ft there was an explosion and white smoke poured over his canopy. The windscreen was soon covered in oil so he could see nothing. Slowly he eased the control column back, speed decaying to a point where he might consider bailing out. He then realized that he had marginal control of the aeroplane so he elected to attempt a landing to preserve the valuable data recorded automatically during the flight. The slipstream cleared away some of the oil. He could not see the propeller but bits of engine were protruding through the battered cowling. Skilfully he glided the 20 miles back to Farnborough and landed safely, finding to his astonishment, that the whole of the reduction gear and propeller had broken away.

In the following month he was extremely unlucky. On a similar flight the supercharger blew up at 600 mph and the engine caught fire. Farnborough was enveloped in cloud so he was forced to attempt a landing in a field. At the last minute he saw high tension cables across his path and swerved to avoid them, crashing into a wood. In spite of spinal injuries he courageously returned to the burning wreck to rescue the data recorder. For this he was awarded the AFC. After the war he returned to his old firm, Rolls-Royce, from which he had entered the RAF.

When, in 1946, a conference was held between senior RAE and Supermarine officials to discuss the present state of the high Mach number tests, the Spitfire was reported to be the best of fifteen aircraft dived in the trials. It was only limited in achievable Mach number by airframe drag. Other types showed violent pitching characteristics whilst the American aircraft had experienced aileron buzz, a very high frequency vibration, often the precursor of immediate structural failure.

It is significant that the limiting Mach number of the Spitfire Mk IX at 0.90 was superior to the 1946 Vampire jet fighter at 0.80. Longitudinal instability was also a problem with this type. Similarly the Meteor 1 was prevented by buffeting from reaching a figure higher than 0.80. Further development of the type with longer nacelles, as

recorded in chapter ten, achieved a critical Mach number of 0.84.

Apart from its immense value as a research project, this series of trials was yet another accolade for R. J. Mitchell and his design team at Supermarine in 1935, when speeds of this magnitude were inconceivable. Much valuable data emerged from these trials and the wind tunnel tests which preceded them.

The principle of the laminar flow wing had been investigated in model and full-scale tests in Britain and America, with encouraging results. Such a wing is thin in section with large radius curves on the surfaces so that the air flows smoothly over them with uniform separation between the layers. If the curve changes abruptly the air leaves the surfaces and becomes turbulent with rapidly increasing drag and loss of lift. In practice the slightest imperfection in the surface finish, even dead insects upon the leading edge, can nullify the advantages of such a wing.

It became clear that Supermarines would have to think about a successor to the Spitfire, which could no longer be considered adequate for the new engines under development. A new wing was required to reduce profile drag – this is the total drag of the aeroplane less the drag induced by the lift of the wing. This would enable the critical Mach number to be increased. It was also necessary to increase the rate of roll. The new wing was built and fitted to a Griffon-engined Spitfire XIV with a Rotol five-bladed propeller. Jeffrey Quill flew it for the first time from High Post on 30 June 1944. The speed increase was found to be disappointing and behaviour at the stall inferior to the Spitfire's impeccable manners. Jeffrey likened it to a fidgety but otherwise well mannered horse which the rider had to get to know before he could trust it. He felt that this would not be acceptable to A&AEE.

By 11 September Quill had carried out 32 flights. Some had been carried out by Frank Furlong who, on 13 September, was engaged in a mock dogfight with Philip Wigley in a Spitfire XIV. At low level Frank hauled his aircraft round in a high G-turn. Suddenly it flicked on its back and dived into the ground, killing Furlong instantly. The reasons were obscure. It was possible that aileron trouble had developed, snatch was experienced near the stall, and a sharp wing drop occurred. He may have been taken unawares whilst assuming that he could fly this machine as he did the Spitfire.

The next prototype was a complete re-design. It was named Spiteful and was flown by Jeffrey Quill on 8 January 1945. Various modifications incorporated during the test programme resulted in acceptable handling characteristics but the performance increase due to the laminar flow wing remained disappointing; it proved to be a snare and a delusion due to the impossibility of maintaining the high standards of surface finish necessary in production and in squadron service. 17 of the original 190 on order were completed, the remainder being converted to the naval version, named Seafang.

By 1943 Supermarine had decided that they must enter the new jet era and designed a fuselage to be fitted to the Spiteful wing; the aeroplane to be powered by the new Rolls-Royce gas turbine, later named Nene. Jeffrey Quill flew the new E10/44 from the long runway at Boscombe Down in July 1946. During the 64 sorties which he carried out upon the aeroplane various problems arose. The pressure cabin did not operate so he spent many hours at high altitude in an unpressurized cockpit. The elevators were heavy and longitudinal stability left much to be desired. A spring tab elevator was fitted. In such an elevator the servo tab at the trailing edge is spring loaded so that for gentle control movements the tab remains aligned with the elevator. Where the control forces are high the tab assists in moving the elevator.

On one flight, at 600 mph, the tab fluttered, the control column and the aircraft vibrating so violently that Jeffrey thought it was about to break up. Being at low-level he pulled the nose up and throttled back; as speed decayed the vibration ceased and he made a safe landing. The spring tab was removed. As the Attacker, the E10/44 went into production, but it still suffered from heavy elevator control and the critical Mach number was only 0.82, the same as the Spiteful.

In June 1947 Jeffrey Quill was flying the E10/44 at 35,000 ft when he passed out. Having realized what was about to happen he reduced power and trimmed to a gentle dive. At 10,000 ft he revived. Assuming that the oxygen system had failed he returned to Chilbolton, by this time Supermarine's test flight base. To his dismay he found that the oxygen supply was quite satisfactory. A series of medical tests at the Aviation Medicine centre at Farnborough were inconclusive. He had spent 16 years in continuous and often difficult test flying with few breaks and such pressure had taken its toll. After a period of leave and further checks he decided that he must resign. As he said, so poignantly in his book, 'I went home full of sad and bitter thoughts. I could never again be a test pilot; I would have to learn to fly a desk.' His

outstanding career was far from over. As head of the military aircraft office at Weybridge he was deeply involved with the TSR.2 from its early days. As sales director of the Anglo-French company Sepecat he was involved with the Jaguar. As director of marketing of Panavia until his retirement in December 1978 he played a major part in the Tornado programme.

Quill was very fortunate to be involved with four outstanding military aeroplanes: the Spitfire, TSR.2, Jaguar and Tornado. It is probably not overstating the case to suggest that a major contribution to the outstanding performance of these aircraft was Jeffrey Quill's own unrivalled experience and dedication. The Spitfire was arguably the greatest fighter aeroplane of the piston engine era and Jeffrey Quill's contribution to it assures him an honoured place in the history of British aviation.

In 1947 Quill recruited a new pilot named John Derry who had learned to fly in 1943 and served with distinction in Fighter Command during the war. After the war Sqn Ldr Derry commanded the Tempest squadron at the Day Fighter Leader School, a part of the Central Fighter Establishment at West Raynham. The other squadrons in the unit were commanded by Sqn Ldr Bill Waterton, later to become chief test pilot of Gloster, and Sqn Ldr J. S. Fifield, whose work with Martin Baker helped perfect the ejector seat. In command of the DFLS was Sqn Ldr T. S. 'Wimpy' Wade, also to make a name for himself as a leading test pilot with Hawkers.

Derry soon made a fine reputation as a demonstration pilot flying the civil registered two-seat Spitfire VIII G-AIDN, so familiar to air show visitors at that time. He began work on high Mach number research using a Seafang. On 23 June 1947 he dived it from 27,000 ft to 20,000 ft reaching 0.75 without any compressibility problems. Suddenly a violent pitching motion at high frequency commenced. At the peak and trough of the phugoid, high negative and positive G forces, already excessive, threatened to break the aeroplane. At 16,000 ft the pitching decreased to a point where he could recover control and climb to 26,000 ft again for a repeat performance, gradually increasing speed to 0.7 when elevator problems developed. At 0.74–75 it became clear that the violent phugoid was beginning to develop again, so a slight reduction in power returned the Seafang to normal control. Various modifications were made and a speed of 0.83 finally achieved.

These tests established yet again how critical the surface profile of a laminar flow wing is. A distortion of only 0.020 ins in the upper surface or 0.006 ins in the lower surface was sufficient to change flow from laminar to turbulent beyond a line 10 per cent from the leading edge of the wing. If the surface distortion could be controlled to plus or minus 0.002 ins – an impossibly expensive task on a production line, the transition to turbulent flow would be delayed to a line 60 per cent of the chord of the wing, giving a critical Mach number of 0.80. Derry's sorties, carried out so skilfully and methodically, provided extremely valuable data for the forthcoming generation of fast jets.

De Havilland planned to develop an advanced airliner after the war. It was envisaged as a revolutionary sweptwing tail-less aeroplane powered by four de Havilland Goblin gas turbines. Wind tunnel tests commenced before the end of the war and it was decided to build a half-scale model based upon the Vampire. A metal wing, swept back 40 degrees, and a swept rudder were fitted. Lateral and longitudinal control was achieved by elevons at the outer trailing edges of the wing. The elevons acted differentially to roll the machine, and in unison for control in pitch.

The D.H.108 Swallow was flown for the first time by Geoffrey de Havilland Junior from RAF Woodbridge in Suffolk on 15 May 1946. RAE Farnborough had warned that wind tunnel model tests had indicated a tendency to dutch roll, a wallowing flight path with longitudinal and directional instability. There was also a possibility that the aircraft might drop into a spin at low speeds. Forewarned, Geoffrey took-off and was agreeably surprised by its handling qualities. From Hatfield he carried out a series of tests and it soon became evident that the sweptwing had been entirely successful in delaying the onset of compressibility problems, although this particular prototype had been designed for research at the lower end of the speed range.

It had already been decided that the tail-less configuration for the new D.H.106 airliner was not practical for reasons of inadequate engine power and excessive weight. The 108 trials proved conclusively that the decision was sound. Geoffrey de Havilland flew the second prototype, designed for high-speed research, on 21 August 1946, demonstrating it at the SBAC show at Radlett in September.

To check the speed measurement instrumentation it was decided to fly it along the south coast course used by the RAF High Speed Flight when, on 7 November 1945, Group Captain H. J. 'Willie' Wilson, commandant of the ETPS set up a new

world record of 606.262 mph in a specially modified Meteor. On 7 September 1946 Group Captain E. M. Donaldson increased it to 616 mph. The back-up pilots were Sqn Ldr Eric Greenwood, chief test pilot of Glosters, and his successor, Sqn Ldr W. A. Waterton.

Initially there was no intention of trying to beat the record. On 27 September Geoffrey took off from Hatfield in the calm of the evening for a final test flight before flying to the speed course base at Tangmere next day. His colleagues at the aerodrome became concerned when the 108 failed to return at the scheduled time. A report came in that an aeroplane had been seen falling into the Thames Estuary in pieces. Next day the wreckage was found in Egypt Bay near Gravesend.

Geoffrey de Havilland Senior had now lost his second, and eldest, son at the controls of a de Havilland aeroplane. The tests planned for this disastrous flight were a dive from 10,000 ft at high Mach number to investigate controllability and, if there was no problem, a high speed level run. It became clear that the 108 disintegrated during the second test and that the pilot died of a broken neck before his body hit the mudflats. Part of a recorder trace found in the wreckage proved that violent instability had occurred before the aeroplane broke up.

John Cunningham, chief test pilot of the de Havilland Engine Company, was appointed to succeed Geoffrey de Havilland. At the Lympne Air Show in August 1947 John Cunningham saw John Derry's demonstration in the Spitfire trainer and realized that he was a pilot of outstanding ability so he offered him a position at Hatfield. Derry, keen on the prospect of the transonic development programme in the 108, accepted the invitation with enthusiasm.

Cunningham had already flown the surviving prototype at Mach 0.88 after the installation of a more powerful engine with 3,750 lb of thrust and powered boosters for the elevon controls, so Derry took over the responsibility for this machine. On 24 July 1947 a new high speed 108 had been flown by Cunningham and demonstrated at the SBAC show at Radlett in September.

Derry decided that the only way in which the test programme could be conducted efficiently with minimal risk, was to move in increments towards the critical Mach number in a series of carefully planned and controlled experiments – the calculated risk technique, as described earlier. Pressure plotting points were installed over the wing from tip to tip with specialized instrumentation to record

Top left *John Derry (1952).*
Top right *John Cunningham and high altitude Vampire (1948).*
Below *D.H.108.*

chordwise and spanwise pressures, from which aerodynamic loads could be calculated. In February 1948 John Derry carried out ten sorties gradually increasing diving speeds until high Mach numbers were reached. The pattern of the onset of instability in pitch was becoming clearer. His test reports were sent to RAE Farnborough who were keenly interested.

De Havilland decided to enter the 108 for the 100 km closed circuit speed record held by Mike Lithgow of Supermarines who flew an Attacker at 564.88 mph over a four-sided course near Chilbolton. On 12 April, after a fuel leak had caused him to return to base soon after take-off, Derry lapped the course at 605.23 mph. For this he was awarded the 1947 Segrave Trophy for the greatest performance that year on land, sea or in the air.

The press had conceived the phrase 'breaking the sound barrier' and it now appeared that the D.H.108 was capable of accomplishing this feat, already achieved in America by Chuck Yeager in the Bell X-1, although this aeroplane could not take off unaided, being taken into the air and dropped at altitude by a B-29 bomber.

John Derry continued his programme of dives at high Mach number, increasing his knowledge of pitching and oscillation so that the aerodynamicists could analyse what was happening. On one occasion he was within a split second of emulating Geoffrey de Havilland's last flight. Pitching began very suddenly, the recorder showing that in less than 1½ seconds the aircraft had been subjected to positive and negative accelerations of 3½ G. Fortunately, throttling back saved his life. It indicated with startling clarity just how Geoffrey died.

John Cunningham set up another world record for de Havilland when he flew a Ghost-engined Vampire to a height of 59,492 ft, beating the existing record held by the Italian Colonel Mario Pezzi who flew his Caproni biplane to 56,049 ft in 1938.

Derry had a dreadful experience on 6 September 1948. He climbed to 45,000 ft to take pressure plots with the trimmer flaps up and down. Commencing a 30 degree dive to gain speed, at Mach 0.91 he noticed a tendency to nose heaviness. At 0.93 a wallowing motion developed, and at 0.94 pitching became more marked but was not too serious. He increased revs from 10,600 to 10,750 rpm but found no corresponding increase in speed. He thought that this was due to a rapid increase in drag so steepened the dive to maintain the Mach number at lower altitudes. Suddenly a sharp nose down attitude developed with a feeling of instability. The dive steepened still further, the nose down pitch and the instability developing violently with accelerations up to −2G.

Believing that he could still pull out he decided to continue in an even steeper dive. Suddenly the aircraft went beyond the vertical at 38,000 ft, pulling −3G as it did so. It was completely uncontrollable on the elevons and was heading for the ground − less than a minute away. Derry saw the Machmeter needle move past 1.00 − he had flown faster than any other British pilot, but if he could not pull out it would be a hollow victory. He closed the throttle but no reduction in speed followed. As a last resort he deployed the trim flaps; immediately a slow recovery commenced with the Machmeter registering 1.04. As 0.98 was reached the elevons

began to operate again so the flaps were partially retracted, the 108 levelling out at 23,850 ft with 0.94 on the meter, an indicated airspeed of 500 mph. An undamped pitching was still being experienced but complete retraction of the trim flaps eliminated it.

Derry cruised at low power back to Hatfield wondering whether the Machmeter was accurate. The flight had lasted for 45 minutes, the dive only one minute. Careful checks on the meter proved its accuracy so John Derry had indeed achieved the distinction of being the first British pilot to fly at a speed in excess of Mach 1.0 in a British aeroplane. Unquestionably his survival had been a matter of luck as well as his masterly handling of the 108 under extremely difficult conditions.

A decision was made to explore the supersonic régime even further. In February 1949 Derry made nine more dives from 44,000 ft achieving speeds up to Mach 0.99 and acquiring more valuable data. On 1 March he had a repeat performance of his flight of 6 September 1948. This time the trim flaps were not effective. As before, throttling back the engine was also ineffectual, negative G increased and the dive steepened, the 108 commencing a roll to port. Opposite aileron had little effect and the aircraft began a vertical dive, completely out of control, at a speed in excess of Mach 1.0.

Negative G increased and the spiral motion abated. The 108 executed the downward half of a bunt, or inverted loop, flew level at high speed, still inverted, then slowly Derry rolled it out, and by careful operation of the trim flaps and elevons brought it under control again. There was little doubt that recovery was assisted by the increased drag at lower altitudes, a phenomenon to which George Bulman had drawn attention in his 1943 recommendations to test pilots faced with compressibility problems. It was concluded that the trim flaps had little effect.

From the extensive data obtained during these exceptionally dangerous flights John Derry concluded that the critical Mach number of the D.H.108 was 0.70, at which speed nose-down pitch increased without a chance of controlling it. In the latter stages of the programme Derry was assisted by Sqn Ldr John Wilson who had joined the firm in 1948. On completion of the test series the high speed version was flown to Farnborough to join the other one for further tests by Service pilots. The CO of the Aerodynamics Flight was Eric Brown who carried out a number of flights in the 108. He too experienced the phenomena reported by Derry and the vicious stall which took place at 86 mph with no warning, when the wing dropped to vertical and then, if immediate action was not taken, the 108 would roll on to its back.

Brown was due to complete his tour of duty at Farnborough in August 1949: his successor was to be Flt Lt Stewart Muller-Rowland, an experienced test pilot who had been at RAE for two years. He was introduced to the high speed 108 whilst Sqn Ldr G. E. C. 'Jumbo' Genders began testing the slow speed machine, with emphasis upon its spinning characteristics, for which purpose spin recovery parachutes were fitted at each wing tip. Sqn Ldr Muller-Rowland concentrated upon longitudinal stability at high speed. On 15 February 1950 he was flying near Birkhall in Buckinghamshire when the aircraft broke up, crashing and killing the pilot. No defect in the machine was found and it was concluded that Muller-Rowland had exhausted or mis-managed his oxygen supply resulting in loss of consciousness.

During the morning of 1 May 1950 Sqn Ldr Genders took off from Farnborough in the low speed prototype to record, by automatic observer, the behaviour of the aircraft during the three phases of the stall: the approach, the actual stall, and recovery with various configurations of flaps and undercarriage. Fifteen minutes later the 108 crashed at Hartley Wintney. It appeared, from eye witness accounts, that it recovered from a dive and then entered a high speed stall or flick roll and then began a spin to starboard from which the pilot was unable to recover. He left the aircraft, descending at the same rate, until he hit the ground nearby, his parachute did not deploy. Although anti-spin parachutes were fitted they were ineffective, one of them having failed to operate. Three remarkable 108s had been lost with their pilots after a test programme which can boast of few equals in terms of cost effectiveness. In 1948 John Derry received the gold medal of the Royal Aero Club for outstanding achievement in the air.

Derry's reputation as a demonstration pilot rose to a peak at the Farnborough Air show in 1949. His aerobatic display in the de Havilland Venom prototype, which he had flown for the first time only a few days previously, was brilliant. The test programme for this aeroplane revealed some fairly serious problems. It had a much thinner wing than the Vampire and a more powerful engine. At Mach 0.84 it dropped a wing violently and dived, becoming uncontrollable until much lower altitudes were reached. At high speed in rough air it was unpleasant, being prone to aileron flutter at certain speeds. Both Derry and Wilson made many flights with cameras mounted on the wing to photograph wool tufts for study by the aerodynamicists. A re-design of the trailing edge of the aileron made a slight improvement. John Derry concluded that irreversible powered controls were essential for high speed flight. Cable operated controls were completely outdated as they were prone to stretching so the control surfaces could not move through their full arc; additionally the sloppiness due to stretch was an invitation to the evils of flutter.

A&AEE handling reports were also slightly caustic, but the aircraft went on to service in a number of RAF squadrons until the Hawker Hunter came into service in 1954. The last RAF Venom was retired in July 1962.

POST-WAR EUPHORIA II

The end of the Second World War saw Britain impoverished but the undoubted leader in practical jet propulsion technology. Germany had many advanced projects under development, but fortunately for the Allies, lack of high level direction and continual interference from Hitler prevented most of them reaching the operational stage in any quantity.

In 1943, at a time when the outcome of the war was uncertain, a committee under the chairmanship of Lord Brabazon of Tara, sat to consider recommendations for the shape of post-war civil aviation. Five types of aircraft were considered, ranging from an airliner capable of flying a regular service directly from London to New York, to a small feeder liner. The requirements were to be considered by design staffs as and when the exigencies of their war work permitted.

By the end of the war the Americans had established a commanding lead with the Douglas C-54 Skymaster and the Lockheed C-69, which became the Constellation. Both were well entrenched on the transatlantic routes and were flying personnel and stores all over the world. The C-54 had been in production since 1942 and hundreds were in service.

The industry, represented by the élite SBAC, was still led by the great pioneers, Sir Thomas Sopwith, Sir Roy Dobson and Sir Frank Spencer Spriggs in the Hawker Siddeley Group. Fairey was still in the family with Sir Charles casting a cold eye upon affairs. The White family still controlled the Bristol Aeroplane Company as did Sir George Nelson at English Electric, the company which was soon to develop the outstanding Canberra bomber. Rex Pierson and George Smith were at the helm of Vickers with George Edwards their brilliant young designer.

Sir Frederick Handley Page was still a law unto himself, ruling Radlett with a rod of iron whilst Geoffrey de Havilland, surrounded by many of his original 1920 team such as Frank Hearle and Charles Walker, ran the Hatfield firm, which now included Airspeed as a wholly owned subsidiary. Elsewhere there were a number of smaller constructors hoping to exploit what they saw as the burgeoning civil aeroplane market.

Several new machines were flown soon after the war. The 'Dakota replacement' was the objective of a number of manufacturers but it proved to be a mythical bird. To meet this need Cunliffe-Owen at Southampton designed the Concordia; only two prototypes were built. Among the smaller aircraft were the Percival Merganser, Miles Aerovan, and Miles Merchantman with a crop of prototypes likely to be of interest to the private owner. They were shown at the 1947 Radlett SBAC show.

First in the field among the larger companies were Bristol, de Havilland, Vickers and Avro. Bristol had designed a twin-engined transport sufficiently rugged to operate from jungle airstrips. As the war ended it was realized that such an aircraft would be a useful freighter in undeveloped countries. L. G. Frise, the technical director, and Archibald E. Russell, the chief designer, developed the Bristol 170, Britain's first post-war civil transport, which was first flown by Cyril Uwins on 2 December 1945.

In the twin-engined airliner class Vickers' 21-seat Viking prototype for BEA had been flown by Mutt Summers from Wisley on 22 June 1945. To put it into service as quickly as possible many Wellington components were joined to the new metal, stressed skin fuselage; the geodetic outer wing panels (albeit fabric covered), and the nacelle/undercarriage assemblies were used. Later, metal wings were fitted. Flight trials were uneventful and the machine gave good service with BEA and charter operators until around 1970.

On 25 September 1945 Geoffrey de Havilland had flown the D.H.104 Dove for the first time. Designed to meet one of the Brabazon Committee recommendations it was a modern replacement of the Dragon Rapide biplane, but a much more expensive machine with twin D.H. Gipsy Queen supercharged engines driving three bladed de Havilland Hydromatic feathering and braking propellers. Apart from directional stability deficiencies, cured by the addition of a dorsal fin, the flight test programme, mainly conducted by Geoffrey Pike, was satisfactory, the Dove becoming a popular aeroplane throughout the world and the precursor of a number of small and medium size civil aeroplanes which were built in the late 1940s.

In 1946 an 'industry only' SBAC show was held at Radlett aerodrome. The highlight was one of Geoffrey de Havilland's superb demonstrations in the D.H.108 tail-less research aircraft just two weeks before he was killed in it. It was believed that this machine was a small scale model of the new de Havilland airliner design so it aroused great interest. None of the new and advanced post-war projects had been completed but engine flying testbeds were flown including the Nene Lancastrian and a Sabre-powered Warwick.

Percival Aircraft at Luton had built Oxfords and Mosquitoes during the war although the redoubtable Edgar W. Percival had relinquished control of the business. After the war they built the Prentice trainer which was flown for the first time by Capt L. T. Carruthers on 31 March 1946. Carruthers had succeeded David Bay, who before the war, had been Percival's demonstration pilot and finally chief test pilot before joining the Fleet Air Arm and serving in the Air Fighting Development Unit. He was shot down and spent much of the war in a POW camp.

The Prentice showed marked lateral instability and turned over on its back in gentle turns. To cure this tendency the characteristic up-turned wing tips were devised. The spinning performance was unacceptable so a larger rudder was installed and anti-spin strakes fitted to the rear fuselage. There was little improvement; the machine spun in a potentially dangerous flat attitude. Major modifications, including twin rudders, were tried but with little success. Finally re-design of the elevators improved the aeroplane sufficiently to permit production to proceed for the RAF.

Avro was producing the Lancastrian, a converted Lancaster bomber, a completely uneconomic and noisy aeroplane. A few Yorks were in service, not in the same class as the Douglas C-54 but useful workhorses with four Merlin engines. The ubiquitous Anson, 'Faithful Annie', had been built in large numbers and many were sold as war surplus. Avro wanted to sell their new Mk XIX and let it be known that the war surplus machines

were not to a standard appropriate to post-war civil aircraft; nevertheless many were used by charter firms. Meanwhile Airspeed bought back Oxford trainers from the Air Ministry for conversion to the Consul, a practical 5–6 seater feederliner cum executive transport, which was sold for £5,500 and returned a handsome profit, keeping the Portsmouth and Christchurch factories active whilst the Ambassador airliner was being designed and tooled.

The British national airline had been divided into three Corporations; British European Airways, British Overseas Airways, and British South American Airways, the names reflecting their sphere of influence. One of the white hopes for long range operations was the Avro Tudor. Great optimism was felt as it had come from the design office of Roy Chadwick who had been responsible for the remarkable Lancaster. In the event it was the biggest disappointment in the long history of that great company. Work commenced in 1944, the Tudor being an interim type pending the introduction of more advanced designs.

Based upon the Lincoln, the 12-seat prototype first flew on 14 June 1945, with S. A. Thorn and J. H. Orrell at the controls. Bill Thorn had succeeded H. A. Brown as chief test pilot. Fourteen Tudors were on order for BOAC with another six to follow. It seems incredible that orders for 12-seat airliners were placed by the national carrier when the C-54 carried 44 passengers and the Constellation, which BOAC ordered when the Tudor was obviously going to be delayed, carried 43 passengers. Clearly the order should have been cancelled and reinstated with the 60-seat Tudor Mk 2. Another of the first ill-considered decisions which have bedevilled the British aircraft industry and the airlines since the war.

The maiden flight revealed many problems. The Tudor was unstable directionally and longitudinally whilst the steep ground angle resulted in unacceptable landing bounce. Three prototypes went to A&AEE at Boscombe Down, a continual stream of modifications being called for. A larger tailplane, fin and rudder were fitted, the undercarriage oleo legs were shortened to reduce the bouncing tendency, wing root fillets were modified and the inboard engine nacelles were lengthened to improve airflow over the tail. A design conference with BOAC in March 1946 tabled 346 modifications and alterations which the airline considered necessary. It seemed to be a case of 'We don't know what we want and we won't be happy till we get it'. Tropical trials at Nairobi sounded the death

Capt 'Jimmy' Orrell at the controls of a Lancastrian (1945).

knell of the Tudor I in December 1946, the order being cancelled.

On 23 August 1947 the prototype Tudor 2, which had been flying since March 1946, and had shown the same defects as the Mk I, taxied out for take-off with Bill Thorn, Roy Chadwick and Sir Roy Dobson, the Avro managing director. A red lamp from the control tower brought the machine to a halt as a messenger ran out to call Dobson to the telephone. He instructed Thorn to fly without him – the most momentous decision of his life. Shortly after take-off a bank developed, growing steeper until the Tudor plunged into a pond just outside the aerodrome. Thorn and Chadwick were killed. It was reported that the accident was due to the incorrect assembly of aileron control cables reversing the effect of the wheel.

Capt J. H. 'Jimmy' Orrell was appointed chief test pilot. He learned to fly as a Sergeant Pilot in the RAF in 1926. Another member of his course was Geoffrey Tyson, also to have a distinguished career as a test pilot. Leaving the service in 1931 Jimmy worked with a small airline, joined the Avro design office for a time and was delighted to be approached by Imperial Airways who invited him to join their flying staff on the European and Empire routes.

In those halcyon days passengers on the long Empire routes stayed overnight in hotels. Jimmy told the author, 'In the 1930s we were very decent to our customers. The captain was expected to take a keen personal interest in the welfare of his passengers and he always had a dinner jacket in his luggage. Navigational decisions were made upon the principle that the mail may be lost but not delayed, the passengers may be delayed but not lost!' On the outbreak of war he was flying the de Havilland Albatross and Armstrong Whitworth Ensign. All were impressed into National Air Communications and, after some hair-raising experiences flying Ensigns in and out of France at the time of Dunkirk, he entered an even more dangerous period of his career flying Hudsons on the 'ball bearing run' to Stockholm, running the gauntlet of the *Luftwaffe* on every flight. In 1942 Jimmy Orrell joined Avro as a test pilot, seeing the last of the Manchesters and all the Lancasters through flight test.

Tudor 4s were flown on the South American route by BSAA but the hoodoo remained. *Star Tiger* and *Star Ariel* were both lost under mysterious circumstances never satisfactorily explained. The type was withdrawn from passenger service and relegated to freight carrying. From the Mk 8 was developed the Ashton with four Rolls-Royce Nene turbines. It was the world's first four-jet civil aeroplane and Jimmy Orrell recalled the fascination of the first flights. Take-off procedures were quite different, altitude and speed were vastly increased whilst the absence of propeller drag required a complete review of landing procedures. The only snag was the 'taildragger' attitude which caused the jet efflux to batter the tailplane and burn off the runway surface. Once airborne, he realized that he had entered a different era of aviation, 'The smoothness and quietness of the flight made it so different and pleasant.'

Handley Page were also extremely unfortunate with their post-war airliner. Halifax bombers were being converted to carry large freight panniers underneath the fuselage and were popular with

Avro Tudor IV.

Handley Page Hermes IV in BOAC livery.

charter companies. In the meantime the design office was working on a new airliner/military transport, the civil machine to be built first. In 1944 work had been carried out to investigate the potential of a swept-wing tail-less aeroplane, which had first been the subject of ground runs with Major Cordes at the controls in 1940. Not until June 1943 was it actually flown by Jamie Talbot, who followed Cordes as chief test pilot, when Cordes took over the management of No 7 Aircraft Assembly Unit at Hooton Park near Manchester in 1941. It was evident from the test flights that the possibility of developing a large aeroplane using this configuration was too remote to be considered further. Accordingly, an orthodox low wing monoplane with four Bristol Hercules engines was designed. As the Cricklewood design office was short of draughtsmen the tail unit was sub-contracted to Blackburn at Brough.

On 1 December 1945 Jamie Talbot and Ginger Wright began taxying trials at Radlett. The Bristol Freighter, D.H. Dove, and Avro Tudor had flown and Sir Frederick Handley Page was anxious to see the Hermes fly next. On Sunday 2 December Talbot and Wright took off. It was clear immediately that they were in serious trouble; the Hermes climbed in a violent switchback path, diving steeply and then climbing again as the pilots fought to retain control. Finally it stalled, turned upon its back, and crashed on farmland three miles from the aerodrome, miraculously missing Radlett itself. Both pilots were killed and the wreckage destroyed by fire. Little evidence remained, but it was concluded that the elevators were seriously overbalanced to a level which the pilot was quite unable to control. As speed rose the control column would move violently fore-and-aft until the inevitable disaster occurred.

As a result of the investigation the tailplane was increased in span by 8 ft, the fin area was also increased whilst control tabs were adjusted to increase the stick-free stability margin.

The next Handley Page prototype to fly was the military version, to be known as Hastings. To ensure that short hops could be made before the first take-off, a practice which would probably have prevented the Hermes disaster, the new machine was flown first from RAF Wittering by Sqn Ldr Maurice Hartford, on loan from the Service. The initial trials were uneventful and it was flown back to Radlett after ten hours flying. At the end of the year it was delivered to A&AEE at Boscombe Down whilst production of the type began at Cricklewood.

On 25 April 1947 the first production aircraft was flown from Radlett by the new chief test pilot,

Sqn Ldr Hedley Hazelden who, after a distinguished career in Bomber Command, had joined the first course at the ETPS in 1943. Having graduated he was posted to the heavy aircraft squadron at A&AEE. One of his tasks was to evaluate the handling of the Lancaster carrying the 22,000 lb 'Grand Slam' bomb which increased the all up weight from 65,000 to 72,000 lb. The bomb was, of course, inert, but as the slips had not been fully developed, it was chained into the bomb bay. There was therefore no chance of jettisoning it in the event of trouble.

As the European war drew towards its end attention was directed to the airworthiness requirements for the new breed of civil aircraft which were under development. A civil aircraft testing section was opened at Boscombe Down with Sqn Ldr Hazelden in command. A major element of the work was to achieve adequate safety parameters in the 'engine out on take-off' situation. 'Hazel' said that he hardly ever carried out a take-off in any aeroplane with all the engines running!

On 8 April 1947 he joined Handley Page, soon to be told by R. S. Stafford, the technical director, that the company was designing a new jet bomber to fly at 500 knots for 5,000 miles at 50,000 ft with 50,000 lb of bombs. To the question, 'What do you feel about flying it?' Hazel answered, 'You find out how to make it and I will find out how to fly it!' In the meantime there was much to be done to prepare the Hastings for service. An original tail vibration problem had been cured by cording the trailing edge of the rudder; as the test weight rose to 78,000 lb longitudinal instability developed. Many unsuccessful modifications were made to the tailplane: 10 degrees of dihedral, 15 degrees of dihedral, 10 degrees and 15 degrees of anhedral. The centre flaps were rigged 5 degrees then 10 degrees down, they were inter-connected with the elevators to give trim compensation at touch down but none of these expedients completely solved the problem. Ultimately a stall warning indicator permitted the Mk 1 to go into service at the restricted all-up weight of 75,000 lb.

The second Hermes prototype was flown by Hazelden from Radlett on 2 September 1947. It did not share all the stability problems of its military counterpart but various modifications were found to be necessary. The tailplane was lowered, bulbous nosed elevators were fitted and the trim tabs were locked. A tricycle undercarriage version commenced taxying trials in August 1948. Hazel experienced violent nose wheel shimmy; this was soon cured and the first flight took place on 5

September just in time to put in the qualifying hours for the SBAC show which moved, in 1948, from Radlett to Farnborough. Westland's last fixed wing aircraft, the Wyvern, was flown for the first time by Harald Penrose on 12 December 1946.

This massive naval fighter, with a Rolls-Royce Eagle engine driving contra-rotating four-blade propellers, caused Penrose and his assistant, Peter Garner much pain and grief, and ultimately cost Garner his life. Engine failure was frequent and a dead-stick landing very hazardous because of the braking effect of the eight large propeller blades which could not be feathered.

A photographic sortie was to be made and a coin was tossed by the two pilots. Peter Garner took the assignment. His propeller translation unit bearing failed and the Wyvern crash landed in a field, Garner dying in the ensuing fire.

Rolls-Royce abandoned development of the Eagle engine so an Armstrong Siddeley Python was installed. Another Westland test pilot, Mike Graves, was demonstrating the prototype before a group of naval and Air Ministry officials when the engine flamed out. He attempted to return downwind to the airfield, overshot and crashed through the boundary hedge into a house, killing the two occupants and losing his own life.

For six years Harald Penrose worked at full pressure to solve the endless problems of the Wyvern, ultimately developing it into a first class naval aeroplane. He carried out 500 dives from high altitude to overcome propeller control problems – he faced disaster on six occasions, and the machine killed three test pilots. On one occasion he was approaching Yeovil airfield at 800 ft when the Wyvern suddenly, and without warning, turned on its back. Penrose, heading for the houses of Yeovil 500 ft away, recovered control with consummate skill, drawing upon his instinctive reactions in aerobatic flight. One aileron had become disconnected so both were hard up against the stops. He managed to roll level again and returned to a safe landing.

In his book, *No echo in the sky*, he gives a vivid and, indeed, poetic description of this awful experience, ending, 'Few had escaped so close a call.'

A promising exhibit at the 1948 SBAC show was the all magnesium alloy Planet Satellite. Designed by a civil engineer and sponsored by ICI and a subsidiary of the Distillers Company, Magnesium Elektron, who saw in it a sound way of promoting their magnesium alloys, the Satellite was a very elegant butterfly tail monoplane with the engine

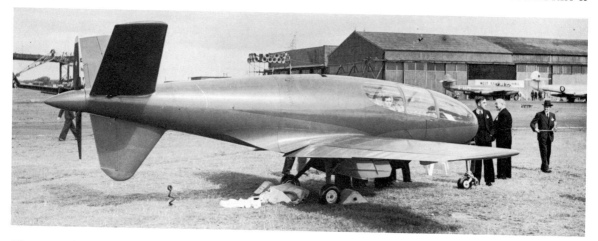

Planet Satellite.

and propeller behind the passenger cabin – a configuration shared by the new Lear Fan business-aircraft.

Group Captain H. J. Wilson resigned his commission to become test pilot to Planet Aircraft and was soon appointed managing director. His account of the 'test programme' affords a little light relief in the often tragic events of that period. The Satellite was taken to Blackbushe for flight trials and the story is best told in Willie's own words, published in the *Distillers Gazette*. 'After the first hop which resulted in the undercarriage collapsing, the Air Registration Board called for an investigation into the stressing. After numerous delays the machine was prepared for a second test flight and once more I carried out a hop to about 20 ft, then executed what I thought to be quite a reasonable landing. When, on inspection, it was found that the main keel had broken, that really brought the wrath of the ARB upon us, insisting that the aircraft had to be completely re-stressed . . . my own view was that we should, in the old phrase, 'jack up the windscreen and run a new aeroplane underneath', and I recommended to Distillers that they pack up the venture and sack H. J. Wilson. To give them their due they appreciated my endeavours and did very kindly offer me a job in one of their divisions; but I considered that the profession of flogging whisky was probably more dangerous than test flying'! Wilson became associated with Blackburns in connection with the Turbomeca gas turbine, later becoming sales manager for the Buccaneer and Beverley and sales director of the Blackburn Engine Company in 1959.

Scottish Aviation at Prestwick had maintained and carried out conversion of Liberators during the war. Their managing director, Group Captain David F. McIntyre, decided to build a short take-off and landing (STOL) aeroplane. N. J. Capper and R. C. W. Ellison flew the prototype Pioneer in time to demonstrate it at the Radlett SBAC show in 1947. As an exercise in the use of slots and flaps it was very successful, a speed as low as 30 mph being achieved. 59 were built for service for the RAF and the Royal Ceylon Air Force.

Raoul Hafner, the helicopter designer, had joined Bristols to work on their first helicopter, the Type 171, later to be known as the Sycamore, one of the few elegant specimens of the breed. The prototype was flown by H. Alan Marsh of Cierva, on 27 July 1947; the second one took to the air on 25 April 1949. It was the recipient of the first C of A issued to a British helicopter.

In 1947 the veteran Cyril Uwins retired as chief test pilot having made 54 first flights. A. J. 'Bill'

Bristol Sycamore prototype.

Bristol Brabazon.

Pegg, who had been assistant chief test pilot since 1935 succeeded him.

His first maiden flight was at the controls of the giant Type 167 Brabazon airliner which was the largest of the projects recommended by the Brabazon Committee, with the capability of flying non-stop to New York. Eight 2,500 hp Centaurus engines in coupled pairs driving co-axial contra-rotating propellers were installed in the prototype. Pegg spent many months delving into the complexities of this aeroplane, the controls of which were hydraulically operated. An extensive test rig had been built to prove the integrity of the system which was also flight tested in a Lancaster. A Buckmaster trainer was used to test the combustion heaters for wing and tailplane de-icing. A half-scale wing was tested to destruction in the RAE test rig and a section of the fuselage was pressure-tested at Farnborough.

At Filton the complex engine and propeller installation was run for hundreds of hours on a rig whilst the runway was extended by demolishing part of a village. An eight acre assembly hall was built, later to be used for Concorde.

A fashionable interior designer was inflicted upon the design staff to preside over the cabin interiors. The large fuselage mock-up was the scene of wordy battles! Bill Pegg recorded his irritation with the controversy which arose over trivia, 'I felt like saying "what the hell are you worrying about the colour of the bar for when we don't know if it will fly yet – if it does it will probably fly like a rocking horse and you won't be able to stand, let alone drink"!'

On 3 September 1949 Pegg and his crew of nine technicians boarded the 230 ft span aircraft for taxying trials at an all-up weight of 250,000 lb.

The test pilot had spent several weeks in America flying the giant B-36 bomber – almost as large as the Brabazon, so he was conditioned to the massive scale of the new aircraft. Problems having arisen with the nose wheel steering, this was disconnected, only the brakes being used for directional control on the ground. Several runs were made, with the nose being lifted off the ground so that Pegg could 'feel' the controls.

After an all-night inspection conditions were satisfactory for the first flight although the absence of nose wheel steering created a potential hazard in the slight cross wind. This had to be carefully watched particularly as the Brabazon had shown a tendency to weathercock into wind during the taxying trials.

Take-off was satisfactory and a slow climb with undercarriage down was made. Bill Pegg's impression of the enormous size of the aircraft was summed up in his response to the question, 'What is it like to fly?' 'We just fly the cockpit and the rest of it trails along behind!' Undercarriage retraction was a major undertaking with a definite sequence of operations to avoid such troubles as the wheel well doors being closed as the chassis came up. The flaps were built in eight sections to avoid problems with wing flexure. They were operated initially in symmetrical pairs so that when Pegg raised the inner pair a sharp nose-down pitch was induced, a phenomenon which had to be investigated on later flights. The landing was perfect, Pegg marvelling at the absence of any real problems with such an advanced aeroplane.

As he left the Brabazon to join the throng of pressmen he was appalled to see nearby the prototype Mark II Sycamore helicopter, about to make its second flight, rise ten feet and then fall back to the ground as the rotor blades disintegrated. The vibration characteristics of the Alvis Leonides engine had created unexpected resonance and thus weakness in the trailing edge of the new rotor design. It was miraculous that the failure occurred so near the ground. The pilot was uninjured.

Bill Pegg carefully steered the press away from the forlorn Sycamore. One man, who saw the accident, was told nonchalantly, 'Oh, it is just a routine test!'

Data gathering was a major element in the Brabazon test programme. Twelve cine cameras filmed continuously the twelve separate instrument panels with over 1,000 dials monitoring every aspect of the operation of the aeroplane. Analysis of the data was an immense task and took hundreds of hours for each flying hour.

Bill Pegg, his aeroplane and his Bristol car.

As the Mark II with Proteus gas turbine engines was designed to fly at 330 mph at 35,000 ft, the wings were vulnerable to gust loads. Stiffening the structure would have imposed an unacceptable weight penalty so a gust alleviator system was devised. A detector was to be mounted on the nose, eighty feet ahead of the wing, to feed a signal back to the aileron actuators, moving them in unison and symmetrically to counteract the effect of the gust. The system was flight tested in a Lancaster but was not sufficiently promising to be installed in the Brabazon.

The Brabazon was the largest aeroplane studied by the ARB which had been revived in 1946. Until 1937 the airworthiness certification of all civil land-planes was the responsibility of A&AEE at Martlesham Heath. In 1937 the Board was formed to take over the certification of aeroplanes with an all-up weight of less than 12,500 lb. Towards the end of the war the Civil Aircraft Test Squadron was

formed at Boscombe Down under the command of Sqn Ldr Hedley Hazelden, with the objective of establishing airworthiness requirements for the postwar breed of large civil aeroplanes. The first test pilot of the ARB after it was re-formed was Capt Digby, formerly a pilot with Imperial Airways. He was involved in certification of the D.H. Dove and Vickers Viking and was then succeeded by Douglas Wakeman who was a trained test pilot. There was hardly enough work to occupy all his time so, in his slack periods, he assisted Bill Pegg in testing production Brigand bombers at Filton. His career ended tragically. He was flying a Brigand when a propeller broke away. It dropped below the machine, rose on the other side and took off the propeller and engine on that side. Wakeman made a masterly forced landing but the Brigand hit a tree which fell upon the cockpit, killing the pilot.

Lt David P. Davies joined the ARB in 1949 as a test pilot. He entered the Navy in 1940 and flew Swordfish and Avengers, being awarded the DSC. After squadron service he took a MU test pilots

D.P. Davies, chief test pilot of the Air Registration Board (1968).

course, graduated at ETPS and spent four years in the Handling Squadron at Hullavington. The only other test pilot in ARB was Geoff Howett who had been one of Group Captain John Cunningham's night fighter pilots. Dave Davies and Geoff Howett did most of the certification flying for fifteen years, to be joined by Gordon Corps who served for nineteen years, John Carrodus who served for ten years, and Nick Warner who is, at the time of writing, the chief test pilot of the ARB, whose test parameters are defined in British civil airworthiness requirements which have developed in line with the increasing complexity of civil aircraft. With the Handley Page Hermes IV, in 1949, the Civil Aircraft Test Squadron ceased to take an active part in certification.

Dave Davies was involved in the Brabazon project and recalled an experience surely unique in the annals of British test flying. On a five-hour flight with Bill Pegg, Dave was surprised to hear, 'We will go for lunch now.' Handing over to his co-pilot Pegg took Davies into one of the cabins where a good lunch was served in a most civilized manner by a steward in a white uniform! 'Right!' said Bill afterwards, 'We will go back to work now'!

Dave was surprised by the remarkably soft undercarriage of the Brabazon; it was quite impossible to detect when it had actually landed so a red warning light was activated as the oleo legs compressed.

Sadly the Brabazon was the airliner which nobody wanted. When its 400-hour inspection was due there was no enthusiasm on the part of Bristols, the Ministry or BOAC to pay for it, so the project which should never have been commenced was abandoned. Like its maritime counterpart, Brunel's *Great Eastern*, Brabazon was ahead of its time. Today, the Boeing 747 of 195 ft span and an all-up weight of 710,000 lb will fly 370 passengers 5,790 miles non-stop at almost 600 mph.

The Brabazon was broken up in 1953 and all that is left of this handsome aeroplane is the nose wheel assembly in the London Science Museum and a length of fuselage skin bearing the name *Brabazon* in the Shuttleworth Trust Museum at Old Warden.

On 30 May 1947, Lindsay Neale flew the Boulton Paul Balliol for the first time. Intended as a replacement for the ageing Master trainers, it was in competition with the Avro Athena which flew later; both were intended as prop-jet aeroplanes. Initially the Balliol flew with a Bristol Mercury engine. The second prototype, flown on 17 May 1948, was the world's first single-engined turboprop aircraft. The first machine was re-engined with a Mamba. Problems with the Mamba led to the decision to fit Merlin engines of which there were large numbers in storage.

Lindsay Neale discovered serious control problems; elevator reversal occurred at 320 mph so he flew at 420 mph to see what the effect was. The windscreen disintegrated, the Balliol diving into the ground, killing Neale and his co-pilot, Peter Tishaw.

In 'A' Squadron at Boscombe Down was Flt Lt A. E. 'Ben' Gunn. He had served, in 1944, in No 501 Sqn raiding occupied territory in Spitfires. The squadron was re-equipped with Tempest Vs in which they shot down V1 flying bombs and destroyed rolling stock on the French railways as part of the softening-up operation for the invasion of Europe. After 200 hours of ops on Spits and 200 on Tempests, he was posted to Boscombe Down on VE Day, 6 June 1945, to work on Tempest development and armament trials on Vampires. An investigation into the possibilities of the Vampire as a dive bomber began, but it was soon realized that the current designs of 500 lb and 1,000 lb bombs were useless; they tumbled. Launching

Above *Boulton Paul Balliol.*
Below *Avro Athena prototype.*

rockets from zero length rails was another aspect of his work. On one occasion, after firing them at targets in Lyme Bay, he was extremely surprised when his engine stopped as he ran down the runway at the end of the sortie. All his fuel had gone. It was discovered that the two fuel pipes from the wing tanks were proud of the lower surface at the root of the wing and covered by a light aluminium fairing; as the rockets fired they rose towards the wing, the fins cutting into the fairings and the pipes.

Realizing that life for him in the peace-time Air Force was not ideal unless he could continue test flying, he was able to join the 1948 ETPS course, returning to Boscombe Down in June 1949. By this time the Avro Athena and the Balliol were being evaluated with some urgency as there were spinning problems with both.

Capt James Orrell had first flown the prototype Athena with a Mamba engine on 12 June 1948. At 1,000 ft, after two minutes in the air, the jet pipe temperature reading went off the clock. 'Jimmy' shut down the engine and, already being in a turn, continued into the circuit and landed safely, his limited experience in the air indicating that there were no apparent control problems. The forward blading of the turbine rotor had rubbed against the stator fixed blades and bent them severely.

The second prototype was fitted with a Dart turbine which behaved perfectly. But as with the Balliol, the decision was taken to instal the Merlin. It was necessary to move the wing forward 27 inches to compensate for the greater weight.

Both trainers shared peculiar spinning characteristics regardless of the type of engine fitted. As the spin developed the tail snaked up to the horizon again and resumed a normal spin with no tendency to tighten up. To prove this, Ben Gunn took a Balliol to 27,000 ft and carried out a 25 turn spin which A&AEE technicians watched through binoculars.

During these tests news of the death of Lindsay Neale was received. Gunn was detached to Boulton Paul to continue the test flight development of their trainer.

The second prototype was dived at 320 mph; control feel on the stick was neutral, whereas at 330 mph a degree of overbalance occurred. Gunn recommended that the tailplane be strengthened and a 2 degree alteration be made in its angle of incidence. This solved the reversal problem but the spinning difficulties remained intractable.

When the Athena arrived at Boscombe Down it was known to have similar spinning characteristics. The Athena was evaluated against the Balliol and if its spinning qualities proved inferior, the latter would be ordered. On the first flight in the hands of an A&AEE pilot the spin was so violent that half the fin and rudder broke away. The Balliol received the contract.

Within a month Ben Gunn was invited to join Boulton Paul as chief test pilot where he soon became involved in the flight trials of the Lancaster being used to test Boulton Paul powered controls, including the gust alleviator system, designed for the Bristol Brabazon. Carefully screened from prying eyes were the two delta research aircraft which he would soon fly, and in one of which, he nearly lost his life.

For a number of years Armstrong Whitworth had been involved in laminar flow and boundary layer research applied to flying wing aircraft. In 1942 chief designer John Lloyd had designed a section of a wing which had been tested in the wind tunnel at the National Physical Laboratory. A twin-boom single-seat fighter design followed, but it was not built and a jet bomber with four Metro-Vick Beryl turbines and no tail was projected in

1942. It was decided to build a one-third scale glider to investigate the configuration.

NPL tests on the wing model indicated that full scale tests were essential. A Hurricane IIb was fitted with a laminar flow wing, which permitted the firm to investigate the production problems inherent in the tight tolerances required to make a wing having its transition point from laminar to turbulent flow as far back as 50 per cent chord. In simple terms the smooth flow of air over the wing surface must be maintained until it reaches a point half way between leading and trailing edges; thereafter, turbulent flow as the air leaves the surfaces is not so important.

Charles Turner-Hughes flew the Hurricane on 23 March 1945. Later it went to RAE where Eric 'Winkle' Brown became involved in the test programme which showed disappointing results, the transition point being at only 40 per cent of the chord. Profile drag of the tail section was investigated by a pitot-static comb and automatic observer, one of the earliest uses of such a recorder.

It was suspected that undulating wing surface was the reason for such poor results. The Hurricane was returned to the works and the wing skin carefully filled and re-finished to remain within plus/minus one-thousandth of an inch tolerance on a two inch length of surface. Armstrong Whitworth test pilot R. Midgeley flew the Hurricane back to Farnborough in April 1946.

Further tests indicated that the wing now gave the drag co-efficients required, but it proved to be impracticable.

At the end of the war Professor A. A. Griffith at RAE designed an aerofoil section which he believed could achieve laminar flow from leading to trailing edge, if used with boundary layer suction on both upper and lower surfaces of the wing. After inconclusive model tests it was decided to carry out full scale trials on a Meteor FIII.

The suction system required a 0.05 inch-wide slot along the surfaces of the wing on the aileron hinge line which continued from root to tip of the new outer panels.

Sqn Ldr Eric Franklin succeeded Charles Turner-Hughes as chief test pilot in April 1947. On the outbreak of war he was called up as a pilot in the RAFVR, serving in Bomber Command until the end of his second tour in 1943, followed by an interesting detachment to 'B' Squadron at Boscombe Down. He was awarded a DFC with an AFC for his work in the formation of the first Halifax conversion units. At the end of his second tour he returned to A&AEE for a lengthy period testing heavy bombers including, in 1943, tropical trials in Khartoum and, in 1944, winter trials of a Lancaster in Canada, the first of many such test programmes which have now become established practice. He then took a course at the ETPS, joining Armstrong Whitworth on special release to assist Turner-Hughes.

Eric Franklin flew the Meteor in January 1947; blizzard conditions during that winter prevented further flying until March. After eleven flights which showed little improvement in performance the Meteor was flown to RAE in October. 'Winkle' Brown carried out a further series of flights with equally inconclusive results. Clearly theory and practice were not in accord.

John Lloyd concluded that a flying wing was essential if maximum benefit was to be obtained from boundary layer control. It was decided to build the glider which had been projected in 1942.

To reduce building time a wooden structure was chosen. The machine was equipped with appropriate instruments for pressure plotting, strain gauging, and measurement of control surface movement and was flown first by Turner-Hughes, towed by a Whitley (the last one built) in March 1945. Trials were satisfactory and continued until March 1950 when the glider was delivered to the Airborne Forces Experimental Establishment at RAF Beaulieu.

Armstrong Whitworth and the Ministry were content with the test data and work commenced

AW.52 G glider with Eric Franklin in front seat (1946).

in 1944 on two powered aircraft of similar configuration, to be known as the A.W.52, and powered, in the case of the first one, with two Rolls-Royce Nenes of 5,000 lb thrust. The second one would have two 3,500 lb thrust Derwents. The use of gas turbines permitted a high degree of suction to be available for boundary layer control. An innovation was the installation of the new Martin-Baker ejector seat in both aircraft.

Eric Franklin commenced taxying trials at Baginton on 1 April 1947 and the machine was then taken to Boscombe Down for the first flight.

Taxying trials were resumed in October 1947 and a few runs made at speeds up to 75 knots. The nosewheel rose off the runway and Franklin had trouble in dropping it back to the surface; he was forced to close the throttles as longitudinal control was inadequate. A brake fire brought the tests to a halt whilst modifications were made to the nosewheel assembly and the controls.

Further runs and a short hop were made with a lengthened but fixed front oleo leg; the problem was cured. It became apparent, however, that as predicted the elevator control was very sensitive. This received further confirmation when Eric Franklin made the first flight on 13 November 1947. During the approach and flare-out the slightest movement of the control column would initiate a rapid fore-and-aft oscillation at about two cycles per second. The problem also arose on the third flight in bumpy air when a pitching oscillation began soon after take-off. The aeroplane was shaking to an uncomfortable degree although a climb into calmer air improved the situation.

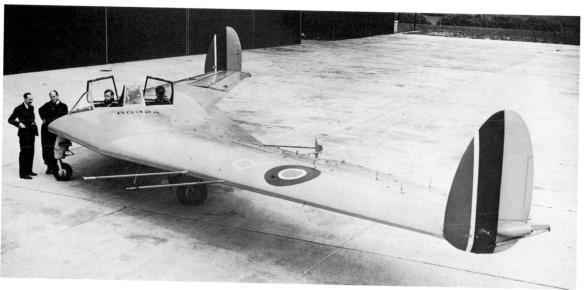

Having met the Ministry of Supply requirement for five flights and three hours airborne at Boscombe Down, Franklin flew the AW.52 to Bitteswell on 1 December for modification and further tests. At the end of December a further flight was made carrying a test observer – he noticed a flexing of the wing which could have been responsible for the vibration arising at 250 knots.

In April 1948 Flt Lt W. H. Else entered the test programme. Having joined the RAF in 1940 he served in No 182 Sqn operating Hurricanes. Later, A&AEE required three experienced Typhoon pilots for work concerning attacks on Japanese tanks and parked aircraft. Bill Else was one of those selected and he recalled the realism and excitement of strafing the targets with the great advantage that there was no answering fire – aim was greatly improved!

In 1944 he was invited to join 'A' Squadron and was nominated for No 4 course at the ETPS which had moved to Cranfield. His room mate was Sqn Ldr Neville Duke. In January 1944 Else returned to A&AEE and, with Neville Duke, evaluated the first de Havilland Canada Chipmunk to arrive in Britain. Both pilots were impressed with the machine and reported accordingly.

Eric Franklin, at the time known by the unusual title of senior pilot, was looking for an assistant. A mutual friend, Sqn Ldr 'Tich' Havercroft, made the introduction. Else resigned his commission and joined Armstrong Whitworth in June 1947. Eric Franklin was appointed chief test pilot immediately after the first flight of the AW.52.

Bill Else soon took an equal share in the work on the AW.52. The controls left much to be desired;

AW.52 with Rolls-Royce Nene engines.

Bill Else in Meteor IV cockpit (1947).

harmonization was non-existent, they were spongy and, still, the longitudinal control was much too sensitive.

The prototype flew to Farnborough for the 1948 SBAC show in September; it was joined there by the newly completed second prototype. Subsequently the first one was modified at Baginton in a further attempt to cure some of the defects. The second machine shared all the problems of the first, with the additional headache that its low power resulted in inferior performance.

The work continued until March 1949 when Bill Else, flying with an observer, Arthur Payne, carried out a low pass at Baginton for the benefit of the factory workers who had not seen the AW.52 in the air. The day was calm but, as he climbed away, he entered turbulent air and violent pitching commenced with the aeroplane shuddering and banging. The pilot immediately closed the throttles; as the machine was climbing speed soon decayed and peace reigned again at 170 knots. This was the first time that the short 2 CPS pitching had been experienced with the Derwent engined prototype. It was thought that flutter of a tab or control surface had occurred but, as Bill Else had not noticed any undue input to the control column, this was unlikely. Accelerometer readings showed an alarming plus 12G to minus 4G so the aircraft was grounded for a thorough structural check.

On 3 May 1949 Flt Lt John O. Lancaster joined the test team. Having served in Bomber Command since the beginning of the war and completed two tours of ops for which he was awarded the DFC, he joined 'B' Squadron at Boscombe Down in November 1943. In 1945 he graduated from No 3 course at ETPS and was de-mobilized in January 1946. Before joining AW he had a short period with Lindsay Neale at Boulton Paul and was assistant to Geoffrey Tyson at Saunders Roe.

On his third familiarization flight in the Nene-engined AW.52 he descended from 12,000 ft into turbulent air at 5,000 ft at an indicated air speed of 320 knots. The violent oscillation, not hitherto experienced on this prototype began during the descent, rising to such a pitch that the pilot was becoming totally disorientated and feared unconsciousness. For the first time 'in anger', the Martin Baker ejection seat was used and Lancaster landed safely in his parachute. The pilotless prototype regained stability and flew on to make a heavy landing in open country, tearing out the engines and writing off the aircraft after 65 flights totalling 36 hours.

Not until October 1949 did the second prototype fly again with severe speed restrictions limiting it to 250 knots. The next phase of the test programme investigated the boundary layer transition point with many pressure plots being recorded. In October 1950 the remaining AW.52 was delivered by Farnborough where it was used for further research into airflow over swept wings.

Once again surface undulation had a most adverse effect upon the boundary layer, again the results were improved by carefully filling and smoothing the surfaces. To isolate the problem of dead insects on its leading edges, the AW.52 was taxied to the end of the runway with sheets of paper over the wings. By September 1953, the type had come to the end of its useful life and the AW.52 was ignominiously despatched to the Proof and Experimental Establishment at Shoeburyness to act as a target for weapon trials.

The protracted test programme had proved yet again what had already been learned on the Supermarine Attacker and the special Meteor; whilst boundary layer control of laminar flow wings is attractive theoretically, it is almost impossible to achieve worthwhile results in practice. Also, as the D.H.108 had proved, swept-back wing, tail-less aeroplanes present exceptionally difficult problems of fore and aft stability. The failure to resolve this problem destroyed Armstrong Whitworth's hopes of building a large flying wing bomber or transport aeroplane.

At the end of the war Faireys were building Firefly aircraft for the Royal Navy. Foster Dixon was the chief test pilot, having succeeded the great Chris Staniland who was killed in a flying accident in 1942.

The company had been displaced from its original Great West Road aerodrome when it was requisitioned to be part of Heathrow, now London Airport; flying was transferred to Heston until this airfield was also affected by the Heathrow complex. The flight test department then moved to White Waltham near Maidenhead, not an ideal site as it was the operational headquarters of the Air Tranport Auxiliary, the famous wartime civilian ferrying organization.

In 1945 Sqn Ldr David Masters was seconded to Faireys from Bomber Command and was posted to Ringway near Manchester to join Sam Moseley and Geoffrey Alington. David resigned his commission, joined the Fairey staff and was sent to take a course at ETPS.

Two serious accidents resulted when cockpit canopies broke away from two Fireflies in a dive; Ken Seth-Smith and Colin Evans were knocked unconscious and died. The enquiry into these accidents created a tense atmosphere between Foster Dixon and a senior official in Faireys and, to resolve it, Dixon was invited to become chief test pilot of the newly formed rotary wing division. Tim Wood and Ralph Munday were recruited to the fixed-wing side.

Fairey had considered in depth the future path of development in rotary wing flight. The autogiro was fairly simple but had no real ability to rise vertically. The helicopter was extremely complicated and costly and wasted power by having a small rotor at the tail to counteract the torque of the main rotor, the machine having a tendency to rotate in the opposite direction to the rotor.

Fairey designed the Gyrodyne to adopt the best features of the autogiro and helicopter with none of the obvious penalties. It had stub wings and, on the starboard one, was a propeller driven by the Alvis Leonides engine. This replaced the normal tail rotor and, at the same time, produced a useful amount of thrust.

By September 1947 the first of two prototypes had flown 56 hours in a tethered rig. On 12 December Basil Arkell, an experienced helicopter pilot, flew it untethered for the first time. As the test programme proceeded satisfactorily Arkell increased speeds and duration of flights until it became clear that Fairey had a potential record breaker. Arkell broke the international three kilometre closed circuit record for helicopters on 28 June 1948 establishing a speed of 124.3 mph.

Fairey Jet Gyrodyne at 1955 SBAC show.

Development flying continued. In April 1949 Foster Dixon telephoned David Masters at Ringway to invite him to join the rotary wing test team as 'he wanted a man with no experience of helicopters or autogiros so that he could bring an entirely fresh mind to bear upon the problems.' David said that he would consider it and give Dixon an answer within a few days. Three days later the chief test pilot, with his observer Derek Garraway, were carrying out a high speed run when a fatigue failure occurred in the rotor assembly. The aircraft crashed at Ufton near Reading, both crew members being killed.

Work on the project continued under the control of Group Captain Gordon Slade who had joined Fairey on detachment from the RAF in 1945 and became chief test pilot in 1946. He joined the RAF in 1933 and Slade became a test pilot at Martlesham Heath, moving, in 1940, with the A&AEE to Boscombe Down where he served in 'C' Squadron, ultimately commanding it. One of the highlights in his career at Boscombe was the responsibility of testing the Mosquito bomber and fighter prototypes. In 1941 Slade decided that he must have a period of operational flying. He took a night fighter course at Church Fenton, was promoted to Wg Cdr, and joined John Cunningham's crack No 604 Sqn.

In 1943 he commanded the Handling Squadron at Central Flying School, Hullavington, returning to operational flying in February 1944. As Fairey's chief test pilot he had a first class team, which since the death of Foster Dixon, had no direction and was in disarray. A strict disciplinarian, he was most unpopular with all but his pilots whom he

supported fully in the quest for optimum performance and quality in the aircraft being delivered to the Navy. To everyone but the pilots he was 'Group Captain Slade' – 'Gordon' was out!

Slade became responsible for the Gyrodyne and, in 1953, the second prototype appeared with two propellers on the stub wings powered by the Alvis engine whilst rotor power was provided by a fuel burner at each tip giving jet propulsion. John N. Dennis carried out flight trials in this machine and a major effort was required to master the techniques of transition from auto-rotational flight in the autogiro mode to helicopter flight with direct lift after the tip jets had been re-lit.

In 1954 Sqn Ldr Ron Gellatly flew a new Fairey ultralight helicopter with tip jet propulsion of the rotor; intended as an air observation post it was not put into production. From these early experiments was developed the most advanced helicopter in the world at that time, the Fairey Rotodyne.

Another officer attached to Faireys after the two Firefly crashes was Lt Cdr E. Peter Twiss from the Naval Test Squadron at Boscombe Down, whose early naval career has already been referred to in chapter nine.

Twiss flew Fulmars and Seafires on operations in the Mediterranean, being awarded the DSC in 1942. He was awarded a bar to it in the same year for his work associated with the North African landings, reconnoitring the French positions for an American tank commander. During one of many desert landings he broke his Seafire's tailwheel, but found a crashed Spitfire and removed its tailwheel to make his own machine airworthy again.

After night fighter and intruder ops from British bases he was appointed night fighter representative with the British Air Purchasing Commission, going to Washington in 1944. With the European war in its final stages he was selected for a course at ETPS and afterwards joined the Naval Test Squadron at Boscombe Down, an appointment which indicated to him that his postwar career should be in test flying. Peter Twiss took part in the Firefly test programme under Gordon Slade and was soon invited to resign his commission and join the staff of Fairey.

The end of the war saw the RAF in a transitional phase of fighter development. First-line equipment included the Meteor and Vampire jet fighters, Tempest and Spitfire Mk 21 propeller-driven single-seat fighters and the imminent introduction of the D.H. Hornet single-seat twin, all armed with four 20mm cannon.

Money was scarce for any development projects between 1945 and 1948 and the RAF had no swept-wing fighters in service when the Korean war broke out. The appearance of the superlative Soviet MiG-15 swept-wing jet fighter over Korea galvanized the Government into a 'Super Priority' programme which accelerated the development and production of the Hawker Hunter, Supermarine Swift, and the English Electric Canberra.

It was left largely to the aircraft industry to sponsor the considerable development expenditure required on both engines and airframes. Hawker began in 1944 a design which became the P.1040 with a Nene turbine exhausting through a bifurcated outlet on each side of the fuselage. The Air Ministry was not interested but there was encouragement from the Navy – from it was developed the Sea Hawk which caused Sydney Camm to comment in 1946, 'Thank God for the Navy.'

In 1947 Bill Humble was chief test pilot to Hawker, having succeeded Philip Lucas in 1946. A mining engineer by profession, he flew before the war as a hobby and was on the Reserve of Air Force Officers. He was called up and spent ten weeks at No 11 FTS at Shawbury as an instructor. Red tape caught up with him and he was consigned by Government edict back to the mines. Eventually he persuaded officialdom that he was more valuable to the nation in a cockpit than down a mine. He was posted to Sealand for flying duties. En route he called at Hawkers and was persuaded to remain as a test pilot concentrating upon production aeroplanes until he began prototype flying in 1942.

Bill Humble recruited Sqn Ldr T. S. 'Wimpy' Wade in 1947. Wade had flown since he joined the RAFVR at Gatwick in 1938. He flew Spitfires with No 92 Sqn from May 1940 to October 1941,

Above *Hawker P.1040.*
Below *'Wimpy' Wade in Hawker P.1081 (1950).*

being awarded a DFC for gallantry in the Battle of Britain. After a period of instructing he was appointed OC flying at the Air Fighting Development Unit, being awarded an AFC in 1944. After a postwar period in aviation journalism he was offered the Hawker job as assistant test pilot.

Wade flew the P.1040 for the first time from Boscombe Down on 2 September 1947. There were a few problems although the general handling of the aeroplane was excellent. A&AEE criticized the absence of air brakes and an aileron trimmer whilst stick force per G was said to be too low at low speeds but excessive at high speeds. For carrier work the take-off run was unacceptably long. Wimpy's demonstration flying was in a class of its own as visitors to the 1947 SBAC show would confirm.

An increase in wing span of 2 ft 6 inch, and the provision of wing folding plus the usual equipment for carrier borne operation resulted in the Sea Hawk, which became a successful naval aircraft and certainly one of the most handsome fighters ever designed.

Two P.1040s were converted to have swept wings, of which the aerodynamics were not fully understood in Britain. The American forces had arrived at the German research centres first so had taken much of the data on the work of Lippisch and the Horten brothers to the US to the immense benefit of the American aircraft industry. 'Wimpy' Wade made the first flight in the prototype, known as P.1052, on 19 November 1948 from Boscombe Down. In July 1949 A&AEE took over the machine for evaluation as an interceptor fighter. The P.1052 was liked by all who flew it, with slow speed handling characteristics superior to the P.1040. In mock combat with a Meteor F.4 elevator control was too heavy and ineffective, but the ailerons were light and highly responsive, giving a rapid roll rate.

For the first time the phenomenon known as 'Dutch Roll' was experienced. Associated specifically with early swept-wing aeroplanes it takes the form of a lateral oscillation with the aircraft yawing and rolling simultaneously.

Whilst Hawker was working on the P.1052s which gave good service in the research role, Supermarine was developing the Type 510, again, as a research vehicle, with a 40 degree swept wing and a swept tailplane – the tail of the P.1040 was unswept. The fuselage of the Attacker was used for the 510, still retaining the tailwheel undercarriage and the Nene engine. Mike Lithgow flew the prototype on 29 December 1948. Due to official parsimony only the one machine was built and development was protracted. A&AEE returned it to works for an investigation of serious vibration at low engine speeds as the throttle was closed.

From the 510 came the Type 535 with a tricycle undercarriage and an early type of afterburner fitted to the Nene engine. It was the first new British aircraft to have this thrust augmenter. Mike Lithgow flew it on 13 August 1951; take-off run of 3,000 ft was dangerously long but the team of test pilots at Chilbolton which included Les Colquhoun, Peter Roberts, 'PeeWee' Judge, Dave Morgan and 'Chunky' Judge did a marvellous job with an inadequate aeroplane and equally inadequate test facilities.

From the 510 was developed the Type 541 prototype, much nearer to the first Swift in design. Extra power and less drag gave greater speed and more flutter problems. There was high frequency buffeting and the Rolls-Royce Avon RA.7 engine was unreliable. On the third flight it failed due to a broken fuel control link. Dave Morgan had a total failure a few days before the 1951 Farnborough Show and made a crash landing, damaging himself and the aeroplane.

On 18 July 1952 the first true Swift was flown for the first time. This had an 'all-flying' tailplane like the North American Sabre which had proved its worth at high subsonic speeds. Dave Morgan soon ran into aileron flutter of a particularly dangerous character which necessitated immediate action as production of the fighter was already underway at Long Marston near Swindon. The first production model F.1 flew only four weeks after the prototype. The problem was traced to the aileron spring tabs. They were removed, to the detriment of lateral control, but, at last, the speed restriction could be lifted. In February 1953 Morgan dived at Mach 1.0 plus and created a sonic boom at Chilbolton.

A minor modification to the leading edge of the wing of the F.2 caused serious pitch-up at Mach 0.85. This was quite unacceptable in a fighter and various modifications were tried: wing fences, vortex generators, even a re-designed leading edge. The RA.7 engine was failing with monotonous regularity; as it was behaving in exemplary fashion in other aeroplanes the Swift installation became suspect and attention was directed to the air intake design. In the event it was the engine which was at fault; blade root fixings in the compressor, purchased from a sub-contractor, were not to specification. The F.3 and F.4 Swifts were fitted with stiffened outer wings and irreversible powered ailerons; this cured the flutter problem.

Supermarine Swift, second production prototype.

In July 1953 Mike Lithgow flew the prototype F.4 from London to Paris at 669.3 mph and on 25 September in the same year, he established a short-lived world speed record of 737.7 mph in Libya, where the hot air permitted higher speeds before the critical Mach number was exceeded.

Soon more problems arose. Not until January 1954 were two F.1s sent to Boscombe Down for service clearance, by which time most of the F.1s and F.2s had been delivered. Sqn Ldr Peter Thorne, the 'A' Squadron test pilot responsible for the Swift made 97 supersonic dives over the South of England, no complaints about sonic booms were received! Wg Cdr H. Bird-Wilson, OC of the Air Fighting Development Squadron of the Central Fighter Establishment, first flew the type at Chilbolton in October 1953. In tight turns he discovered that the engine flamed out, a phenomenon that had not been apparent in the tests carried out at Chilbolton which had not included pulling G at low speeds and a high angle of attack. The trouble was traced to yet another new problem, axial flow compressor stall. A re-design of the intakes was again necessary.

Other problems that arose at AFDS led to the conclusion that because some of the test pilots had not had experience of flying other advanced jet fighters, they had an inadequate background to evaluate their own products against the operational requirement. This may well have been true, but this was not the fault of the pilots. The system which prevailed at Boscombe Down during the war when company pilots were able to fly rival aeroplanes to the advantage of the industry and the Service ended with the war; in any case there were few advanced British fighters to be flown.

The Swift staggered from crisis to crisis. By the time the F.4 had been developed with a slab tail and other modifications it was beginning to improve, but the programme was cancelled in February 1955, leaving the fighter field open to Hawker.

To return to the civil market, two of the outstanding events in post-war aviation were the development of the Airspeed Ambassador and the Vickers Viscount, the world's first turboprop airliner.

Both were designed to meet the recommendations of the Brabazon Committee; the Ambassador with two Bristol Centaurus radial engines, later intended to be developed with Dart turbines, whilst the Viscount began life with Darts. George Erring-

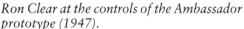

Ron Clear at the controls of the Ambassador prototype (1947).

Above *Airspeed Ambassador prototype.*
Below *Ambassador at Christchurch after mishap during trials with CG right forward. Ron Clear found himself with inadequate elevator control as he tried to flare out for landing. Both engines broke away on impact and the 'glider' climbed to 40 ft before Clear was able to make a landing with the column right forward.*

ton first flew the beautiful Ambassador from Christchurch on 10 July 1947. The flight lasted fifty minutes; the aircraft behaved well although the centre rudder shed its spring tab and a partial electrical failure caused the loss of some services for a short time.

In September the Ambassador was demonstrated at the Radlett SBAC show where George Errington created a favourable impression with his polished flying.

By this time Vickers were well advanced with their Type 609, the 'small Viscount', which flew for the first time with Mutt Summers at the controls on 16 July 1948. By this time Airspeed had suffered a serious set-back. After 50 hours flying the bolts retaining the hydraulic actuation ram of the port undercarriage leg failed as the prototype was flying at high speed. The leg dropped and locked in the 'down' position, fortunately without tearing the wing off. All hydraulic fluid was lost through the ruptured piping, making it impossible to lower the flaps for landing, so the Ambassador was landed

at a fairly high speed on the one locked down undercarriage leg. The outcome was a remarkable vindication of the 'crash-worthiness' of the high wing layout. The wing and engine nacelles were undamaged and repairs to the fuselage underside were completed in 18 days.

Flight trials soon revealed that the aircraft had remarkable characteristics in single engine flight. It was fully controllable with one propeller feathered down to a speed of 110 knots. At the 1948 SBAC show at Farnborough, Errington flew the second prototype on only one engine from take-off to landing, steering on the ground with the nosewheel.

Various set-backs and problems delayed production whilst BEA were undecided whether to pin their faith in the new Viscount propjet. Mutt

Summers' first flight from Wisley in the Type 609, designed as a 32-seater, was uneventful. Test pilots are often called upon by the public relations experts to suggest, after a first flight, that the aeroplane is the most perfect machine ever flown but Mutt's comment had a ring of truth about it: 'The smoothest and best I have ever known'. A comment which will be echoed by the millions of passengers who have flown in this superb machine which is one of Britain's few postwar aviation success stories. 446 were sold to a total value of £177 million.

Mutt Summers' co-pilot on the first flight was G. R. 'Jock' Bryce. Jock joined the RAFVR in 1937, learning to fly in 1939 and being posted to a special duty Blenheim flight charged with investigating the *Knickebein* radio bombing aid beams in use by the *Luftwaffe*. In 1942 he joined a squadron at Chivenor hunting U-boats over the Atlantic and then moved to ATERFO, the Atlantic Ferry Organization. In 1945 Jock was posted to No 232 Sqn, the only RAF squadron to operate the Douglas C-54 Skymaster, a very advanced transport for its day. His commanding officer was Wg Cdr E. H. 'Mouse' Fielden who for many years commanded the Royal Flight with distinction and who had, before the war, been personal pilot to the Prince of Wales.

After the war Jock, with his C-54 crew, was invited to join the King's Flight at Benson to fly the third Viking, used to carry the Royal staff such as hairdressers and valets. Jock was not amused when, on a flight to Aberdeen, he said to the hairdresser, 'What about a short back and sides before we land?' 'I only cut the hair of gentlemen!' was the lofty reply!

When Jock's co-pilot was demobilized, his replacement was F/O E. Brian Trubshaw. In 1946 it was Jock's turn to be de-mobbed in the rank of Flt Lt. He met Mutt Summers at Wisley who invited him to join the Vickers team. He told the author this began 20 years of the most interesting flying imaginable. Mutt and his assistant George Lowdell were of the old school, flying by the seat of their pants to a degree. Jock, from his C-54 experience, had much more knowledge of modern airliner technology so his contribution was invaluable. He learned a great deal by flying with Mutt and recalls with amusement his first flight with him in the prototype Viscount 630. As he walked out to the machine he felt like a new boy eager to learn from the master. He was astonished to see the great man begin his pre-flight checks by relieving himself alongside the main wheels! 'A bit of advice for you, boy,' said Mutt. 'Never fly with a full bladder, I

know people who crashed with one and it killed them!' Jock always observed the appropriate precaution, but more discreetly!

An interesting aspect of the test flying programme was the establishment of the true drag of the airframe, a vital element in the economy of the aeroplane. Rolls-Royce were unable to quote a figure for the thrust contribution made by the tail pipes of the Darts so Jock and Hugh Hemsley, the flight test manager, set to work to find the answers. A series of flights was carried out at speeds ranging from 100 knots to the designed diving speed of 295 knots in increments of 10 knots with all propellers feathered, auxiliary batteries having been fitted to ensure that they could all be unfeathered without pain and grief. A weather restriction was imposed and flights could only be carried out in clear weather. The distance to descend from 25,000 ft to 10,000 ft was carefully calculated so that the run ended over Boscombe Down airfield; at 10,000 ft a bell rang and nothing was allowed to delay an immediate engine start. Jock was surprised to find that to meet the requirements of the test procedure he had to commence the run at Cardiff, nearly 100 miles away. The tests took months to complete and produced a mass of technical information. Jock said that the Viscount taught him many valuable lessons in test flying. 'The machine was right from the word GO, breathtaking!'

In direct competition with the Viscount was the Armstrong Whitworth Apollo with four Arm-

Eric Franklin, Air Marshal Sir Alec Coryton and Bill Else with Apollo at Baginton (1949).

strong Siddeley Mamba turboprops. Eric Franklin and Bill Else flew the prototype on 10 April 1949. The engines were not sufficiently developed and, although the machine had very good handling and performance characteristics, it was abandoned.

Shown for the first time at the 1949 SBAC show was Cierva's 17-ton helicopter, the Air Horse, with three rotors driven by one Merlin engine of 1,620 hp. First flown by Alan Marsh on 12 December 1948, Sqn Ldr Basil Arkell also flew this giant machine. In a letter to the author he described it as looking like an elephant in the air but flying more like a pig! To achieve blade interchangeability the rotors all rotated in the same direction, so, to counteract torque they were set at a permanent tilt which had a curious effect upon handling. It could be turned to the right easily but was very difficult to turn left.

On 13 June 1960, during a routine test flight, a fatigue failure in one of the rotor assemblies caused the machine to dive to the ground, Alan Marsh, 'Jeep' Cable and the test crew being killed.

Sqn Ldr Arkell commented that testing a helicopter may seem rather less glamorous than a fixed wing aircraft but the pilot has just as many problems as his fixed wing counterpart. Although the first take-off is a hover operation a few feet from the ground, the rotor tip speed may be around 500 mph and, at this speed, problems can arise with little warning. Control response and vibration are the main problems, and the rotor head must be in perfect balance and track for smooth response to control input. These problems were particularly difficult in the tests of the Fairey Gyrodyne where the combination of a tilting, powered rotor head and the anti-torque propeller, providing thrust, produced some difficulties in control which reduced the initial test flights to durations of half minutes.

In 1947, Wg Cdr H. P. 'Sandy' Powell, chief test pilot of the Percival Aircraft Company, had flown the first of the postwar products of that company, the twin D.H. Gipsy Queen-engined Merganser.

Cierva Air Horse.

Supply problems with the engine doomed this small feeder airliner which was then developed into the Prince with Alvis Leonides radial engines. Sandy Powell flew this prototype from Luton on 13 May 1948, slight directional instability soon being cured by fitting a dorsal fin. The Prince was the first of a series of similar machines, including the President and the Pembroke trainer, the latter being used in the RAF.

After service in light and medium bomber squadrons, Powell's test flying career began in 1941, when he joined the performance testing squadron at Boscombe Down. He was involved in the trials of the Mosquito and was the first pilot to fire its guns and rocket armament and to drop the 4,000 lb bomb from the Mk IV Series 2 conversion. He became a flight commander and was awarded the AFC for his work at A&AEE.

In 1943 he became deputy commandant and chief flying instructor at the newly formed ETPS. Leaving the service in 1946 he became chief test pilot of Air Service Training and made the first flights of the Lancaster test-bed used for trials of the Armstrong Siddeley Mamba.

1949 saw the first flight of the new and revolutionary de Havilland D.H.106 Comet. John Cunningham, who became chief test pilot after the death of Geoffrey de Havilland Junior, had no experience of transport aircraft so, in 1946, he began to study the problems and techniques in depth. For three years he flew as a supernumerary crew member on BOAC routes after a full conversion course on the Lockheed Constellation, at the time the most advanced passenger aeroplane in service.

The de Havilland Ghost turbines to be fitted to the Comet were test flown in two Lancastrians, each with a pair of Ghosts in the outboard engine positions. The power controls were also flown extensively in one of the D.H.108s. They were installed so that various alterations could be made at will; indeed, some characteristics could be altered in flight. As John Cunningham said, 'We learned a great deal about powered controls; it was an extremely useful exercise.'

An interesting experiment checked the ability of the windscreens to shed rain effectively by building a Comet nose upon an Airspeed Horsa military glider which was towed around the skies searching for rain clouds.

The Comet was recognized as an aeroplane which would experience stresses at its operating altitude of 35,000 ft quite unknown to earlier transport aircraft and de Havillands carried out an

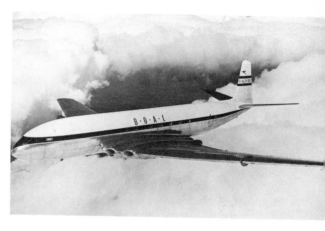

D.H.106 Comet I.

exhaustive series of cyclic load tests in special rigs at Hatfield. On 27 July 1949 John Cunningham and a crew of four flew this beautiful aeroplane for the first time. General handling was investigated in the 31 minute flight and Cunningham pronounced himself well satisfied with the machine. It then entered an intensive test programme which proved that throughout the performance envelope all the targets had been met. The Achilles heel of the Comet I was the symmetrical wing section. Due to the relatively small angle of incidence required to stall the wing it was possible for a pilot to rotate for lift-off too early and too far, stalling the wing and preventing a successful take-off. This happened to a BOAC Comet at Rome in 1952, fortunately without casualties, and at Karachi on the delivery flight of a Canadian Pacific machine in 1953. In this case all aboard died.

Later marks of the Comet had a wing with a drooped leading edge. This cured the problem.

The elevator control was also subject to criticism and was suitably modified but, generally, for such an advanced design it was remarkably trouble-free, and put Britain, and de Havilland, in the forefront of world civil aviation. As is well known the disasters in 1953 and 1954 caused the C of A to be withdrawn and, at one fell swoop the lead was lost to the Soviet Union and America, de Havilland being almost bankrupted in the process. From the ashes rose the Comet 3 and 4 and they gave good service on the routes and with charter operators for many years. Vestigially, the Comet airframe remains in the Nimrod maritime reconnaissance and airborne early warning aircraft.

From Woodford, in August 1949, a small aeroplane was taken to Boscombe Down for its first flight. This was the Avro 707, a one-third scale model of the new Avro 698 bomber design, later to be named Vulcan. On 4 September 1949 S. E. Esler flew it for the first time; sadly, on 30 September it crashed, killing him. Not until the following year did the next scale model, the 707B, fly in the hands of Wg Cdr R. J. 'Roly' Falk who had just joined Avro as superintendent of flying.

The period embraced by chapter fourteen saw the increasing importance of the ejector seat, and it is appropriate to end the chapter with an account of the development testing of this device, which has saved the lives of over 5,000 pilots of all nationalities. Reference has already been made in chapter ten to the use of a Defiant and a Meteor in the early stages of Sir James Martin's work; but it is impossible to praise too highly the courage of Bernard Lynch, who braved quite unknown hazards in being fired upward on the test-rig, at a time when the degree of acceleration which the human spine could sustain without injury was a matter of sheer guesswork. By the time he had experienced 180 sequences on the rig he had suffered a crushed vertebra.

In June 1946 flight testing began at Chalgrove when a dummy ejection took place at 415 mph from a Meteor. This was unsuccessful, the parachute burst and the seat was lost. A subsequent test with a modified release was equally unsuccessful. It was then discovered that the stabilizing drogue parachute was drawn in the wake of the seat and became entangled in it. Martin then introduced a gun to eject the drogue; this was most successful and reliability was achieved.

After this Lynch made his historic ejection at 8,000 ft from a Meteor travelling at 320 mph. On 29 August 1947 he repeated the ejection at 12,000 ft at a speed of 420 mph.

Capt J. E. D. Scott and Sqn Ldr J. S. Fifield flew the test aircraft and Scott recalls the occasion when one of the dummy tests went wrong, the seat drifting off the airfield to descend with some force through the roof of a near-by pig-sty. The farmer was exceedingly aggrieved and claimed that the seat had caused one of his sows to farrow prematurely! Soothing words and new slates mollified the gentleman.

Lt Cartier of the French Air Force was another volunteer parachutist; on his first flight with Scott at Chalgrove he delayed his ejection by a second or so and narrowly missed a noisome touch-down in a nearby sewage farm!

As most flying accidents occurred in the landing or take-off phase it became clear that a seat must be designed to permit safe ejection at ground level.

Early examples, requiring manual operation of the canopy release, seat release, and parachute deployment were only of use for ejection above about 1,200 ft. Further development took place in 1960, after the successful ejection by W. T. 'Doddy' Hay from a rearward facing seat designed for a Valiant bomber at a speed of 250 mph at 1,000 ft. This followed a series of dummy tests at ground level with the aeroplane travelling at 110 mph. The parachute was fully open in 4.3 seconds giving a controlled drop of 38 ft. On 1 April 1961 'Doddy' Hay made a zero-height zero-speed ejection at Chalgrove, a descent of 200 ft on a fully developed parachute being achieved – the zero-zero seat had arrived.

On 13 March 1962 Sqn Ldr Peter Howard tested a rocket propelled seat at an altitude of 250 ft with the Meteor flying at 290 mph. Peter Howard was surprised by the comparative comfort of the experience, commenting that, 'The greatest hazard was the risk of landing on top of Mr Martin's car'!

Underwater ejection was another aspect of development which occupied Martin Baker. John Rawlins, of the Institute of Aviation Medicine, was the guinea pig in a series of hazardous experiments and by 1962 a safe method had been developed. In June 1962 the automatic underwater escape system was tested at HMS *Dolphin*, Gosport. Surgeon Lieutenant Sandy Davidson made the first live test through a dummy cockpit canopy with complete success. These underwater trials were undoubtedly some of the most dangerous operations in which the IAM had been involved.

Wg Cdr R. H. Winfield, an ex-mercantile marine surgeon and general practitioner, joined the airborne forces training station at Ringway. A system was devised by which agents could be picked up from enemy territory by an aeroplane flying slowly over the site plucking the man from the ground by a winch line which was allowed to pay out and was then wound in again as the agent accelerated into the air. Trials were carried out at Booker in Buckinghamshire; Winfield was a volunteer, another was W. K. 'Bill' Stewart who joined the IAM in 1940 and in 1946 became head of it.

The hazards of such an operation hardly need emphasis.

Martin Baker have continued to develop the 'bang seat' to keep pace with the ever increasing demands of higher performance aeroplanes. Indeed, part of the system now includes a winch which will enable a pilot unfortunate enough to land in a tall tree to descend to ground level easily and safely.

15

THE DANGEROUS TRANSONIC YEARS

By 1950 the necessary requirements for flight at high subsonic speed were clear, design factors for transonic speeds were becoming clearer and it appeared that success in this regime would probably result in smooth supersonic flight, but there was much to learn.

Although the Bell X-1 had achieved Mach 1.0 with a thin aerofoil section and orthodox configuration, it was clear that swept wing/tail surfaces and irreversible controls (the ability of the pilot to move the controls by means of the stick without aerodynamic forces being able to reverse the movement) were vital, as was the necessity for an all-moving tailplane without separate elevators, trim and balance tabs. The mechanical linkages to orthodox controls were a source of weakness at high Mach, wear in the pin joints and flexure of the airframe permitting catastrophic flutter in surfaces with only the slightest freedom to move.

Boulton Paul Aircraft had moved into the manufacture of powered controls under the guidance of their managing director, John D. North. Ben Gunn flew many hours in the Lancaster test-bed which was used for developing them.

As a result of the pitching problems of the de Havilland D.H.108 the RAE had considered the possibility of linking the automatic pilot into the control loop, but it was decided that the instrument, being designed for level steady flight, would not have sufficiently rapid response characteristics to control the fast and violent motion experienced in the 108. These discussions paved the way to the modern system of auto-stabilization which is now commonplace on high speed aircraft.

Aeroelasticity had become a serious problem in high speed airframes; the inter-action of aerodynamic forces with the normal flexure of which the structure was capable under dynamic loads created de-stabilizing forces which could be totally destructive. Aeroelasticity has always been a problem in aircraft design but high speed flight has compounded it.

Journalistic phrases such as 'breaking the sound barrier' were used to describe transonic flight in terms of drama rather than accuracy and the mark of success was the sonic boom which, in the next decade, was one of the attractions at air shows until the environmentalists became strong enough to have it banned.

Gas turbine development was reversing the trend which had handicapped aircraft designers since the days of the early pioneers. They always claimed, sometimes correctly, that they were in advance of engine technology and could do much better if they had more powerful engines. The turbine was reaching a stage where development was outstripping airframe design. British designers and engineers were handicapped by inadequate research facilities and the low-priority of Government funding.

As the war ended it was clear that Farnborough's runway and other facilities would not meet the future needs of the industry. It was decided to establish a National Aeronautical Establishment. It was originally intended to join up three wartime airfields, Thurleigh, Twinwoods and Little Staughton, located north of Bedford. This would enable a five mile runway to be built by linking Thurleigh and Little Staughton. This did not materialize in the grandiose manner intended but, by 1946, the airfield and wind tunnel complex was under construction. Not until 1952 were the high speed laboratory, transonic tunnel and spinning tunnel completed, to be followed in 1954 by the low speed tunnel and, in 1957, the supersonic tunnel. In 1960 a high supersonic tunnel was opened.

In 1955 the site became known as RAE Bedford. It has a 10,500 ft runway and carries out a vast range of work through its various sections; the flying wing, flight systems, aircraft department, aerodynamics department, engineering services and general administration.

Airshows in the 1950s were exciting, none more so than the SBAC show at Farnborough. A regular and elegant performer was the new English Electric Canberra twin-Avon-powered bomber which had been flown for the first time on 13 May 1949 with Wg Cdr Roland P. Beamont at the controls. Beamont had been a distinguished fighter pilot during the war and had spent two periods of 'rest' between ops testing Hurricanes, Typhoons and Tempests for Hawker. He formed and commanded the first Tempest wing; being promoted to Wg Cdr at the age of 23. In 1944 he was shot down over Germany and returned from POW camp in 1945 to command the Air Fighting Development Unit at the Central Fighter Establishment, joining English Electric as chief test pilot in May 1947. During his service in the RAF Beamont was awarded a DSO and bar, DFC and bar and the American DFC. He had been mentioned in despatches during the Battle of Britain.

'Bee' Beamont was already familiar with the Meteor, having joined Glosters in 1946 to test the Meteor IV prototypes and the machines being prepared for the 1946 High Speed Flight's attempt upon the world's air speed record. When he joined English Electric he had no aeroplane and no aerodrome, being located in the design office over a garage in Preston until the company took over Warton airfield from the RAF in 1948.

Beamont went to America in 1948 to fly the North American XP-86 Sabre prototype and ac-quire experience of an advanced fighter. His American friends boasted of its supersonic capability so he decided to try it, exceeding Mach 1.0 in a dive. Only one other man, George Welch, had flown it to this limit. Beamont became a founder member, with John Derry, of the very exclusive supersonic club – there were no other British members.

Vampires, a Meteor IV and a Halifax were used to test various aspects of the new Canberra's potential performance and a cockpit canopy failure in the Ghost-engined Vampire left Beamont semi-conscious at 43,000 ft; he recovered at 38,000 ft in time for a draughty ride back to Warton.

In May 1949 taxying trials of the prototype began with short hops being made. On Friday 13th, Beamont, ignoring superstition and satisfied from his short hops that the controls were satisfactory, took the Canberra into the air accompanied by another test pilot, Johnnie Squier, in a Vampire Mk 5 as chase aircraft.

This was probably the first time that the technique of test flying with a chase machine had been practised in the UK. Essentially the chase pilot must be good at formation flying, familiar with the design concept of the subject aircraft, and alert for any malfunction which can be seen from outside. The operation of flaps, undercarriage and doors may be checked, and the integrity of access panels is of importance. The chase pilot is in radio communication with base and the subject pilot who, with his crew, is busy checking aircraft systems on

English Electric Canberra prototype.

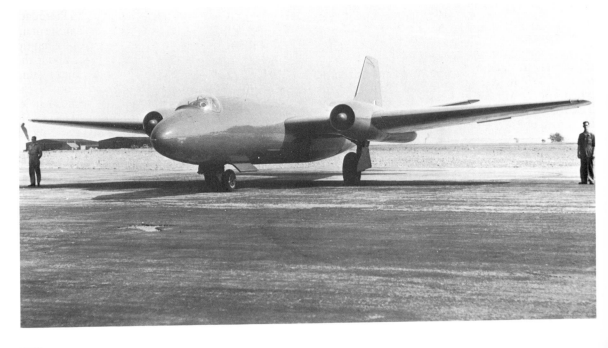

a first flight. The crew may be informed of traffic intruding into their airspace, or of the onset of turbulence which may be mistaken by the test crew for a malfunction in the new aeroplane.

The chase aircraft will have a carefully calibrated air speed indicator so the ASI of the prototype may be checked right through the airspeed envelope, whilst stalling speeds may be checked with equal accuracy.

For 27 minutes Roland Beamont flew the Canberra, but few problems were reported. The rudder was slightly overbalanced and was reduced in height to cut down the area of the horn. From 1 June to 5 July the machine was in the hangar for various minor alterations; then the whole of the initial design flight envelope was cleared in 36 flights, during which slight 'snaking' due to wake turbulence behind the canopy was cleared by a small fairing, and elevator modifications were made to cure an eight-cycle flutter which developed.

The Canberra proved to be an outstanding aeroplane, entirely free from vices. It was demonstrated publicly for the first time at the 1949 Farnborough show when Beamont astounded the visitors by his spectacular routine which had evolved after careful consideration of the many virtues of the new machine, particularly the manoeuvrability, which designer 'Teddy' Petter's insistence upon a low wing loading had given it. The Canberra stole the limelight from the fighters which, customarily, provided the excitement.

In May 1951 No 101 Sqn became the first jet bomber squadron in the RAF when it received its Canberras, and it soon proved to be a jet-age Mosquito with a bomb load of 6,000 lb, and a top speed of 570 mph at 40,000 ft, and a ceiling of over 50,000 ft. It received its ultimate accolade when Glenn Martin at Baltimore built it under licence as the B-57A. It was also made in Australia. In 1984 many Canberras are still flying.

It became clear after the war that the RAF must have the capability of delivering a nuclear bomb, so the Air Staff drafted a specification for both aircraft and bomb. Without going into the detail of the evolution of the aircraft specification, it is sufficient to say that it led to the production of the Short Sperrin prototypes; the Vickers Valiant, Avro Vulcan and the Handley Page Victor. In retrospect the sheer extravagance of four prototypes in the programme was incredible, but there were valid reasons for it, notably that the two most promising designs, Vulcan and Victor, were so far ahead of current practice that both appeared to be major

gambles. Britain could not afford a failure in this crucial area of an effective strategic bomber.

The most advanced specification was B5/46, issued in 1947 for a machine to carry 10,000 lb of bombs for 3,500 nautical miles at 500 knots, i.e. 4,030 miles at 576 mph, with a ceiling of 50,000 ft. Avro, Handley Page, Shorts and Vickers submitted designs. In August 1947 another specification, B14/46, was issued as a safeguard against delay in meeting the demanding needs of B5/46. It called for an orthodox aeroplane flying at 390 knots, 449 mph, for the same distance at a height of 45,000 ft.

Britain was at a grave disadvantage in having inadequate wind tunnel facilities at that time. The Americans had managed to acquire most of the German technical data on transonic flight. Competition was tough for this prime contract. Vickers worked on the swept-wing Valiant design, Avro the tail-less delta Vulcan, and Handley Page favoured the crescent wing Victor. Short's design, the Sperrin, had a thin unswept wing and four Rolls-Royce Avon engines mounted in pairs, one above the other, in wing nacelles. In 1954 David Keith-Lucas had been appointed chief designer and he had inherited this design. He was extremely doubtful of the high Mach number potential of its wing, but he was well aware of the difficulties he would face if he attempted to change, at that late stage, to a swept wing. Aeroelasticity problems were in the forefront of his mind. He knew that Professor Geoffrey Hill had, in the 1930s, overcome such problems in the Westland Hill Pterodactyl (see chapter five) by careful location of the main spar further aft than usual, and the use of wing-tip controllers — in effect pivoting the tips about the axis of the spar had entirely eliminated the twisting moment inevitable with orthodox ailerons.

Keith-Lucas and Hill devised an 'aero-isoclinic' wing using this technique, and submitted proposals to the Air Ministry in the form of a new Sperrin design. It was rejected but work went ahead on this wing for use in another project to specification NA.39, ultimately met by the Blackburn Buccaneer. Whilst the Sperrin was under construction it had been decided that the aero-isoclinic wing could be evaluated quickly and inexpensively in the form of a glider which would enable chief test pilot Tom Brooke-Smith to check control and stability characteristics with the moving wing tips.

Having learned to fly privately before the war, Brooke-Smith joined Air Transport Auxiliary in 1940 and was invited, in 1941, to set up a ferrypool to deliver Stirlings from the Belfast factory of Shorts to the squadrons. His ability was soon noticed by the chief test pilot, John Lankester Parker, who invited him to join the test flying team. With 83 different types in his log book Tom achieved his ambition and entered the realm of experimental flying at the age of 23! Throughout the war he tested Stirlings and, when Lankester Parker retired in 1948 after 32 years with Shorts, Brooke-Smith was appointed chief test pilot. He was selected for a place at the ETPS and, in July 1951, was ready to fly the SB.1 glider with the new wing.

Winch launches were made on 14 and 15 July, and no obvious difficulties arose. To reduce slip-stream turbulence in the wake of the tug, Brooke-Smith decided to use the new Short Sturgeon, which had two engines rotating in opposite directions, and which had climb power in excess of requirements. On 30 July Jock Eassie, flying the Sturgeon, towed the SB.1 for the first time. 'Brookie' quickly realized that winch launches had induced a sense of false security. It was clear that the wing configuration demanded heavier stick forces in the slip-stream of the tug, and consequently the glider was extremely unpleasant and tiring to fly. He was towed to 15,000 ft and slipped the towline. The SB.1 handled beautifully in free flight and the pilot was impressed. He decided to lengthen the towline for the next flight in an attempt to reduce the effect of turbulence. He also decided to take off at a higher speed, the tug pilot calling out his take-off run speeds on the radio telephone. Suddenly, at 70 knots, communication ceased, the glider was becoming unstable upon its undercarriage. He rotated, but the slipstream effect was much more severe, and he could not climb up through it to the

Short SB.1 glider.

'tow-high' position; instability in pitch developed. The tow was slipped and Brooke-Smith tried unsuccessfully to edge sideways out of the turbulent air. Suddenly the SB.1 went into a dive at 100 knots, and, as it hit the runway the nosewheel collapsed, and the machine bounced into a steep nose-up attitude.

'Brookie', even if he had not been knocked unconscious, could have done nothing about this, as any attempt to stabilize the aeroplane with the wing tip controllers would have stalled them and made matters worse. The SB.1 eventually stalled, rolled to port through 90 degrees, crashed on its side and disintegrated.

Brooke-Smith recovered consciousness lying on soft grass by the side of the runway. A shaken and ashen faced Keith-Lucas looked at him, marvelling that he was still alive. Suddenly 'Brookie' realized that he had no feeling below his waist – his back was broken, but after many months in hospital he returned to duty, completely recovered. Later the SB.1 was rebuilt with a metal fuselage and two small French Turbomeca turbines. Re-numbered SB.4 and later named Sherpa, it was flown by 'Brookie' within six months of his crash and proved the soundness of the aero-isoclinic wing. It is surprising that development of it ceased with the Sherpa; in fact, Brookie believes to this day that it could have been the progenitor of a superb carrier-borne aeroplane with transonic performance and good handling characteristics at low speed.

On 10 August 1951, just before the SB.1 disaster, Tom Brooke-Smith flew the prototype Sperrin for the first time from Aldergrove. Fundamentally, it was a conventional bomber powered by turbines, but it had a number of interesting innovations. It was the first aircraft to have a 4,000 PSI hydraulic system, and the first to have four-wheel undercarriage bogies with Dunlop Maxaret non-locking brakes. The flying controls were advanced for their day, there being no direct link between the pilot's controls and the main control surfaces. He operated full-span flaps on the trailing edge of each control surface. To the onlooker, take-off appeared most disconcerting – with the surfaces free to move anywhere until speed rose sufficiently for the servo controls to operate. Initially a Sperrin fin and rudder were mounted upon a Sunderland flying boat which carried out a series of runs off the step and on it at increasing speeds, using the 14 mile length of Belfast Lough.

There was no feedback to indicate to the pilot the magnitude of control forces and it was necessary to introduce it artificially by means of springs.

Short Sperrin.

Restrictors to compensate for varying airspeeds were also built into the system to avoid dangerous loads upon the airframe.

Another innovation was Tom Brooke-Smith's own idea. He thought that the use of a separate wheel to steer an aeroplane on the ground was primitive in the extreme, so Sperrin had its nose-wheel connected to the rudder pedals only when the weight of the aeroplane was on the undercarriage; thereafter it was disconnected.

Because the Sperrin had only one ejector seat 'Brookie' made the first flight alone. It proved a delightful aeroplane to fly. The only two prototypes were used for research and development at RAE and as an engine test bed for the big experimental de Havilland Gyron turbines.

Wg Cdr 'Jimpy' Shaw was in Aero Flight at Farnborough and flew the Sperrin which he, too, thought was a delight to fly. He recalled with some amusement the high altitude sorties which required the crew to carry a tin of glycerine and a cloth padded stick to de-ice the windscreens before landing!

On 19 May 1951 the prototype Vickers Valiant made its first flight from Wisley with 'Mutt' Summers in command and Jock Bryce as co-pilot. After three flights with Summers, Jock was checked out as first pilot and took over as chief test pilot when Summers retired shortly afterwards. Sadly, his retirement was brief. He died after an operation two years later.

On 12 January 1952 disaster struck the Valiant prototype. Bryce took off with Sqn Ldr Brian Foster as co-pilot and a crew of three to carry out engine re-light tests. Bomb-door problems had already arisen and one of the large units had torn away with a loud bang. Modifications had been made and were to be checked on this flight. Some difficulty was experienced in starting No 3 engine. During the attempt the bomb-door selector was operated. Suddenly there was a loud bang. 'Damn!' said Bryce. 'The lousy door has gone again!' Roy Holland, the senior technician in the back, reported that the door was intact. A few minutes later he announced that he had lost all his instrument readings for the starboard engines, and soon he had lost all data from the starboard wing, too. Bryce, flying near Tangmere, decided to abandon the sortie and return to Hurn, which was being used as the base whilst a new runway was being built at Wisley. En route he was horrified to realize that he had lost aileron control and thought, 'We really are in big trouble now.' He immediately called for clearance to the long runway at Boscombe Down, but it was Saturday afternoon, it was closed. Suddenly the co-pilot reported flames emerging from the leading edge of the starboard wing, well out from the root. Bryce was having serious handling problems as the fire was weakening the main spar, causing the wing incidence to vary, and the aeroplane to yaw to the left. He ordered the crew to bail out and headed for Boscombe in the hope that he could save the machine. Brian Foster ejected as the angle of bank reached 60 degrees. Sadly, he hit the fin and was

Vickers Valiant, August 1951.

killed. Bryce believed that his ejection coincided with an explosion in one of the fuel tanks and the blast reduced his escape velocity to a fatal level. Jock just managed to get out 'by courtesy of Sir James Martin, bless him!' He said, 'I landed heavily and found myself flat on my back, sure that I had broken it. Suddenly a woman appeared and offered me a cup of tea. Suddenly I had the feeling I had been here before, and so I had. I had landed in the middle of No 6 site at the old Holmsley South aerodrome and was alongside the hut in which I was billeted during my Douglas C-54 conversion course in 1945!'

The fire was caused by fuel from the previous unsuccessful engine start leaking into the wing structure. A sealing shroud was fitted around the tailpipe: a modification which was later incorporated in all turbine installations. Serious though the loss of the prototype was, it caused little delay to the test programme and the second prototype was flown by Jock Bryce with Brian Trubshaw as co-pilot on 11 April 1952.

One of the first five production Valiants shed both its ailerons in a high speed run at medium height, but in a brilliant display of skill test pilot Bill Aston carried out a safe landing at Boscombe Down.

Brian Trubshaw recalls a rather disturbing experience when flying the Valiant in an attempt to drop a dummy atom bomb. It was necessary to prove the operation of the bomb slip and the trajectory of the weapon. The dummy was of exactly the same shape and weight as the actual bomb. Soon after take-off the crew heard the bomb fall off the slip and roll about in the bay. As they were flying over Dorking it was fortunate that the door locks were sufficiently strong to contain this massive projectile until it could be dropped safely in the Thames Estuary.

Another Service test pilot involved in the Valiant programme was Wg Cdr Ralph 'Tich' Havercroft. He was in the RAFVR at the outbreak of war and carried out about 200 sorties in the Battle of Britain, flying Spitfires and Blenheim fighters. From his Blenheim squadron he applied to go to Spitfires because he was too short to control the Blenheim effectively! Tich had wide experience in armament test flying from 1942 until he was selected for the ETPS course which began in March 1944. At the end of this course Jeffrey Quill was desperate for assistance in testing production Spitfires at High Post, so Havercroft and a fellow graduate, Mike Lithgow, joined Jeffrey, Mike staying with Supermarines and Havercroft returning in December of the same year to join 'A' Flight at Boscombe Down. In 1946 he became an instructor at ETPS at

Wg Cdr Ralph Havercroft (1946).

Cranfield, returning to Boscombe with the School in 1947, to become chief test flying instructor.

A posting overseas in 1948 appeared to be the end of his test flying career, but in 1955 he was stationed at Defford, the base of the telecommunications flying unit of the Royal Radar Establishment, commanding one of the squadrons. He was told that a Valiant was coming to Defford for trials of the H2S-9 bombing radar but as the Ministry had decreed that only qualified ETPS pilots were to fly it, it became Havercroft's responsibility. He went to Wisley to fly with Jock Bryce and Brian Trubshaw, spending six months there, but returned to Defford for the radar trials which had to be flown from Gaydon's longer runway. After the trials Havercroft was appointed to command a Valiant squadron, No. 543, at RAF Wyton.

The Valiant was very popular with its crews, it handled well throughout the flight envelope and had few vices. A slight nose-up change of trim occurred at Mach 0.84 and application of G was not desirable above 0.78, as buffeting became severe. Ten squadrons were equipped with this elegant aeroplane which served as a flying tanker until wing fatigue caused its withdrawal in 1964.

The flights of the first two Avro 707 delta research aircraft have been recorded in chapter four-

teen. 'Roly' Falk flew the second one, which was to be used for low speed research, and a third one, to be used for high speed work was flown by Falk from Boscombe Down on 14 July 1951. Two others were built, another high speed version was flown on 20 February 1953, and a side-by-side two-seat version was airborne on 1 July 1953. The RAE employed them for trials of automatic throttle systems and powered controls.

The small deltas created a tremendous impression when they flew at Farnborough in 1953 with the two prototype Vulcans, the first of which was flown by Falk from Woodford on 30 August 1952. He had learned to fly in 1932, and flew for the press covering the 1935/36 Abyssinian war and the Spanish Civil War in 1936. From 1939 to 1946 he served in the RAF, becoming chief test pilot at the RAE in 1943. For a short period he was an experimental test pilot with Vickers-Armstrongs and joined Avro in 1950.

Falk's experience in the small deltas gave him complete confidence in this giant and highly unconventional aeroplane, taxi runs were very encouraging and, as there was no ejector seat for a second pilot, the maiden flight was a solo operation. Handling in the air was excellent so he returned to Woodford. As he lowered the undercarriage his controller warned him that something had fallen off the aircraft. He waited for a Vampire to make an inspection run and it reported that a fairing behind the undercarriage legs had come adrift. Falk

'Roly' Falk (1951).

Four Avro 707 research aircraft in formation with two Vulcan prototypes over Thorney Island.

landed using the braking parachute which was to be standard on the Vulcan. After two more short flights the prototype was flown to Farnborough where it created a tremendous impression of power and speed.

As development progressed, it became clear that buffet boundaries were unacceptably low and the familiar kinked leading edge was designed. It was too late to incorporate this on the first production aeroplanes, but it became the phase 2 wing to be incorporated as soon as possible.

Eight squadrons were equipped with this magnificent bomber which was later used in the flight re-fuelling role, finally being withdrawn from service in 1984.

Handley Page's new and highly unorthodox crescent wing design, drawn to meet the heavy bomber specification, was completed when their tender was accepted in November 1947. There were so many unknowns, such as the tailplane location on top of

the fin, that it was decided to build a 10 ft span radio controlled scale model. This was flown at Farnborough but crashed on its first flight. It was then decided to build a one-third scale aircraft using the fuselage of a Supermarine 510 and building upon it a replica of the unusual crescent wing which Reginald Stafford, the chief designer, with Godfrey Lee and Charles Joy, had conceived, with the idea of maintaining the critical Mach number at a constant figure from root to tip.

The HP.88, as the machine was known, was built by Blackburn at Brough and was first flown from the wartime emergency landing strip at Carnaby, near Bridlington, on 21 June 1951, by chief test pilot G. R. I. 'Sailor' Parker. Events and design changes had overtaken it, as with the Avro 707s, the research machine could not keep pace with the big bomber. A number of flights were made from Carnaby by Parker and Douglas Broomfield, Sqn Ldr Hedley Hazelden's assistant. Hazelden himself never flew it; he was too big to be comfortable in the cockpit! It is said that during one of his annual medical checks his doctor said, 'According to my weight, height and age tables you should be 130 years old and 10 ft 6 inches high!' 'Hazel' was unrepentant and passed his medical.

Douglas Broomfield, who had joined Hazelden's test team from Boscombe Down, was flying the HP.88 on 26 August when, during a low-level, high speed run, practising for the Farnborough air show, the aeroplane developed a violent pitching motion, eventually breaking up and killing the pilot. It was fitted with powered controls and it was deduced that the rear fuselage was too weak to withstand the inputs from the powered all-flying slab tailplane. As the tailplane moved, the fuselage bent upwards or downwards, the distortion being self-generating and increasing in frequency until failure occurred.

At the time of the HP.88 crash, construction of the first of the two bomber prototypes was well advanced and it was hoped to fly it at Farnborough in 1952. Various problems arose, the CG was too far aft, necessitating the addition of 1,000 lb of ballast in the nose. The Air Ministry decided that the runway at Radlett was not long enough for the first flight. The aircraft was dismantled and taken to Boscombe Down in great secrecy and to ensure security a frame was built over the low-loader with a tarpaulin draped over it to simulate the lines of a boat hull! It even had the name of a boat stencilled on the side: GHELEAPANDY, an anagram of Handley Page!

Assembly was seriously delayed by a fire in the hydraulic bay of the machine, which injured an electrician, Eddie Eyles, so severely that he died. Not until Christmas Eve 1952 was Hazelden able to take off for the first time with his test observer, Ian Bennett. The 17 minute flight was entirely satisfactory and included a successful overshoot.

On the fourth flight the parking brake had been left on, and as the Victor landed all 16 tyres burst. With only one prototype, delays were inevitable while new test equipment was being fitted and modifications made. On one flight Hazelden lowered his flaps on the approach, but the machine immediately began to roll. He selected them up again and repeated the approach; again a roll began to develop so he made a landing without flaps, thinking that one of the actuation rams on one side had failed. On inspection it was found that one of the flaps had broken away.

An interesting feature of the prototype was its ability to virtually land itself. Once it had been set up on final approach it would begin to flare out upon its own ground cushion with no further initiative on the part of the pilot. However, as a result of the disastrous crash of the prototype on 14 July

Victor at the 1955 SBAC show.

1954, the fin and rudder were reduced in height to cut down bending loads and this seriously affected this unusual facility.

In July 1954 the aeroplane was to be subjected to a series of tests to check the position error of the airspeed indicator. Some preliminary work had been carried out at Radlett, but complaints from the local people caused the trials to be moved to the less heavily populated Cranfield area. Hazelden had decided on the course to be flown, and on the following day, the fourteenth, he picked up his flying helmet to walk out of his office to the aeroplane. The telephone rang to inform him that a Japanese admiral who was interested in buying the Marathon small airliner (which was being built at the Woodley factory of the now-defunct Miles company, taken over by HP), had arrived to see the machine and fly in it. Hazelden was in a dilemma. Ronald 'Taffy' Ecclestone, who had joined him from Boscombe, had just been checked out on the Victor but had little experience of flying it. He had no knowledge of the Marathon but had overheard the conversation. 'Why don't I take the Victor?' Hazelden agreed and gave him a thorough briefing on the PE flights. He then drove to Woodley, flew the admiral in the Marathon and took him to lunch in a Sonning hotel. As he arrived the manager asked him to telephone flying control at Radlett most urgently. He was told that the Victor had crashed and all aboard were dead. Utterly shocked he returned to Radlett to find that during high speed runs at low level down the runway at Cranfield the tailplane had broken off the fin due to fatigue failure of the fixing bolts. The whole hideous sequence was captured in about four seconds by the timing camera in which the frame interval was 1.1 seconds. Frame one showed the Victor, fast and low with a small gap appearing between the top of the fin and the leading edge of the tailplane, the second one showed the aeroplane still level but with the gap opening up, the third one showed it without the tailplane and diving at 30–40 degrees, the fourth frame showed a ball of flame at the runway intersection. As Hazelden said, 'It was so quick, thank God, that nobody in the four-man crew would have known anything about it.'

Handley Page had gone to extraordinary lengths to prove the structural integrity of the unusual fin mounted tailplane configuration, with wind tunnel tests on a model to check flutter potential, and ground resonance tests on the actual prototype. In spite of all this research, the utterly unexpected happened. The second prototype flew in September 1954. At A&AEE Boscombe Down the OC 'B' Sqn at the time when the Victor was evaluated was Wg Cdr Geoffrey Fletcher. He had joined the RAF in 1946, graduated at Cranwell, and was posted to fly Wellingtons at Swinderby, later moving to a Lincoln squadron at Scampton, and the last Lancaster squadron in service, No 7, at Upwood. In 1951 he flew his first jet aircraft, a Canberra being flown by Rolls-Royce as an Avon test-bed.

In February 1953 Geoffrey Fletcher joined No 12 course at ETPS and recalls his surprise at receiving from Group Captain Arthur Clouston, the Commandant, a personal letter welcoming him to Boscombe. When he graduated and was appointed to 'B' Sqn the V-bombers were in development and eagerly awaited. He recalls the Valiant as a magnificent, very stable aeroplane, marvellous for its time. He was equally impressed with the Vulcan in spite of the nickname, 'the Greater Crested Dragmaster' which it acquired in its earlier days until the wing form was changed. It has always been suspected that the name originated in the design office of Handley Page! Fletcher also rated the Victor a fine aircraft and noticed a considerable improvement in each of the V-bombers as they came into squadron service. This was particularly evident in the electrical systems.

A tricky situation arose during the photoflash dropping trials of the Victor. The flares were of two-million candlepower, and their detonation was equivalent to a 500 lb bomb. Trouble had been experienced with the detonators, and a number had been specially assembled at Farnborough for the trials. A time delay of seven seconds from release was achieved by a small propeller at the nose of the canister, which unscrewed the safety device. On the first drop, the flare left the bomb bay, but as soon as it reached the slipstream, it rose into the bomb bay again, finally leaving the

Wg Cdr Geoffrey Fletcher in the cockpit of an American F-111 fighter bomber, 16 December 1965. He was the first RAF officer to fly it and, on this sortie, both engines flamed out whilst decelerating from Mach 1.95.

aeroplane and detonating close to the underside with a great blast which dislodged the other flares and left them rolling about on the bomb doors which had been closed. To avoid them skidding forward and detonating against the forward bulkhead, Fletcher decided not to use the brakes on landing. The sortie ended with no further problems.

Development continued, and No 232 OCU at Gaydon received its first BMk 1s at the end of November 1957. No 10 Sqn at Cottesmore received its Victors in April 1958. This superb bomber remained in its main role until 1974, when many were converted to tankers.

On the fighter front Hawker had carried out a major test programme on the two P.1052s and had decided that the reason for their inadequate elevator control in mock combat and a tendency to dutch roll (a defect not shared with the rival Supermarine 510), was the combination of sweptwing and unswept tailplane. Sydney Camm produced various alternative design projects, finally deciding upon one known as P.1067, a single-seat fighter with wing root air intakes and a single jet pipe for the Armstrong Siddeley Sapphire or Rolls-Royce Avon engine. Construction of three prototypes began, two of them with Sapphires, the other with an Avon. In the meantime, one of the P.1052s was converted to a swept tailplane configuration, becoming the P.1081, first flown by Sqn Ldr 'Wimpy' Wade on 19 June 1950. Most of the problems of the P.1052 appeared to have been solved, and after various minor modifications it achieved a speed of Mach 0.89 at 36,000 ft.

In August 1948 Sqn Ldr Neville Duke, one of the most distinguished fighter pilots of the war, joined Wade with whom he had served in the famous No 92 Sqn in 1941–42.

Neville Duke joined the RAF in 1940 as an Aircraftman, Second Class. 'The lowest form of life but the grandest title I could imagine, "AC 2 under pilot training".' When he joined No 92 Sqn at Biggin Hill in March 1941 many of the immortals of the Battle of Britain were operating there: Wg Cdr A. G. 'Sailor' Malan DSO, DFC, Sqn Ldr Jamie Rankine DSO, DFC, Sqn Ldr Mungo Park DFC, Sqn Ldr Robinson DFC and Flt Lt Brian Kingcombe DSO, DFC. In this distinguished company he served his apprenticeship in aerial warfare.

He spent three years in the Middle East flying Curtiss P-40s in which he proved that thirteen was not his lucky number.

His first flight in a P-40 on 13 November ended in a ground loop, and the number has haunted him ever since. During this period he was shot down and posted missing twice in five days. By March 1944 he had been awarded a DFC and bar, and was informed personally by the C-in-C, Air Vice Marshal Harry Broadhurst, of the immediate award of a DSO.

In 1944 Duke moved to the Desert Air Force in Italy to command No 145 Sqn, receiving a second bar to his DFC. He was incredibly lucky on one operation when his Spitfire was hit, forcing him to bail out in cloud. The parachute snagged on the cockpit and he was hurtling towards a large lake. He managed to release himself just in time and fell into the lake, a high wind dragging him across the surface until the canopy sank and almost took him with it. He was rescued by some Italian partisans and hidden until American forces reached the hide-out.

After operational tours totalling 712 hours in 486 sorties during which he destroyed 28 enemy aircraft, was awarded three probables and five damaged, he returned to the UK where, from 1

January 1945 to 1 1946 he was on detachment to Hawkers for test flying duty. Although he had a permanent commission, his time at Langley gave him a taste for test flying, and he applied for nomination to the ETPS, joining No 4 course just after his 24th birthday.

Towards the end of the course Duke was informed by the Commandant, Group Captain H. J. Wilson, that he would be posted to the new High Speed Flight at Tangmere where Group Captain 'Teddy' Donaldson and Sqn Ldr 'Bill' Waterton were to make an attempt to beat Group Captain Wilson's own 1946 record. Due to the low temperature over the south coast the best that Donaldson could achieve was 616 mph. Duke returned to ETPS and passed out as a graduate.

He was posted to 'A' Sqn at Boscombe Down, and began research work at high Mach numbers in Meteors at altitudes up to 50,000 ft. His enjoyment of this phase of his career caused him to ponder upon his next appointment, where, if he was to proceed through the Service to achieve high rank, he would be confined to an office flying a 'mahogany bomber'. He had been flying for 8 years, 3½ of which had been on test work. 'Bill' Humble, Hawker's chief test pilot, who lived near the Dukes at Bray in Berkshire, mentioned that he would be delighted to welcome him into the Hawker team. Humble was to move into a senior administrative position when his No 2, 'Wimpy' Wade, would become chief test pilot. Duke would then become Wade's No 2.

In August 1948 Duke joined Hawker and flew, among other aircraft, the new P.1040 which he raced in the Elmdon closed circuit events in 1949, competing with Hawker test pilots 'Doc' Morell and Frank Murphy in Furys, John Cunningham in a Vampire and Group Captain Allen Wheeler in a Spitfire V. Peter Lawrence of Blackburns flew a Firebrand and R. W. Jamieson a de Havilland Hornet. In the Kemsley Trophy race Neville Duke came first on handicap at an average speed of 508 mph. In the series Hawker pilots were awarded two first prizes and a third.

A Snarler rocket motor was installed in the tail of a P.1040 which then became known as P.1072. The climb performance on both the Nene and the Snarler was spectacular. During Duke's last flight in it the Snarler exploded and the tail of the machine caught fire. He shut the rocket down and landed safely.

The high speed flights in P.1052 and P.1081 required the recording of more information than could be gathered on the pilot's knee pad. Wire recorders were fitted. John Cunningham and John Derry showed interest in this development and asked to come to Langley for a demonstration. Duke and Wade thought that a special tape might interest their visitors from de Havilland. With a vacuum cleaner in the next office, providing a fair imitation of engine noise, Wade talked into the microphone to record an imaginary flight. When Cunningham and Derry heard him reporting 'Mach .98, Mach .99 . . .' in a calm voice, they were astounded but tried to appear unconcerned. The faces of the two conspirators gave the game away!

Wade went to the USA to fly American jet aircraft and in his absence Duke flew the P.1081. On Wade's return to Langley he flew the P.1081 which crashed at Lewes under most mysterious circumstances. The accident was never explained: Wade bailed out, but he did not release himself from the ejector seat. The aeroplane was totally destroyed and Wade killed instantly. Neville Duke was appointed to succeed his old friend and colleague. He regarded the appointment as a great honour but it was tinged with sadness.

Neville Duke had joined No 615 County of London Royal Auxiliary Air Force Squadron, of which Sir Winston Churchill was Honorary Air Commodore. He was appointed their OC, but with his new duties he felt he had insufficient time to devote to the squadron, so he resigned.

The P.1067 was at the cockpit mock-up stage, and by the spring of 1951 construction of the prototype was well advanced. To prepare for its first flight the new chief test pilot flew an Avon-engined Canberra to practise re-lights; he also flew an American F-86A Sabre. In June, the P.1067 was ready at Boscombe Down for the flight. Painted a pale duck egg green with RAF roundels, the machine looked beautiful. Taxying trials were satisfactory, although a short hop to check the unstick speed and feel the controls, ended with burned out brakes as the high idling speed of the Avon moved the machine too fast for comfort. On 20 July 1951 the prototype took off. It handled beautifully and was a delight to fly, a real pilot's aeroplane. There was slight lateral instability due to over-sensitivity of the power boosted ailerons, and the elevators were heavy as the booster had been disconnected for the maiden flight. The machine was named Hunter in 1952 and was clearly destined to become a classic.

At the September SBAC show, with only 11 hours in the log book, Neville Duke flew the Hunter over the Farnborough crowd at 700 mph. By

Above *Hawker Hunter, second prototype.*
Below *Neville Duke, chief test pilot, and Frank Bullen, chief production test pilot, in two-seat Hunter trainer (1956).*

January 1952 Mach 1.0 was attained in a 40 degree dive and, in April, Mach 1.03 produced airflow breakaway and tail buffeting. Various remedies were tried without success; finally the joint between the elevators and the rudder was faired in with a 'bullet', and this proved to be the answer. By June 1952 the Mach number had risen to 1.06 without buffet and on 10 July 1952, Duke flew to Brussels in 25 minutes to give its first supersonic demonstration before the public.

Gloster's Javelin, with its two Metrovick F9 axial flow turbines of 7,000 lb thrust each, had been flown for the first time by Bill Waterton on 26 November 1951. During its high speed taxying trials in October the tendency for the machine to rear-up when the flaps were lowered necessitated modifications to the range of incidence of the tail-plane.

Soon after take-off the pilot noticed a tendency towards buffeting at the rear end, and by the time speed had risen to 200 mph, the whole aeroplane was shaking violently. Speed was reduced to 150 mph, and after 30 minutes in the air Waterton returned to base, to report that the Javelin was easy to fly, performed well and was generally a promising design but had revealed a few nasty habits. Near the stall the machine would tend to tighten into a turn and when the flaps were lowered a nose-up pitching moment would develop. Appropriate modifications were made.

On 2 June 1952, after 60 hours flying, Bill Waterton took off in the prototype for a high speed run at 3,000 ft. Suddenly, at 90 per cent power, violent flutter developed. Two bangs heralded the departure of the elevators. The pilot found that the machine was pointing towards the ground and the stick moved freely fore-and-aft. His immediate impulse was to get out as fast as possible but he realized that a safe departure was unlikely. By winding the tailplane trimmer wheel he managed to arrest the dive and climbed to 10,000 ft at 300 mph. He flew towards the Bristol Channel where the machine would cause no damage if he bailed out, but decided that he might have a chance of saving the aircraft. He experimented with control in the landing configuration and headed for the long runway at Boscombe Down having found that, at a speed of 60 mph above normal, he could retain his limited control over the aeroplane.

He was congratulating himself on a perfect touch-down when a gust of wind or a bump in the runway surface suddenly initiated a fast lift-off, the nose rising high as the Javelin bounced along the ground in a series of hops, each one higher and slower than the last, whilst Waterton sat there wondering how it was going to end. He did not have long to wait. With a crash, the port undercarriage leg came up through the wing and sheets of flame rose from the ruptured fuel tank. The other two undercarriage legs collapsed and more fuel tanks exploded, but fortunately the Javelin did not turn over. After a terrifying ride to a standstill, Waterton tried to open the canopy in the middle of a mass of flames which, miraculously, had not reached the cockpit. The electric motor would not move the canopy and in sheer desperation, he thumped the melting perspex and the actuating button, until it slid back sufficiently for him to leap out of the wreck. He suddenly remembered the flight recorder, grabbed a foam hose from one of the fire tenders, and managed to retrieve the valuable instrument. For his efforts he was awarded a George Medal.

At the Farnborough air show the second prototype was demonstrated, but it soon became clear that the thick wing would seriously handicap the type and that the required Mach number could not be achieved. It was returned to the works to be fitted with re-designed wings which were intended to improve its aerodynamics and reduce the tendency to tip stalling which caused the Javelin to tighten into turns. It was the first British aeroplane to use a flight resonance system during its trials. Geoffrey Longford and another Gloster technician designed a trace recorder which received signals from eccentric weights within the airframe, rotated at varying speeds by motors. The exitation could, therefore, be varied in frequency. At increments of ten knots throughout the speed range the pilot was able to reproduce a whole range of frequencies in the airframe and detect instantly where there was a resonant one which could be an embarrassment.

At the end of May 1953 the modified machine was ready for test by Bill Waterton, who then passed responsibility to Peter Lawrence, formerly a naval pilot, who had joined Gloster from Blackburn in 1952. Waterton wanted a second opinion on the elevator control which was sluggish at low speed. After a briefing on the new machine,

Gloster GA5 Javelin, August 1952.

Lawrence made two flights: 30 minutes after the second take-off an RT message came from the Javelin, 'I'm in trouble!' Contact was then lost. The machine had gone into a deep stall from which Lawrence was unable to recover, dropping vertically with little forward speed. He ejected, but left it too late, his body being found in the seat near the burnt out wreckage. This was the first of a number of such fatal accidents which arose when jet aircraft with high mounted tailplanes deepstalled and descended in this stabilized condition with no useful airflow over the tailplane to achieve recovery. Work continued in an attempt to overcome the problems inherent in the type, which had now been fitted with Sapphire engines.

In March 1954 Wg Cdr R. F. Martin succeeded Bill Waterton as chief test pilot, with Flt Lt Peter Varley as his assistant. 'Dicky' Martin joined the RAF in 1937, determined to become a technical officer. Passing out from Cranwell, he joined a

Wg Cdr Dick Martin in front of the 1912 Blackburn monoplane which he still flies for the Shuttleworth collection (1950).

Hurricane squadron and fought in France. After a period in the Western Desert flying Curtiss Tomahawk fighters and a year testing American aircraft at a Maintenance Unit in Egypt, he moved into accident investigation, and was selected for No 4 course at ETPS and served for three years at the RAE, taking command of Aero Flight on the death of Sqn Ldr Muller-Rowland in the D.H.108. He became an instructor at ETPS and, in 1951, took a course at the RAF Flying College at Manby. After a spell at the Air Ministry he resigned his commission to join Gloster. Varley was in 'A' Flight at Farnborough and was attracted by the prospect of developing the Javelin.

'Dicky' Martin achieved some notoriety in the press when he was named as the pilot who aimed a sonic-boom at London, causing questions to be asked in the House of Commons! Newspaper reports had stated that the new Javelin was unable to fly at supersonic speeds. Gloster, naturally, apologized for the unseemly intrusion but the point had been made!

Many hours of test flying and the introduction of an all-moving slab tailplane without elevators –

Short SB.5.

one of the first to be fitted to a British aeroplane – enabled the Javelin to be delivered to squadrons in February 1956. 428 were built and were generally liked by their pilots. The type was to be replaced by a new thin-wing version, expected to be supersonic in level flight, and scheduled to fly in 1957. The notorious Sandys' edict, the Defence White Paper of 1957, caused the contract to be cancelled, and hastened the end of Gloster Aircraft. At the time of writing Martin is still flying as an airline pilot with Monarch and delighting the visitors to Shuttleworth with demonstrations of veteran aeroplanes.

The first and only all-British truly supersonic fighter, the English Electric Lightning, was first flown in its P1 prototype form, by Wg Cdr Roland Beamont on 4 August 1954. Its origins lay in the belated realization, in 1947, that Britain, among the pioneers of jet propulsion, was far behind in supersonic flight. A specification was issued for an experimental aeroplane. Fairey designed the FD.2 (later to set up a world speed record), and the brilliant E. W. Petter designed the P.1 for English Electric before he resigned in 1950 to join Folland, where he began work on the lightweight Midge and Gnat fighters.

Petter realized that to achieve the major jump in performance necessary to catch up, an advanced design with swept wings and tail would be necess-

ary. The prototype was powered by two Sapphire engines without re-heat, mounted on top of each other in the fuselage. Eventually two Avons, with reheat, were to power the P.1B fighter version to a speed of Mach 2-plus. RAE were concerned about the 60 degree sweep proposal, so they ordered from Short Brothers another research aircraft, the Short SB.5, the wings of which could be varied in sweep on the ground, and which could have its tailplane mounted in different positions. Not until December 1952 was it flown by Tom Brooke-Smith in the 50 degree sweep configuration and in January 1954 it flew with the wings at 60 degrees. By this time work on the P.1 was well advanced, and the only contribution the SB.5 made to the P.1 was to prove that the calculations and predictions on slow speed handling of the aeroplane, made by the young design team at Warton, were accurate. Nevertheless, the SB.5 was used for valuable research work at RAE Bedford.

The wings presented serious stress calculation problems as no precedent existed. The National Physical Laboratory at Teddington were developing their ACE computer and for the first time, programmes were run through it and many equations quickly solved. To investigate flutter potential one-seventh scale rocket-powered models were made and tested at the Larkhill army range.

Reheat was little more than a theory in 1948. The P.1 had to go supersonic without it. Powered controls and an all-moving tailplane were considered essential, whilst, for the first time, kinetic heating (caused by the passage of the aircraft through the air at high speed) had to receive serious consideration. Wind tunnel tests indicated that one of the SB.5 configurations with the tailplane mounted on top of the fin would be troublesome, and that a deep-stall would be likely – early evidence of the phenomenon which was to cost lives in the Javelin, Trident and BAC One-Eleven airliners. The tailplane of the P.1 was located low down and proved to be extremely efficient in avoiding pitch-up as the machine achieved Mach 1.0 – announced in August 1954. After the first flight of the Lightning fighter version in May 1957, Mach 2.0 was reached, with Beamont at the controls, on 25 November 1958.

The first aircraft simulator to be developed in Britain had been built by English Electric and RAE at Farnborough. Roland Beamont was able to put in a number of hours on the simulator before the first flight. He was delighted with the handling of the P.1, and its performance was better than predicted. Slight problems of aileron gearing emerged but were soon overcome. Unfortunately it was not possible to fly the 10 hours necessary for participation in the 1954 SBAC show, but by the end of September, 22 flights had proved the soundness of the design and work proceeded to turn it into a fighting machine, a process which necessitated a considerable increase in fuel capacity by fitting a large belly tank and a radar weapons system. Intensive development work resulted in an exceptional interceptor fighter which went into service with the RAF at Central Fighter Establishment, Coltishall, in December 1959. In addition to the three P.1 prototypes 12 pre-production aircraft were built, a policy which was followed later when the Tornado was developed. The significance of the Lightning as an advanced weapons system, as distinct from just a fighter aircraft, was emphasized by the attachment of Sqn Ldr James Dell, from Central Fighter Establishment, to the flight operations department at Warton. He made a large number of test sorties, and joined the Company as a civilian test pilot on 1 January 1960. In 1961 he became deputy chief test pilot.

The prototype trainer T.4 Lightning gave its pilot an extremely unpleasant experience on 1 October 1959. J. W. C. 'Johnny' Squier climbed to 35,000 ft, selected reheat, accelerated to Mach 1.7 and continued climbing to 40,000 ft. Half-way between the Isle of Man and the mainland he initiated a high-rate roll. As it terminated there was a loud bang, and the aeroplane went out of control so

Above *English Electric P.1 prototype.*
Centre *Wg Cdr R. P. Beamont after his thousandth flight in a Lightning (April 1963).*
Below *Lightning T.5.*

Johnny Squier (1975).

a loud bang. The P.120 began a series of high speed rolls to port. Gunn threw the control column over to the other side, reducing the roll rate and then put on full starboard rudder, the rolling then ceased, but the machine was diving to earth. With the controls set to eliminate the roll he had little chance of a pull-out so decided, as a last resort, to use the all-moving tailplane trimmer. To his relief it worked. He set, as best he could, a course for Boscombe Down where he hoped to land a virtually uncontrollable aeroplane on the long runway. Realizing that the chances of success were slim, he jettisoned the canopy. At 3,000 ft turbulence destroyed the modest level of stability which he had achieved, and the P.120 began to roll. He decided to get out and pulled the blind.

He ejected when the machine was upside down, far too near the ground for comfort. In his haste to jettison the seat he pulled the parachute ripcord in error, then released the seat. The error saved his life; as the canopy deployed, he crashed through some trees.

The air traffic control officer at RNAS Lee-on-Solent had seen the aircraft break up as it passed overhead and collected the pieces. The main

Montage prepared by Boulton Paul Aircraft Ltd to mark Ben Gunn's 21 years of test flying, 1945–66.

violently that the pilot began to fear loss of consciousness. He reached up to pull the face blind of the Martin Baker ejection seat, realizing that nowhere in the world had a pilot escaped successfully at supersonic speed. He left the aircraft holding the blind tightly over his face, the forces were agonizing and he thought he would lose his arms. Nevertheless, he slowed down, the seat released him, and the parachute, which should have opened automatically, failed to do so. Fortunately, he pulled the manual over-ride handle at 1,000 ft and fell into the sea, managing to climb into the dinghy. In spite of the various devices, such as the SARBE homing beacon, he could not be sighted by searching aircraft, several of which were seen by him.

Squier spent 28½ hours in the sea before the tide, and a piece of driftwood which he used as a paddle, enabled him to land in Wigtown Bay on the Scottish coast, 30 miles away. Six months after his ordeal he was flying again. It was established that the fin had broken away from his aircraft.

Another catastrophic attempt at supersonic flight in the early 1950s nearly cost the life of Ben Gunn, Boulton Paul's chief test pilot. On 28 August 1952 he was flying along the south coast at 5,000 ft in the P.120 delta research aircraft, when, at high speed, he suddenly heard a loud buzz followed by component was the port elevon with all the signs of hinge failure caused by flutter.

This chapter has recorded a period in the history of British test flying which was marked by high endeavour, great achievement and a measure of tragedy. It marked the end of an era in which design was still directed towards solving problems which, in themselves, were not fully understood although great progress had been made. Computer studies had not yet joined the armoury of the design offices, simulators were in their infancy, and analysis of in-flight data was still within the realm of the cine-photography of instrumentation and the wire recorder supplementing the pilot's knee pad.

It is appropriate to end this sombre account on a lighter note. Auster Aircraft of Rearsby, Leicestershire, had for many years specialized in small single-engined high wing monoplanes for private owners, pilot training, crop dusting and, during the war, army observation machines. Their chief test pilot, Ranald Porteous, was always a most welcome visitor at postwar SBAC and at other air shows. He claims, most modestly, to be Scotland's greatest living poet! – clearly on a par with Mike Daunt whose talent in that sphere has been revealed earlier in this book.

Ranald's talent in demonstrating light aeroplanes is without question, indeed, many pilots considered him to be the finest ever to have appeared at Farnborough. Trained at the de Havilland Technical School before the war, he learned to fly there, and had his first experience of test flying in a small monoplane, the Chilton, built at Hungerford by two ex-Tech School students, the Hon Andrew Dalrymple and A. R. Ward in 1937. In 1947 Ranald broke the 100 km international closed circuit record at 124.5 mph in the Folkestone Trophy Race at Lympne, flying one of the surviving Chiltons.

He joined Phillips and Powis at Woodley as a flying instructor and trainee test pilot, becoming experienced on the Miles range of light aircraft. Serving in RAF Flying Training Command throughout the war, much of it in Rhodesia, where he became president of the central examination board, he also had a period at CFS as a flight commander. After the war he joined Auster as sales manager and chief test pilot – soon appreciating the conflict inherent in this dual role. As Ranald explained, 'As sales manager I must tell my customers how good the aeroplane is, but I am forced to tell my colleagues how bad it is!'

His reputation as a pilot is only matched by his reputation as a raconteur. He claims to have had

Ranald Porteous crazy-flying in an Auster Autocrat at the Swansea Air Display, 1950.

few noteworthy or alarming experiences in the air, but tells, with relish, two stories. He took off in an Auster IX air observation post to carry out spinning trials with the CG well aft. He commenced a spin at a safe height, but recovery action was ineffective. Ranald reached up to push the roof-mounted operating lever for the anti-spin parachute. Suddenly, the seat collapsed, pilot and seat being held firmly to the floor by centrifugal force. Porteous was not sure if the lever had been moved far enough to release the parachute, so decided that his chances of survival were 50:50. Suddenly the Auster came out of the spin and dived vertically into cloud, pilot and seat then being projected forward upon the control column and instrument panel. With great difficulty control was regained, and a landing made in gusty conditions with Porteous just able to see over the coaming. As his radio link had been in circuit throughout the performance, flying control were aware of his problems. One of his happiest memories is that of his charming secretary walking out to the aeroplane with a silver salver upon which reposed a glass of brandy!

On one of his many overseas demonstration flights he was met by Auster's Indian agent who told him that his personal Aiglet had been entered for the all-India crazy-flying contest at Cawnpore and that Porteous was to fly it. Being out of practice in this esoteric art he was not amused but, as the Aiglet was particularly well suited to such routines he agreed to perform, his efforts being received with acclaim by the large audience. The next pilot stalled and spun in, producing a cloud of dust and smoke. Suddenly the shocked silence was broken by a public address system announcer, 'Ladies and gentlemen, there has been a terrible accident, we do not know whether the pilot is dead. Joy riding will now commence!'

16

HIGH TECHNOLOGY

The decade between 1955 and 1965 saw great changes in the structure of the British aircraft industry. 25 builders of aeroplanes were still in business. General Aircraft and Blackburn had joined forces whilst Cierva and Saunders Roe had formed the Saro Helicopter Division. On the engine side Armstrong Siddeley Motors had taken over Metropolitan Vickers turbine interests.

The complexity of aircraft, and consequent development costs, were rising steeply. One researcher stated in 1965 that, in 1954, 155 combat machines cost £6.2 million whilst four years later the same number cost £25.25 million. He also pointed out that, from 1953 to 1955, the average annual production of aircraft was 2,000, dropping, in 1957, to 968. The writing was on the wall, but the inevitable mergers were several years ahead.

Avro, Handley Page and Vickers were busy with the three V-bombers, hopelessly uneconomical, involving as they did three huge development bills spread over a small number of aircraft. Avro were also working on the 748 airliner and HP competed with their Herald design. Vickers were busy with the hugely successful Viscount. De Havilland were turning the ill-fated D.H.110 into the Sea Vixen and hoping to sell the new Comet 4 to the world's airlines whilst production of the Dove and Heron proceeded apace. Shorts at Belfast had produced the anti-submarine Seamew and were studying the possibilities of vertical take-off.

Armstrong Whitworth were working on the Argosy freighter and were building later marks of Meteor, whilst Blackburn's huge Beverley freighter was soon to be joined on the production line by the outstanding Buccaneer. Supermarine was still struggling with the Swift and was almost ready to fly the Scimitar naval fighter.

The Hawker Hunter was in production at Kingston, and a new supersonic fighter was on Sydney Camm's drawing boards. In contrast to the sleek Hawker types, Gordon Slade and Peter Twiss were busy eliminating the bugs from the complex Gannet twin-engined search and strike aircraft for the Royal Navy, and preparing for the first flight of the attractive FD.2 delta, their last fixed wing aeroplane. They were active, on the helicopter side, with developments of the ill-fated Gyrodyne which was considered to be a breakthrough in the field of rotary wing technology. Bristol's helicopter division was also making progress in this field, whilst the frustrations attendant upon the Britannia airliner programme harassed the aircraft division.

The engine companies were producing power units for these projects so the future for the industry looked reasonably healthy with a quarter of a million people employed in it.

At Bristol, Raoul Hafner had followed his successful Sycamore helicopter with a twin Alvis Leonides engined design, the Type 173.

In 1948 C. T. D. 'Sox' Hosegood had joined the helicopter division as a test pilot. Hosegood had served in the Fleet Air Arm from 1939 to 1943, and had been trained to fly helicopters in America in 1944. On his return he joined the Airborne Forces Experimental Establishment at Beaulieu.

After ground running and tethered trials he made the maiden flight of the first prototype on 9 November 1956. The second one was fitted with stub wings but they were removed as it was too slow for them to be effective. The Navy showed great interest in the 173 and ordered 100 of them. Development of the Type 192, to meet the naval requirements, called for an extremely strong four-wheel undercarriage and various other features which were included in the 25 aircraft ordered for RAF service. The cancellation of the naval order, just after the establishment of the helicopter division at Weston Super Mare, was a severe blow to Bristol. 'Sox' told the author, wryly, 'It was the biggest order ever for helicopters, and the biggest cancelled order ever!'

The first flight revealed an unexpected problem. It was thought that twin-tandem rotors would entirely eliminate the torque effect which necessitates

Bristol Type 173 helicopter, third prototype.

the use of a tail rotor in a single rotor machine. As the 173 accelerated down the long runway at Filton, Hosegood was forced to apply an increasing degree of port rudder, with the machine drifting away to starboard. He noticed Hafner following behind in a jeep, shouting loudly. His observer tried to hear his comments, without success. As the runway intersection was reached Hosegood was able to continue along another one until he brought the machine back to the ground.

Hafner appeared and announced that they had a problem! When it was carefully considered, the explanation was obvious; although the tail rotor was unnecessary in a tandem configuration, each of the main rotors would have a tendency to turn the machine in the direction of their rotation, so a perfect turning couple was established. The axis of rotation was canted sideways on each shaft to compensate, and no further trouble was experienced.

Trials with the RAF version, the Belvedere, caused some difficulty when hovering with the CG fully forward. Flying slowly backwards at very low altitude, Hosegood suddenly felt the nose dropping, and he had insufficient height or speed to do anything about it. The airspeed indicator probe on

the nose dug into the earth and then he found his suede shoes covered in mud – all rather embarrassing, but no-one was hurt. The Belvedere was one of the first helicopters to be fitted with duplicated powered controls.

Bristol's chief test pilot, Bill Pegg, had flown the prototype Britannia airliner on 16 August 1951 and had experienced a number of problems. The elevator control was far too light, and generated a switchback flight path. When he selected undercarriage down, no green light appeared for one of the main wheels; one of the four wheel bogies had failed to rotate to the landing position, and jerking the controls failed to free it. Pegg suddenly smelt burning, and saw smoke rising from the cockpit floor. He decided to make an immediate landing in the hope that the bogie would rotate on impact. Fortunately it did so before touch down, so the new aeroplane landed safely. The smoke came from an overheated motor in the systems bay, but the undercarriage problem was persistent.

Finally, it was found that during taxying, excessive heat coming from the brakes was being transmitted to the main bogie bearing which seized upon its shaft. During the next flight the nosewheel failed to lock down. As he was due to demonstrate the Britannia at the 1952 SBAC show two weeks hence, Pegg was extremely worried by this incident, so he

First take-off of Bristol Britannia prototype.

landed with the nosewheel held off for as long as possible to lessen the damage in the event of its retraction. Fortunately, as the main wheels touched, the green light came up on the nosewheel indicator.

A serious incident occurred on 4 February 1954, when the second prototype, G-ALRX, suffered a major engine failure after only 51 hours in the air. Ten minutes after take-off, with a group of KLM airline executives and Dr A. E. Russell, the chief designer, on board, the oil temperature on No 3 engine rose; Pegg decided to shut down the engine, ostensibly to demonstrate to the Dutchmen how well the Britannia flew on three. Perhaps rashly, he then decided to re-start it, run at low rpm and watch the temperature. It rose immediately, so another shut-down was initiated. Suddenly there was a loud bang. Dr Russell came forward to report, 'A hell of a fire in No 3 with flames going back almost as far as the tailplane.'

Fire drill had little effect and the situation was extremely serious; they were at 10,000 ft with 2,000 gallons of fuel in the wing. There followed what must be one of the worst experiences in a test pilot's life – rapid decision making, each of which held the key to life or death for 12 people, to

say nothing of the reputation of Bristols and an important new aeroplane. How long would it be before the wing spar was so weakened by the fire that the wing broke away? Would aileron control go first? The answers, if they could be predicted, would determine whether an immediate crash landing or a return to Filton should be attempted. Alternatively, the mud flats of the River Severn offered a chance of survival.

The Britannia was over the Welsh mountains and a landing there was out of the question. Burning metal began to emerge from No 3 engine, so Pegg shut down the adjacent one. It was now either the mud or Filton.

If he elected to go to Filton, would the wing hold? What state would the undercarriage be in, could he lower it? Would the flaps work properly? If the actuators on the starboard side were damaged by fire, the Britannia would roll into the ground. If they were not used and the brakes were inoperative, even if the tyres had survived, the petrol filling station on the road at the end of the runway seemed a dangerous stopping place for a blazing airliner.

The chief designer leaned over to the sales manager to say that he had heard of a few engine fires in his life in aviation, but none which had burned for as long as this without the wing coming off! Pegg, unaware of this encouraging analysis of his situation, saw that the tide was out, and was convinced that a touchdown on the mud between Avonmouth and Sharpness offered the best chance of survival. As he came in at 200 mph with flaps and undercarriage up, both port engines stopped due to a short circuit. Ahead was a deep gully across the mud which might have been disastrous, but swift work by Ken Fitzgerald and Gareth Jones, two technicians from the flight test department, re-started the engines and enabled Pegg to fly over the gully and put down safely in the mud, where the machine ran smoothly for 400 yards before stopping safely.

Across the mud was a brickyard to which the bedraggled party trudged, Bill Pegg staying behind in the office whilst the rest of the party returned to Filton by car. He was amused to be offered an order for a substantial quantity of bricks by a man who suddenly appeared!

The cause of the fire was the failure of the engine reduction gearing to the propeller which permitted

the compressor turbine to overspeed and disintegrate.

The Britannia was plagued by troubles with flaming out of the Proteus turbines, even after delivery to BOAC. In May 1954, Walter Gibb, Pegg's assistant, who became chief test pilot in 1957, had an unpleasant experience in the prototype when a torque tube linking the flaps broke during stalling tests, and a 3G overload was applied to correct the violent half roll which followed.

On 6 November 1957 the Britannia programme sustained a tragic setback. G-ANCA, on a test flight, dived into a wood near Bristol, killing the pilot and his test crew of 14. An electrical fault causing autopilot runaway was believed to be the explanation. Shortly afterwards, Godfrey Auty, another Bristol test pilot, was training crews of Aeronaves de Mexico who had bought two Britannias. Over Brownsville, Texas, the aircraft entered a rapidly steepening banked turn which was becoming uncontrollable. Recalling the previous crash, he instantly disconnected the electrical supply to the autopilot and control was regained. Immediate circuitry modifications were made.

Fairey FD.1 with airbrakes out as it approaches photographic aircraft.

Peter Twiss (1956).

Fairey FD.2.

In 1947, Fairey had been invited by the Ministry of Supply to initiate a design study into an aircraft capable of transonic flight. This became the FD.1 fitted with a Rolls-Royce Derwent engine, and it was taxied for the first time by Gordon Slade and Peter Twiss at Ringway, Manchester, on 12 May 1950. The first flight was made from Boscombe Down by Gordon Slade on 12 March 1951. Originally intended for ramp launching it was a tricky aeroplane. Slade disliked it and Peter Twiss described it as a 'very dicey little box'. Whilst being flown by a Service pilot, it swung on landing and the undercarriage was torn off.

The FD.2 was in a different class. An outstanding technical achievement, it permitted a quantum jump in performance of which Peter Twiss took full advantage when he set up a new world speed record in 1956. He made the first flight in the FD.2 at Boscombe Down on 6 October 1954, by which time Gordon Slade had retired and Twiss had been appointed chief test pilot.

The first 12 flights were entirely uneventful with all systems operating satisfactorily and the aeroplane handling sweetly. Flight number 13 was distinctly fraught. 40 miles north of Boscombe Down,

at 20,000 ft, the engine stopped, the fuel warning light came on, and the fuel gauge moved from full to empty in five seconds. By this time the pilot was talking earnestly to Boscombe tower, asking for a course to bring him in with the minimum of control movement. This was essential as FD.2 had no back-up manual controls; a reservoir was available but its capacity was only sufficient for limited control movement, so return to base was a case of 'hands off, feet off, move nothing unless you have to!' The directions from the tower were so good, that, as Twiss broke cloud at 3,000 ft, flying at 350 mph, the aeroplane was well aligned for the runway. Selection of wheels down to kill some of the excess speed resulted in the nosewheel locking down but no response from the main wheels. There was just enough power left in the control system to bring the nose up for a landing at 170 mph on the rear of the fuselage and the nosewheel. As speed decayed and lateral control was reduced, the machine swung off the runway and came to rest without much serious damage.

The reason for the incident was the failure of a rubber seal in the air intake. It had blown out and allowed high pressure air to enter the wing and partially collapse the bag tanks. The distortion of the bags caused the fuel valves to jam, leaving the contents unusable.

Peter Twiss was awarded the Queen's Commendation for Valuable Services in the Air for saving this valuable prototype under extremely difficult circumstances. The programme was delayed for six months but, on 10 March 1956, he established his new world air speed record of 1,132 mph, 310

219

mph faster than the record held by an American F-100C Super Sabre.

For such an early project in transonic and supersonic flight the FD.2 was remarkably successful. The pilot noted only a slight change of trim at Mach 0.95 and a flick of the ASI needle as the shock waves passed the static vent. RAE pilots reported, however, that it was not an easy machine to fly. It was a great credit to the design and development teams, and to Peter Twiss, who received the OBE for his work.

Both prototypes were based at RAE Bedford where valuable research flights were made. To take advantage of more favourable weather conditions, one was based at Cazaux, near Bordeaux, a sparsely populated area, where many supersonic flights were made at altitudes down to 3,500 ft. This provided valuable information for the Concorde programme which began in 1957. The prototype FD.2 was later converted by Bristols to the ogival delta wing as a scale model of Concorde. The Bristol 221, later BAC.221, is now on show, with a Concorde prototype and another research aeroplane used in the programme, the HP.115, at the Fleet Air Arm Museum at Yeovilton.

In the Fairey rotary wing organization Ron Gellatly and John Morton were busy with a major development of the Gyrodyne helicopter with tip powered rotors. After many hours of engine running and ground resonance tests Gellatly and Mor-

Bristol BAC.221 research aircraft at the 1966 SBAC show.

ton made the first flight of the twin Napier Eland turbine powered machine on 6 November 1957. It proved to be a successful design and was fast, setting up a new closed circuit record for helicopters in 1959 with a speed of 190.0 mph over a 100 km course.

Development continued. BEA showed interest although the high noise levels created by the tip jets were considered intolerable. In February 1960 Westlands took over the rotary wing interests of Fairey and Bristol Aeroplane Company, so a degree of indecision was apparent. New York Airways had ordered a larger model but saw that delivery would be greatly extended and cancelled. The Rotodyne drifted on in limbo until the programme was cancelled in February 1962.

1957 also saw the first flight of a remarkable new design which had great potential, but which was yet another casualty of the disastrous 1957 White Paper. This was the Saunders Roe SR.53 mixed powerplant fighter with a de Havilland Spectre variable thrust rocket motor to give primary power, with an Armstrong Siddeley Viper gas turbine for secondary power. Sqn Ldr J. S. Booth flew the first of two prototypes from Boscombe Down on 16 May 1957. Projected top speed was Mach 2.2 at 45,000 ft plus, with the incredible rate of climb of 52,800 ft per minute.

Trials were encouraging, and the aircraft was demonstrated by John Booth at the 1957 SBAC show. Taking off in the second prototype on 5 June 1958, from the shorter runway at Boscombe Down, the rocket motor stopped whilst he was still on the

ground. It was never established whether it failed or the take-off was aborted. Booth streamed the braking parachute, but went through the boundary fence into a field. Control heard him say, in a calm voice, 'Come and get me.' Sadly, what should have been a very minor incident ended in disaster. The SR.53 hit a pole carrying an approach light, the pole broke and fell upon the aircraft, killing the pilot. An explosion followed immediately, and the aircraft was destroyed. A development of the SR.53 in which the Royal Navy and the *Luftwaffe* showed interest was yet another casualty of the Sandys bludgeon, also what could have been a world-beating Mach 2.35 fighter was lost to the nation. Another victim of this folly was a fighter, the Hawker P.1121, also designed to achieve Mach 2.35. The prototype was approaching completion when the project was cancelled.

Handley Page's attempt to return to the civil market after the war was in the Dakota replacement category. On 25 August 1955 Sqn Ldr Hedley Hazelden flew the Herald for the first time. It was a 37 seat (later, in its turboprop form, stretched to 50 seats), with four Alvis Leonides radial engines. Clear evidence of the success of the R-R Dart turbines in the new Viscount and in the Herald's strongest competitor, the Dutch Fokker Friendship, led to the decision, in 1957, to abandon piston engines and fit two Darts, from which Rolls-Royce had obtained useful increases in power. The prototype was converted and flown from Woodley, by Hazelden on 11 March 1958. En route to the SBAC show at Farnborough on 30 August the opportunity was taken to obtain some air-to-air photographs of the Herald, and an accompanying Victor, from a Hastings.

Just before beginning his descent to Farnborough, with the aeroplane at 6,000 ft, there was a bang from the starboard engine which then caught fire. Hazelden closed the fuel cocks, feathered the propeller and activated the fire extinguishers. There was no response; the fire continued to burn furiously. With eight other people, including his wife, on board, an immediate forced landing was imperative. He throttled back the port engine as he studied the heavily wooded countryside ahead in a search for a suitable site. The aircraft descended at about 160 knots but, as the fire progressed, considerable vibration occurred and control became difficult. As a possible landing field was identified, the machine commenced a rapid roll to starboard. Instinctively Hazelden applied opposite aileron, thinking, calmly, 'The wing is coming off, so this is it!' Unknown to him, the starboard engine had

The burnt out Handley Page Herald; and Sqn Ldr Hedley Hazelden inspecting the wreckage.

dropped off and this allowed the Herald to respond to the aileron correction. Once more, level flight was regained, but control was now even worse with increased vibration and pitching caused by the loss of the starboard tailplane, which was burned away by flames streaming from the wing. As the chosen field was approached, he saw that the approach was compromised by an 80 ft high tree and a farm roller parked on the best touchdown spot, whilst further on, high tension cables crossed the landing run. To land beyond them would leave insufficient room to stop. He therefore went over the tree, belly landed at about 130 knots, and slid under the cables.

An unseen tree stump tore a hole in the fuselage, just ahead of the burning wing. After slewing to the right and coming to rest, the occupants escaped through this hole, whilst the aircraft continued to burn out – a happy ending to what could have been total disaster had been brought about by Hazelden's superb airmanship, aided by the rugged Herald airframe which sustained, for a considerable period, a major fire in the wing which in many aeroplanes would have caused major structural failure.

The engine had sustained a turbine disintegration caused by failure of a layshaft which caused loss of oil to the main bearings. As the bearing failed, the turbine disc moved so that it rubbed against the fixed guide vanes. The heat generated weakened the turbine disc which then broke under centrifugal force. A large piece of the disc passed through the engine casing and severed the main fuel line and one of the engine bearer struts. The volume of fuel escaping fed a fire which no extinguisher could contain, and the fire eventually severed two more bearer struts which caused the engine to fall away. The wing, however, was, by then, so seriously on fire that it continued to burn.

Hazelden told the author that Sir Frederick Handley Page telephoned him and his first thought was for the occupants of his aircraft. He gave the pilot a gold watch in recognition of his skill. He

Rolls-Royce Thrust Measuring Rig – the Flying Bedstead.

was also awarded the Queen's Commendation for his work at Boscombe Down on British civil airworthiness requirements.

In a quest for a flying machine to enable agents to enter and leave enemy territory, Marcel Lobelle, formerly chief designer of Fairey, designed a strange inflatable device, a rubberised fabric delta wing with a nacelle carrying a 60 hp Mikron engine and pusher propeller. The idea was to be able to fold it up for stowage in a valise. First flown in 1953 by Sq Lr R. Harvey, it was publicly demonstrated in 1955, its nickname changing from the 'flying mattress' to the 'Durex delta'. David Masters gave a demonstration at White Waltham in 1957 when it was inflated and flying in about 20 minutes. Peter Twiss also flew it, but was not too enthusiastic about risking his life in an aircraft that relied upon a motor car pressure gauge for a structural check! It did not go into production.

In the early 1950s vertical take-off and landing was being seriously considered by designers all over the world. Dr A. A. Griffith, of Rolls-Royce, proposed the construction of a flying test bed to evaluate the problems of VTOL, as the principle became known. Called the thrust measuring rig by Lord Hives, the chairman of Rolls, and the 'Flying Bedstead' by almost everyone else, the strange device was 'flown' in 1954 by Capt R. T. Shepherd, the chief test pilot. Two Rolls-Royce Nene turbines

produced the thrust which was deflected downwards; jets of compressed air ejected from 'puffer pipes' gave lateral and directional stability. The success of this ungainly rig persuaded Rolls that the principle was feasible and that they should develop a gas turbine for the specific function of providing lift for vertical take-off aeroplanes. The RB.108 was the result of this decision.

Shorts were interested and decided to collaborate with Rolls-Royce in developing the world's first jet propelled VTOL aircraft. Tom Brooke-Smith, who had only just recovered from his serious crash in the Short SB.1 glider, was at Boscombe Down when he received a telephone call from his chairman telling him of the new project. He reflected upon this news, and decided that he must have experience in helicopters. He spoke to Sq Ldr Ron Gellatly who was OC 'D' Sqn, and asked his advice. 'Be down at "D" at 0900 tomorrow and I will have you solo before tea!' By sacrificing lunch, Brookie was solo at 16.15.

Rolls-Royce invited him to fly the 'Bedstead', and a Hiller helicopter was sent to Belfast, whilst he also flew the Sikorsky and Bristol Sycamore helicopters.

He became totally absorbed in the multitude of potential problems. Highly experimental, the two prototypes bristled with engineering and aerodynamic problems, with a number of thermodynamic ones for good measure. Every degree rise in the ambient temperature above standard resulted in a loss of vertical thrust totalling 100 lb for the four lift engines. Even a cloud passing over the sun significantly affected the unstick performance in vertical flight. Even his own weight was rudely commented upon by the weight control department, but he was quite unrepentant and refused to diet!

It was originally intended that forward thrust and deceleration should be achieved by tilting the four engines hydraulically 30 degrees either side of their vertical locations. Brooke-Smith prevailed upon the designers to fit a fifth engine to give thrust. For its first wingborne flight from the long runway at Boscombe Down on 2 April 1954 it used most of the runway, unsticking at 150–160 knots. The propulsion engine had no governor so its rpm was affected by both the speed of the aircraft and its attitude on the runway. The propulsion engine flamed out, so a dead-stick landing was made.

Whilst these preliminary trials were in progress the second prototype was being built to make its first tethered flight in the vertical mode on 23 May 1958. In this phase Brookie ensured that all four lift engines would start together, sustain 'idle' running

satisfactorily and accelerate or decelerate to any point within the operating range to provide the crispness of response essential to hovering flight. Control in hover was achieved, as in the prototype, by jets of high velocity air bled from the compressors. He approached the transitional stage very stealthily. Flow patterns of high speed air would alter when the lift engines started and he suspected that the propulsion engine could flame out. They might not start in unison, indeed they might not start at all. After careful sequential tests it became clear that there were no apparent problems.

After three years hard work all the tests had been successfully completed within the sphere of known and avoidable risks which every test pilot may identify and analyse – the next part of the programme was a major step into unknown, and to a great extent, unpredictable territory.

Limitations of climb performance and fuel load dictated a height of 8,000 ft for the light-up trials of the lift engines. His visit to the Farnborough vertical tunnel to watch spinning trials of a model of the SC.1 was not encouraging. A loss of height in the spin of 20,000 ft/min left him with less than 20 seconds before he hit the ground if he went into a spin whilst passing through the 1G stall regime in the course of the tests.

On 6 April 1960, with a chase aircraft in attendance, Tom Brooke-Smith started the four lift engines at 8,000 ft. They lit, 'Like the top of a gas cooker!' A major problem of nose pitch-up arose later in the flight. As speed reduced he required more vertical power; at this point the nose rose until he ran out of trim and the stick was right forward on the instrument panel. A number of expedients were tried to enable the machine to be flown at the Farnborough air show; eventually the linkage of the elevon controls had to be re-designed.

Space forbids a full account of the remarkable series of trials which Brooke-Smith conducted through the vital and very hazardous transition stage but, after five years of unremitting concentration and first class airmanship, he announced his satisfaction with the SC.1, which was demonstrated at the 1960 SBAC show as the world's first practical jet propelled vertical take-off and landing aeroplane.

'Brookie' carried out his intention to retire after the completion of his work on the SC.1. His assistant was to take the machine to RAE Bedford for further tests, but he was taken ill. Due to limited fuel capacity it could not fly to Thurleigh after a vertical take-off and the Farnborough runway was not long enough for a full load wingborne depar-

Tom Brooke-Smith (1960).

Short SC.1.

ture, so he decided to carry out the delivery flight himself and refuel at Boscombe Down where the long runway was adequate.

Describing the take-off after refuelling he said 'At about 155 knots there was a hell of a bang – two tyres on the port undercarriage and one on the nose had burst simultaneously. I thought, my God, this thing's only got to yaw and it will roll over and that's the end – it's full of fuel. So I called over the RT for the arrestor net at the end of the runway to be triggered and fought to keep the aircraft straight in spite of the burst tyres. The SC.1 came to rest on the grass overshoot area beyond the end of the runway.'

The Air League awarded him the Founder's Medal for his outstanding achievement in bringing jet VTOL into the realm of reality. He received the Medal from the Duke of Hamilton at Grosvenor House Hotel. Having spoken of Tom's achievements he gave him a parcel which he insisted should be opened immediately. Inside was a pair of car number plates 1 VTO which grace the Brooke-Smith barouche in perpetuity!

Another equally outstanding design in the same field was germinating at Bristol Siddeley and Hawker Aircraft, a project which required a similar degree of skill and courage from Bill Bedford and John Farley, as chief test pilots, and their teams.

Sqn Ldr A. W. Bedford had graduated from ETPS in 1949/50, served as a tutor there, before moving to RAE. He joined Neville Duke at Hawker in 1951. In August 1955 Duke was carrying out gun firing trials in a Hunter off Littlehampton when a turbine failed. He coaxed it back to Ford and received the Queen's Commendation for his work.

The engine was changed, and Neville returned to Ford to collect the machine. At 1,000 ft over Chichester the engine slowed to idling thrust. His options were strictly limited. Thorney Island, near Portsmouth, was the nearest aerodrome, but he arrived at too high a speed for a normal landing, with insufficient excess speed to turn on to the runway. He touched down on the rough grass surface at 200 mph, the Hunter immediately developing a series of galloping bounces characteristic of tricycle undercarriage aeroplanes with the CG well aft. The machine was practically out of control when Duke decided to select undercarriage up. Only one main leg retracted but, at least, it saved a fatal stall at the top of one of the rapidly increasing bounces. The Hunter careered on in a series of arcs with the pilot sitting there utterly incapable of any control. At the aerodrome perimeter it hurtled over a ridge and crashed nose first into a hollow.

From the disintegrated wreckage Neville Duke emerged, cut, bruised and aching. When he looked at the scene of devastation around him he realised how lucky he had been in spite of the fact which, at that moment occurred to him, the serial number of his Hunter, 562, added up to thirteen, as did the number of his Tomahawk, AN 337, in which he crashed in the Western Desert in 1941!

It was discovered that his spine had been fractured in the crash which was caused by a small piece of fluff in a fuel vent valve. After a protracted period on his back whilst the spine healed he returned to test flying but was in pain when G forces were experienced. He felt that this was a totally unsatisfactory state of affairs for a chief test pilot so, in October 1956, he handed over the reins to 'Bill' Bedford.

Neville continued to fly as personal pilot to Sir George Dowty, and carried out a number of freelance test flying assignments. At the time of writing he is carrying out certification flying on John Edgley's remarkable Optica observation aeroplane. The prototype of this was designed and built by Edgley himself, who now runs a computer-aided aircraft works at Old Sarum, one of the oldest aerodromes in the world, where he is building the first batch of over 80 orders for this machine, originally test flown at Cranfield by Sqn Ldr Angus McVitie.

In September 1983, 30 years to the day after his world record breaking flight at a sea-level speed of 726.6 mph, Neville Duke was invited to fly Michael Carlton's red Hunter trainer over the Bognor/Littlehampton/Worthing course, to re-create the atmosphere of those exciting days, and to raise money for the Stoke Mandeville Hospital, a cause of particular interest to Neville Duke after his recovery from a broken spine.

Another Hawker pilot who had a similar remarkable escape in a Hunter was Frank Murphy. Just before Neville Duke's crash at Thorney Island, Frank was carrying out fuel system tests which necessitated turning the booster pumps off, an action which was likely to stop the engine. This happened, and a re-light was impossible. With clouds from 1,000 ft up to 6,000 ft he had to rely upon guidance from the control tower at Ford near Chichester, an aerodrome where he had already made four forced landings in various aeroplanes! He carefully planned his approach to Ford with a possible diversion to nearby Tangmere.

Suddenly radio contact was lost as the batteries had been exhausted by the attempts to re-light. As he broke cloud his alignment was fairly good but he could not lower the flaps. Determined to save the machine, he remained with it and landed at

The remains of Frank Murphy's Hunter.

230 mph with the undercarriage retracted. The Hunter developed a violent bounce which was quite uncontrollable and the pilot almost lost consciousness. Eyewitnesses counted 15 bounces and the Hunter then slewed sideways through a caravan park, where two people were killed. It hurtled on over the Clymping road where it broke into three pieces. The cockpit went on rolling for another 100 yards; the weight of the gun pack underneath caused it to come to rest in an upright position with the top of the ejector seat battered. Marks of all the bolt ends in the cockpit canopy were found in the sides and top of Frank Murphy's helmet, which was split from front to back. This was the

first occasion on which a new British 'bone dome' had been tested in a crash. The Institute of Aviation Medicine was well satisfied with the outcome of it. Frank spent many months in hospital recovering from his injuries.

In 1954 Neville Duke recruited, from the Royal Air Force, Duncan Simpson, who had trained, and become a qualified aircraft engineer, at the de Havilland Technical School. He completed an operational tour in No 222 Fighter Squadron and was posted to Central Fighter Establishment, West Raynham, where he joined the Day Fighter Trials Unit, flying, among other types, the outstanding American Sabre. In February 1954 the first Swift F.1s appeared for test and, in July 1954, the first three Hunters were delivered. Soon afterwards Duncan joined the Hawker team with Hugh Merewether who Neville Duke had brought in from his Auxiliary Air Force Squadron, No 615. Hugh was a highly qualified engineer who had worked in the Vickers Advanced Projects Office under Barnes Wallis. He was quite outstanding, and his work on the Hunter, particularly in connection with the demanding, difficult and highly unpleasant inverted spinning programme deserves to be better known.

Hawker was developing, in 1957, the P.1121 high speed, high altitude interceptor, whilst in France the veteran designer Michel Wibault was working on a machine known as the Gyroptère, in which a turbine drove, through shafts, four compressors arranged like car wheels on the sides of the fuselage; the jets from these compressors could be directed downwards for thrust or aft for propulsion. Sir Stanley Hooker, who had left Rolls-Royce in 1949 to join Bristol Siddeley as chief engineer, became involved in discussion on the Wibault project. Hooker was not optimistic of the success of the R-R/Short SC.1 principle, which in essence required the wasteful transport around the sky of lift engines which only performed a function at the beginning and end of a flight; he considered the new idea to be a much more satisfactory system.

Sydney Camm was equally unimpressed with the lift engine concept and wrote to Hooker asking what he was doing about vertical take-off engines. Hooker sent him a drawing of a proposal which had been sketched out at Bristol, and which ultimately became the Pegasus. Camm suddenly demanded that a meeting be held as his designers had produced drawings of an aeroplane based on the vectored thrust engine, at that time known as the B.E.53.

The Bristol team went to Kingston and saw the drawings of the P.1127. It was agreed to develop, from the Bristol Orion engine, one with four outlet 'elbows', one on each side of the front of the engine taking air from the compressors with two aft, taking hot gases from the jet pipe which was split into two sections, one for each outlet duct. The ducts could be swivelled in unison so that lift could be generated through the CG of the aircraft or, if they were turned by the pilot to face aft, the machine would be translated by the changing direction of the jets, into wingborne flight. A major step forward in assisting stability in the hover mode, was the decision to arrange for the high pressure and low pressure turbines to rotate in opposite directions, so that the gyroscopic forces created by their rotation would cancel out. Following the principle of the R-R Flying Bedstead, control of pitch and roll in the hover mode would be achieved by air jets at the extremities of the aeroplane. These would be operated by the movement of the control column only when the nozzles were turned into the hover position. The jet at the tail could be rotated to act as a rudder.

The Sandys axe fell upon the Hawker P.1121, a very advanced project for a strike fighter which was almost completed. It was powered by a powerful de Havilland Gyron engine. So all the Hawker effort was directed towards the new 'jump jet', as it became known. Sir Sydney and Roy Chaplin were in charge of the design; but, after Camm's death in 1966, and the retirement of Chaplin, the task was given to two brilliant young designers: Ralph Hooper and John Fozard. Development of the Pegasus engine at Bristol was the responsibility of Charles Marchant and John Dale with Hooker in charge.

Sir Sydney Camm was not an innovator but certainly he was one of the most competent aircraft designers in the world in his day. Conventional and highly practical, he always demanded the simple solution to a problem – a formula which ensured that Hawker aircraft have been in service with the RAF for the whole of its existence. Weight was obviously a major problem in the P.1127. The structural weight of the Hunter was about 30 per cent of the total. This percentage would have been intolerable in the case of the P.1127 as it would only just manage to leave the ground with negligible payload. So weight control was crucial and dictated the short, squat appearance of it.

In conformity with Camm's passion for simplicity, it was decided that autostabilization would not be used. Bill Bedford and his deputy, Hugh

Merewether, concurred, and were convinced that manual control would be entirely satisfactory. The Ministry of Supply was equally convinced that autostabilization in hover was essential. To confound the Ministry pundits, Hawker carried out a computer exercise, and fed into it all the parameters associated with a man riding a bicycle. The computer concluded that it was quite impossible for a man to ride a bicycle unless it was autostabilized!

Bill Bedford went to America to watch experiments being carried out by NASA on a 1/6 scale model of P.1127 in a free flight wind tunnel. Four pilots sat in cubicles watching the model through windows, and actually flew them through their own controls in the cubicles. One handled pitch, the second, roll, the third, yaw and the fourth controlled height. They flew the model successfully right through from take-off to wingborne flight. NASA also gave Bedford access to a simulator which proved to be much more difficult to fly than the actual P.1127, but it revealed a weakness in that more power was shown to be required in the lateral and fore-and-aft hover controls than was actually planned. The later test flights confirmed this prediction. NASA had a variable stability helicopter which Bedford also flew. Predicted characteristics of P.1127 were fed into it.

Bedford also had a short 'flight' in the SC.1 mounted within a gantry which did not contribute much to his experience, particularly as it was fully autostabilized. Later, he flew it in free flight at Belfast. A few days before the projected first tethered flight in the P.1127 on 21 October 1960, Bedford was involved in a car accident in Germany when his German driver failed to negotiate a bend and ran into a tree. A large plaster was put on his broken leg so his prospects for the first flight looked grim. Nevertheless he managed to convince the RAF medical board that he could still fly, and persuaded them to grant him approval with the unique proviso 'tethered hovering only'.

21 hovering flights were made between 3 November and 19 November 1960 and it was soon clear that there was inadequate power in the 'puffer' controls, and also that the undercarriage was not wholly satisfactory. On 19 November Bedford flew in free hover with no restraints. In March 1961 taxying trials were carried out at RAE Bedford. Further problems with the undercarriage necessitated a number of modifications.

Bedford flew a number of sorties in a Hunter converted to reproduce, as far as possible, the lift/drag characteristics of P.1127, the engine of which was as new as the airframe, so a number of flights were made in the Hunter to simulate the possibility of engine failure on take-off.

Even the first cross-country flight was carefully planned well in advance to enable the pilot to remain within gliding distance of four aerodromes with long runways, should an engine failure occur.

Bedford was well satisfied with the first wing-borne flight on 13 March. Considering the unique nature of the control system, it was crisp and precise. When he tested, at altitude, the effect of the flaps he found that a severe nose-down pitch developed so the landing was made without flaps.

The long test programme revealed many problems associated with the relationship between the three fundamental factors, the centre of lift, centre of gravity and the thrust line. Various alterations were made to the reaction control system and many wingborne flights were made by Bedford and Hugh Merewether. The second prototype entered the programme which, within six months, reached the stage of clearing the aeroplane for transitional flight – a remarkable achievement for such a radical and difficult project.

On 12 September 1961 Bedford took off from Dunsfold, rose to a safe altitude and rotated the nozzles, smoothly accelerating to wingborne flight amid the cheers of the assembled spectators, including John Fozard and Ralph Hooper. Hugh Merewether repeated the performance.

The test programme was so successful that the directors of the company decided to demonstrate the P.1127 to the C-in-C Fighter Command, Air Marshal Sir Hector McGregor. Bedford took off vertically and flew off in transition, he attempted to turn but the machine simply yawed; it rotated several times before the pilot was able to bring it under control again. At the time the C-in-C thought it was part of the demonstration but it was the first manifestation of a potentially dangerous phenomenon known as intake momentum drag yaw. This occurs when the aeroplane is flying so slowly that the rudder is ineffectual; enormous volumes of air are entering the intakes, which are ahead of the CG, so if the wind is slightly off the nose, the machine will be turned away from the wind by intake drag. As it turns, it presents the windward wing to the wind; more lift is generated by this wing, as the other is, by now, heavily swept in relation to the wind, so the machine rolls away from the wind with the pilot quite unable to recover control. Bedford was in a situation where he almost lost control at 200 ft; fortunately his skill and experience with the P.1127 saved the day. An American pilot was killed at Dunsfold when he

Hawker P.1127 prototype hovering.

rolled through 90 degrees, realized he had lost control and ejected, only to hurtle into the ground in his seat.

Ultimately devices on the rudder pedals were fitted to indicate to the pilot which pedal to push if a sideslip developed. Together with the limited authority autostabilizer this device made the later Harrier a straightforward aeroplane to fly.

Bedford had an alarming experience during flutter tests. He flew the aircraft through the speed range and hit the stick with a metal 'bonker' to induce an input of vibration. Suddenly at 5,000 ft and 400 knots there was roughness and a roaring noise. He decided to land at nearby Yeovilton Royal Naval Air Station. Hugh Merewether, in the chase Hunter, could see nothing wrong with the aircraft so Bedford began his final approach at 200 knots, lowered the undercarriage and selected flaps down; at 200 ft the aeroplane began an uncontrollable roll to port. The desperate urgency of his situation reminded him of advice given to him by Jimmy Martin, 'To save time, don't bother with the blind release above your head, just grab the lever between your legs!' This saved his life, he made a perfect ejection and, almost as soon as the parachute had deployed, he was on the ground. A two or three second delay could have been fatal. There was little left of the P.1127 to indicate the nature of the malfunction, but, a day or so later, a

farmer appeared with the port forward engine nozzle which had broken away. It had been made of glass reinforced plastic to save weight. The specification was immediately changed to steel.

The 11,200 lb thrust of the original Pegasus was insufficient for a payload likely to interest air forces and a number of senior officers were besotted with the idea that only a supersonic fighter had any real merit. The protagonists of the Rolls-Royce

Sqn Ldr Bill Bedford and Hugh Merewether with P.1127.

multi-engine system and the Bristol Siddeley vectored thrust system were vehemently putting their cases to the Ministry and to learned societies in the form of technical papers. This chapter is not concerned with the politics of the project, since much has been written in a number of books on the overall development strategy of this remarkable aeroplane. It is sufficient to say that engine development increased power to well over 20,000 lb and improved the combat value of the aeroplane with every step.

Interest was aroused in the US Forces and the *Luftwaffe* and it was decided to form a tri-partite evaluation squadron. This was to be equipped with P.1127s up-dated with the latest design improvements.

In the meantime development flying proceeded at Dunsfold and RAE Bedford where Sqn Ldr Jack Henderson and Flt Lt John Farley carried out most of the trials. Sqn Ldr Henderson had served in Fighter Command and graduated from ETPS in late 1959, being posted, in 1960, to Aerodynamics Flight, of which he became OC in 1962. Both pilots recall the fascination of the work in the flight at that time. Farley had already had experience in the wind tunnel department ten years before, when he was an RAE engineering apprentice, and is convinced that the three and a half years of his second spell at Bedford was undoubtedly the high point of interest in test flying. There were only four pilots in the unit, and they had a wide range of aeroplanes to fly, piston engined, turboprop powered, pure jet, even hovercraft. They were expected to fly them all. Every research aircraft flying in Britain at that time was there: the HP.115 slender delta research machine was working in the Concorde slow speed programme, whilst the Fairey FD.2 and the derivative Bristol/BAC.221 were researching the high speed end of the flight envelope. Two Short SC.1s were flown there and the jet-flap Hunting H.126 was a useful aircraft. John Farley flew no fewer than 40 different types, as distinct from marks, during his time at Bedford.

Sqn Ldr Henderson was the third pilot to fly the P.1127, Hugh Merewether being the second one. He was present at Dunsfold when John Farley was converted to the type. John recalled that the engine had a one hour life in the vertical lift mode at that time, or 25 hours in wingborne flight. It was then returned to Rolls-Royce for an overhaul which cost £60,000. Conversion had to be carried out efficiently and swiftly. 'People became excited,' said John. 'If you sat in the hover for 30 seconds, you had spent £500, the price of a good car in those

Sqn Ldr Jack Henderson (1960).

days! You were allowed a quarter of the engine life – 15 minutes – to convert; at the end of that period you must have carried out satisfactorily all the VSTOL manoeuvres of which the aircraft was capable.' He flew the machine to RAE Bedford for evaluation.

An early problem which arose with the P.1127 was the design of the engine air intakes. A bulbous profile for the leading edge was required for the hover with a thin, sharp edge for high speed flight. An ingenious idea was tried; the forward lip being made of rubber which could be inflated to the bulbous shape and evacuated to the thin profile. Unfortunately it was vulnerable and easily damaged. There was, in fact, an insurmountable problem; with the rapid transit from take-off to high speed it was impossible, in the time available, to deflate the rubber sections to a firm, smooth profile. During deflation the airflow pressed the rubber rearwards as the increasing speed created folds in them and the metal stiffeners inside them pierced the bag. As Bill Bedford graphically described the outcome, 'They flapped like spaniel's ears!' The designers mercifully brought this interesting development exercise to a halt by developing a compromise profile which was suitable for both extremes of flight.

1962–63 saw attempts by the Kingston drawing office to reconcile the diametrically opposed needs of the RAF and the Navy for the next generation of fighter. The Navy required a powerful twin-engined machine such as the Phantom to operate from the new 50,000 ton carrier which was being designed – but which was ultimately cancelled. Single-engined aircraft were not liked for carrier operations and the Navy offered every conceivable reason why VTOL was quite unacceptable – probably realizing that the success of the P.1127 concept would sound the death knell of the big carrier.

On 8 February 1963 Bedford took off from Dunsfold, which was officially closed by deep snow which covered the south of England, and flew, in company with two RN Hunters, to land on HMS *Ark Royal* off Portland Bill. Trials of the Blackburn Buccaneer were in progress and Bedford experienced a certain amount of condescension among the 'fishheads' who were rather cynical about this little aeroplane with only one engine aboard their big ship. He had carried out various simulated deck landings before flying out to the vessel and he found that operation from the actual deck was even easier with the visual cues of the bridge superstructure. During the week a series of take-offs and vertical landings were made and the demonstration proceeded very smoothly. The Flag Officer, Aircraft Carriers, Rear Admiral Donald Gibson commented on reversal of the usual trend that new aeroplanes were usually much heavier and arrived much faster. He said, 'The thing that impressed me most was the complete absence of fright among those watching!'

At the 1963 Paris Air Show Bedford had one of his most embarrassing experiences. He gave a sparkling demonstration in front of 150,000 people at the airfield and countless millions of television viewers. As he came in to land the nozzles of the Pegasus engine suddenly rotated from the lift position to the thrust position; the P.1127 fell out of the sky upon a concrete platform used for the take-off and landing of its French competitor, the Balzac VTOL aircraft. A shower of wheels, undercarriage legs, dust and dirt accompanied its arrival and Bedford miraculously stepped out of the wreck uninjured! Fortunately there was no lasting damage to the cause of the P.1127. The technical *cognoscenti* who mattered, learned that a piece of dirt in an air reducing valve to the air motors driving the nozzles had jammed the valve and allowed them to move of their own volition.

From 1962 work had proceeded upon the aircraft for the tri-partite evaluation squadron. The Kestrels had a new wing, anhedralled tailplane and an engine up-rated to 15,000 lb thrust. The squadron began operations with nine Kestrels from October 1964, and, in April 1969, the definitive Harrier went into operational service. It embodied lessons learned from the squadron; it had an advanced navigational system and a head-up display for the pilot, this device enabling the pilot to see information projected upon a transparent screen level with the windscreen. An auxiliary power unit for starting the engine was also fitted to ensure independence of ground facilities. A full range of stores and armament was also available.

Even at this stage the RAF did not show much enthusiasm for this remarkable aeroplane, indeed it was probably the Falklands campaign (which could not have been launched without the Harrier, and flight-refuelling) that revealed the true potential of the design.

Harrier development required a sustained flight test programme probably unequalled in risk to the test pilots since the 1930s. 'Bill' Bedford and John

Hugh Merewether and Duncan Simpson (1969).

John Farley and Dr John Fozard, chief designer Harrier, with a Sea Harrier at the 1984 SBAC show.

Farley have talked to the author about 'interesting incidents', for the truth is that many of their sorties were exceptionally dangerous, particularly John Farley's work in overcoming the problems of intake momentum drag yaw after the death of Major Chuck Rosburg of the US Air Force, who was killed at Dunsfold in 1969. John spent many months in low speed and hover manoeuvres at a height of 50 ft to analyse the problem, and check out possible methods of overcoming it. Much of the time he was right on the edge of instability and therefore at high risk.

It is, perhaps, quite invidious to compare one test pilot with another, but there can be no possible doubt that John Farley, with his engineering background and analytical, enquiring mind, is one of the finest in the world, a judgement with which most test pilots would concur. In 1967 Bill Bedford retired, to be succeeded by Hugh Merewether. In 1969 Duncan Simpson had a serious accident in a two-seat Harrier, but after recovery from his injuries he was appointed to succeed Hugh Merew-

ether, who retired, John Farley becoming deputy chief test pilot, succeeding Simpson in 1978.

Simpson had been involved in the P.1127 programme since June 1962. In April 1969 Hugh Merewether and John Farley made several flights in the prototype two-seat Harrier. On Simpson's first flight, to carry out low level flutter clearance tests at 3,000 ft and an indicated air speed of 450 knots, Boscombe Down was in control of the flight as he flew westward from the airfield en route from Dunsfold. Suddenly the engine ran down to sub-idling speed and no response to the throttle could be obtained.

Relight procedures were initiated but were unsuccessful. So an immediate 180 degree turn towards Boscombe Down was made although it soon became clear that the chances of arrival there were slim – as Simpson said, 'A two-seater Harrier full of fuel is not the greatest of gliders.'

The best that could be done was to attempt an arrival in a field near Stonehenge. To reduce the destruction as much as possible the flaps and wheels were lowered and the aircraft trimmed for a final glide to impact. Simpson used the new Martin Baker Mk 9 seat for the first emergency ejection. The powerful new rocket saved him from a mere

100 ft above the ground, although he received severe back and neck injuries from sections of the perspex canopy. As the Harrier broke up and exploded he found himself in the unhealthy position of descending towards the fireball. Fortunately the wind drifted him clear of it.

A helicopter and doctor arrived from Boscombe Down within minutes and he was soon in hospital. Fortunately the tail of the aircraft, with all the flight instrumentation, had broken away on impact. So the test records were recovered and also the fuel control unit which was believed to have caused the accident by becoming blocked.

Another failure, which was attributed to a blockage in the fuel system, occurred almost exactly a year later, in 1970. On this occasion Barrie Tonkinson was flying a two-seat Harrier with extra large, long-range fuel tanks to be used for ferrying the aircraft. Flying at medium altitude he tried to restart the Pegasus as he descended towards Boscombe Down, jettisoning the tanks, en route. As he was working with London Military Radar, he informed them of his intention to set up a visual forced landing at Boscombe, which he knew well from his days as a test pilot in 'A' Squadron. As it was a Saturday morning he knew he could not expect crash facilities or air traffic services, in particular, the vital information on wind conditions.

The landing, clearly, was a hazardous undertaking. His attempt should have met with complete success. As it was, he touched down on the grass trials strip at the side of the runway, where the main undercarriage leg came adrift whilst the aeroplane remained, otherwise, intact. He was subjected to an extremely rough passage in a landing where the touch-down had to be made at 170 knots. Mercifully, the wings remained level, so the Harrier ran true before skidding to a standstill on the runway.

London Radar had telephoned Boscombe tower and the fire section hurriedly mustered a scratch crew. Barrie managed to extricate himself from the aeroplane which was, by now, well alight; walking away from the flames as fast as his injuries would permit. He was picked up by the fire crew. By the time he had arrived at sick quarters the Boscombe emergency services were moving fast; doctors had been called out and numerous people were assisting. Barrie Tonkinson has remained ever grateful to the many people who acted so swiftly and effectively at Boscombe Down and Tidworth Military Hospital on that Saturday morning.

To avoid any further problems with blockages in the very complex automatic fuel control system, it was decided to include a manual device by which the pilot could, in the event of a malfunction, feed fuel by virtually turning a tap. John Farley tested the system, first on the ground and then in the air. It proved to be effective, and has saved many Harrier pilots from disaster.

The introduction of Harrier into naval service made the large carrier redundant and the necessity of fast steaming into wind for take-off and recovery of the ship's aircraft was eliminated. Clearly, however, if the Harrier can achieve a short take-off run, its load carrying capacity is increased. For every foot of run the payload is increased by 6 lb and it increases by 60 lb for every knot of ship's speed.

The US Marine Corps showed considerable interest in the aircraft – an interest which resulted in collaboration between British Aerospace and McDonnell Douglas to develop the AV-8B or 'Super Harrier'.

A Royal Navy engineer officer, Lt Cmdr Douglas Taylor, conceived the idea of the ski-jump take-off aid. At the bow of the ship is built a curved ramp, the Harrier runs, at speed, upon this ramp and the upward thrust created by its slope enables the

Developed by British Aerospace in conjunction with Dowty Boulton Paul, the Sky Hook was demonstrated for the first time at BAe Dunsfold on 26 April 1985.

machine to take off safely at an all-up weight much higher than would otherwise be possible. At the time of writing yet another ingenious technique of operating the Harrier is being evaluated, the 'Sky Hook', an idea dreamed up by Heinz Frick, one of the Dunsfold test pilots. It is a crane of roughly the same size as a ship's derrick, suitably stabilized so that the crane head is always located at a fixed height above the sea. The Harrier then flies under the crane hook where a pick-up probe locks on to a point just above the CG of the aircraft. The Harrier is then drawn up to a set of docking pads and may be re-armed and refuelled on the crane. If successful it will extend the range of naval air power far beyond the large warships now required; any small merchant ship could be armed with a Harrier, with few modifications to the structure.

Another pilot who carried out splendid work in the Harrier programme was Don Riches. He was an RAF pilot attached to Dunsfold for Harrier liaison duties, became a civilian test pilot and stayed at Dunsfold until 1979. Currently flying the Harriers and Hawks, under the direction of Andy Jones, who became chief test pilot when John Farley retired from the post in 1983, are Mike Snelling as deputy chief, Jim Hawkins, an ex-Red Arrows pilot, Heinz Frick, Chris Roberts and Taylor Scott, an ex-RN Lt Cdr who was recalled to the Navy during the Falklands crisis and became a Harrier flight commander aboard HMS *Illustrious*.

The range of experience available at Dunsfold is remarkable. Andy Jones was trained at Cranwell, and in his thirteen years in the RAF he served in Training Command as a Qualified Flying Instructor, had a tour on Lightnings and graduated from ETPS in 1966. After two years in 'A' Sqn, at Boscombe Down and six months with a USAF unit in the States he decided that his next posting was likely to be to fly a mahogany bomber, so he joined British Aerospace in September 1970.

All the pilots, with the exception of Taylor Scott, are ex-'A' Squadron men. Mike Snelling is uniquely qualified as an engineer, flying instructor and test pilot, a source of considerable strength in his present position and experience of equal value in the Hawk trainer programme, a programme which has been remarkably successful and entirely free of serious problems. Jim Hawkins is a graduate of the French test pilots school, and, with Mike Snelling, he is one of the original project pilots on the Hawk with ten years experience on the type, and one of the four Qualified Flying Instructors in the team. Both Mike and Jim are also Qualified Weapons Instructors.

Heinz Frick, too, is a weapons expert, whilst Taylor Scott graduated from an avionics test pilot school in the USA, served an exchange tour with the American Navy, and contributes this very valuable experience to the joint British Aerospace/McDonnell Douglas Harrier AV-8B, and to the development of the Sea Harrier of Falklands fame.

The Hawker Aircraft Company was always famed for the quality of its test pilots; their successors, clearly, maintain the tradition.

To revert to the early 1960s, Bristol built two research aircraft to be capable of prolonged flight at Mach 2.75, to enable the effect of kinetic heating to be investigated at high speeds. The final design, the Bristol 188, was a striking looking aeroplane which was powered by two relatively undeveloped de Havilland Gyron Junior engines with re-heat and a variable orifice tail nozzle. Structural problems were serious, the machine having to be built of stainless steel. Boulton Paul powered control actuators were used and cockpit air conditioning was required.

A major programme of data transmission by telemetry was necessary, and RAE designed a system which transmitted outputs from hundreds of transducers measuring strain, vibration, pressure, temperature, attitude, acceleration and other data. A ground control unit was set up so that a pilot and an engineer in the control room could relieve Godfrey Auty, the pilot, of responsibility for everything but his flight programme, and warn him of any malfunction which might arise.

After wartime service in the RAF, with experience on Hampdens, Mosquitoes and Dakotas, Auty joined Bill Pegg's staff at Bristol in April 1951 and flew many different aircraft. In 1957 Walter Gibb followed Bill Pegg as chief test pilot and Auty was appointed deputy chief, becoming chief when Gibb retired in 1960. He flew a number of high performance aircraft at RAE Bedford, and in the USA, in preparation for the first flight of the 188 which was delayed until 14 April 1961. As he took off from Filton the undercarriage began to retract and then lowered again – a hydraulic pipe had burst. He had a tape recorder strapped to his thigh, and, to make matters worse, a spring loaded button on the recorder came adrift and jammed all radio communication with the chase aircraft and with the ground controller. He continued to Boscombe Down where he was able to lock the undercarriage down by emergency power. Godfrey then found that the wind had changed through 180 degrees, so the runway safety barrier was at the wrong end. Nevertheless he made a safe landing.

Above *Bristol 188 research aircraft.*
Below *Godfrey Auty boarding the 188 (1963).*

The under-developed Gyron engines were beset with surging problems which were a serious handicap to the programme. The second 188 was flown in April 1963. Auty enjoyed flying the two machines, the handling qualities were excellent with no change of trim at Mach 1.0. Flight time on both was limited and in January 1964 the programme was abandoned. By this time the preliminary design studies on the supersonic airliner, which became Concorde, had indicated that the ogival delta configuration would be a likely one, so the 188 was completely superseded. The benefit to the Concorde programme lay, mainly, in the data telemetry system which was valuable and was developed to a high level of efficiency.

The 188 was the first jet-propelled aeroplane to be built by the Bristol Aeroplane Company and the last to carry that proud name.

In the field of civil aviation 1962/63 saw triumph and tragedy for the British industry. John Cunningham flew the new D.H.121 Trident airliner on 1 January 1962. This followed the pattern set by the French Sud-Aviation Caravelle in having engines at the tail, as did the Vickers VC10, first flown by Jock Bryce, from Brooklands on 29 June 1962. It was originally planned to fly it from Wisley's 2,200 yard runway but Jock thought that he could safely

Above *Jock Bryce (at foot of steps), Brian Trubshaw, Bill Dairns (flight engineer) and Ernie Marshall (senior design project engineer) leaving the prototype VC10 after its first flight.*

Below *Vickers VC10*

lift off the 1,460 yards at Brooklands and save six months dismantling and re-assembling the airliner.

Calculations proved him correct. With various devices to ensure that the angle of incidence at lift-off speed was exactly right, he became airborne, with Brian Trubshaw in the right-hand seat, in 560 yards and flew to Wisley. It was the last take-off of a Vickers designed and built aeroplane from Brooklands, and, indeed, the last aircraft to bear the great name of that company which had entered the British Aircraft Corporation. It was fortunate that Jock's idea of take-off from Brooklands saved so much time and money, as it cost the company £1½ million to cure the stall and drag problems which the flight development programme revealed.

In April 1964 this magnificent airliner went into service with BOAC and was warmly welcomed by passengers. Unfortunately, three months before, Sir Giles Guthrie had become chairman of the airline. The damage which his policies inflicted upon the prospects of the VC10 was enormous. Although it had been built to a BOAC specification, he wished to reduce an order for 30 Super VC10s to seven, later he decided to cancel them all and buy Boeing 707-320Cs. Finally he was ordered by the Government to take twelve Supers, but the damage had been done. Only 37 Standards and 27 Supers were built, and so Britain's last chance of remaining in the subsonic, long haul, transport business was lost irrevocably to the Americans.

On 20 August 1963 Mike Lithgow flew the BAC One-Eleven twin-engined airliner from Hurn. This

BAC One-Eleven.

new machine was intended as a successor to the Viscount, and had its engines mounted at the tail with the tailplane high on the fin. On 22 October Lithgow and Dickie Rymer, who had been BEA's chief Viscount training captain before joining the Vickers team at Wisley, took the prototype on its 53rd flight with a test crew of five, to measure stability in approaches to the stall, with the CG as far aft as possible. 42 of the previous flights had explored the regime up to CG aft, with varying angles of flap; on this ill-fated flight the approach to the stall had been checked 'clean'. 8 degrees of flap was selected and a further stall initiated; the aircraft reached a high angle of incidence but no pitch-down followed. It was in a catastrophic deep-stall from which no recovery was possible in the absence of engine-induced slipstream over the elevators. The aircraft descended at high vertical velocity with little forward speed, the whole crew being killed in the crash.

The flight recorder revealed the circumstances of the disaster·and modifications were made to the wing leading edge to give a more positive nose-down tendency after the stall. Powered elevators, a stick-shaker and an automatic stall warning indi-

cator were also fitted. The accident happened in a flight regime never likely to be encountered in commercial operation, but the world-wide publicity did nothing to improve the prospects of the new airliner. More trouble was soon to follow. The second prototype was fitted with an anti-spin parachute; whilst continuing the stalling trials, a pilot, probably slightly apprehensive after the Lithgow disaster, deployed the parachute, at what appeared to be the stall, although instrumentation later confirmed that he had emerged from it. He continued to fly with the parachute trailing astern until the drag caused him to land in a field. It was a complete aberration, which he admitted – he merely had to release the parachute and fly home. In spite of all these setbacks the BAC One-Eleven proved to be a fine aeroplane and operates worldwide.

The deep-stall was an ever-present risk to test pilots exploring the outer extremities of the flight envelope of high-tailed jet aircraft.

'Spud' Murphy, a Handley Page test pilot, encountered a deep-stall in a Victor, a flat spin developed and recovery was impossible. At 500 ft Murphy and his co-pilot ejected. Murphy blacked-out momentarily and, as he descended, felt that he was numb from the waist downwards. Concerned by the prospect of landing hard on a road, he steered his parachute, and fell upon a run of telephone wires which broke progressively beneath him, until his canopy caught in the wires and lowered him gently and mercifully to the ground. His back had been broken in the ejection. The RAF Medical Service returned him, after many months, to full flying duties.

A Trident test crew lost their lives on a routine test flight from Hatfield on 3 June 1966. Peter Barlow and George Errington, both experienced pilots, with their test crew, E. Brackstone-Brown and G. W. Patterson, took off to carry out tests to qualify the aircraft for C of A. The stall warning and recovery systems were checked in three approaches to the stall, in the landing configuration. According to the flight engineer's log, the stick shaker operated at 102 knots and the stall recovery system at 93 knots. It was then necessary to disconnect the systems and take the aircraft, which was loaded to CG aft, to the edge of stall to determine the margin left after the warnings had been given. Two hours after take-off Peter Barlow reported on his radio-telephone, 'We are in a superstall at the moment.' Nothing more was heard from the Trident which was seen over Felthorpe, near Norwich flying slowly at 10,000 ft. As the nose went up to 30/40 degrees, the airliner turned to port, the starboard wing dropped sharply, the engines being given full power for a short period before the

machine developed a flat spin, hitting the ground a minute and a half later, killing everybody on board.

It was concluded that the pilot, who had taken part in no fewer than 2,195 stalls in Trident, had delayed positive recovery action a few seconds too long. No anti-spin parachute was fitted.

The Trident was the first airliner in the world to make entirely automatic landings in passenger service, when it carried out the first one in June 1965. It was the outcome of many years of pioneering work by RAE and civilian firms which began in 1916 in the RNAS which devised an aircraft height indicator consisting of a weight attached to a length of cord wound on a drum. Hanging some 15 ft below the aeroplane, the weight activated a light in the cockpit as soon as it touched the ground, warning the pilot to commence his flare-out. During the Second World War the problems faced by crews returning from operations in bad weather led to the introduction of FIDO – Fog, Intensive, Dispersal Of – at several aerodromes. The runway was lined with petroleum burners which were ignited to burn off the fog, enabling the aircraft to land between the lines of flame whilst the crew prayed that a tyre would not burst on touch-down. Clearly, it was impracticable for civil use.

Collaboration between the Telecommunications Research Establishment, later Royal Radar Establishment, at Malvern, and RAE, under the overall control of the Ministr of Aircraft Production, led, in January 1945, to a demonstration, at RAF Def-

De Havilland Trident II.

TSR.2.

ford, of a blind landing system in a Boeing 247D. This was carried out in complete darkness and was almost certainly the world's first blind landing. Encouraged by this success the Ministry established, later in 1945, the Blind Landing Experimental Unit at Woodbridge, a wartime emergency landing strip with a long runway. By the time the unit moved to RAE Bedford in 1957, many thousands of flying hours had been carried out with different parts of a system in various aircraft including a D.H. Devon, a Varsity and a Canberra.

One of the outstanding achievements of Britain's aircraft industry in the 1960s was the TSR.2 advanced low-level strike and reconnaissance aircraft, sacrificed at the altar of political expediency. Designed and built by English Electric and Vickers at Weybridge, by then in the British Aircraft Corporation, two Bristol Olympus 22R engines were fitted although serious problems caused a limitation of available power until vibration in the low pressure turbine shaft was cured. This defect was discovered at Filton, when a Vulcan used as a flying test-bed, with this engine in a nacelle underneath, disintegrated during ground running. Failure of another engine during a rig test blew the roof off the test house.

When Roland Beamont flew the TSR.2 from Boscombe Down for the first time the engines, severely de-rated in output, were approved for only one flight. Nevertheless Beamont and his observer, Don Bowen, were impressed with the handling of the aeroplane which, in almost every respect, was a vast leap ahead of any in Western Europe. It was designed to fly at 200 ft, at sonic speed, under terrain following radar control. Sortie data was fed into the navigational system in the form of punched tape, both cockpits had advanced head-up displays for pilot and navigator. The short delta wing, with blown flaps, was designed to give a comfortable ride for the crew at low-level, sonic speed, normally a rough affair, with a high level of buffet. Indeed, there were many similarities with the Tornado –

Bristol Siddeley Olympus engine for TSR.2 being flown in Vulcan test bed. Note new profile of wing leading edge.

described in the next chapter – which undoubtedly benefited from the work carried out on TSR.2.

After two months, during which new engines were prepared, TSR.2 flew again. The vociferous anti-TSR.2 political lobby used this delay as an excuse to claim that the aircraft was useless and that the American F-111 swing-wing bomber should be purchased instead. It was planned to build 20 development prototypes. Four were completed, only one being flown. The main problems of the machine were solved in the early part of 1965. Roland Beamont and James Dell found it a delight to fly and it met all its design requirements. Cost was high, as might have been expected in the case of such a complex aeroplane. This was used as the excuse for its cancellation by the Labour Government. In the event this was utter nonsense. A price of £750 million was quoted for a run of 150 aircraft, a similar number of F-111s was quoted at £450 million. The Royal Australian Air Force bought F-111s and are said to have paid three times the originally quoted price by the time the bugs had been eliminated, years later.

The effect of cancellation upon the workforce in BAC was devastating with many redundancies. The Warton management suggested to the Government that TSR.2 was the only aircraft available which could be used for research at the speeds envisaged for Concorde and they put forward a 'last ditch' proposal that a flight test programme of 100 hours should be carried out for the very modest sum of £2½ million. It was summarily brushed aside and the company was peremptorily told to proceed with the destruction of jigs and aircraft at once. There is no doubt that the Concorde development programme would have been shortened and would have cost less if this eminently logical suggestion had been listened to.

Many people believe that the abandonment of the TSR.2 was the price exacted upon the Wilson Government for the rescue by the Americans of the disastrous British economy at that time – a price which included the order for F-111s. Later, that too, was cancelled.

The crowning stroke of political perfidy was the order to destroy immediately all the jigs and cease flying the prototype unless BAC was prepared to meet all the costs. During a visit to Warton in 1966 the author asked a senior BAC official why they were not permitted to continue flying the machine which would have provided invaluable data for future designs and, particularly, Concorde. His answer was, 'Wouldn't it have been embarrassing

for the Government when the tests revealed the true measure of TSR.2's superiority over the F-111!'

The other prototypes were destroyed, leaving one which is now in the Imperial War Museum collection at Duxford.

A happier story is the development of the world's first jet airliner, the D.H. Comet, into a remarkably successful maritime reconnaissance aircraft, the Nimrod, now the responsibility of British Aerospace at Woodford, Manchester, who also took over the support of the Victor bomber after the tragic liquidation of Handley Page.

It is a tribute to the original design of the Comet that such radical alterations could be made to its structure and to its aerodynamic form, without affecting adversely its flying characteristics.

Since the retirement of 'Roly' Falk in 1957, the responsibility of chief test pilot rested upon Wg Cdr Jimmy Harrison who, during the war served as a flying instructor and joined 2nd Tactical Air Force as a pilot in No 605 Sqn. From 1950 to 1952 he was in Aero Flight at the RAE and became a test pilot at Avro in 1954. Harrison was succeeded by Tony Blackman in 1970. He, in turn, was followed by Charles Masefield, the very able son of Sir Peter Masefield. Charles joined Avro on the demise of the Beagle Aircraft Company at Shoreham where he was responsible for test flying. He gives full credit to Jimmy Harrison for the final development of the Vulcan. His analytical mind resolved the many problems which he inherited.

Wg Cdr J. A. Robinson was trained at Cranwell in 1957, and served in Bomber Command, flying Canberras and Valiants. In 1962 he graduated from ETPS returning to the school in 1968 as a tutor after periods at Staff College and the Ministry of Defence. For three years he remained at ETPS, went back to MoD and then became Deputy Superintendent of Flying at A&AEE Boscombe Down, a post which led to his appointment as chief instructor at ETPS, a title which is now that of commanding officer.

Tony Blackman succeeded Charles Masefield who had achieved the remarkable distinction for a test pilot of being appointed production director at Woodford. Blackman had persuaded Robby to join him as a test pilot so, when Blackman left, he took over as chief at a time when the last of the Victor tanker conversions was being completed, the Nimrod AEW.3 was ready for test, and the long-lived 748 airliner was in production.

The brief for the handling characteristics of the Nimrod was that they should not be inferior to the Comet 4 from which it was developed. Robby

Above *Jimmy Harrison (1982)*.
Below *Tony Blackman (1972)*.

Above *Charles Masefield (1982)*.
Below *Robbie Robinson (1983)*.

British Aerospace Nimrod AEW.3 airborne early warning aircraft.

considers that the Mk 1 and 2 were slightly better than the Comet because the rudder area was increased, and the AEW.3, in spite of the enormous protruberances at nose and tail, is even better.

Problems have been few. In 1981 Robby and his deputy, John Cruse were flying an AEW3 on an altitude test when the two inboard engines burned out. The intensive investigation which followed this extraordinary occurrence established that a hitherto unexpected high energy vortex was being generated off the new nose; it went straight into the intake causing major disruption to the airflow in the turbines. Robby was extremely impressed with the elegantly simple solution achieved by the aerodynamics department: 'A bit of bent tin in front of the windscreen!' In fact, a small vortex generator on each side of the nose in front of the windscreen diverted the vortex and cured the fault.

Problems of a different nature occur on the civil side of the Woodford test pilots' job. All eight of them have to be qualified on military and civil aircraft with both British and American airline pilot's licences. Robinson was indignant when he left the RAF, after 28 years flying, to be virtually sent back to school by the CAA to re-learn such subjects as basic magnetism! He was surprised to find that no tests of his flying ability were required. Peter Henley, his present deputy, is the former CO of No 74 Sqn with many hours on Hercules aircraft.

Another test pilot, Kevin Moorhouse, followed an unusual path to the left-hand seat. In 1983 he received his Twenty Year clock from the company. He joined as an apprentice, became a flight test observer and took his private pilot's licence. He then became a flight engineer and co-pilot on the communications Dove, obtained his commercial pilot's licence and qualified as captain of the Dove and co-pilot on the 748. When Robinson joined the company Kevin was about to achieve his 748 captaincy. He has since become a Nimrod captain and is a qualified test pilot on all types of aircraft – a remarkable achievement.

In common with other test pilots of commercial aeroplanes, the Woodford team is called upon to train the pilots of airlines who buy the 748. Experiences range from the humdrum to the hairy. Robinson tells the story of one foreign captain who was flying the 748 at night. In the right-hand seat, Robinson was rather disconcerted to find that the brilliant stars around had suddenly disappeared, and, what seemed to be jungle had replaced them. The pilot had, quite unknowingly, allowed the 748 to roll slowly upon its back!

Resulting from technical feasibility studies made in 1955, a Supersonic Transport Aircraft Committee was formed which included representatives of nine airframe builders, four engine companies, BOAC, BEA and the RAE. In the chair was Morien Morgan, the deputy director of RAE. By 1960 it had become clear that only international collaboration could finance such a complex project and

Handley Page HP.115 research aircraft.

that Mach 2.0 would be the target speed to ensure that most of the structure could be built of existing light alloys, without recourse to the more difficult alloys and stainless steel required to sustain the kinetic heating experienced at higher speeds. In November 1961 an agreement was signed with the French Government which led to the production of two prototypes and whatever production aircraft could be sold. Pan American gave a major boost to the project by taking options.

One of the imponderables was low speed control with the slender delta wing envisaged. An intensive programme of model flying was embarked upon to support the computer and wind tunnel studies in progress. Much had been learned about swept-wing and delta-wing characteristics from the supersonic Lightning fighter and the two Fairey FD.2s. From Handley Page was ordered one of the most valuable and cheapest research aircraft ever built, the HP.115. Built largely of light alloy and powered by a Viper turbine, it was designed to explore the slow speed characteristics of the narrow delta and had 75 degrees of sweepback on the leading edges of the wing. Computer studies had indicated that it would be a rather unpleasant machine to fly but, when Sqn Ldr Jack Henderson flew it for the first time from RAE Bedford on 17 August 1961, he was very pleased with it, saying, in a Royal Aeronautical Society Lecture, in 1962, 'The HP.115 has turned out to be a simple and delightful aeroplane to fly and one that can be flown very accurately with a minimum of effort throughout a flight envelope that has now been extended beyond even the most optimistic of our early hopes.'

The lift of a slender delta at low speeds is dependent upon the angle of incidence of the wing, the airflow separates into powerful vortices which increase in power as the angle increases, the lift increasing proportionately. No true stall can occur, but this hazard is replaced by another one – speed can decay to such a level that the aircraft begins to descend at high vertical velocity. It was found that the 115 had a remarkable degree of lateral stability when flying slowly at high angles, it could be rocked through 60 degrees each side and still remain under perfect control. It had a designed life of 500 hours and the 493 hours flown produced data out of all proportion to the cost. This remarkable little aeroplane occupies a hangar at Yeovilton with the BAC 221 and a Concorde prototype. Together they produced the data which gave the confidence to proceed with Concorde, and ensured the technical success which it has enjoyed right from the first flight made by André Turcat, chief test pilot of the French partner, Aérospatiale, on 2 March 1969 from Toulouse.

In parallel with the aerodynamic research being carried out in France and in Britain, a comprehensive engine research and development programme was in hand on ground rigs, and in a Vulcan, with one of the Concorde's Olympus 593 turbines mounted in a nacelle underneath the fuselage. Huge ground test rigs were built to simulate kinetic heating whilst hydraulic jacks exerted forces equivalent to predicted flight loads upon a test airframe.

To compensate for centre of pressure shift, as the aircraft achieved sonic speed, fuel was transferred from one set of tanks to another. A rig was built to verify the integrity of this very important innovation.

Brian Trubshaw had been nominated as the British project pilot at an early stage, and spent several years studying the technology of the new aircraft, whilst the politicians argued about it. The Wilson Government tried to cancel it at the time of the TSR.2 purge. Fortunately the French Government insisted, on pain of substantial contractual penalties, that Britain should not renege on the solemn agreement. The enormous enthusiasm for, and pride in, Concorde, which was so obvious at Bristol and the other BAC plants concerned, carried the project along to a successful first flight of the British prototype on 9 April 1969. By then Trubshaw had been appointed director of flight test of the BAC Commercial Aircraft Division, his co-pilot was John Cochrane, the deputy chief test pilot. A 42-minute flight ended at RAF Station, Fairford which became the base for British flight test operations.

Concorde 001, the French machine, concentrated upon the flight qualitative tests and investigation of the autopilot and navigation systems, whilst the British machine's programme concentrated upon power plant testing including intakes, silencers and reverse thrust with tests upon electrical and fuel systems, together with the establishment of performance characteristics.

It was possible for the Vulcan flying test bed, operated by the Rolls-Royce-Bristol Engine Division, under the control of their chief test pilot, T. P. Frost, to clear the installation of the Olympus 593 within the flight envelope of the Vulcan which almost coincided with the subsonic element of Concorde's own flight envelope. Several hundred flying hours solved many problems and revealed the 593 to be an outstanding reliable engine.

Problems of surging at fast rates of acceleration were encountered and overcome on the Vulcan but when the Concorde began its supersonic phase of flight test the problem recurred. Brian Trubshaw likened it to a loud and rapid backfiring, Not

acceptable with the champagne and roast beef! as he put it. The shape of the nacelle intakes was a complex aspect of design and the success of the technology could only be determined when the engines were flown in Concorde. Brian Trubshaw commented to the author that the intakes were undoubtedly the most difficult development jobs in the programme and the first flight to Mach 2.0 generated some unpleasantness.

The experience of telemetry, gained with the Bristol 188, was of considerable benefit during the test operations. The two prototypes and the first two pre-production aeroplanes, with their longer fuselages, carried almost twelve tons of test instrumentation and data transmitting equipment. Some was telemetered to the ground station, much of it was recorded on magnetic tape for analysis later. Altogether some 4,000 different parameters were recorded on each of the prototypes, these parameters being derived from various types of transducer introduced into all the aircraft systems, engines and sources of structural load measurement. Three flight observers monitored the on-board instrumentation.

Few dramas were experienced during the test programme. In August 1974, 002 was practising a display routine for the SBAC show, and as the undercarriage was lowered on the approach to Fairford a loud bang and an impact was observed. A hatch in the cabin floor revealed that there was a doubt if the port undercarriage leg was locked down whilst the main retraction jack was disconnected. A careful landing was made to reduce landing loads as much as possible; fortunately there was just enough strength left in the structure to permit a safe touch down but the undercarriage was in a critical condition, a pin attaching a strut to the main leg having sheared as the undercarriage lowered whilst Concorde was turning.

On January 1971 the French machine, 001, encountered trouble on a flight over the Atlantic near Ireland. At Mach 1.98 re-heat on number one and number three engines was under test. As the engines were reduced to normal power violent vibrations developed and warning lights appeared for all four engines. Number three had overspeeded and surged, causing number four to surge in sympathy. The violence of the surge was enough to blow out the forward intake ramp, damaging the lower nacelle lip, metal from which was ingested into number four.

Special tests upon 002 allowed surges to be induced in flight so that a full analysis of the problem could be made. The wing leading edge profile was

Concorde.

changed slightly, to avoid the vortices under the wing entering the intake, whilst a more refined control system was developed for the intake ramp.

Much of the test flying involved long overseas flights which were a severe test for such a new and complex aeroplane, but it performed exceptionally well. Commenting on the programme, Brian Trubshaw said, 'It was an experience one can never forget, everything else is dwarfed by it, those seven years at Fairford were so memorable. I look back with great joy upon the things we used to do with the aeroplane, we stuck our necks out a bit as we were so totally confident. We were ambitious and believed in it, we went all over the world with the two prototypes, people thought we were mad! In a 30,000 mile tour to Australia we only had to cancel one demonstration!'

5,495 hours were spent in development flying of which a little over 1,000 hours were spent in obtaining certification. David Davies, who was the Air Registration Board chief test pilot at the time, finds it difficult to decide which of two aeroplanes he enjoyed flying most, the Boeing 747 or Concorde. He considers both of them to be quite outstanding pilot's aeroplanes – the ultimate accolade.

On 5 December 1975 Concorde was granted a full C of A and scheduled services were started simultaneously by British Airways and Air France, on 21 January 1976. The startling increase in fuel cost since the inception of the project ensured that high fares would be required to achieve profitable operation. Total production costs of £654 million offset by sales to the value of £278 million, meant that development charges could never be recovered. In spite of these problems, and the vociferous anti-Concorde lobby in Britain and America, this magnificent aeroplane has given spendid and reliable service over the Atlantic, with high load factors. With its auto-stabilisation system and fly-by-wire

Brian Trubshaw with deputy chief test pilot, John Cochrane, on flight deck of Concorde prototype 002.

controls it is easy to fly, and, even in the event of a failure of these complex systems, it can be flown manually without undue difficulty.

In November 1978 the British Concordes were cleared for automatic landing in Category 3 conditions of a 50 yard runway visual range.

By any standards Concorde is a stupendous technical achievement and no Briton, or Frenchman, seeing this beautiful aeroplane flying overhead can fail to feel a glow of pride in the sheer professionalism it represents.

The stories of British test flying narrated in this book span a mere 75 years or so, in which the design of aeroplanes has moved from sheer guesswork and faith to a highly scientific operation involving computers, simulators and wind tunnels of considerable power and complexity. The guesswork has largely disappeared although, as John Farley suggested to the author, 'Flutter is still a bit of a black art!'

The immense cost of new aircraft makes it imperative that designers get it right first time. The test pilots will apply the final polish.

It has been suggested that 'the fun has gone out of test flying'. Fun is perhaps the wrong word to use for such a serious occupation, but there is no doubt that the present breed of test pilot obtains as much pleasure from his far more complex task as did his predecessors. Very fortunately, although the margins for error at high speed are much smaller, so are the number of dramas that beset the test crews. Less frequently can they describe 'an interesting situation', which often meant that they were within a hairsbreadth of sudden death. The next chapter concludes the book with an account of yet another technological triumph, in the military field this time – the Panavia Tornado.

Above *A revival, after fifty years, of an early form of VTOL is the Airship Industries range of dirigibles. Built of advanced materials and inflated with helium, these modern technology non-rigid ships are powered by two Porsche car engines driving five bladed ducted fans. The propulsors can be vectored downwards or upwards to assist manoeuvring.*

This photograph shows the SKS 500, and its larger sister ship SKS 600, flying over London. Four 500s are in service, one with a subsidiary of Japanese Airlines. A 600 has been sold to a Canadian company for geographical survey work whilst a further 600 is being evaluated by the French Navy.

The flight test programme is under the control of Commander N. T. 'Nick' Bennett AFC, who served in the Fleet Air Arm from 1955 to 1977. He graduated at the ETPS in 1960 and carried out the Service trials of the Blackburn Buccaneer 1 and 2 from 1961 to 1968 when be became CO of the RN's Hovercraft Trials Unit.

In June 1980 Cdr Bennett was appointed chief test pilot of Airship Industries and carried out the maiden flight of both the new ships. The SKS 500 is certified for operation in the public transport category and is the only airship in the world permitted to carry fare-paying passengers.

Below *Skyship 600 being drawn out of its hangar at RAF Cardington. The vehicle is a mobile mooring mast. Note the castering wheel under the 20-passenger gondola and the ducted fan propulsors.*

17

VERY HIGH TECHNOLOGY

The last chapter examines the flight test programme of what is unquestionably the most advanced military aeroplane in service in large numbers anywhere in the world.

The product of a three nation design and production team, the Panavia Tornado presented major problems in engineering and aerodynamics at the outset. All were triumphantly overcome and it is widely acclaimed by those who fly it as one of the finest pilot's aeroplanes ever built whilst the very smooth way in which the development of this complex machine proceeded spoke volumes for the remarkable talents of those Britons, Germans and Italians who were responsible for it.

Originating as a Multi-Role Combat Aircraft, the design parameters were highly contradictory with the spectre of the enormous cost escalation of the TSR.2 poised over the project. To achieve the lowest cost, size must be minimal. Supersonic speed at low level requires a highly swept wing of minimum span to give the crew a reasonably comfortable ride and reduce the fatigue problems resulting from gusts.

A highly swept wing is incompatible with short take-off and landing where a complex array of high lift devices must be spread over maximum span. So variable geometry became inevitable. The swing wing, advocated by that great engineer, Sir Barnes Wallis, was in the initial design specification for TSR.2 but was rejected as being too far in advance of the state of the art at that time. The American F-111 swing wing fighter-bomber had experienced serious problems with its wing root box and the wing bearing so the difficulties were not unknown to the design team at Warton. In turn they developed a highly satisfactory bearing using polytetrafluorethylene, better known as Teflon, the material originating in the American space programme which also made the non-stick frying pan possible – a versatile material, indeed. Exhaustive full scale tests proved the bearing to be entirely trouble-free, in service it has been extremely reliable. Resulting from a remarkable degree of political and inter-Service harmony between Great Britain, Germany and Italy, the international company, Panavia GmbH, was registered in Munich in March 1969 with the express purpose of building the MRCA upon which there was close agreement among the participants, with keen interest in Holland as well. The present production aeroplane is almost identical with the preliminary drawings published at that time and is of orthodox light alloy construction, the highly stressed 'carry-through' wing box supporting the wing pivots being built of titanium welded by electron beam.

The wings sweep from 25 degrees at the leading edge to 67 degrees and are actuated by an hydraulic motor on each side. Through a screw jack motion

Is this the design of the future? Sir Barnes Wallis with a model of his hypersonic design.

they are interconnected mechanically. Movement is under manual control of the pilot with automatic sweep on the air defence variant. As the whole span of the wing is used for the four section double slotted trailing edge flaps, lateral control is achieved by the 'tailerons', an all-moving tailplane, the two sections of which operate in unison for control in pitch and differentially for roll control. Triple section leading edge slats are fitted and inboard of them, close to the fuselage on the fixed part of the wing, is fitted a pair of Kruger flaps. Spoilers on the upper surface of the wing dump lift at touch down but are used primarily to control the rate of roll with the wing in positions up to medium sweep, used for maximum manoeuvrability in combat.

Tornado is one of the first aeroplanes to use a 'fly-by-wire' control system, giving an outstanding result. The prime control is a command/stability augmentation system, CSAS, which accepts inputs from the cockpit controls and feeds them, via computers and power control units, to the actual control surfaces. Rates of roll, pitch and yaw are sensed through gyros and the information fed into the CSAS which is also connected to the autopilot. A feel unit is connected to the control column. So the controls are superbly harmonized regardless of wing sweep or the type and weight of stores carried. The machine responds to control inputs in exactly the same way throughout the whole of the flight envelope.

Performance and airframe stresses will vary with stores loading and it was essential to study carefully the way in which stresses develop in various configurations. A 'rate demand system' was built into the CSAS based upon the principle that unit stick displacement should result in unit roll rate, this ensures that the roll rate is constant throughout the flight envelope. With heavy stores on the outboard pylons the initial roll is more difficult to generate and more difficult to stop. With full wing sweep Tornado will roll more easily, both damping and inertia being lower, so the control system is programmed to compensate accordingly.

All high performance aeroplanes show slight buffeting tendencies with wing drop in certain manoeuvres. The 'black boxes' compensate for this, but the resulting superb handling qualities of Tornado could mask a serious hazard which was studied deeply during the flight test programme. It is possible for the pilot to be unaware, from the feel of the aircraft, that he is approaching a manoeuvre in which structural limits may be exceeded; he must therefore monitor his accelerometer, mach meter and air speed indicator.

The 'fly-by-wire' system is protected by triple circuitry for all controls except the tailerons, which have four circuits. Each control computer compares itself with the performance of the others, a suspect unit is automatically switched out of circuit. A mechanical drive to the tailerons is connected if, at any time, two malfunctions occur in any one channel.

The two engines of Tornado are Rolls-Royce RB.199s, production being shared, as with the airframe, between the three countries through a holding company, Turbo Union. The maximum static thrust of each engine is in excess of 8,000 lb dry and 15,000 lb with full operation of the afterburner.

Engine development test flying was a major element in the programme and was carried out initially in the Avro Vulcan used for testing the Olympus engines for Concorde. The Vulcan was already well instrumented and stressed for the large belly pod which carried the simulated engine installation.

On 19 April 1973, after a year of bench testing at Bristol, Munich and Turin, John Pollitt, chief test pilot of Rolls-Royce Filton, flew the engine in the Vulcan for the first time to investigate its behaviour and performance up to 50,000 ft at Mach 0.92. Mach 2.0 operation was simulated in a test cell at the National Gas Turbine Establishment at Pyestock. Various modifications were required, but, in general, the trials were extremely successful. Slight fan blade flutter problems at high revs in one corner of the flight envelope were cured by widening the blades slightly. There was a tendency to shed blades from the high pressure turbine; remarkably, this was not discovered until the engine was inspected after a flight. A twenty hour period of simulated combat sorties was carried out with blades missing. No adverse effect was apparent. After a long and detailed investigation the reason for the blade failures was found to be a resonance causing interference between blade tip shrouds.

Another problem which caused a few headaches was engine surging, which occurs when gas and air flow inside the engine become unstable, with violent backfires which, in some earlier engines, had caused structural failure. Smoke emission was high originally but production engines are virtually smokeless.

The avionics systems for Tornado are exceptionally complex to cover the remarkable range of missions within the capability of the type. The three air forces involved had different operational and technical requirements so all the systems had to be compatible with each other. The RAF, with its wide experience in attack systems for use in all weather, naturally favoured the most comprehensive equipment which would remain operationally serviceable until the end of the century. The *Luftwaffe*, mindful of its disastrous experience with the much simpler Lockheed F-104G Starfighter, was dedicated to the idea of simplicity and minimum cost. However, the Germans and the Italians, in the spirit of co-operation and mutual understanding which has infused the Tornado programme from its inception, accepted the British proposals.

An inertial system feeds the autopilot/flight director and the main navigational attack computer. The pilot has a head-up display in front of him, this presents vital data on a glass screen so that he can read it whilst studying the terrain ahead. The navigator has tabulator displays upon which he can obtain any information required for his part of the action, whilst he also has a moving map/radar display.

Two Hawker Siddeley S.2 Buccaneers played a valuable part in the test programme by proving the avionics, including elements of the terrain following radar installation, before the Tornado prototype flew.

A remarkable feature of the test programme is the manner in which the weapons system has remained almost the same as the one originally drafted over fifteen years ago. The proving of it formed a major part of the development work with such stores as the Hunting Engineering JP233 low-level airfield denial weapon. In an egg-crate style container under each engine bay are stored a series of munitions ranging from runway cratering bombs to direct and delayed-action vehicle destruction and anti-personnel mines. Guided by its single pass attack system, a Tornado can make a high speed, low level pass dispensing these munitions in any desired sequence to create havoc on an airfield and ensure the maximum dislocation and danger for rescue and repair parties. The dropping characteristics of all types of bombs had to be tested to ensure that they left the pylons cleanly with no tendency to float about in the airflow or, as has happened in some cases, rise towards the aircraft. To prove the trajectory the bombs were painted with markings so that a chase machine equipped with high speed cine cameras can record the drop.

A pair of IWKA-Mauser 27 mm cannon with a high muzzle velocity and two alternative rates of fire is fitted as standard. Firing such a weapon from an aircraft causes heavy vibration forces and a

discharge of hot gas. Prototype 06 was fitted with comprehensive instrumentation to analyse all the forces arising during the short period of weapon firing to ensure that the relatively delicate avionics system was not affected, whilst ammunition feed problems and the effect of gas ingestion into the engines was also studied.

The background testing work carried out long before the prototype flew was in itself a gigantic task. At Warton, Manching, 50 miles north of Munich, and Turin, test rigs were built to check, over many years, the whole of the complex engineering of Tornado, and wind tunnel testing was carried out by the three partners to study every aspect of aerodynamics and performance. Fatigue tests of components and a complete airframe have been extensive and will continue for most of the Service life of the aircraft.

All three test centres were involved, as were the national test establishments such as RAE Farnborough and A&AEE Boscombe Down. The engine manufacturers, too, had a major part to play as did the manufacturers of the external stores and avionics systems.

The Panavia companies each selected, in 1973, two test pilots as project pilots for the MRCA. The British pair were Paul Millett and 'Dave' Eagles. Paul Millett joined the Royal Navy as an aircrew cadet in 1949, his flying training was followed by service with squadrons in UK, Mediterranean and Korean waters, a flying instructor's course at RAF Central Flying School and various instructional and flight examining posts.

After graduation at ETPS in 1958 he served as a test pilot at RAE Farnborough, initially in Armament and Guided Weapons Flight, later moving to RAE Bedford. Joining Aerodynamics Flight he was project pilot on the Handley Page 115, the Short SB.5 and the Bristol 188. In 1964 he joined the Hawker Siddeley Aviation test team at Brough and retired from the RN to continue testing the Buccaneer as a civilian test pilot.

In 1968 he became senior experimental test pilot at British Aircraft Corporation, Warton, and project pilot for the Jaguar. Promoted to chief test pilot in 1970, he was responsible for Jaguar development flying at the time of his new appointment to Tornado.

John David Eagles joined the Royal Navy in 1953 and trained with the US Navy at Pensacola and Corpus Christi, Texas. On loan for two years to the Australian Navy he flew the Firefly and Sea Fury. Returning to the Royal Navy he served in various carriers and squadrons before graduating

Paul Millet (1984)

David Eagles (1984).

from ETPS in 1963. He served with the Naval Test Squadron at Boscombe Down for two years and was senior pilot of No 809 Sqn in 1968, leading the Buccaneer aerobatic team at the Farnborough Show in that year.

He resigned from the Navy to join BAC as an experimental test pilot at Warton.

Britain had wide experience of airborne telemetry in the flight development of Concorde but her two partners had little experience of the techniques. A very advanced system was set up at Warton, Manching and Caselle, and a major communications network was required between these centres and Panavia headquarters at Munich, with facilities for rapid contact with material and component suppliers. At an early stage simulators were built to train the test pilots and assist the engineering staff in solving some of their problems. It was decided to build ten prototypes, one of which would spend its life in a static test rig, a further six were to be pre-production aircraft.

Flight test was under the control of Roland Beamont, Panavia Director of Flight Operations. It was to be carried out at the three test centres and, later, the national air force test establishments would become involved. There was overlap in some areas such as general handling and performance, and avionics, where each centre would be in close

touch with its air force customer to ensure that specific requirements were met.

Messerschmitt-Bolkow-Blohm had responsibility for general avionics as distinct from attack avionics. Aeritalia were to test the aeroplane with its large range of external stores, whilst Britain concentrated upon general handling and exploration of the flight envelope without stores, and the development of the dual pilot version. Warton would also concentrate upon satisfying the RAF in terms of avionics and other special requirements.

On 14 August 1974 Paul Millett, with Nils Meister, his German opposite number, made the first flight in the prototype from Manching flanked by two chase aircraft, a German Lockheed F-104G and an Italian Fiat G.91. The wings were unswept, partial flap was used with full afterburner power. At 10,000 ft, with power at cruise setting, an approach was simulated in case it was necessary to abort the flight in a hurry. Millett retracted the undercarriage and flaps and checked handling up to 300 knots. After a number of other function tests he returned after a completely successful thirty minute flight. He flew a simulated approach with afterburners operating, went round again and landed. The complete programme had proceeded without a malfunction of any kind. A week later another flight was made by the same two pilots, the wings were swept to 45 degrees, single engine flight, approach and overshoot were checked and the effect of air brakes and several failure modes were explored – another flight of fifty minutes with no malfunction. On the third flight Meister was in the front seat. He swept the wings to 67 degrees and reached a speed of Mach 1.15.

Both of these very experienced pilots were delighted with the handling of the aeroplane, indeed, they both rated it the best they had ever flown. For a machine of such complexity serviceability had been remarkable. The engines were not yet representative of the production standard but it was clear that performance with the production engines would be up to specification.

To test the 27 mm cannon, initially, independently of Tornado, the weapon was fitted to a Lightning F.2A. This aircraft was based at Warton and trials with live ammunition were carried out on ranges at West Freugh in Scotland, and Eskmeals off the Cumbrian coast. There were few problems with it.

The flight control system proved to be oversensitive, tending to move the control surfaces slightly too fast and too far so that the pilot had to make final control adjustments. This was easily overcome by modifications to the CSAS.

The very complex avionics system was a major element in the test programme. The primary strike roles for the aircraft are battlefield interdiction, interdiction strike and naval strike, the IDS version was built for these purposes. The ADV, air defence variant, was designed for air defence interception. Reconnaissance and training is also within the capability of this versatile aeroplane which replaces in Germany and Italy the F-104G Starfighter and, in the RAF, the IDS version is replacing Vulcan, Buccaneer and Canberra, whilst the ADV is to replace the Lightning and Phantom. It will be apparent that the advantages in operational efficiency, cost effectiveness of stores inventories and manpower utilization are very substantial.

The navigational system will direct the Tornado to its target, regardless of weather, with no ground aids being required. The radar scanner in the nose will monitor a small section of the terrain ahead and it is also effective along a curved manoeuvring path. The signals from the scanner are converted by the appropriate computer into instructions to the flight control system which the autopilot then processes into signals causing the controls to operate. The terrain following system can be used in two modes, one in which the terrain is followed very closely at a height of 200 ft, but giving a fairly

rough ride to the crew or, in the second mode, a smoother ride is achieved by following the terrain less closely by smoothing out the peaks. There is little doubt that Tornado is the fastest aeroplane in the world at tree-top height.

A Doppler radar and an inertial platform form the heart of the navigational system which enables the aeroplane to approach its target with a very high degree of accuracy and effectiveness in the attack. Exceptionally accurate gyros stabilize a platform mounted on gimbals. On the platform is mounted a group of equally sensitive accelerometers, one for each plane of movement. Once the system has been zeroed by the co-ordinates for the point of departure, the accelerometers will register every change of direction or height and integrate them with speed sensors and the navigational requirements which were fed into the computer. The position of the aircraft, to within a few yards at any given moment, is available to the crew through their display consoles in the cockpit. The ADV version has a similar, though simpler, navigation system.

Flight control modes can be selected according to the requirements of the particular sortie, so much of the test flying was directed towards an evaluation of the results of various circuit failures. In the event of failure of the CSAS, direct signalling to the controls, by-passing the computer, is established; after the two pre-determined circuit failures, direct manual control of the tailerons is switched into the system, this being sufficient to control the aeroplane. The outcome of the failure mode tests was found to be considerably more satisfactory than had been predicted, or indeed, required. It quickly emerged that the reliability of the avionics system was quite exceptional. As prototype 01 became increasingly unrepresentative of the breed it was used for engine development, and proved the thrust reverser.

Paul Millett flew 02 on 30 October 1974. This had fully variable engine air inlets so was able to explore the top end of the speed range. It focused upon the whole of the flight envelope concentrating on spinning and the stall, or 'departure', in the current jargon. In May 1977 a high speed level run was made by 02, the pilot throttling back as the machmeter showed a speed increasing beyond 1.93. A slight temperature problem had arisen in the re-heat system but it was quite clear that maximum speed would exceed Mach 2 by a comfortable margin.

02 explored high angle of attack regimes; angles in excess of 30 degrees were found to be well within

Tornado prototype 02 (ADV) posing behind a Hercules to show its four Sky Flash missiles under the fuselage, two Sidewinder missiles on the inboard wing pylons and two long-range fuel tanks; and being put to the test in a dive.

the capability of Tornado with the wings unswept. For these trials 02 was fitted with an emergency power unit, in case of engine flame-out, and a spin recovery parachute. Even after departures from angles of attack well beyond 30 degrees the spin was straightforward and recovery entirely satisfactory.

In July 1975 flight refuelling trials were carried out with a Victor K.2 tanker of No 57 Sqn. Film records were taken from the tanker and from a Canberra chase aircraft. They showed the extraordinary steadiness of the Tornado's approach to the drogue coupling, a steadiness maintained throughout the operation which was so satisfactory that immediate clearance was given on the basis of this one flight. A valuable bonus was the use of tanker aircraft to prolong test sorties and enable complete programmes to be carried out over several hours in the air.

02 was also used to investigate the effect of mounting the larger stores on the underwing pylons. It will be appreciated that, as the wings swing, these stores must remain aligned with the centre line of the aircraft, therefore the pylons are moved by a mechanical linkage within the wings. The first of these stores to be proved was the 330 gallon fuel tank on the inner pylons. Flutter mode tests showed no adverse effects although, later in the programme, it was found that with full tanks and the wings at 67 degree sweep aeroelastic deflection could cause the wing and leading edge of the tailerons to be too close for comfort, so a small section was removed from the leading edge at the tip of the taileron.

One of the few accidents in the test programme befell Tim Ferguson on 4 October 1976 when landing 03 on the rain-swept runway at Warton, the tyres aquaplaned and the aeroplane slid diagonally off the concrete. A main undercarriage leg collapsed, the wing on that side and the fuselage being damaged. It was a fortuitous accident as, clearly, it revealed a problem which could be met by squadron pilots with less experience. The thrust reversers were modified to improve directional control on the ground, nose wheel steering was improved and the undercarriage mounting points strengthened. Two months later 03 began full load trials. At 58,000 lb there were no problems in

Prototype 03 carrying ECM pods on the outboard wing pylons, long-range fuel tanks on the inboard pylons and eight 1,000 lb bombs on the fuselage shoulder pylons – the standard weapons configuration for low-level strike.

manoeuvring with the appropriate underwing stores.

At Casselle in June 1976 Italy's first prototype, already dogged by engine delivery delays, made a heavy landing due to a control system malfunction, the nose hit the ground and severe damage resulted. Not until March 1978 was this aircraft, 05, back in the programme.

In the early part of 1978 the Aircraft and Armament Experimental Establishment at Boscombe Down began to take a major part in the flight test programme. Group Captain David Scouller, at present Officer Commanding Experimental Flying at RAE Farnborough, was 'A' Sqn commander at Boscombe Down. David Scouller made his first solo flight at the RAF College, Cranwell in May 1955, having had an unswerving dedication to a flying career from a very early age. He flew Provosts and Vampires, joined a Hunter squadron at Odiham, moved to the Central Flying School and instructed on piston Provosts at Tern Hill and

Acklington. He was nominated for the ETPS course, joining it in January 1962. Fellow students on the course were Manx Kelly, famous for his leadership of the Rothman Pitts special aerobatic team, killed whilst flying a small private aeroplane in the USA, and Neil Williams, the aerobatic champion whose incredible skill in landing a Zlin trainer after failure of the upper wing fixing bolts has become a legend in aviation circles, and who was killed in the Pyrenees ferrying a Spanish built Heinkel 2111 back to Britain. From ETPS David Scouller joined the Fighter Test Squadron at Boscombe Down in January 1963, becoming project pilot for release to the service of the Lightning T.5.

Group Captain Scouller summarized the function of A&AEE succinctly by saying that it must decide if the aeroplane is good enough to go into service, and if so, what limitations should be specified and what techniques should be recommended for its use. A&AEE does not become involved, other than in a peripheral manner, with the tactical exploitation of the aeroplane. The work of the Establishment and the aircraft manufacturer is closely related, as has been the case with Tornado. The Group Captain is obviously very impressed with the degree of co-operation which has been established between the RAF and the manu-

Group Captain David Scouller (1984).

facturers but also between the three participating countries, a co-operation which has resulted in an exceptional aeroplane. If he has any criticism it is a mild one that he would like to have seen A&AEE participation commence at an earlier stage.

With such a complex aircraft no test pilot could be expert in all aspects of it so, as with the manufacturers' pilots, there were specialists in the major elements: engine handling, avionics, terrain following radar, weapons systems and general handling. As Squadron Commander, David Scouller acted as one of the specialists, but frequently flew test sorties in the Tornado. His technique in starting work on a new aeroplane is to walk around it, studying it thoroughly. From its shape, its flying controls and other significant detail much can be deduced; in his mind he synthesizes how it will fly. The philosophy of the designer is being probed so, whilst it is impossible to assimilate the whole of the system detail and retain it in the mind, the overall logic must be clearly understood. Then, if a malfunction occurs in the air, the pilot can analyse the problem. Trying to memorize the whole of the check list is equally unsatisfactory so it is important to decide which are the main areas of critical malfunction;

there are rarely more than three, often only one, in any aeroplane.

In his present position, Group Captain Scouller, in assessing pilots for a position on his staff, looks for a man with this particular outlook and the ability to sense and identify potential problems before a test sortie. He defines three facets in authorizing the sortie; the job, the people and the environment in which it is to be carried out, such as the weather and air traffic situations.

The people must be keen on the job – this is obviously what they have been trained for. Equally the CO must know his staff very well – a streak of vanity is a killer and a test pilot must have a 'healthy yellow streak,' as the Group Captain stressed to the author several times. In some circumstances a Service test pilot with relatively limited hours on a type is expected to fly it right to the limit of the flight envelope. Pilot selection is based, therefore, upon the assumption that, in spite of the low number of hours on Tornado or Jaguar or whatever it may be, his wide experience in test flying will enable him to analyse and recognize instantly any difficulties in flying to the outer limits of the envelope, – the 'Softy, softly, catchee monkey' technique. David Scouller commented, 'My job, now, is to avoid killing people and breaking aeroplanes, this is what I am paid for.'

Normal service conversion to Tornado takes about 60 hours of flying in two 13-week courses at the Tri-National Training Establishment at RAF Cottesmore and the Tornado Weapons Conversion Unit at RAF Honington. In July 1978 Group Captain Scouller was 'thrown in at the deep end'. It was planned that he would have one back seat trip with Paul Millett, followed by a front seat trip with Dave Eagles in the back. Thereafter he would have to be productive, as he put it. As it turned out he had two back seat rides. During the first he had a mere ten minutes in command during a sortie testing negative G load points. The next one, two months later, was a back seat trip from Farnborough to Warton after the 1978 SBAC show. He then experienced, from the front seat, a genuine conversion sortie of 50 minutes with Dave Eagles covering, among other items, possible problem areas such as wing sweep mechanism failure. From that point he was cleared for solo flying.

Wing sweep failure was a remote possibility due to cross-coupling electrically and mechanically but it had to be investigated. At 45 degree sweep there is no problem in landing the aircraft but at full sweep it is more difficult as the steep nose-up angle on the approach seriously impairs the view. There

Tornado prototype 12 on low-level tests with the wings fully swept at 67 degrees.

is also a risk of the rear end striking the ground in the flare-out, so the approach is made at 210–215 knots with rapid use of the thrust reversers after touch-down. The reverser buckets can be deployed in one second after automatic activation by a switch as soon as the undercarriage touches the runway.

The only wing sweep crisis was the entirely unforeseen one when an Italian pilot converting at Cottesmore experienced the sweep control handle coming off in his hand! A safe landing was made with the wings swept.

A modern aeroplane with its high inertia levels and large mass will lose considerable height if it departs from controlled flight, so, such a departure, or spin, as it was once called, is not an escape route from a combat. Pilots may need to go to the limit of controlled flight but not beyond it, so Tornado, in common with other modern high performance aircraft, has a spin prevention and incidence limit-

ing system which prevents the critical angle of attack being exceeded. In co-operation with the manufacturer's test team the A&AEE pilots had to determine what the critical angle was before the Tornado was cleared for service. The system works laterally and directionally, because a swept-wing aeroplane does not, typically, just drop its nose in a stall, it tends to 'nose-slice' into a yaw and roll into an inverted position.

One of the problems of data transmission by telemetry is that of maintaining the aircraft aerial in constant alignment with the ground aerial – spins and rolls are particularly difficult. The knee pad is still used by the test pilot for his qualitative assessment notes. Group Captain Scouller stressed that there is no substitute for the subjective judgement of the test pilot regardless of the comprehensive instrumentation, data recording and automatic flight control equipment currently available. The basic criterion must be 'Can the average Service pilot fly the aeroplane successfully? If the work load is such that an expert pilot can fly it but the average pilot cannot do so, then the aircraft is not satisfactory.'

As the test programme continued and further prototypes became available it became clear that the full complement of nine prototypes was barely enough to carry out all the work – even the much simpler Lightning test programme had 15 aircraft at its disposal, whilst, on the other hand, 'Jimmy' Dell, the Warton chief test pilot at the time the Jaguar flew from 1969, had to be content to share only eight prototypes with his French opposite number. It became increasingly difficult to recognize which of the various modifications in the development machines was to be representative of the production standard. To overcome this problem a Difference Assessment Exercise was carried out. This unique procedure required the first production aircraft to be flown through a comprehensive test schedule of four sorties by day and by night, to ensure that it was up to the standard agreed.

Inevitably, minor anomalies were found, such details as warning systems and lighting were among the few problems. On the subject of lighting, David Scouller quoted one flight early in the test programme when supersonic flight was required for thirty-five minutes by day and forty minutes by night. Shortly after he took off, darkness fell, he turned up the cockpit lights and said to his navigator, 'I can't understand it, here we have 13 million pounds worth of aeroplane strapped to our backsides and the lighting is as dim as a down-town casino!'

He spoke to the ground crew about this at de-briefing, when the manufacturer's representative was present – in the hot seat! He said, 'You should not have been flying that particular aeroplane at night!' All the prototypes had a build statement to indicate the modification state and it transpired that the one for this prototype showed that the red cockpit lights were functional but the white ones had been disconnected. This statement had not been brought to the attention of the crew.

Keeping track of the test programme paperwork generated by test teams at the various centres was a major undertaking in itself.

Rigid control was exercised upon the cost of the aircraft which, because of its complexity, is an expensive one. Tornado has been the butt of ill-informed criticism for years as, since the Concorde began to fly the routes so successfully, another subject had to be found by those papers who delight in knocking the aircraft industry without troubling to investigate the subject in detail. Certainly a less expensive aeroplane could have been built with much less avionic equipment and a much higher

The pilot's cockpit of an RAF Tornado GR.1; and two fully operational GR.1s from No 9 Sqn, RAF Honington.

workload for the crew, but combat capability would have been degraded and, in war, attrition rates could be expected to be higher, hence, more aeroplanes would have been needed and more crews trained at great expense. There seems little economic logic in that. Fortunately for Britain, its superb aircraft industry, for which this author has unbounded admiration, appears to thrive on a diet of press and Parliamentary vitriol.

Two serious crashes marred what has otherwise been a classic test programme, one of the most complex and successful achieved anywhere in the world. In June 1979 Russ Pengelly, an outstanding Warton test pilot, and Sqn Ldr John Gray of A&AEE, were lost in 08 when it flew into the mist covered Irish Sea on a low-level sortie. The other one was at Manching, killing the German crew.

Flight development of Tornado will continue as long as the type remains in service so that its operational capability remains matched to the threat of enemy potential. The first fully operational machine was delivered to RAF Cottesmore, on 1 July 1980, six years after the maiden flight, by Paul Millett and 'Ollie' Heath, Panavia systems engineering director.

The contribution of this aeroplane to the NATO deterrent is immense. Its versatility is legendary. It

Air Commodore Allen Wheeler, as a Group Captain, with his private Spitfire (1950).

can deliver a large conventional weapon load in all weathers, by day and night, with very high accuracy. Its ability to fly at transonic speed in terrain following flight and return at supersonic speed at low level ensures greatly reduced vulnerability from enemy interception, whilst the low specific fuel consumption of the engines results in a much greater combat range than contemporary combat aircraft. The ferry range, which can be further increased by in-flight refuelling, is 2,100 miles. Tornado can operate from any strip 3,000 ft long; during tests, take-off and landing runs of below 1,700 ft have been demonstrated.

The outstandingly efficient RB.199 engines are robust, as they must be to withstand the effect of bird strike in the terrain following mode. Rolls-Royce consider that with relatively minor modifications to the engine and increases in maximum operating temperature, an increase in thrust of around 20 per cent is feasible with minimal effect upon fuel economy.

This outstanding aeroplane is the legacy left to Great Britain by the design teams of this great industry and its pioneering predecessors, now sadly anonymous in the monolithic British Aerospace organization. It is a legacy from generations of test pilots from Busk, Cody and Hawker, Sayer, Uwins and Bulman, Orrell, Wroath and Cordes, Penrose, the Heyworth brothers, Quill, Summers and Daunt, de Havilland, Derry and Davie, Twiss, Duke and Bryce, to name but a few.

Now the torch is borne by very highly qualified, but much less familiar names, such as John Farley, Andy Jones, David Eagles, and the Service teams led by David Scouller, David Bywater and Robin Hargreaves. Highly educated in the sciences and in engineering, they integrate their exceptional flying ability into a team of equally scientific designers and engineers who judge their technical input as being of value equal to their own. In common with their great predecessors they all love flying and, no doubt, all have that keen sense of smell which Air Commodore Allen Wheeler told the author is so essential to a test pilot. 'So that he can tell when the thing is on fire!'

Clearly Britain's future in aviation is in competent hands if only the politicians will let them exercise their expertise.

Lest the paucity of dramatic incidents in the recent test flight programmes indicate that computer and simulator studies have largely eliminated the risks from test flying, it is chastening to realize that three very skilled and experienced chief test pilots lost their lives in prototypes during 1984.

In America, Doug Benefield, of Rockwell, died in an escape capsule failure when the new B-1 bomber crashed. Northrop's F-20 Tigershark fighter, after a brilliant display at Farnborough, in September, by Darrell Cornell, was destroyed in a crash in South Korea, Cornell losing his life. In Italy, Aeritalia's Manlio Quarantelli died when the prototype AMX aircraft crashed in May.

Flight International commenting upon these tragedies said, 'There is no single cause . . . For all pilots, part of the problem lies in their own professional pride. The greater the pilot's professionalism, the nearer he wants to get to the performance limits of his aircraft.' This is what test flying is about.

As an epilogue it seems appropriate to record Group Captain David Scouller's quotation from an RAF flight safety poster in 1976: *A superior pilot is a man who uses his superior judgement to avoid the exercise of his superior skill.*

Sadly, however, it is inevitable that there will be occasions when even the most superior skill is not enough.

GLOSSARY

AID — Aeronautical Inspection Directorate

Aeroelastic forces — Forces created by aerodynamically induced bending and twisting loads upon an aircraft structure

Aileron — Control surface, usually located on each outer wing to form part of the trailing edge. Used for control about longitudinal axis – i.e. in roll. Now largely replaced or augmented in high speed aeroplanes by such devices as elevons or tailerons.

Air log — Instrument which measures air distance flown.

Air Transport Auxiliary — Civilian ferrying service set up in WW2 to deliver aircraft from the manufacturer to operational squadrons.

All flying tailplane — Variable incidence tailplane, without elevators, used for control in pitch.

Aneroid — A thin walled airtight capsule which responds dimensionally to differences in air pressure within and outside it. The basis of pressure type altimeters.

Angle of incidence — Angle between the chord line of the wing and the fore and aft datum line of the fuselage. Not to be confused with angle of attack, which is the angle between the chord line and the direction of undisturbed air flowing over the wing.

Autostabilizer — Aircraft system to detect and correct automatically, changes of trim and altitude.

Axial flow ducted fan — An engine driven fan within a duct which drives compressed air straight into a combustion system without any variation of flow direction.

BEA — British European Airways.

BEM — British Empire Medal.

Back lash — Lost motion due to wear or excessive tolerance in a linear motion control system.

Barbette — Gun position in large aircraft, usually remotely controlled.

Barograph — A continuously recording barometer.

Blind flying — Flight by manual control of the aeroplane but without external visual cues.

Blown flaps — Flaps with high velocity air blown across the upper surface to retain airflow close to the surface.

Bone dome (colloquial) — Hard, internally padded flying helmet.

Brakes, hydraulic — Wheel brakes actuated by oil pressure.

Brakes, pneumatic — Wheel brakes actuated by air pressure.

Brakes, Dunlop Maxaret — Wheel brakes incorporating a device to prevent locking of the wheels in hard braking.

Buffet — Vibration of aircraft due to turbulent airflow.

Buffet boundary — Speeds at specified altitudes when buffet becomes unacceptable.

CG — Centre of Gravity.

Carbon fibre — A composite material, containing fine fibres, which gives outstanding structural strength for a very low weight.

Cathode ray oscilloscope	Instrument to transform electrical signals into visible traces upon the face of a cathode ray tube.
Certificate of airworthiness	Certificate issued by appropriate national aviation authority certifying that the subject aircraft meets all the safety and performance requirements of that authority.
CFS	Central Flying School.
Chord line (of wing)	Line joining centres of curvature at leading and trailing edges of a wing section.
Constant speed unit	Device connected to propeller pitch change mechanism which varies blade angle to retain engine revolutions at a constant, pre-set speed.
Control harmonization	The establishment of a satisfactory and constant relationship between the controls in all axes and at all speeds throughout the aircraft speed range.
Control surface over-balance	Control surface is overbalanced with too much area forward of the hinge line, resulting in loss of 'feel'. The surface may, in extreme cases, move to full deflection by itself.
Cooling, evaporative cooling steam	Cooling system based upon the latent heat of evaporation of the coolant liquid. Coolant is allowed to boil, then condensed before re-entering the cycle.
Critical Mach number	Mach number at which the controllability of the aircraft is affected by compressibility problems.
Desynn	A device which can be used to record in the cockpit the exact angular displacement of a control surface or any other parameter which it is capable of measuring.
Drag coefficient	Non-dimensional measure of drag generated by an aircraft.
Ducted radiator	Radiator installed in a duct designed to achieve a measure of extra thrust.
Dutch roll	Lateral oscillation in both rolling and yawing planes simultaneously.

Dynamometer	Device for measuring power developed by an engine.
Ejector exhausts	Exhaust outlets designed to achieve a measure of extra thrust.
Ejection seat (Colloquial) bang seat	Seat designed for high speed ejection of occupant in the event of an emergency.
Elevons	Usually fitted to tail-less aircraft to act as combined ailerons and elevators.
Engine, in-line	Piston engine with the cylinders arranged on axes parallel with the axis of the crankshaft.
Engine, radial	Piston engine with the cylinders arranged radially to the crankshaft.
Exhausts, rams horn	Shroud over engine exhaust ports to reduce noise and flame emission.
Fatigue failure	Failure of a member due to repeated overloading.
Flame out	Uncontrolled extinction of combustion in a gas turbine, due to causes other than intentional fuel cut-off.
Flick roll	A very fast roll.
Flight envelope	Curves defining altitude and performance limitations within which the aircraft must be operated.
Flow meter	Instrument used to measure rate of flow of fuel, oxygen or other liquid or gas.
Flutter	High frequency oscillation of aircraft structure induced by aerodynamic and aeroelastic forces.
Fly-by-wire	Flight control system with electrical links between pilot's controls and control surface actuators.
Gas turbine	A power unit with a turbine rotated by the expansion of hot gases.
Geared tabs	Control surface tab for balance purposes, mechanically linked to the control surface so that its angular movement remains in the same relationship with the surface.

Geodetic Construction	Framework consisting of spirally crossing members forming a space frame, the members being in tension or compression.	**Layshaft**	A subsidiary shaft driving an engine auxiliary.
Glide path	Path followed by aircraft in gliding flight, usually to a landing.	**Lift coefficient**	Non-dimensional measure of lift generated by a surface.
Gravity, centre of	The point through which the resultant forces of gravity act.	**Limited authority auto-stabilizer**	An automatic stabilizing system which leaves the pilot with a major element of over-ride control.
'G'	Acceleration due to gravity of the earth, for example, a pilot making a 2G turn will weigh double his normal weight.	**Longeron**	Main structural member of fuselage.
Ground resonance test	A test to determine the presence of dangerous natural vibration in an aircraft structure.	**Longitudinal instability**	Inability to return automatically to level flight after a dive or climb.
Heat sink	Means of withdrawing heat from a thermodynamic system which may create excessive heat.	**MAEE**	Marine Aircraft Experimental Establishment.
		MoD	Ministry of Defence
Helmeted cylinder head	A means of reducing the diameter of a radial engine cowling by covering the tops of the cylinders with streamlined fairings.	**Machmeter**	A cockpit instrument giving a direct and almost instant read-out of Mach number.
High speed stall	A stall at a speed well above the normal stalling speed. Occurs when an excessively high angle of attack is achieved.	**Mach number**	The ratio of the true speed of the aircraft to the speed of sound in air at the altitude flown.
Hinge moments	Force required to move control surface under aerodynamic loads applied to the surface.	**Mae West** (colloquial)	Aircrew life jacket of WW2, reminiscent of the contours of a famous actress of the period.
Hot wire anemometer	An instrument capable of measuring very low air velocity.	**Manual pump**	Hand operated hydraulic pump for emergency operation, usually, of the undercarriage.
Hucks starter	An early method of starting an engine by engaging a shaft driven dog on a suitable motor vehicle, generally a T model Ford, with a similar dog on the propeller boss.	**Marstrand tail wheel**	Tail wheel designed to prevent shimmy (oscillation about vertical axis) of tail wheel assembly. Tyre has two thick ribs circumferentially around outside edges, with a deep groove between them.
Initial Training Wing (ITW)	Training centre for RAF recruits. A high level of discipline was required with much 'square-bashing'.	**Mass balance**	A weight attached to a control surface by a fixed bracket, usually forward of the hinge line, to reduce tendency to flutter.
Inter-plane strut	Strut joining wings of biplane.	**Monocoque**	Description, usually applied to fuselage, where the structure has all its strength built into the skin with no internal bracing.
Kinetic heating	Heating of airframe by the friction created by its passage through the air.	**OCU**	Operational Conversion Unit.
		Ogival delta wing	A wing profile with a radius of curvature at the leading edge which gradually develops into an almost straight line towards the trailing edge. Gothic arch shape. (See Concorde.)
Laminar flow wing	Wing designed to ensure smooth flow of air over its surfaces with uniform separation between the layers of air.	**Oleo leg**	Shock absorbing undercarriage strut which absorbs landing loads

by allowing its hydraulic fluid content to pass under pressure through a small orifice, with a suitable device to prevent rapid rebound.

Oxometer (colloquial) — An imaginary instrument of WW2 origin, for measuring 'bull'.

Phugoid — Switchback profile oscillation of aircraft about its flight path.

Pitching moment — Force causing an aircraft to pitch about its lateral axis, nose-up or nose-down.

Pitot head (or tube) — Sensing pressure head for airspeed indicator.

Pitot comb — Vertical row of pitot tubes, usually located behind a wing.

Pitot traverse — Successive measurements of pitot pressures in different places along, say, the trailing edge of a wing.

Powered controls — A flight control system in which the pilot's controls move the surfaces by means of a powered, irreversible, mechanism.

Pressure plotting points — Small orifices in the surface of a wing or other component which can be connected to suitable pressure reading or recording instruments.

Private venture prototype — Prototype financed by its builders.

Profile drag — Drag created by the shape of the aeroplane plus the surface friction drag.

Propeller, bracket type — Propeller in which centrifugal force, acting on counterweights on brackets fitted to the blade roots, move the blades into coarse pitch, oil pressure being used to move them into fine pitch.

Propeller, constant speed — Propeller controlled by means of a governor which adjusts blade angle to maintain a pre-set rpm regardless of the attitude of the aeroplane.

Propeller, constant speed, fully feathering — As constant speed but with additional facility that the blades may be moved past the coarse pitch position to lie edge-on to the line-of-flight. Stops propeller windmilling and reduces drag.

propeller, constant speed, fully feathering and braking — As above but with extra facility to move blades to reverse pitch angle, through fine pitch position, to achieve braking effect on the ground.

Propeller, contra-rotating — Two propellers on two co-axial shafts rotating in opposite directions to balance the effect of engine and propeller torque.

propeller, pusher — Propeller mounted behind engine.

Propeller, variable pitch — Propeller in which the blade pitch angle can be varied in flight, usually by manual control to one of two positions, fine or coarse.

Prop-jet (also prop-turbine, turbo-prop) — A gas turbine engine driving a propeller, or propellers, to give a proportion of thrust additional to the thrust from the turbine exhaust.

PSI — Pressure in pounds per square inch.

Queen Mary (colloquial) — Large low-loading, articulated vehicle used for transporting aircraft.

Quill shaft — Splined, slim shaft for component drive.

RNAS — Royal Naval Air Service.

SBAC — Society of British Aircraft Construction. Later, Society of British Aerospace Companies.

Shock waves — Powerful pressure waves formed at speeds at, and above, subsonic, usually perpendicular to the airflow.

Simulator — Replica of an aircraft cockpit, designed to reproduce for the pilot the sensory experience of flying the actual aeroplane.

Slot — Gap contrived between the leading edge of the wing, at the tip, and a suitably shaped slat above the leading edge to accelerate airflow at high angles of attack to delay flow breakaway. Can be operated manually but is usually automatically deployed.

Spar — Main structural member of a

Spin A spiral descent, usually resulting from a stall.

Spring tab Control surface servo tab loaded by a torsion bar so that for small control inputs the tab is ineffective, for large control inputs the tab deflects to give extra power to the surface.

Stall Caused by excessive angle of attack and consequent breakaway of airflow from upper surface of aerofoil or control surface. The modern terminology is 'departure'.

Stall warning indicator Visual or audible warning to pilot of imminence of stall.

Stick shaker Device which indicates the imminence of a stall by shaking the control column in a fore and aft direction.

Strain gauge Device for converting strain into an electrical signal.

Stressing analysis Investigation of all stresses borne by an aircraft structure in all conditions of operation.

Supersonic flight Flight at speeds above the speed of sound.

super stall, deep stall A phenomenon experienced, usually with T tailed, rear engined aeroplanes. As the pilot raises the nose at low airspeeds, drag rises faster than lift and the increasing angle of attack leads to a stabilized stall; the absence of slipstream over the tailplane then prevents recovery without a tail parachute.

Surging Major breakdown of airflow in a gas turbine, usually of axial flow design. Results in backfiring and rapid increase in operating temperature.

Sutton harness Pilot or passenger seat harness with two shoulder straps and two lap straps with a quick release for the four of them, over the wearer's abdomen.

Tail dragger (colloquial) Refers to the attitude of an aircraft with a tail skid or tail wheel.

Taileron Horizontal control surfaces of a swept wing aircraft, used as ailerons by deflecting them differentially and as elevators by deflecting them in unison about their transverse axis.

Telemetry Transmission of in-flight test data by radio link from aircraft to ground station.

Thermal stress Structural stresses caused by temperature.

Thrust reverser Device, such as clam-shell shrouds, to deflect jet efflux partially forward to achieve a braking effect on the ground.

Torque tube Tube joining the sections of a flap or elevator on each side of the aircraft.

Transducer Device for converting energy from one form to another, usually into an electrical signal.

Transition point Point on wing, or other surface of the aircraft, where the boundary layer of air changes from laminar to turbulent flow.

Transonic Speed range around Mach 1.0 where, over some parts of the aeroplane, the airflow velocity is below Mach 1.0 whilst, over other parts, it is above Mach 1.0.

Trousered undercarriage Undercarriage assembly faired in with a trouser-shaped fairing to reduce drag.

Turbulence Air disturbance which can vary from the mild to the violent, either in the air through which the aeroplane flies, or in the airflow passing over its structure.

Type test A test, which, if passed, will entitle the manufacturer of the engine or aircraft to receive an official Certificate of Approval.

Variable geometry Ability to make major changes in the configuration of an aircraft, by, for example, swinging or slewing the wing.

Variable stability aircraft Experimental aircraft in which a range of stability factors can be altered at will for test purposes.

wing. May be of several spars linked by ribs, or, in the form of a strong box section to which leading and trailing edge sections are fitted.

Vortex Generator	A small metal fin set at an angle perpendicularly to the skin of an aircraft to create a vortex in the boundary layer of air.
Wheel spats	Close fitting fairings over the main undercarriage wheels of a fixed undercarriage aircraft.
Wing fences	A vertical metal plate, often starting around the leading edge of the wing, and continuing to the trailing edge to prevent spanwise flow of air, particularly in swept wing aircraft.
Wing Rib	A primary structural member which joins the leading edge to the trailing edge of a wing and maintains the correct aerodynamic profile.
Wing root fillet	A streamlined fairing to improve airflow where the wing joins the fuselage.
Wing tip controllers	Control surfaces like extended wing tips, arranged to rotate about a spanwise axis to give roll control.
Yaw	Rotary movement of aircraft about its vertical axis.
Youngman flaps	Trailing edge flaps designed and patented by Fairey. Mounted on struts below the wing, they could be used as conventional flaps or deflected upwards for use as air brakes.

LIST OF TEST PILOTS
AND OTHERS CONSULTED

Geoffrey Alington.
† Squadron Leader Basil H. Arkell AFRAeS.
Leslie Ash.
Godfrey L. Auty AFRAeS.
David M. Bay ARAeS.
Wing Commander Roland P. Beamont CBE,
    DSO*, DFC*, DL, FRAeS.
A. W. 'Bill' Bedford OBE, AFC, FRAeS.
Commander N. T. 'Nick' Bennett AFC.
E. W. 'Jock' Bonar GC.
Squadron Leader M. C. Brooke AFC, MRAeS.
Tom W. Brooke-Smith CEng, FRAeS, MIPR.
Captain Eric M. Brown CBE, MBE, DSC, AFC,
    MA, FRAeS, RN Retd.
G. R. 'Jock' Bryce OBE.
Hugh Burroughes (Gloster Aircraft Company Ltd).
Group Captain David L. Bywater MRAeS, MBIM.
† Peter Cadbury.
Ron E. Clear AFRAeS.
† Air Commodore Arthur E. Clouston CBE, DSO,
    DFC, AFC*.
Group Captain John Cunningham CBE, DSO**,
    DFC*, DL, FRAeS.
Major James L. B. H. Cordes, FRSA, MRAeS.
N. Michael Daunt OBE.
David P. Davies, OBE, DSC, FRAeS.
Squadron Leader A. W. Debuse BSc, MSc, CEng,
    MIMechE, MRAeS.
Squadron Leader Neville F. Duke DSO, OBE,
    DFC**, AFC, FRSA, AFRAeS, Czech MC.
† J. David Eagles AFC, FRAeS.
W. H. 'Bill' Else.
John F. Farley OBE, AFC, CEng, MRAeS.
Wing Commander Geoffrey R. K. Fletcher AFC.
† Squadron Leader Eric Franklin DFC, AFRAeS.
Harry Fraser-Mitchell.
A. E. 'Ben' Gunn OBE, MRAeS.
Wing Commander Robin Hargreaves BSc Eng.
Wing Commander Ralph E. Havercroft AFC.
Squadron Leader Hedley G. Hazelden DFC*,
    AFRAeS.
Wing Commander Jack M. Henderson OBE,
    AFC*, AFRAeS.
† Alex H. Henshaw MBE.
A. James Heyworth DFC*, AFRAeS.
Charles T. D. Hosegood AFRAeS.

Charles F. Hughesdon AFC.
Andy P. S. Jones.
Wing Commander Charles G. B. McClure AFC,
    DL, MA, FRAeS.
Wing Commander Richard F. Martin OBE, DFC*,
    AFC, AFRAeS.
Charles B. G. Masefield MA, MRAeS.
David J. Masters DFC, AFRAeS.
Robert E. M. B. Milne.
Mrs Mary Morrison.
Squadron Leader Frank Murphy DFC, AFRAeS.
† P. 'Spud' Murphy.
Captain James H. Orrell OBE.
Harald J. Penrose OBE, CEng, FRAeS, MRINA.
Mrs Olga Pike.
Ranald Porteous FRAeS, MIEx, MInstM.
Jeffrey K. Quill OBE, AFC, FRAeS.
Squadron Leader D. C. Reid.
Wing Commander J. A. 'Robby' Robinson AFC,
    MRAeS.
Captain H. C. 'Cliff' Rogers OBE, DFC*, CEng,
    FRAeS.
Sir Archibald E. Russell CBE, FRS, CEng, FIAeS,
    HonFRAeS.
Frederick C. Sanders (Gloster Aircraft).
† Hugh R. Scanlan.
† Captain J. E. D. Scott.
Group Captain David C. Scouller AFC, MRAeS.
† Wing Commander E. J. 'Jimpy' Shaw AFC.
Duncan M. S. Simpson OBE, CEng, FRAeS.
Group Captain Leonard S. Snaith CB, AFC.
Air Commodore R. J. 'Reggie' Spiers OBE, FRAeS.
Mrs Miriam Tiltman.
Barrie J. Tonkinson.
E. Brian Trubshaw CBE, OBE, MVO, FRAeS.
L. Peter Twiss OBE, DSC.*
Air Commodore Allen H. Wheeler CBE,
    MA(Cantab), FRAeS, Dutch DFC.
Mrs Barbara Wheeler.
Group Captain H. J. 'Willie' Wilson CBE, AFC**,
    MRAeS.
Group Captain S. 'Sammy' Wroath CBE, AFC*,
    MRAeS.

† Not interviewed personally

BIBLIOGRAPHY

Allward, Maurice. *Buccaneer*. Ian Allan, 1981. *History of Seaplanes and Flying Boats*. Moorland, 1981.

Andrews, C. F. and Morgan, E. B. *Supermarine Aircraft since 1914*. Putnam, 1981.

Babington Smith, Constance. *Testing Time*. Cassell, 1961.

Banks, Air Commodore F. R. *I Kept no Diary*. Airlife, 1978.

Barnes, C. H. *Handley Page Aircraft since 1907*. Putnam, 1976.

Beamont, Wing Commander Roland P. *Testing Years*. Ian Allan, 1980. (see also Lanchbery)

Birtles, Philip. *Concorde*. Ian Allan, 1984.

Brookes, A. *V Force*. Jane's, 1982.

Brown, Captain Eric M. *Wings of the Weird and Wonderful*. Airlife, 1983. *Wings of the Navy*. Pilot, 1980.

Bullen, A. and Rivas, B. *John Derry*. Kimber, 1982.

Burnet, Charles. *Three Centuries to Concorde*. Mechanical Engineering Publications, 1979.

Cobham, Sir Alan J. *A Time to Fly*. Shepheard-Walwyn, 1978.

Cooksley, P. G. *Skystreak*. Hale, 1980.

Courtney, Captain Frank. *Flight Path*. Kimber, 1973.

Deighton, Len. *Airshipwreck*. Cape, 1978.

Donne, M. *Leaders of the Sky* (Rolls-Royce). Muller, 1981.

Duke, Squadron Leader Neville F. and Mitchell, H. W. *Test Pilot*. Allen Wingate, 1953.

Gardner, Charles. *British Aircraft Corporation*. Batsford, 1981.

Gibson, T. M. and Harrison, M. H. *Into the Air: A History of Aviation Medicine in the RAF*. Hale, 1984.

Gillman, Captain R. E. *Croydon to Concorde*. Murray, 1980.

Grierson, John. *Jet Flight*. Sampson Low, 1946.

Gunston, Bill. *Panavia Tornado*. Ian Allan, 1980. *Early Supersonic Fighters of the West*. Ian Allan, 1976.

Hannah, D. *Avro*. Key Publishing, 1983. *Shorts*. Flypast Reference Library, 1983.

Hardy, M. J. *Avro*. Patrick Stephens, 1982.

Harvey-Bailey, Alec. *Rolls-Royce, the Formative Years*. R-R Heritage Trust, 1982. *The Merlin in Perspective*. R-R Heritage Trust, 1983.

Hedley, M. *Vickers VC 10*. Ian Allan, 1982.

Henshaw, Alex. *Sigh for a Merlin*. Murray, 1979. *The Flight of the Mew Gull*. Murray, 1980.

Hooker, Sir Stanley G. *Not Much of an Engineer*. Airlife, 1984.

Jackson, A. J. *British Civil Aircraft since 1919*. Vols 1–3. Putnam, 1959–60 et seq.

Jackson, Robert. *The Jet Age*. Barker, 1980. *The V Bombers*. Ian Allan, 1981.

Jewell, John. *Engineering for Life*. Martin Baker Aircraft Co Ltd, 1979.

Johnson, Brian and Heffernan, Terry. *Boscombe Down: a Most Secret Place*. Jane's, 1982.

Kinsey, Gordon. *Martlesham Heath*. Terence Dalton, 1975. *Seaplanes-Felixstowe*. Terence Dalton, 1978.

Lanchbery, Edward. *Against the Sun* (Roland Beamont). Cassell, 1955.

Lewis, Peter. *The British Fighter Since 1912*. Putnam, 1965 et seq. *The British Bomber Since 1914*. Putnam, 1967 et seq.

Lithgow, Mike J. *Mach One*. Allen Wingate, 1954.

Mason, Francis K. *Hawker Hunter*. Patrick Stephens, 1981.

Middleton, D. H. *Airspeed: the Company and its Aeroplanes*. Terence Dalton, 1982.

Myles, Bruce. *Jump Jet*. Brassey, 1978.

Pegg, A. J. 'Bill'. *Sent Flying*. Macdonald, 1959.

Penrose, Harald, *British Aviation: The Pioneering Years*. Cassell, 1967. *British Aviation: The Adventuring Years, 1920–29*. Putnam, 1973. *British Aviation: Widening Horizons, 1930–34*. HMSO, 1974. *British Aviation: Ominous Skies, 1935–39*. RAF Museum, 1980. *Adventure with Fate* (autobiography). Airlife, 1984. *No Echo in the Sky*. Cassell, 1958. *Airymouse*. Airlife, 1967 & 1982. *Cloud Cuckooland*. Airlife, 1981.

Powell, Wing Commander H. P. 'Sandy'. *Men with Wings*. Allen Wingate, 1957.

Price, Alfred. *The Spitfire Story*. Jane's, 1982.

Quill, Jeffrey K. *Spitfire: A Test Pilot's Story*. Murray, 1983.

Reed, Arthur. *B.A.C. Lightning*. Ian Allan, 1980. *Sepecat Jaguar*. Ian Allan, 1982.

Sharp, C. Martin. *D.H.: A History of de Havilland*. Faber & Faber/Airlife, 1960 & 1982.

Sharp, C. Martin and Bowyer, M. J. F. *Mosquito*. Faber & Faber, 1967.

Shute, Nevil. *Slide Rule*. Heinemann, 1954.

Sweetman, Bill. *High Speed Flight*. Jane's, 1982.

Tapper, Oliver. *Armstrong Whitworth Aircraft Since 1913*. Putnam, 1973.

Taylor, H. A. *Airspeed Aircraft Since 1931*. Putnam, 1970. *Fairey Aircraft Since 1915*. Putnam, 1974.

Taylor, J. W. R. and Allward, M. *Westland 50*. Ian Allan, 1965.

Thetford, Owen. *Aircraft of the Royal Air Force Since 1918*. Putnam, 1957 et seq.

Turner, P. St. John. *Handbook of the Vickers Viscount*. Ian Allan, 1968.

Wheeler, Air Commodore Allen H. *That Nothing Failed Them*. Foulis, 1963.

ALSO CONSULTED *Centenary Journal*, Royal Aeronautical Society, 1966; *Aviation Year*, Avia/Duciman, 1977/78; *The Rolls-Royce Magazine*, Rolls-Royce Ltd; *Aeroplane Monthly* and *Flight International*, Business Press International; *Aviation Annual*, Jane's; *Aircraft Illustrated* and *Air Extra*, Ian Allan; *Air Enthusiast*, Fine Scroll.

PHOTOGRAPHIC ACKNOWLEDGEMENTS

The author and publishers are indebted to the following individuals and organisations for allowing their photographs to be reproduced in this book:

Airship Industries, 246.
Associated Press, 189 (bottom).
British Aerospace
    Bristol, 61, 65 (bottom), 216, 217, 228 (top), 229, 244, 245.
    Dunsfold, 232.
    Dynamics Group, 102.
    Hatfield, 13, 22, 53, 84, 87 (bottom), 90 (top), 98, 111, 112, 137, 171, 192.
    Kingston, 225, 231.
    Manchester, 28, 63 (bottom), 183 (bottom), 203 (bottom), 240, 241.
    Warton, Front cover, 212 (top and bottom), 213 (top), 238 (top), 250, 252, 253, 255, 256.
    Weybridge, 235 (top).
British Airways, 237.
Captain Eric Brown, 118, 165.
Crown Copyright, 139, 140, 141.
Michael Daunt, 125, 129.
David Davies, 182.
W. H. Else, 30 (top), 186 (top), 193.
Wg Cdr Geoffrey Fletcher, 206.
Flight International, Back cover, 72 (bottom left).
Sqn Ldr Hedley Hazelden, 221.
Handley Page Association, 48.
Wg Cdr Ralph Havercroft, 203 (top).
Alex Henshaw, 167.
Wg Cdr Charles McClure, 105.
Wg Cdr Dick Martin, 210.
Martin Baker Engineering, 134, 135.
Harald Penrose, 41.
Ranald Porteous, 214.
Portsmouth News, 64.
RAF Museum, Hendon, 96.
Richard Riding, 78, 156.
Capt Cliff Rogers, 148.
Rolls-Royce, 132, 148, 150, 151, 153, 155, 157, 158, 159 (Bristol Engineering Division), 160, 222, 238 (bottom).
Gp Cpt David Scouller, 254.
Duncan Simpson, 230.
Vickers, 72 (top and bottom right). 73 (top and centre).
Mrs Barbara Wheeler, 257

All other photographs not mentioned above have been provided from the archives of *Aeroplane Monthly* by courtesy of the editor, Richard Riding.

INDEX

Figures in italic refer to illustrations